The IBM® PS/2® from the Inside Out

The IBM® PS/2®
From the Inside Out

TOM SHANLEY

Addison-Wesley Publishing Company, Inc.
Reading, Massachusetts   Menlo Park, California   New York
Don Mills, Ontario   Wokingham, England   Amsterdam   Bonn
Sydney   Singapore   Tokyo   Madrid   San Juan

Many of the designations used by manufacturers and sellers to distinguish their products are claimed as trademarks. Where those designations appear in this book and Addison-Wesley was aware of a trademark claim, the designations have been printed in initial capital letters.

This book acknowledges the following trademarks:

Registered trademarks of IBM Corporation: IBM, AT, PC/AT, PS/2, PC/XT, PC-DOS, VGA, CGA, MCA, MDA, EGA, OS/2, Micro Channel, Programmable Option Select, POS.
Registered trademarks of Intel Corporation: Intel.
Registered trademarks of Lotus Development Corporation: Lotus, 1-2-3.
Registered trademarks of Motorola Corporation: Motorola.
Registered trademarks of Dallas Semiconductor Corporation: Dallas semiconductor.
Registered trademarks of Microsoft Corporation: Microsoft.
Registered trademarks of AT&T Bell Laboratories: Unix.

Library of Congress Cataloging-in-Publication Data

Shanley, Tom.
    The IBM PS/2 from the inside out / Tom Shanley.
      p. cm.
    Includes index.
    ISBN 0-201-57056-4
    1. IBM Personal System/2 (Computer system)   I. Title.
  QA76.8.I25963S48   1991
  004.165–dc20   90-21069
                                               CIP

Cover design by Doliber Skeffington
Set in 11 pt. Century Schoolbook by Impressions, a division of Edwards Brothers, Inc.

ABCDEFGHIJ-MW-91

First Printing, December 1990

To my wife, Nancy, for her patience, friendship, and good advice.

Contents

1   Introduction to Microprocessor Communications   5

2   I/O and Memory: The World According to Intel   15

3   The Address Decode Logic: Is He Talking to Me?   25

4   Introduction to the Bus Cycle   41

Appendices

Preface

The Purpose of the Book

Using a building-block approach, this book attempts to provide a complete overview of the hardware architecture of the IBM PS/2 products that incorporate the micro channel architecture (MCA). In this book, the term PS/2 refers only to PS/2 products that use MCA. Many of the concepts presented also apply to the earlier IBM PCs and PS/2 products that do not utilize MCA.

Who Should Read This Book

Although this book assumes a relatively small degree of technical knowledge on the part of its audience, readers should have some exposure to PCs in a somewhat technical capacity (buyer, programmer, sales, technical support, repair, and so on). In order to ensure an optimum level of understanding, every attempt is made to explain terminology as it is encountered. (See the Definition List below.)

The majority of the book uses block diagrams rather than logic (wiring) diagrams. Only Chapter 3, which covers address decoders, references some simple logic diagrams, and detailed explanations are provided in the text. The Appendix contains a primer on simple logic for readers unfamiliar with logic symbols. Also, because it is absolutely necessary to represent numbers in binary and hexadecimal when discussing this subject, the Appendix contains a primer on these numbering systems.

Definitions for This Chapter

- A **bus** is a group of signal lines with a single, logical purpose.

- A **bus master** is a device that uses the address, data, and control buses to communicate with other devices.

A Historical Perspective: The IBM PC, PC/XT, and PC/AT

The IBM PC, PC/XT, and PC/AT are all single-processor computers, which means that one microprocessor is in complete control of the machine and can run only one program at a time. The performance of the machine is therefore limited by the speed at which this single processor can fetch and execute instructions. For a number of years, PC manufacturers have been working to improve the speed at which the microprocessor can communicate with the various devices found in the PC. In the final analysis, however, there is a limit to the speed that can be realized from a PC based on a single microprocessor. The PC/XT/AT's expansion slots are simply an extension of the system board microprocessor's address, data, and control **buses**.

For example, the microprocessor's address bus is a set of signal lines used to send an address to the particular device with which the microprocessor wishes to communicate. The microprocessor uses these three buses to communicate with other devices in the system. Some of the devices the microprocessor communicates with are located on the system board. Other devices are inserted into the expansion slots, thereby enabling the microprocessor to communicate with them. Each type of card fulfills a separate function. For example, a parallel port card allows the microprocessor to control a printer or similar device. A video adapter card allows the microprocessor to display information on the screen. In a PC/XT/AT system, the microprocessor on the system board is **bus master** most of the time.

Occasionally, the DMA controller or the RAM refresh logic (two devices also located on the system board) becomes **bus master**. The refresh and DMA logic are discussed in subsequent chapters. Every Intel microprocessor has an input signal that can force the microprocessor to electrically detach itself from the address, data, and control buses. When the microprocessor gives up the buses to another device (such as the DMA controller), that device then becomes the bus master. After using the buses, the device gives the buses back to the microprocessor.

It is possible to design a card that can become bus master when inserted into a PC/XT/AT expansion slot and, in fact, a number of boards on the market use this approach. IBM did not design the PC expansion bus to efficiently support bus master cards, however, since they did not anticipate that the PC would evolve to the point where it required the power of multiple bus masters.

When a card becomes bus master in a PC/XT/AT, it can remain bus master forever, to the total exclusion of the system board microprocessor and the RAM refresh logic on the system board. This creates a very dangerous situation. As long as the bus master card retains ownership of the buses, the system board microprocessor cannot fetch instructions. As a result, the program the microprocessor was running stops. The data in RAM memory may be lost because the refresh logic cannot become bus master. Also, because the bus master card has no way of sensing when another bus master card wants to use the buses, it completely monopolizes the buses so that no other devices can use the buses.

Bus mastering in a PC/XT/AT is risky at best and potentially catastrophic. The PC/XT/AT can therefore never play host safely to a multiple bus master environment. This leaves you back at square one—a single-microprocessor system.

The IBM PS/2: A Multiple-processor Engine

In creating the PS/2 product line, IBM created a PC that can safely play host to a number of bus master cards, each incorporating its own microprocessor and performing part of the overall job. When necessary, any of these microprocessors can communicate with any other device in the system. When a PS/2 is manufactured and sold, the only microprocessor in the system is the one on the system board. On the surface, the PS/2 appears to be just another single-processor PC. Like the PC/XT/AT, PS/2 systems allow the addition of bus master expansion cards.

The true power of a machine using MCA is its ability to handle multiple bus masters in an orderly fashion. In addition to the address, data, and control buses found on the PC/XT/AT's expansion slots, MCA slots have a fourth set of signal lines, the bus arbitration signals. Using these signals, multiple bus masters can safely compete for the use of the buses. When a device becomes bus master, it senses when another bus master requires the use of the buses, and must give them up on a timely basis. The PS/2 therefore lets you create a system with multiple bus master cards plugged into the MCA slots. Each of these bus master cards can be a completely self-contained subsystem, with its own microprocessor, memory, and I/O devices. When it needs to communicate with another device in the system, it can arbitrate, or compete, for the buses and perform all necessary communication as bus master.

As a result of the MCA's orderly handling of multiple bus masters, it is not unusual to find a PS/2 based on an Intel 80386 microprocessor with MCA cards installed incorporating other, even more powerful, microprocessors such as the Intel 80486 or Motorola 68040. The microprocessor on the system board can run a powerful operating system, such as OS/2, which delegates tasks to highly intelligent, microprocessor-based bus master cards such as disk and network controller cards. System throughput, or performance, is greatly enhanced because multiple microprocessors are able to perform tasks in parallel with each other. For example, the operating system software being executed by the host microprocessor (on the system board) can command an intelligent disk card to search for a match on a particular string of characters in a file called "TOM.TXT" while a network controller card is handling a network of PCs attached to the PS/2. At the same time, a highly intelligent communications bus master card can transmit a block of data to a mainframe over a communications line. Each of these bus master cards can communicate with any device on the system board or another MCA card by becoming bus master.

Due to the hardware and software complexity involved in handling this interplay, the full potential of machines incorporating the MCA is only now beginning to be realized.

Organization of This Book

The book is divided into nine parts plus a set of appendices. Brief descriptions of each part and the appendices follow this list.

Part I: The Microprocessor

Part II: The System Board Engine

Part III: The Bus Cycle

Part IV: The Micro Channel Architecture

Part V: Interrupts

Part VI: Direct Memory Access (DMA)

Part VII: Memory

Part VIII: The System Board Peripheral Devices

Part IX: Miscellaneous Subjects

Appendices

Part I: Provides the necessary background for understanding all of the material covered in the book. Part I provides a detailed tutorial on how Intel microprocessors communicate with memory and I/O devices. All of the currently available PS/2 products are based on Intel microprocessors.

Part II: Describes the support logic that allows the microprocessor to communicate with 8-, 16-, and 32-bit devices.

Part III: Continues the communication discussion begun in Part I. Part III provides a detailed view of the microprocessor's communications for the reader who requires a more detailed bus cycle description. Part III also includes timing diagrams.

Part IV: Provides a detailed discussion of the MCA. The following subjects are covered:

The MCA concept

Types of bus masters

Bus arbitration

Basic transfer (bus cycle) types

Programmable option select

The 16-bit MCA

The matched-memory extension

The 32-bit MCA extension

The video extension

New MCA features (MCA-2)

Part V: Provides an in-depth description of how interrupts work in the PS/2 environment.

Part VI: Gives a detailed description of direct memory access as implemented in the PS/2 product line.

Part VII: Provides a detailed description of the various types of memory found in the PS/2 product line. The following subjects are covered:

RAM memory: theory of operation

System board DRAM memory

Cache memory

Channel memory

System board and device ROM memory

The real-time clock and configuration RAM

Part VIII: Provides a functional description of the peripheral device interfaces that are a standard part of the PS/2 system board:

The real-time clock and configuration RAM

The floppy disk interface

The serial port

The parallel port

The keyboard/mouse interface

VGA: the display interface

The numeric coprocessor

Part IX: Discusses miscellaneous subjects such as the timers used in the PS/2 products and the reset logic.

Appendix A: Introduces basic logic devices (such as AND and OR gates).

Appendix B: Introduces the binary and hexadecimal numbering systems.

Appendix C: Provides a complete listing of the I/O addresses used in the PS/2 product line.

Appendix D: The Memory Address Map

Appendix E: Glossary of Terms

Appendix F: MCA Signal Glossary

Conventions Used in This Book

This section describes the typographical conventions used in this book.

Terms

All new terms are listed at the beginning of each chapter under the Definitions heading. The term appears in boldface type the first time it is used in the chapter text. When you see a boldface term, you can turn back to the definition list if you are unsure of its meaning.

Each of these terms can be found in the Glossary of Terms in Appendix E.

Hex Notation

All hex numbers are followed by a subscripted h. For example:

$9A4E_h$

0100_h

Binary Notation

All binary numbers are followed by a subscripted b. For example:

$0001\ 1010_b$

0100_b

Decimal Notation

Some decimal numbers are followed by a subscripted d (when required for clarity). For example:

128_d

1024_d

Interpretation of Signal Names

The name of a signal that performs its allotted task when a logic low (zero volts) is placed on it is immediately followed by a pound sign, "#." This adheres to the new method used by Intel Corporation. For example:

A low (zero volts) on the READY# signal line tells the microprocessor that the currently addressed device is ready to end the transaction in progress.

The microprocessor places a low on the S0# signal line to indicate that the current transaction is a write operation.

Naming Conventions for Dual-purpose Signals

A number of signals perform one task when high and another when low. The naming convention used for signals of this type is X/Y#, where the slash is read as the word "or." An example is M/IO#, which is the memory, or IO, signal. On the left side of the slash, the "M" is not followed by a pound sign, thus indicating that a high on this signal line represents a (M)emory address present on the address bus. On the right side of the slash, the IO# indicates that a low on this signal line represents an I/O address present on the address bus.

Identification of Bit Fields (Logical Groups of Bits or Signals)

All bit fields are designated by separating the first bit and the last bit in the field by a colon, ":." For example:

A0:A23 Refers to the 24 address bus bits (or signal lines) A0 through A23, inclusively.

D0:D15 Refers to the 16 data bus bits (or signal lines).

Recommended Reading

The following Addison-Wesley books provide additional insight into the software aspects of the IBM PS/2 product line.

CBIOS for IBM PS/2 Computers and Compatibles

ABIOS for IBM PS/2 Computers and Compatibles

System BIOS for IBM PC/XT/AT Computers and Compatibles

Acknowledgments

First and foremost, I would like to thank the students I have taught for helping me discover the best way to teach technical material: with plenty of humor and using plain English.

In addition, I would like to thank the Addison-Wesley editorial staff, especially Debbie McKenna and Elizabeth Grose, for their expertise, patience, and good humor.

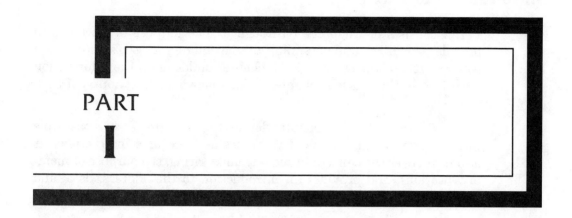

PART

I

The Microprocessor

Introduction to Part I

Part I consists of Chapters 1 through 8. The purpose of Part I is to provide a detailed understanding of the microprocessor's interaction with the rest of the system. Each chapter builds upon the information contained in the previous chapters. The following is a synopsis of each chapter.

Chapter 1: This chapter defines the microprocessor's basic role in the system as an engine that fetches and executes instructions. It also introduces the concept of reading and writing, the purpose of memory locations, and provides an introduction to the address, data, and control buses.

Chapter 2: Starting with the history behind Intel's use of memory and I/O locations, this chapter covers the difference between I/O and memory locations, the definition of an I/O device, the difference between command, status, and data ports, the purpose of the M/IO# microprocessor output signal, and the amount of memory and I/O address space available for the 8080, 8086/8088, 80286, 80386, and 80486 microprocessors.

Chapter 3: This chapter details the purpose of an address decoder, description of data bus contention, and detailed description of three example address decoders.

Chapter 4: This chapter covers an introduction to the subject of state machines, the system clock and the processor clock, an introduction to the microprocessor's bus cycle state machine, and an introduction to the concept of the wait state.

Chapter 5: This chapter describes the rules that provide the basic guidelines for designing systems around Intel microprocessors.

Chapter 6: This chapter provides a description of the 80286 microprocessor. Emphasis is placed on the hardware interface between the 80286 microprocessor and the remainder of the system. There are many good books on the market that provide detailed information about the 80286 from the software perspective. Memory address formation in real mode is covered in detail and an introduction to protected mode is provided.

Chapter 7: This chapter defines the hardware differences between the 80386 and the 80286 microprocessors. It does not cover the 80386 registers, real or protected mode, or any other software-related issues. The discussions of registers, real mode and protected mode found in Chapter 6 apply fully to the 80386 as well as the 80286.

Chapter 8: This chapter details the sequence of operations that occur immediately after a PS/2 is powered on.

Introduction to Microprocessor Communications

Objectives: This chapter defines the microprocessor's basic role in the system as an engine that fetches (reads) and executes instructions. This chapter also introduces the concept of reading and writing, the purpose of memory locations, and provides an introduction to the address, data, and control buses.

Definitions for This Chapter

• **In-line code fetching** is the term used to describe the sequential nature of instruction fetching performed by computers.

• A **JUMP instruction** is an instruction that causes the microprocessor to alter its program flow.

• The **power-on restart address** is the memory location from which the microprocessor always fetches its first instruction after power-up.

• A **register** is an individual storage location found either inside the microprocessor itself or an I/O device.

Instruction Fetch and Execution

The microprocessor is an engine with only one task in life: to continually read instructions from memory and execute them. Instructions are always read from memory, never from I/O devices. I/O devices are described in a later chapter.

The instructions fetched from memory tell the microprocessor what to do. When a microprocessor-based system is first powered up, the microprocessor knows only that it must fetch its first instruction from the **power-on restart address**. From that point forward, the microprocessor is totally dependent on the program to tell it what to do.

An instruction tells the microprocessor to do one of three basic things:

• Read data from an external device.

• Write data to an external device.

• Perform an operation that does not involve reading from or writing to the outside world (such as math functions).

In a properly functioning system, the microprocessor is never idle. At any given moment, the microprocessor is reading data from an external device, writing data to an external device, or executing an instruction that does not require that a read or write take place (for example, an instruction to add together the contents of two of the microprocessor's internal **registers**).

The microprocessor communicates with all external devices by reading data from them or writing data to them. The terms "read" and "write" are extremely important in any discussion of microprocessors and you must think of them from the point of view of the microprocessor rather than from the point of view of the device with which the microprocessor is communicating. Always remember that the microprocessor does the reading and writing, and that devices are read from and written to by the microprocessor. If you think of reading and writing from the device's point of view, the majority of the information in this book will make no sense to you.

As used in this book, the term external device refers to the devices external to the microprocessor chip itself. Figure 1-1 illustrates the relationship between the microprocessor and external devices.

In-Line Code Fetching

When a microprocessor fetches an instruction from a memory location (address) and executes it, one of two things happen:

- Case 1: The instruction does not tell the microprocessor the memory address from which to fetch its next instruction.

- Case 2: The instruction tells the microprocessor the memory address from which to fetch its next instruction.

In Case 1, the microprocessor automatically assumes the next instruction is to be fetched from the next sequential memory location. In Case 2, execution of the instruction causes the microprocessor to alter its program flow, which is usually sequential. Rather than fetching its next instruction from the next sequential memory location, the microprocessor fetches it from the memory location specified by the instruction.

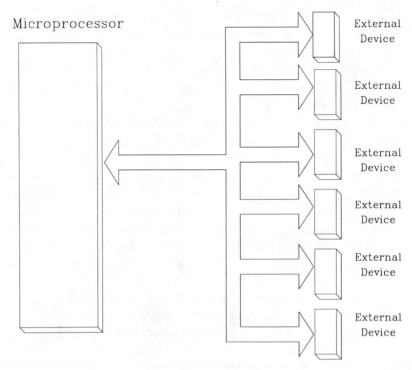

FIGURE 1-1   Microprocessor's Relationship to External Devices

After executing a JUMP instruction, the microprocessor resumes fetching instructions from sequential memory locations until another JUMP instruction is executed. Most well-written programs do not contain an excessive number of JUMPs. Statistically speaking, then, the microprocessor is executing non-jump instructions the majority of the time. This means that the microprocessor is performing **in-line code fetching** most of the time.

For example, refer to Figure 1-2. Assume that the microprocessor has just fetched the ADD instruction from location 0 in memory. The flow of instructions fetched and executed proceeds as follows:

1. The microprocessor executes the ADD instruction fetched from location 0. Since it is not a JUMP instruction, the microprocessor fetches its next instruction from memory location 00001_h.

2. The microprocessor executes the SUBTRACT instruction fetched from location 1. Since it is not a JUMP, the micro-

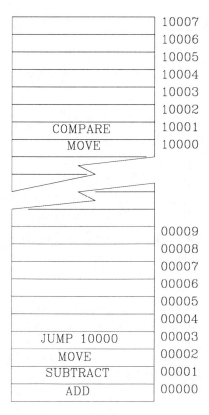

FIGURE 1-2
Sample Instruction Sequence

processor fetches its next instruction from memory location 00002_h.

3. The microprocessor executes the MOVE instruction fetched from location 2. Since it is not a JUMP, the microprocessor fetches its next instruction from memory location 00003_h.

4. The microprocessor executes the JUMP 10000 instruction fetched from location 3. The JUMP instruction alters program flow. Rather than fetch its next instruction from the next sequential memory location (00004_h), the microprocessor fetches it from memory location 10000_h.

5. The microprocessor executes the MOVE instruction fetched from location 10000_h. Since it is not a JUMP, the microprocessor fetches its next instruction from memory location 10001_h.

6. The flow of instruction execution proceeds in this manner.

It should be noted that many instructions actually occupy two or more locations.

Reading and Writing

The microprocessor communicates with external devices under the following circumstances:

- To fetch the next instruction from memory.
- When the currently executing instruction directs the microprocessor to read data from an external device.
- When the currently executing instruction directs the microprocessor to write data to an external device.

Although the microprocessor communicates with external devices under some other special circumstances as well, reading or writing generally occurs for one of the three reasons cited above.

What Kind of Information Is Read from Memory?

The microprocessor reads instructions and data from memory.

The microprocessor reads instructions from memory on an ongoing basis. Data written into a memory location by a previously executed instruction is read from memory when the microprocessor executes an instruction that tells it to read data from the memory location.

What Kind of Information Is Written to Memory?

The microprocessor only writes data into memory locations. Instructions are never written into memory by the microprocessor. Instructions are actually read from disk and written into memory by the DMA controller, not by the microprocessor. DMA is covered in Chapter 20.

Back in the bad old days, programmers sometimes wrote programs that modified themselves on-the-fly by writing new instructions into memory and then executing them. This is known as self-modifying code, and programmers who write this type of program should be cast into the pit. Programs of this nature are a nightmare to understand and maintain, even for the person who wrote them.

The Buses

When the microprocessor must read data from or write data to an external device, it uses address bus, data bus, and control bus signal lines to perform the read or write operation. The following sections introduce the role played by each of these three buses during a read or write operation.

The Address Bus

The microprocessor uses the address bus to identify the external device (and location within the device) with which it wishes to communicate.

The address bus consists of a number of signal lines known as address lines. As an example, the 80286 microprocessor (used in the IBM PS/2 Model 50Z) has 24 address lines, referred to as A0:A23. Refer to Figure 1-3.

When the microprocessor must read data from or write data to an external device, it places the address on the address bus signal lines as a pattern of 1's and 0's. This address pattern identifies the external device and the location within the device. In Figure 1-3, the microprocessor is outputting address 000105_h onto the address bus. Refer to the Appendix for a review of the hexadecimal numbering system.

Each device has an address decoder that decides if the address currently on the address bus is one that is assigned to its respective device. If so, the address decoder tells its device that the microprocessor is talking to it. The device itself then further examines the address to identify the exact location the microprocessor wants to communicate with within the device. This subject is covered in Chapter 3.

The Control Bus: Identifies Transaction Type (Read or Write)

The control bus consists of all the microprocessor's signal lines other than the address bus and data bus lines. The fundamental purposes of the control bus are to:

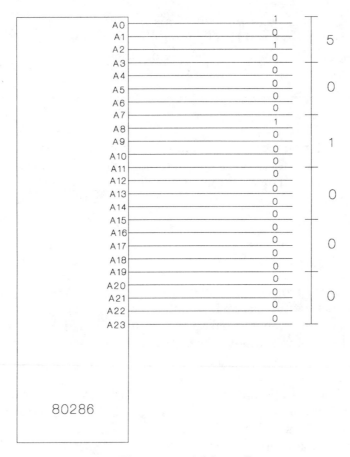

FIGURE 1-3   The 80286 Address Bus

- Identify the type of transaction (for example, as a read or write transaction).
- Synchronize the fast microprocessor to the slow external devices it is reading from or writing to.

The Data Bus: Data Transfer Path

The microprocessor's only purpose in performing a read or write transaction is to transfer data between itself and the currently addressed external device. The sole purpose of the data bus is to provide a data path for the transmission of the data between the two devices. For example, the 80286 microprocessor has 16 data bus signal lines, designated D0:D15. This means that the 80286 microprocessor can read or write 16 bits of information between itself and an external device during a single transaction.

Although the data bus is often referred to as a bi-directional bus, data cannot be transferred in both directions simultaneously. Rather, data can be transferred from the microprocessor to an external device during a write operation, or from an external device to the microprocessor during a read operation. Figure 1-4 illustrates the 80286 microprocessor's data bus.

Note that the 80286 data bus has been illustrated as two 8-bit data paths rather than as one 16-bit data path. Chapter 5 explains why this is done.

Summary

The microprocessor fetches instructions from memory and executes them. Program execution is normally sequential in nature. Only JUMP

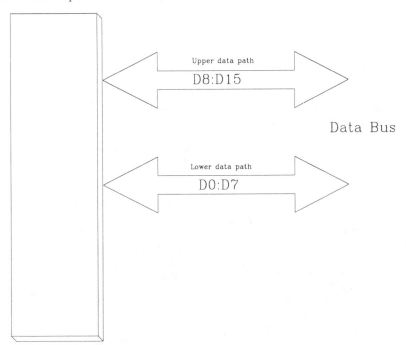

FIGURE 1-4 The 80286 Data Bus

instructions alter program flow. Upon power-up, the microprocessor always reads its first instruction from a pre-defined memory location referred to as the power-on restart address.

The microprocessor communicates with external devices by reading data from them or writing data to them. The address placed on the address bus by the microprocessor identifies the target location. The microprocessor uses the control bus to identify the type of transaction (for example, as a read or write) and to synchronize the fast microprocessor to relatively slow devices. The data bus provides the data transfer path for the data to be read from or written to a device external to the microprocessor.

I/O and Memory: The World According to Intel

Objectives: Starting with the history behind Intel's use of memory and I/O locations, this chapter describes the difference between I/O and memory locations, the definition of an I/O device, and the difference between command, status, and data ports.

The purpose of the M/IO# microprocessor output signal is described.

The amount of memory and I/O address space available for the 8080, 8086/8088, 80286, 80386, and 80486 microprocessors is also specified.

Definitions for This Chapter

• An **I/O device** is any device (except a memory device) that the microprocessor can read data from or write data to.

• An **I/O port** is an I/O address or location.

Some Intel History: The 8080 Microprocessor

The Intel 8080 microprocessor is the ancestor of the entire 80X86 microprocessor family. Many of the family's characteristics stem from this common ancestor.

The 8080 microprocessor's address bus consisted of 16 address lines, A0:A15. With 16 address lines, the microprocessor could place any address pattern on the address bus from all 0's (0000_h) to all 1's ($FFFF_h$). In other words, the 8080 could place any one of 65536 addresses on the address bus and could therefore address any one of 65536 locations located in external devices. In the computer industry, 65536 is referred to as 64K (K stands for kilo, Greek for 1000). Figure 2-1 illustrates a 64K address space. This means that the designer of an 8080-based system could include a maximum of 64K of memory in the system.

In addition to memory devices used for program and data storage, the designer must also use a number of locations in the 8080's 64K address map for I/O ports to communicate with I/O devices. Although implementing these ports certainly is necessary, it depletes the number of addressable locations available to be assigned to memory devices.

If memory locations are actually used for I/O ports, the I/O ports are called memory-mapped I/O locations.

Rather than use up already scarce memory locations to implement I/O devices, Intel added another output pin and two new instruc-

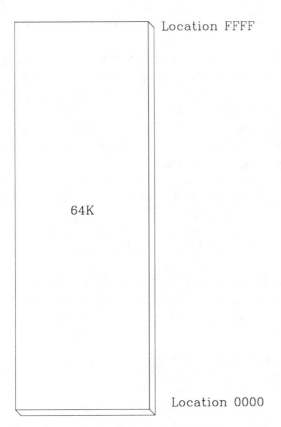

Location FFFF

64K

Location 0000

FIGURE 2-1   Single 64K Address Space

tions to the 8080 microprocessor. The pin was called M/IO#. In Intel signal names, the "/" character should always be read as "or." M/IO# therefore stands for "memory or I/O." The lack of a pound sign after the "M" indicates that a high on this signal line means a memory address is being output by the microprocessor. The pound sign after the "IO" in the signal name indicates that a low signifies the presence of an I/O address on the address bus.

In addition to the M/IO# pin, Intel also added two I/O instructions, IN and OUT, to the 8080's instruction set. When executed, the IN instruction causes the microprocessor to perform a read from the address specified by the programmer. This address is placed on the address bus and the M/IO# pin is set low, thereby indicating the presence of an I/O address on the address bus to external logic. In the same way, the OUT instruction also causes the microprocessor to place an I/O address on the address bus to indicate the address it wishes to write data to.

A separate instruction, MOV (short for Move), is used by the programmer to specify a memory address to move data to or from. When executed, the MOV instruction causes the specified memory address to be placed on the address bus and the M/IO# pin to be set high, thereby indicating the presence of a memory address. Figure 2-2 illustrates the 8080 microprocessor's separate memory and I/O address spaces.

The addition of the M/IO# pin actually created two separate 64K address spaces (or maps), one for memory and the other for I/O. In essence, the M/IO# pin points to the appropriate address space when the microprocessor places an address on the address bus. For example, if the microprocessor places address 0010_h on the address bus and places a low on M/IO#, it is addressing I/O location 0010_h, not memory location 0010_h. On the other hand, if the microprocessor places address 0010_h on the address bus and places a high on M/IO#, it is addressing memory location 0010_h, not I/O location 0010_h. These changes allowed the designer to implement I/O ports without encroaching on memory space.

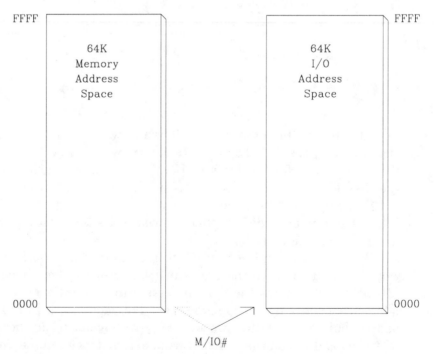

FIGURE 2-2   The 8080's Memory and I/O Address Space

The I/O Device

The **I/O ports** fall into the following basic categories.

1. **Command port**. Data written to this port acts as a command to the associated **I/O device**. The individual bits in the data written to the command port control different aspects of the device's operation. For example, a bit in the data written to the keyboard command port can be a command that either enables or disables the keyboard.

2. **Status port**. Data read from this port represents the current status of the associated I/O device. The individual bits in the data read from the status port reflect different aspects of the device's current status. For example, the state of a bit in the data read from the printer status port might indicate that the printer is out of paper.

3. **Data port**. When an I/O device has data to transfer to the microprocessor, the programmer reads the data from the device's data port. Similarly, when an I/O device is ready for the next character (for example, a character for the printer), the programmer writes the character to the device's data port.

The number of I/O locations it actually takes to control, sense the status of, and read data from or write data to a particular type of I/O device is device-dependent. Simple I/O devices may only require a few I/O locations. For example, the parallel port requires only the command port, status port, and data port.

More complex I/O devices, such as the VGA display interface, can require more I/O locations.

Evolution of Memory and I/O Address Space

The Intel 8086 and 8088 Microprocessors

When Intel designed the 8086 and 8088 microprocessors, it increased the number of address lines from 16 to 20. As a result, the 8086 and 8088 microprocessors can place any address from 00000_h to $FFFFF_h$ on the address bus, which gives them an address range of 1,048,576 locations (2^{20}, commonly referred to as 1M. The "M" is borrowed from the Greek prefix meaning million).

As with the 8080 microprocessor, the 8086/8088's M/IO# pin identifies the address as a memory or I/O address. However, rather than increasing the size of both the memory and I/O address maps to 1M locations, Intel restricts the size of the I/O address space to 64K. The programmer can specify any memory address within the 1M memory address range, but is restricted to I/O addresses in the first 64K locations of address space (0000_h–$FFFF_h$). There were two reasons for this decision.

1. The 8086/8088 microprocessors remain backward-compatible with the I/O instructions in the 8080 instruction set.

2. Virtually no designer requires more than 64K I/O ports (locations) to implement a full complement of I/O devices, no matter how complex they might be.

If you take the example of an IBM PC/AT fully loaded with every conceivable type of add-in I/O expansion boards, no more than 768 I/O ports are used. This is less than 1/64 of the total I/O space available. As previously noted, 64K I/O locations are more than enough for anyone's needs. Figure 2-3 illustrates the 8086 and 8088 microprocessors' memory and I/O address spaces.

The Intel 80286 Microprocessor

With the introduction of the 80286 microprocessor, the number of address lines increased from 20 to 24. Although this increased the size of the memory address space available to the designer from 1M to 16M (2^{24}; 16,777,216 locations), the I/O space was still restricted to 64K. Figure 2-4 illustrates the 80286 microprocessor's memory and I/O address spaces.

The Intel 80386 and 80486 Microprocessors

The 80386 and 80486 microprocessors each have 32 address lines, which provide 4G possible memory locations (2^{32}, or 4,294,967,296 locations. The "G" is borrowed from the Greek word meaning giant; used as prefix, it means billion.). The I/O space is still restricted to 64K locations. Figure 2-5 illustrates the 80386 and 80486 microprocessors' memory and I/O address spaces.

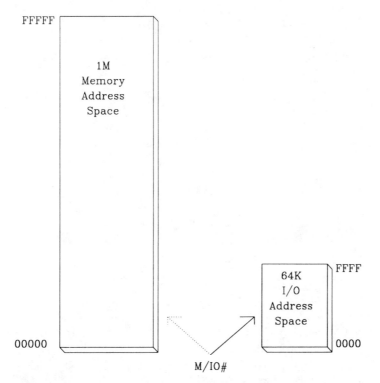

FIGURE 2-3   8086/8088 Memory and I/O Address Space

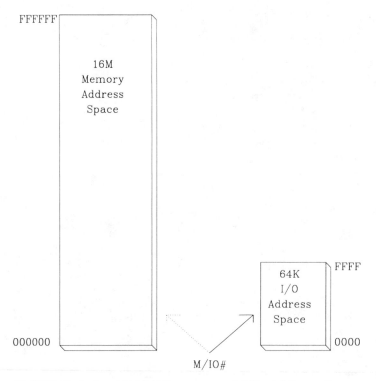

FIGURE 2-4   80286 Memory and I/O Address Space

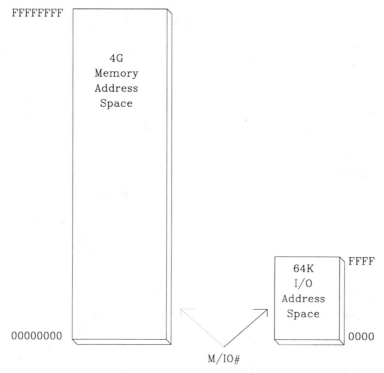

FIGURE 2-5 80386/80486 Memory and I/O Address Space

Summary

Any device other than a memory device (RAM or ROM) that the microprocessor can read data from or write data to is an I/O device. I/O locations are used to control, sense the status of, and read data from or write data to I/O devices. I/O addresses are also referred to as I/O ports. The Intel 80X86 family microprocessors possess separate I/O and memory address spaces. The microprocessor uses the M/IO# pin to indicate which space is currently being addressed. The I/O address space is restricted to addresses 0000_h to $FFFF_h$ (64K locations).

CHAPTER
3

The Address Decode Logic: Is He Talking to Me?

Objectives: Every device that the microprocessor reads from or writes to has an address decoder. The address decoder's only task is to detect addresses assigned to its respective device and alert the device. This chapter describes how address decoders work and explains the conflicts that arise when MCA cards share an address range. This chapter covers the purpose of an address decoder, describes data bus contention, and gives a detailed description of three sample address decoders.

Definitions for This Chapter

• An **address decoder** decodes (examines) the current address being output by the microprocessor to determine if it is within the range of memory or I/O addresses assigned to its respective device.

• The **address map** represents the overall range of memory and/or I/O locations addressable by a particular microprocessor.

• A device's **chip-select** signal line is turned on by the address decoder when an address assigned to its device is detected. An active level on the chip-select line informs the device that the microprocessor is reading from or writing to a location within the device.

• **Data bus contention** occurs when two devices occupy the same address space. A read performed from one device also selects the other, thus causing them to attempt simultaneous use of the data bus. This results in garbled data and, possibly, hardware damage.

• **Don't care bits** are the address lines that need not be examined by an address decoder in order to determine if the address currently on the address bus is assigned to its respective device.

The Address Decoder Concept

When the microprocessor must read data from or write data to an external device, it places the address on the address bus. Every device that can be read from or written to has an associated piece of logic called an **address decoder**.

When an **address decoder** determines that the current address is within the range of memory or I/O addresses assigned to its respective device, it turns on the device's **chip-select** signal line. An active level on the chip-select line informs the device that the microprocessor is reading from or writing to a location within the device. The addressed device then decodes the address to identify the exact location with which the microprocessor wishes to perform a data transfer. Figure 3-1 illustrates the relationship of the address bus, the address decoders, and devices.

A memory or I/O device does not respond to any particular address range. The device's address decode logic informs it that the address currently on the address bus is assigned to one of its internal locations by placing an active level on the device's **chip-select** input pin.

The overall ranges of memory and I/O locations addressable by a particular microprocessor are commonly referred to as address maps. The design of the address decoder, not that of the device itself, defines where a device will "live" within the overall memory or I/O **address map** of a microprocessor.

Data Bus Contention (Address Conflicts)

Under no circumstances should the address decoders for two devices installed in a system be designed so that they both detect the same address ranges. Such a situation causes **data bus contention**.

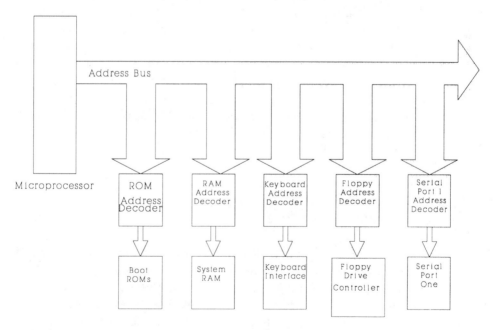

FIGURE 3-1 Relationship of Address Bus, Address Decoders, and Devices

Every expansion card installed in an IBM PC/XT/AT or PS/2 has its own address decode logic that defines the address range the card responds to. Address conflicts are a common problem in the PC world. Problems will arise if the address decoders on two expansion cards are both designed to respond to the same address range. For example, assume that two cards respond to the I/O address range $03F0_h$–$03F7_h$. If the microprocessor executes an instruction that causes a read from I/O location $03F1_h$, both devices are chip-selected by their respective address decoders. Each places the contents of its respective location $03F1_h$ onto the common data bus simultaneously. Both cards may be driving a particular data bus signal line high. In this situation, we have two separate current sources driving five volts onto the same piece of wire. Hardware damage can result.

If one of the cards is placing a low onto a data bus signal line at the same time the other is placing a high on it, the high is forced to a low because the other device effectively grounded the line by placing a low on it. This situation causes garbled data and can also cause hardware damage. This condition, **data bus contention**, is a problem quite common in the PC world because many users populate a PC with cards. This practice increases the prospect of an address conflict.

In order to allow painless resolution of address conflicts, a card designer should allow the user to easily alter the address range to which the board responds. In a PC/XT/AT, this is usually accomplished with configuration switches (or jumpers) on the board. By changing the switch setting, the user causes the card's address decoder to detect a different address range, thereby resolving the conflict.

In a PS/2 incorporating MCA, the configuration switches have been replaced by special I/O locations known as POS registers. This subject is covered in Chapter 12.

How Address Decoders Work

The address decoder function is similar to that performed by the post office. Because it more or less identifies a neighborhood, the zip code is analogous to the high-order part of the address, the upper address bits. The low-order portion of the address identifies the exact location within the neighborhood. In much the same way, the address decoder associated with a device examines the high-order part of the address being output by the microprocessor. It determines if the address is within the range assigned to its device. If it is, the address decoder chip-selects the device. The chip-selected device then examines the lower part of the address to determine the exact location within it that the microprocessor is addressing.

It should be noted that an address decoder need not look at the entire address to determine that it is within the address range assigned to its respective device. If you were traveling in a car and were told to keep an eye out for the two thousand block, you would need to look only at the thousands digit of the address to determine if it was within the desired range. The lower digits would be insignificant to you.

The following three sections describe example address decoders and how they function. (Remember that Appendix A contains a primer on basic logic devices for readers who may need it.) The first example is that of the ROM address decoder in an IBM PC/XT/AT, the second is of the PS/2 ROM address decoder, and the third is of the address decoder that detects many of the addresses assigned to the I/O devices found on a PS/2 system board.

Example 1: PC/XT/AT ROM Address Decoder

The original IBM PC was designed around the 8088 microprocessor. With an address bus consisting of 20 lines designated A0:A19, the 8088 could address any one of one million memory locations. The designers chose to populate this memory map as illustrated in Figure 3-2.

The memory address range from $F0000_h$–$FFFFF_h$ was assigned to the ROM containing the following programs.

1. The power-on self-test (POST).

2. The basic input/output system (BIOS) routines. The PC manufacturer supplies a series of routines (small programs), one for each of the standard I/O devices shipped with a system. These routines are used by applications programmers to facilitate communication with the I/O devices.

3. The interrupt service routines for the standard I/O devices shipped with a system. The interrupt service routines are explained in Chapter 19.

4. The boot program that reads the operating system (PC-DOS, Operating System/2, or another) into memory and executes it.

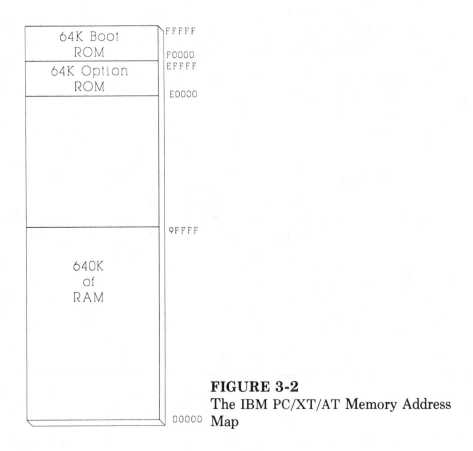

FIGURE 3-2
The IBM PC/XT/AT Memory Address
Map

This ROM is frequently referred to as the boot or POST/BIOS ROM. The 64K addresses from F0000$_h$–FFFFF$_h$ are set aside for the boot ROM. It should therefore be selected whenever the uppermost digit on the address bus is F$_h$ and the M/IO# pin is high, thereby indicating the presence of a memory address on the address bus.

Address Lines

19	18	17	16	15	14	13	12	11	10	09	08	07	06	05	04	03	02	01	00
1	1	1	1	x	x	x	x	x	x	x	x	x	x	x	x	x	x	x	x
			F																

In addition, memory address range E0000$_h$–EFFFF$_h$ was assigned to the optional ROM that could be installed in the empty ROM socket provided on the system board. This capability was provided to allow the installation of a ROM containing the BIOS routines and Interrupt Service routines for optional devices that could be added to the machine. This add-in ROM is referred to as the option ROM. The 64K addresses from $E0000_h$–$EFFFF_h$ are set aside for the option ROM. It should therefore be selected whenever the uppermost digit on the address bus is E_h and the M/IO# pin is high, thereby indicating the presence of a memory address on the address bus.

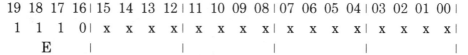

An address decoder to detect addresses for either ROM must look for any memory address that has address lines A17:A19 all set to a 1. That means its high-order digit is either E_h or F_h. To discriminate between addresses for the boot and option ROMs, the decoder then looks at address line A16. If it is low, the high-order digit of the address is E_h and the option ROM should be chip-selected. If address line A16 is high, however, the high-order digit of the address is F_h and the boot ROM should be chip-selected.

The PC/XT/AT ROM Address Decoder Logic

The PC/XT/AT ROM address decoder pictured in Figure 3-3 consists of gates U1, U2, U3, and U4.

The ROM address decoder's inputs consist of address bits A16:A19 and the M/IO# signal from the microprocessor. It has two chip-select outputs, CS EXXXX# and CS FXXXX#. CS EXXXX# is attached to the chip-enable (CE) input of the option ROM and CS FXXXX# is attached to the chip-enable (CE) input of the boot ROM.

To chip-select the option ROM, the signal CS EXXXX# (chip-select $E0000_h$–$EFFFF_h$ range) would go active (low, as indicated by the pound sign). Pins 1 and 2 of gate U4 must both be high in order to set U4-3, CS EXXXX#, low. U4-2 will be high if pins 1, 2, 4, and 5 of U2 are high. This means that M/IO# must be high, thereby indicating that the address is a memory address. In addition, address bus lines A17:A19 must all be 1's. A 0 on A16 is inverted (flipped to its opposite state) by U1, applying a 1 to U4-1. U3-1 will be low, thereby keeping U3-3 high and preventing the boot ROM from being chip-selected.

Address bus lines A0:A15 are not connected to the ROM address decoder and are considered to be **don't care bits** (from the ROM address decoder's view point).

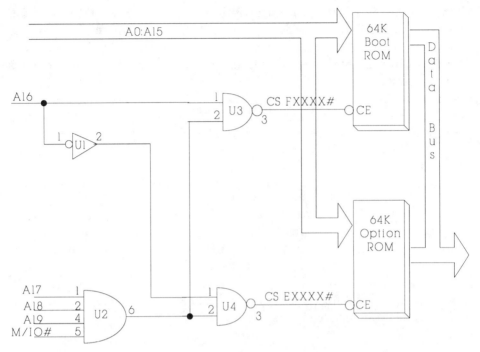

FIGURE 3-3 Example PC/XT/AT ROM Address Decoder

TABLE 3-1 Address Inputs to Chip-Select Option ROM

Address Bus Bits							
19 18 17 16	15 14 13 12	11 10 9 8	7 6 5 4	3 2 1 0			
1 1 1 0	x x x x	x x x x	x x x x	x x x x	Binary
E	x	x	x	x	Hex

Notice, however, that the don't care bits are connected to the boot and option ROMs. Neither of the ROMs looks at these address bus lines unless its respective chip-select signal is set active by the ROM address decoder.

Table 3-1 illustrates the state the address bus inputs (as defined above) must assume in order to chip-select the option ROM.

Address bus lines A0:A15 are shown as "x," which represents a "don't care" condition (can be either a 1 or a 0 because the ROM address decoder does not look at them). If the high-order digit of the memory address on the address bus is an E_h, the address is considered to be for the option ROM and CS EXXXX# is set active (low). This enables the option ROM, which then examines the low-order portion of the memory address, A0:A15, to identify the exact location in the ROM that the microprocessor wishes to read data from. The option ROM then places the contents of the respective location on the data bus to be sent back to the microprocessor. The microprocessor reads the data from the data bus and completes the memory read operation.

To chip-select the boot ROM, the signal CS FXXXX# (chip-select $F0000_h$–$FFFFF_h$ range) must go active (low, as indicated by the pound sign). Pins 1 and 2 of gate U3 must both be high in order to set U3-3, which is CS FXXXX#, low. U3-2 will be high if pins 1, 2, 4, and 5 of U2 are high. This means that M/IO# must be high, thereby indicating that the address is a memory address. In addition, address bus lines A17:A19 must all be 1's. A one on address bus line A16 places a high on U3-1. A16 is inverted by U1, applying a low to U4-1. This prevents the option ROM from being chip-selected by the ROM address decoder. Address bus bits A0:A15 are not connected to the ROM address decoder and are considered to be don't care bits (from the ROM address decoder's view point).

Table 3-2 illustrates the state the address bus lines (as defined in the steps above) must assume in order to chip-select the boot ROM.

Address bus bits A0:A15 are shown as "x," which represents a "don't care" condition (can be either a 1 or a 0 because the ROM address decoder does not look at them). If the high-order digit of the memory address on the address bus is an F_h, the address is for the boot ROM and CS FXXXX# is set active (low). This enables the boot ROM, which then examines the low-order portion of the memory address, A0:A15, to identify the exact location in the ROM the microprocessor wishes to read data from. The boot ROM then places the contents of the respective location on the data bus to be sent back to the microprocessor. The

TABLE 3-2 Address Inputs to Chip-Select Boot ROM

Address Bus Bits																				
19	18	17	16		15	14	13	12		11	10	9	8		7	6	5	4		3	2	1	0		Binary
1	1	1	1		x	x	x	x		x	x	x	x		x	x	x	x		x	x	x	x		Binary
	F					x					x					x					x				Hex

microprocessor reads the data from the data bus and completes the memory read operation.

Example 2: PS/2 ROM Address Decoder

The PS/2 products have expanded the boot ROM to 128K (rather than 64K) and the option ROM has been eliminated. This means the ROM address decoder can be simplified to look like Figure 3-4.

Whenever the microprocessor performs a memory read in the address range from E0000–FFFFF$_h$, A17:A19 and M/IO# are 1's. This causes pins 1 and 2 of U2 to be high, resulting in an active low on U2-3, which is the ROMCS# (ROM chip-select) signal. The enabled ROM then decodes A0:A16 to select the specific location that the microprocessor wishes to read from within the boot ROM. The ROM places the data on the data bus to be sent back to the microprocessor. The microprocessor then reads the data from the data bus and completes the memory read operation.

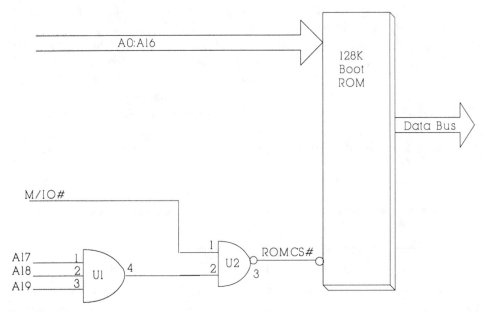

FIGURE 3-4   PS/2 ROM Address Decoder

Example 3: PS/2 System Board I/O Address Decoder

When the microprocessor addresses an I/O location, only address bus lines A0:A15 are used. This is because the microprocessor is restricted to I/O addresses in the range 0000–FFFF$_h$, the 64K I/O address range that has existed unchanged since the days of the 8080 microprocessor. The microprocessor always sets address bus lines above A15 to all 0's when placing I/O addresses on the address bus. This example describes an I/O address decoder that decodes the chip-selects for many of the I/O devices that are integrated on PS/2 system boards.

The address decoder pictured in Figure 3-5 detects most of the I/O addresses assigned to the I/O devices integrated onto the system board. The overall I/O address range detected is from 0000$_h$–00FF$_h$. The address decoder further breaks this address range down into sub-ranges of 32$_d$ locations each. When an I/O address within one of these sub-ranges is detected, the respective chip-select line is activated (set low) to select the addressed I/O device. The sub-ranges and the I/O devices

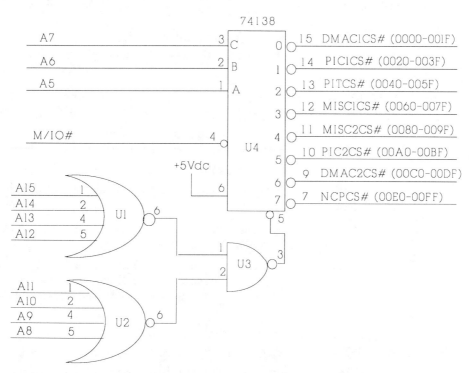

FIGURE 3-5   PS/2 System Board I/O Address Decoder

associated with them are listed in Table 3-3. The I/O devices referred to are described in subsequent chapters.

The system board I/O address decoder consists of three gates and a 74138 one-of-eight decoder.

Operation of the 74138

When the microprocessor begins an I/O read or write operation, it places the I/O address on the address bus and sets the M/IO# line low to indicate the presence of an I/O address. The system board I/O address decoder responds to the address as described in the following paragraphs.

The enabling of the 74138 is fundamental to the operation of the address decoder. This chip has three enable inputs, pins 4, 5, and 6. All three must be active to enable the chip.

1. Pin 6 does not have a state indicator (a bubble), meaning a high is needed on this pin to enable the 74138. The pin 6 enable is tied to a high ($+5V_{dc}$). As a result, this enable is always present.

2. Pin 4 has a state indicator, which indicates that it requires a low input to provide an enable to the chip. The pin 4 enable

TABLE 3-3   System Board I/O Address Sub-Range Assignments

I/O Sub-Range	Device(s) Assigned to Sub-Range
0000–001F$_h$	DMA controller (DMAC) number 1
0020–003F$_h$	Programmable interrupt controller (PIC) number 1
0040–005F$_h$	Programmable interval timers (PIT) 1 and 2
0060–007F$_h$	System control port B, keyboard interface, NMI control, and configuration RAM ports
0080–009F$_h$	DMA page registers, CACP status register, CACP command register, feedback register, system control port A, system board enable/setup register, MCA adapter enable/setup register
00A0–00BF$_h$	Programmable interrupt controller (PIC) number 2
00C0–00DF$_h$	DMA controller (DMAC) number 2
00E0–00FF$_h$	Intel 80X87 numeric coprocessor

input is tied to the M/IO# signal line and is therefore active only when the microprocessor places an I/O address on the address bus.

3. Pin 5 has a state indicator, thereby indicating that it requires a low input to provide an enable to the chip.

Gates U1 and U2 are used to detect all 0's on address lines A8:A15 (an I/O address in the range 0000_h–$00FF_h$). When all of these address lines are low, both gates output highs to U3. This causes U3 to output a low, providing the final enable to the 74138. Only I/O addresses in the range 0000–$00FF_h$ cause the 74138 to receive all three enables, which allows it to decode the low-order address lines to activate the appropriate chip-select line. Assuming that the I/O address currently being output by the microprocessor is within the range 0000–$00FF_h$, the 74138 is enabled and can perform its job.

The 74138 is called a one-of-eight decoder because, when enabled, it uses its A, B, and C inputs to select one of its eight outputs to set active (they are active when low, as indicated by the state indicator on each output). The 74138 uses the binary-weighted value on its inputs to select an output to activate. The A input has a value of 1_d, the B input a value of 2_d, and the C input a value of 4_d. Table 3-4 indicates the output selected for each possible set of inputs.

Assume that the microprocessor is currently performing a read or write with I/O address 0012_h. Address 0012_h is placed on the address

TABLE 3-4   74138 Output Selection Criteria

Inputs			Output	
C	B	A	Selected	On Pin
0	0	0	0	15
0	0	1	1	14
0	1	0	2	13
0	1	1	3	12
1	0	0	4	11
1	0	1	5	10
1	1	0	6	9
1	1	1	7	7

bus and the microprocessor's M/IO# output is set low to indicate it is
an I/O address. Figure 3-6 illustrates how this address appears on the
address bus.

The 74138 is enabled because address bus lines A8:A15 are all
0's and an I/O operation is in progress (as indicated by a low on M/IO#).

Note that address bus lines A5:A7 are all 0's in this address.
Since these three address lines are connected to the 74138's inputs and
have a binary-weighted value of 0, the 74138 activates (sets low) its "0"
output, pin 15. This sets the chip-select line for DMA Controller Number
One active (DMAC1CS# goes low), thereby enabling DMA Controller
Number One. The DMA Controller then decodes address lines A0:A4 to

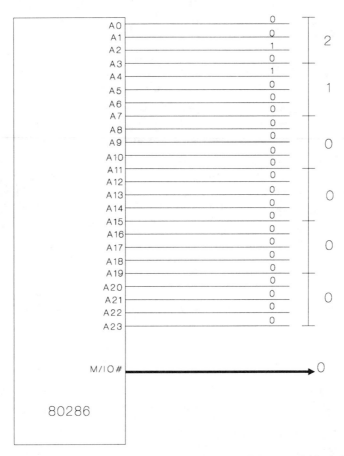

FIGURE 3-6   The Microprocessor Placing I/O Address 0012_h on
the Address Bus.

identify the exact location within it the microprocessor wishes to perform a data transfer with.

To summarize, address lines A8:A15 set to all 0's during an I/O operation enables the system board I/O address decoder. The address decoder then uses address lines A5:A7 to choose the chip-select line to activate. Since address lines A0:A4 are not connected to the system board I/O address decoder, they are "don't care" bits to the address decoder.

This address decoder is designed to detect 32-location I/O address blocks within the overall address range from 0000–00FF$_h$. The designer can implement up to 32 I/O locations for each device to control it, sense its status, and read data from or write data to it. A read or write to any location in the 32-location block assigned to the device by the address decoder causes the device to be chip-selected. The device itself can then decode address lines A0:A4 to select the exact location within itself that the microprocessor wishes to talk to.

Table 3-5 illustrates the I/O address ranges assigned to each of the device chip-selects.

Summary

An address decoder's task is to decode (examine) the current address being output by the microprocessor to determine if it is within the range of memory or I/O addresses assigned to its respective device. When an address assigned to its device is detected, the address decoder turns on

TABLE 3-5 I/O Address Range Assigned to Each Device

I/O Address Sub-Range	Chip-Select	Device
0000–001F$_h$	DMAC1CS#	DMA controller 1
0020–003F$_h$	PIC1CS#	Interrupt controller 1
0040–005F$_h$	PITCS#	Timers
0060–007F$_h$	MISC1CS#	Miscellaneous devices
0080–009F$_h$	MISC2CS#	Miscellaneous devices
00A0–00BF$_h$	PIC2CS#	Interrupt controller 2
00C0–00DF$_h$	DMAC2CS#	DMA controller 2
00E0–00FF$_h$	NCPCS#	Numeric coprocessor

the respective device's chip-select signal line. An active level on the chip-select line informs the device that the microprocessor is reading from or writing to a location within the device. The addressed device then decodes the address to identify the exact location within it the microprocessor wishes to perform a data transfer with.

The "don't care" bits are address lines that need not be examined by an address decoder in order to determine if the address currently on the address bus is assigned to its respective device.

Data bus contention occurs when two devices occupy the same address space. A read performed from one device also selects the other, causing them to attempt simultaneous use of the data bus. This results in garbled data and possibly hardware damage.

CHAPTER
4

Introduction to the Bus Cycle

Objectives: The previous chapters introduced the method the microprocessor uses to communicate with external devices. This chapter introduces the bus cycle, which is the overall sequence of events on the address, control, and data buses when performing a read or a write.

The microprocessor's internal bus unit is a state machine that performs the required bus cycle when the microprocessor must communicate with another device. The concept of the state machine is introduced, as well as the concept of the clock, or timebase, used by the state machine to define the duration of each state. The wait state is also defined.

Definitions for This Chapter

• **Bus cycle** refers to the overall sequence of events on the address, control, and data buses during a read or write.

• A **cycle** of PCLK is the period of time between its positive-going edges (low-to-high transitions).

• A **wait state** is an extra data time inserted into a bus cycle by the microprocessor to allow more time for the currently addressed device to respond to a data transfer request.

• A **0-wait state bus cycle** occurs when the microprocessor samples READY# active at the end of the first data time in a bus cycle.

An Automatic Dishwasher: A Classic State Machine

Any task is easier to do if you divide it into logical steps. A state machine is a device (either mechanical, electronic, or software-based) designed to perform a task that can be divided into steps. Prior to starting the task, the state machine is idle. When commanded to perform the task, the state machine leaves the idle state and moves through a series of steps, or states, performing parts of the overall task during each state. The duration of each state is defined by a clock, or timebase.

In the case of the automatic dishwasher, the dishwasher is idle until you start it. A timer then begins to run, defining the duration of each state the dishwasher must pass through in order to accomplish its overall task of washing dishes. The states are as follows:

- First state—the dishes are wet down.
- Second state—the dishes are washed.
- Third state—the dishes are rinsed.
- Fourth state—the dishes are dried.
- The state machine then returns to the idle state.

Most dishwashers also have one or more switches the user can manipulate to alter the sequence of states or possibly to cause the machine to execute a particular state more than once. A perfect example is the "pot scrubber" button. When pressed, this button causes the state machine to execute the wash state twice instead of just once.

The System Clock: The Metronome

Every Intel microprocessor has an input called CLOCK (or a similar name). This signal is produced when a voltage is applied to a crystal oscillator which then begins to generate an electrical signal of a specific frequency. In essence, the oscillator acts as a highly accurate electronic tuning fork. The signal looks like Figure 4-1.

All microprocessors perform their operations in a highly organized, pre-defined fashion, and each task is always performed during a pre-defined time slot. The duration of each time slot is defined by the output of the crystal oscillator.

Indirectly, the Intel 80286 and 80386 microprocessors use the CLOCK input to define the length of a time slot. They divide the frequency of the CLOCK input by two to yield an internal timebase referred to as the Processor Clock (PCLK). The CLOCK input is referred to as a double-frequency clock because its frequency is double that of PCLK. The 80486 microprocessor, on the other hand, uses the CLOCK input as the PCLK without dividing it. PCLK is the real metronome that defines the duration of the time slots during which the microprocessor performs a task or a pre-defined portion of a task. As illustrated in Figure 4-2, PCLK is half the frequency of CLOCK. When PC manufacturers refer to the operating speed of their computer as 8MHz (mega-

CLOCK

FIGURE 4-1 Crystal Oscillator Output

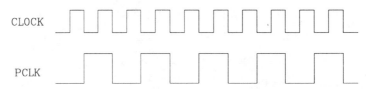

FIGURE 4-2   Relationship of CLOCK and PCLK

hertz, or million cycles-per-second), 10MHz, and so on, they are refer-
ring to the microprocessor's PCLK frequency, not that of CLOCK.

The Microprocessor's Bus Cycle State Machine

When the microprocessor performs a read or a write operation, it begins
a sequence of events called a **bus cycle**.

During a bus cycle, the microprocessor places the address on the
address bus, sets the control bus lines to indicate the type of transaction
(such as a memory read or I/O write bus cycle), and transfers the data
between the target location and itself. This happens in a very orderly
fashion, with each step occurring during the appropriate time slot.

Intel microprocessor chips include a subsystem called a bus unit
that is tasked with the job of running bus cycles when required. The
bus unit is a state machine that is stepped through its various states
by the PCLK signal. The duration of each state is one **cycle** of PCLK.

A **cycle** of PCLK is the period of time between its positive-going
edges (low-to-high transitions). Figure 4-3 illustrates how PCLK is used
to define the duration of each state. For example, if the CLOCK input
frequency is 40MHz (40 million cycles per second), the PCLK frequency
is half that frequency, or 20MHz. In order to determine the duration
of one cycle of PCLK, simply divide 20 million cycles-per-second into
one second. In this example, a PCLK cycle is 50ns in duration (50 nanoseconds, which equals .000000050 seconds or 50 billionths of a second). Since the bus unit states are each one PCLK in duration, each
state is 50ns in duration. If not currently engaged in a bus cycle (a read
or a write operation), the bus unit state machine is said to be in the
idle state. It remains in the idle state until the microprocessor performs
a bus cycle.

Address Time

When the microprocessor must perform a read or a write, its bus unit
initiates a bus cycle. The bus unit leaves the idle state and enters a state

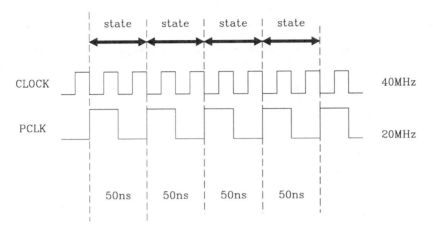

FIGURE 4-3   PCLK States

that will be referred to as address time. (Although Intel uses a different name for this state, address time will be used in this text for clarity's sake.) During address time, one PCLK cycle in duration, the microprocessor places the address on the address bus and the bus cycle definition (type of bus cycle) on the control bus lines.

Data Time

After performing all actions required during address time, the bus unit state machine immediately enters the state we will refer to as data time. As with address time, Intel uses a different name for this state, but data time is the name that will be used in this text for clarity's sake. During data time, one PCLK cycle in duration, the microprocessor expects the data to be transferred between itself and the currently addressed device. At the end (trailing edge) of data time (refer to reference point 1 in Figure 4-4), the microprocessor samples (tests the state of) its READY# input to see if the currently addressed device is ready to complete the bus cycle. If the READY# input is active (low, as indicated by the pound sign), the bus unit state machine terminates the bus cycle.

If a read is in progress, the bus unit interprets an active level on READY# to mean that the currently addressed device has placed the requested data onto the data bus for the microprocessor. The microprocessor reads the data from the data bus and terminates the bus cycle.

If a write is in progress, the bus unit interprets an active level on READY# to mean that the currently addressed device has accepted

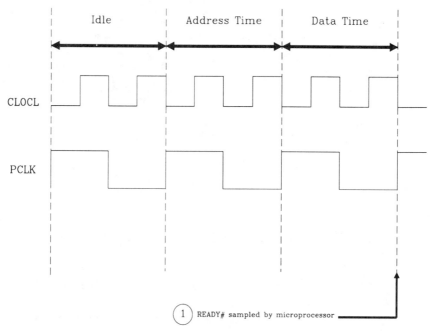

FIGURE 4-4   Bus Cycle Consisting of Address Time and Data
Time

the data being written to it. The microprocessor terminates the bus
cycle. Chapter 11 provides a detailed operational description of the ready
logic in an IBM PS/2.

Figure 4-4 illustrates a bus cycle consisting of address time and
data time. The **0-wait state bus cycle** is the fastest type of bus cycle
the 80286 and 80386 microprocessors can run; the fastest 80286 and
80386 bus cycle takes two "ticks" (cycles) of PCLK. If this were an
80386 running at 20MHz (PCLK speed), a 0-wait state bus cycle would
take 100ns (50ns each for address time and data time).

The Wait State

All bus cycles consist of at least the address time and data time states.
At the end of address time and data time, however, not every device is
ready to end a bus cycle. Some devices are slower than others in responding to the microprocessor's data transfer requests and are referred
to as slow access devices.

Figure 4-5 illustrates a bus cycle with one wait state inserted.
When the microprocessor samples READY# at the end of the first data

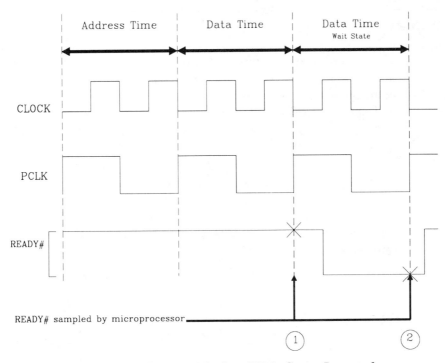

FIGURE 4-5   Bus Cycle with One Wait State Inserted

time (see reference point 1 in Figure 4-5), READY# might not be active. This is the currently addressed device's way of saying "Whoa! Wait up thar big fella!" When the READY# line is sampled inactive, it causes the bus unit state machine to re-enter the data time state again.

During this additional data time, the microprocessor keeps all its outputs the same. In other words, nothing changes; the microprocessor just waits one tick of PCLK. This is referred to as a **wait state**. At the end of this additional data time, the microprocessor samples the READY# input again (see reference point 2 in Figure 4-5) to see if the currently addressed device is ready to complete the transaction.

If READY# is sampled inactive again, the microprocessor inserts another data time or **wait state** into the bus cycle. When READY# is sampled active at the end of data time, the microprocessor terminates the bus cycle.

By holding off the READY# line, the currently addressed device can force the microprocessor to stretch out the bus cycle as long as necessary until the device is ready to complete the data transfer. The currently addressed device turns off READY# until it is ready to end the transaction.

Summary

The overall sequence of events on the address, control, and data buses during a read or write is referred to as a bus cycle. When required, the microprocessor's bus unit performs a bus cycle using the address, control, and data buses. Every bus cycle consists of at least two states, referred to as address time and data time. Each state is one PCLK cycle in duration.

At the end of every data time, the microprocessor's bus unit samples its READY# input to determine if the currently addressed device is ready to complete the bus cycle. The bus cycle ends if the READY# input is sampled active (low). Each time the READY# input is sampled inactive (high), an extra data time is inserted in the bus cycle. This is referred to as a wait state.

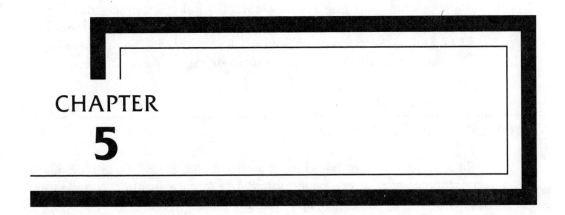

CHAPTER
5

The Cardinal Rules
in the Intel World

Objectives: This chapter describes the three rules that provide the basic guidelines for designing systems around Intel microprocessors. These rules apply directly to the operation of the 80286 microprocessor. The 80386 and 80486 microprocessors use a slight variation on these rules. The chapter on the 80386 microprocessor explains the differences.

Cardinal Rule Number One

Rule: In any system based on the 8086/8088, 80286, 80386, or 80486 microprocessors, every memory and I/O storage location contains exactly one byte (8 bits) of information.

The temptation is great to say that storage locations in a system based on the 80286 microprocessor each contain one word (2 bytes) of information. Many people think this is the case because the 80286 has a 16-bit data bus and can transfer a word at a time. Although its 16-bit data bus allows the 80286 to access two locations simultaneously, this does not alter the fact that each location contains only 1 byte of information.

For the same reason, people are tempted to think that storage locations in an 80386- or 80486-based system each contain a doubleword (4 bytes) of information because the microprocessor has a 32-bit data bus, which allows the 80386 and 80486 to access four locations simultaneously.

Cardinal Rule Number Two

Rule: Every memory and I/O address is considered to be either an even address or an odd address.

The 80286 microprocessor begins a bus cycle when it must read data from or write data to an external device. The address is placed on the address bus signal lines. Logic external to the microprocessor looks at the least-significant address line, A0, to determine if the address is even or odd. Consider the sample addresses in Table 5-1.

The address is even where A0 is 0. The address is odd if A0 is a 1. In itself, this rule may not seem important, but in light of Rule 3, it assumes a great deal of importance.

TABLE 5-1   Examples of Even and Odd Addresses

Address	State of A0	Address Type
000000_h	0	Even
000001_h	1	Odd
$0AFC12_h$	0	Even
$F12345_h$	1	Odd
101003_h	1	Odd

Cardinal Rule Number Three

Rule: When the 80286 microprocessor reads from or writes to an even address, the data (1 byte) is transferred over the lower data path, D0:D7. When reading from or writing to an odd address, the data (1 byte) is transferred over the upper data path, D8:D15.

Figure 5-1 illustrates the 80286 microprocessor's two data paths.

Summary

Every location contains 1 byte of information and is considered to be either an even or an odd location. When communicating with an even location, the 80286 microprocessor always uses the lower data path. When communicating with an odd location, the 80286 microprocessor always uses the upper data path.

These rules are *never* broken. The processor must be surrounded by special logic that guarantees constant adherence to the rules.

80286 Microprocessor

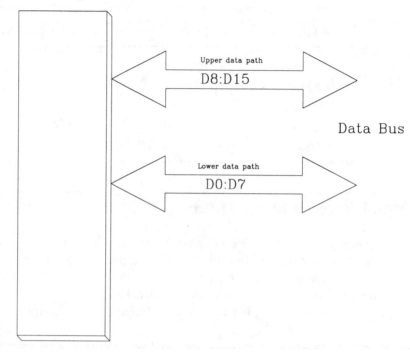

FIGURE 5-1   The 80286 Data Bus

The 80286 Microprocessor

Objectives: This chapter describes the 80286 microprocessor. Emphasis is placed on the hardware interface between the 80286 microprocessor and the remainder of the system. (There are many good books on the market that provide detailed information about the 80286 from the software perspective.) Memory address formation in real mode is covered in detail and an introduction to protected mode is provided.

Definitions for This Chapter

• **Floating the buses** is the term used to describe the process whereby the current bus master electrically disconnects itself from the address, control, and data buses.

• A **queue** is a temporary holding area.

The 80286 Functional Units

Any microprocessor is really a system consisting of a number of functional units. Each unit has a specific job to do and all of the units working together comprise the microprocessor. Figure 6-1 illustrates the units that make up the 80286 microprocessor.

The 80286 microprocessor consists of four functional units.

1. **Bus Unit**. Handles communication with the world outside the microprocessor chip.

2. **Instruction Unit**. Decodes the instruction prior to passing it to the execution unit for execution.

3. **Execution Unit**. Handles the actual execution of the instruction.

4. **Address Unit**. When the microprocessor must address a memory location, the address unit forms the memory address that is driven out onto the address bus by the bus unit during the bus cycle.

The following sections provide a more detailed description of each of these units.

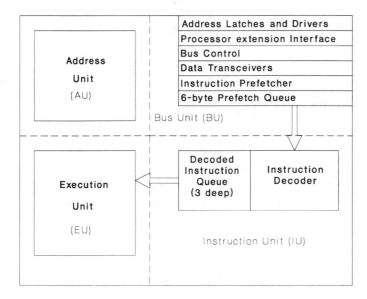

FIGURE 6-1   80286 Microprocessor Block Diagram

The Bus Unit

Whenever the 80286 microprocessor must communicate with an external device, the bus unit performs the required bus cycle using the address, data, and control buses. As illustrated in Figure 6-2, the bus unit consists of the following sub-units.

- Address latches and drivers
- Instruction prefetcher and 6-byte prefetch queue
- Processor extension interface
- Bus control logic
- Data transceivers

The following sections describe the purpose of each of the bus unit sub-units.

   Address Latches and Drivers   When the microprocessor must place an address on the address bus, the address is latched into (held by) the bus unit's internal address latch. (Do not confuse this with the external address latch that is discussed in a subsequent chapter.) The address drivers then drive the latched address out onto the address bus.

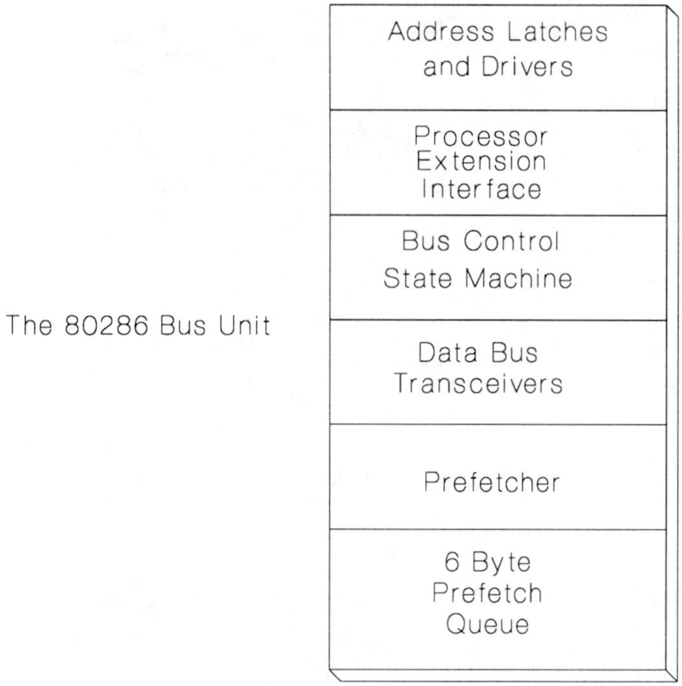

FIGURE 6-2   The 80286 Bus Unit

Instruction Prefetcher and 6-Byte Prefetch Queue   As described in Chapter 1, the microprocessor constantly performs in-line sequential code fetches (instruction fetching). Intel designed the instruction prefetcher to take advantage of in-line code fetching. Rather than waiting for the execution unit to request the next instruction fetch, the prefetcher gambles that the next instruction fetch requested will be from the next sequential memory location and, on its own, performs a memory read bus cycle to get the next instruction. The 80286 instruction prefetcher always fetches two bytes at a time when fetching instructions from memory. It then places these two instruction bytes into the 6-byte prefetch queue.

Since the queue is not full yet, the prefetcher initiates another memory read bus cycle to get the next 2 instruction bytes. These 2 bytes are also placed into the instruction queue. The prefetcher then initiates a third memory read bus cycle to get the next 2 bytes and places them into the instruction queue. The queue is now full. The instructions are decoded by the instruction unit and placed into the decoded instruction queue one at a time. This takes place in parallel with instruction execution by the execution unit and prefetching.

Once the prefetch queue is full, the instruction prefetcher ceases prefetching instructions. If the currently executing instruction is not a JUMP instruction, upon execution completion the execution unit gets the next decoded instruction from the instruction unit's decoded instruction queue. The instruction unit then, in turn, gets the next instruction from the 6-byte prefetch queue, decodes it, and places it into the decoded instruction queue. When 2 or more bytes open up in the prefetch queue, the instruction prefetcher resumes operation to fill the queue back up again.

Most of the time, the execution unit's request for the next instruction can be filled from the on-chip queues rather than by forcing the microprocessor to perform a memory read bus cycle to get the next instruction. When the execution unit executes a JUMP instruction, however, the prefetch queue and decoded instruction queue are "flushed" because the prefetcher gambled and lost. All of the entries in the two queues are marked as invalid. The instruction prefetcher then must initiate a memory read bus cycle to get the requested instruction from memory. This stalls the execution unit until the next instruction becomes available.

Once the instruction has been fetched and placed in the prefetch queue, the prefetcher begins to prefetch once again to get ahead of the game. Since JUMP instructions really do not occur very frequently in most programs, the execution unit may feed off the decoded instruction queue most of the time without having to wait for memory read bus cycles to be performed. In the overall scheme of things, the time lost when the queue must be flushed is minimal when compared to the advantage gained by prefetching.

Processor Extension Interface   This bus unit logic is used by the microprocessor to communicate with the numeric coprocessor (if it is installed). This subject is discussed in Chapter 32.

Bus Control Logic   This is the bus unit's state machine that performs bus cycles upon request. Bus cycles are performed under the following circumstances.

1. Memory-read bus cycle request from the instruction prefetcher.

2. Request from the execution unit to perform a memory read, memory write, I/O read, or I/O write bus cycle.

3. In response to an interrupt request. This subject is discussed in Chapter 19.

Data Transceivers   A transceiver is a device that passes data through itself from left to right or visa versa. During read bus cycles, the bus unit's data transceivers pass the data coming from the currently addressed device into the microprocessor. During write bus cycles, the transceivers pass data from the microprocessor onto the data bus to be written to the currently addressed device.

The Instruction Unit

One at a time, the 80286 instruction unit pops (reads) instructions off the prefetch queue, decodes them into their component parts, and places them into the decoded instruction queue to be forwarded to the execution unit.

The Execution Unit

Instructions are executed by the 80286 execution unit. When the currently executing instruction involves writing or reading a memory or I/O location, the execution unit issues a bus cycle request to the bus unit. The execution unit then stalls until the bus unit completes the requested data transfer.

The Address Unit

When the microprocessor needs to read or write a memory location, the address unit forms the address to be placed on the address bus during the bus cycle. This subject is covered in detail later in this chapter in the section entitled "Addressing Modes."

The 80286 Hardware Interface to External Devices

This section provides a detailed description of the signal lines the 80286 microprocessor uses to communicate with the rest of the system. They have been grouped into address bus, data bus, and control bus. The following sections describe each category.

The Address Bus

The 80286 microprocessor's address bus consists of 25 signal lines including the 24 address lines, A0:A23, and BHE# (Bus High Enable).

Figure 6-3 illustrates the 80286 address bus and BHE#. During a bus cycle, the microprocessor places the full 24-bit address of the target location on the address lines A0:A23. A 24-bit address bus allows the 80286 to address any of 16,777,216 individual addresses from location 000000_h–$FFFFFF_h$. In addition, the microprocessor sets BHE# active (low) when performing a data transfer between itself and an odd address

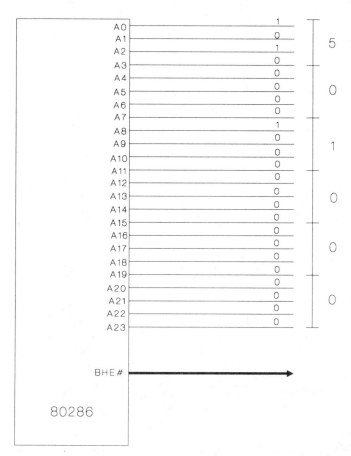

FIGURE 6-3 The 80286 Address Bus and BHE#

(Rule #3). During a bus cycle, the 80286 microprocessor can address just an even-addressed location, just an odd-addressed location, or both an even and the next sequential odd-addressed location simultaneously.

Table 6-1 specifies the binary weighted value of the 80286's address lines. Address bit 0 (A0) has a weighted value of 1. When the microprocessor outputs an address, a 0 on A0 indicates that the address is an even address; a 1 on A0 indicates that it is an odd address. For

TABLE 6-1   Binary Weighted Value of Each Address Line

Address Line	Binary Weighted Value
A0	1
A1	2
A2	4
A3	8
A4	16
A5	32
A6	64
A7	128
A8	256
A9	512
A10	1024
A11	2048
A12	4096
A13	8192
A14	16384
A15	32768
A16	65536
A17	131072
A18	262144
A19	524288
A20	1048576
A21	2097152
A22	4194304
A23	8388608

example, address 000100_h is an even address (A0 = 0); address 000509_h is an odd address (A0 = 1). Since the microprocessor can place only one 24-bit address on the address bus at a time, it is incapable of telling external logic that it wants to address an even address and an odd address during the same bus cycle. A0 would have to be low and high at the same time, which is impossible.

To indicate that it wishes to address an even and an odd address simultaneously, the 80286 microprocessor places the even address out on the address bus and sets its bus high enable output (BHE#) active. External logic interprets this to mean that the microprocessor wishes to perform a data transfer with the currently addressed even address and the next sequential odd address during the same bus cycle.

The data to be transferred between the microprocessor and the even address will be routed over the lower data path, D0:D7, while the data to be transferred with the odd address will be transferred over the upper data path, D8:D15. This action corresponds to Rule 3 in Chapter 5.

When the microprocessor outputs an address at the start of a bus cycle, external logic interprets A0 and BHE# as indicated in Table 6-2. Remember that BHE# is active when low.

The Data Bus

Although it is technically correct to say that the 80286 microprocessor has a 16-bit data bus, it is more correct to say that it has two 8-bit data paths. The lower data path consists of data lines D0:D7 and the upper path consists of D8:D15. Rule 3 described the usage of these two data paths. Figure 6-4 illustrates them.

The Control Bus

The control bus consists of all the 80286 signal lines other than the address bus and the data bus. The control bus signal lines can be separated into the following subcategories:

- bus cycle definition lines
- bus mastering lines
- ready line

TABLE 6-2   Transfer Size Indicated by A0 and BHE#

A0	BHE#	Type of Transfer
0	0	The microprocessor is addressing an even address (A0 = 0) and will therefore use the lower data path to transfer the data byte between itself and the addressed location. Since the microprocessor uses only the upper data path to transfer data between itself and odd addresses, the active level on BHE# indicates that it wants to perform a data transfer with the odd location immediately following the even address it is outputting. This is a 16-bit data transfer using both data paths.
0	1	The microprocessor is addressing an even address (A0 = 0) and will therefore use the lower data path to transfer the data byte between itself and the addressed location. The inactive level on BHE# indicates that the microprocessor will not be using the upper data path to talk to an odd address. This is therefore an 8-bit data transfer using the lower data path.
1	0	The microprocessor is addressing an odd address (A0 = 1) and will therefore use the upper data path to transfer the data byte between itself and the addressed location. The active level on BHE# indicates that the microprocessor will use the upper data path to talk to the odd address. This is an 8-bit data transfer using the upper data path.
1	1	Illegal (will not occur).

- interrupt lines
- processor extension lines
- the clock line
- the reset line

The following sections describe each of these signal groups.

Bus Cycle Definition Lines   When the 80286 bus unit must read data from or write data to an external location, it must run a bus cycle to do so. During the bus cycle, the microprocessor indicates the type of bus cycle by placing the proper pattern on the bus cycle definition signal lines. Table 6-3 indicates each type of bus cycle and the respective pattern which is output onto the bus cycle definition lines.

80286 Microprocessor

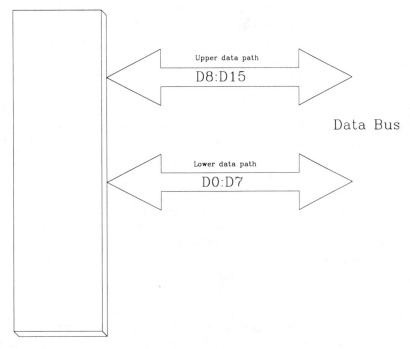

FIGURE 6-4 The 80286 Data Bus

TABLE 6-3 Bus Cycle Definition

M/IO#	S1#	S0#	Bus Cycle Type
0	0	0	Interrupt acknowledge
0	0	1	I/O read
0	1	0	I/O write
1	0	0	Halt or shutdown
1	0	1	Memory read
1	1	0	Memory write

Technically speaking, there is a fourth bus cycle definition line, COD/INTA#. It is the code or interrupt acknowledge line and has something in common with your appendix: if you lost it, you would not miss it. A system needs to use this line only if it must differentiate between a memory read to get data versus a memory read to get an instruction. In most systems, this pin is not even hooked up.

Bus Mastering Lines   Most of the time, the microprocessor on the System Board "owns" the three buses and uses them to communicate with external devices. The microprocessor is the bus master.

There are situations, however, where it is necessary to surrender the buses to other bus masters. For example, when a device other than the microprocessor wishes to use the buses to communicate with another device, it sets the microprocessor's hold request (HOLD) input active. When HOLD is set active, the manner in which the microprocessor responds depends on whether or not a microprocessor bus cycle (data transfer) is currently in progress.

If a bus cycle is in progress when HOLD is set active by the prospective bus master, the microprocessor completes the current bus cycle prior to responding to the HOLD. If a bus cycle is not in progress, the microprocessor responds to the hold request immediately.

In response to HOLD, the microprocessor electrically disconnects itself from the address, data, and control buses. It is just as if the microprocessor opens dozens of switches, thereby disconnecting itself from the external buses. This disconnect process is commonly referred to as "floating" the buses. The microprocessor then sets its hold acknowledge output (HLDA) active to inform the requesting bus master that it now owns the buses and is therefore bus master.

The new bus master can then use the three buses to communicate with any other device in the system. It may remain bus master as long as it keeps the microprocessor's HOLD input active. It should be noted that bus mastering can be dangerous if the proper protection mechanisms are not in place. Since the new bus master can keep the buses as long as it wants to, it can completely lock out the microprocessor. This would have catastrophic effects on the program currently being run by the microprocessor. In addition, it would also lock out the RAM refresh logic from using the buses to refresh RAM memory. In a PS/2, this problem is prevented by the Central Arbitration Control Point (CACP). These subjects are thoroughly explored in Part IV, "The Micro Channel Architecture (MCA)" and Part VII, "Memory."

In addition to HOLD and HLDA, there is a third microprocessor line involved in bus mastering. In a system that takes advantage of it, the 80286's LOCK# output can be used by the programmer to prevent other bus masters from stealing the buses away from the microprocessor. Figure 6-5 illustrates the use of the microprocessor's LOCK# output.

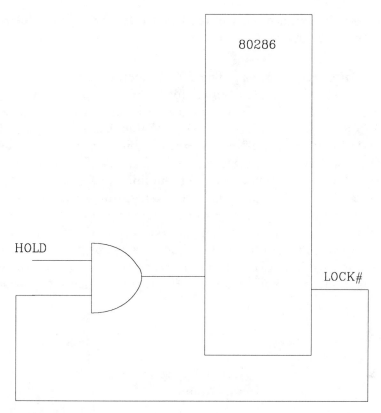

FIGURE 6-5 The Lock Output

If the programmer does not want the microprocessor to give up the buses during a series of instructions, each instruction should be prefaced by a LOCK prefix. Each time that the microprocessor sees a LOCK prefix in front of an instruction, it will set the LOCK# output active while the instruction is executed. The low on the LOCK# line will force the microprocessor's HOLD input to remain inactive, thus preventing any bus master from stealing the buses.

Further discussion of bus mastering can be found in Part IV, "The Micro Channel Architecture (MCA)."

Ready Line   In a nutshell, the READY# input allows slow access devices to stretch out the microprocessor's bus cycles to match their own slow response time. This subject was introduced in Chapter 4, "Introduction To the bus cycle" and is explored in more depth in

Chapter 10, "Detailed View of the Bus Cycle." Figure 6-6 illustrates the state sequence during a bus cycle.

Interrupt Lines The 80286 microprocessor has two inputs used by external logic to "interrupt" the microprocessor. These two inputs are INTR and NMI. The microprocessor's interrupt request input (INTR) is frequently referred to as maskable interrupt request. INTR is generated by the Intel 8259A programmable interrupt controller when an external hardware device requires servicing (for example, the keyboard interface has a keystroke for the microprocessor).

INTR is called the maskable interrupt request input because the programmer has the ability to mask out, or ignore, this input. If the programmer has a piece of critical code (instructions) that he or she does not want interrupted, the instructions can be prefaced with a Clear Interrupt Enable (CLI) instruction. Once the microprocessor executes this instruction, it will ignore the INTR input until recognition of ex-

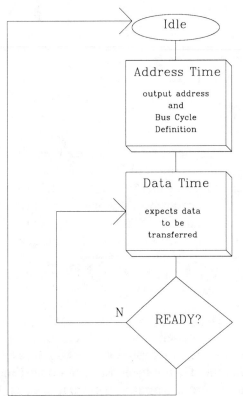

FIGURE 6-6
Flowchart of Bus Cycle States

ternal hardware interrupts is once again re-enabled by the programmer. When the critical series of instructions has been executed without interruption, the programmer should then execute the STI (Set Interrupt Enable) instruction, re-enabling recognition of external hardware interrupts on the INTR input line.

Since interrupts arriving on the INTR line are not recognized while the programmer has interrupts disabled, the programmer should not disable interrupt recognition for extended periods of time. If INTR is ignored for too long, important events can be missed by the microprocessor.

The non-maskable interrupt request (NMI) input to the microprocessor is typically used by external logic to alert the microprocessor that a critical hardware or software failure has been detected (for example, a memory parity error). It is called the Non-Maskable Interrupt Request line because the programmer has no way of masking out recognition of NMI if it should go active. The microprocessor will service NMI interrupts immediately.

A complete explanation of both maskable and non-maskable interrupts can be found in Chapter 19.

Processor Extension Interface Lines   Processor extension is another name for the numeric coprocessor. These four signal lines are used to connect the numeric coprocessor to the microprocessor.

Figure 6-7 illustrates the use of the four processor extension signal lines. Processor extension request (PEREQ) is an output from the numeric coprocessor and an input to the microprocessor. It is used by the numeric coprocessor to ask the microprocessor to perform a memory transfer.

Processor extension acknowledge (PEACK#) is an output from the microprocessor and an input to the numeric coprocessor. The microprocessor uses PEACK# to respond to the PEREQ issued by the numeric coprocessor. It informs the numeric coprocessor that the requested memory transfer is in progress.

BUSY# is an output from the numeric coprocessor to the microprocessor. The numeric coprocessor sets BUSY# active when it begins execution of an instruction received from the microprocessor. While BUSY# is active, the microprocessor should not forward any more instructions to the numeric coprocessor.

ERROR# is an output from the numeric coprocessor to the microprocessor. It informs the microprocessor that the numeric coprocessor has incurred an error while executing an instruction. It causes a

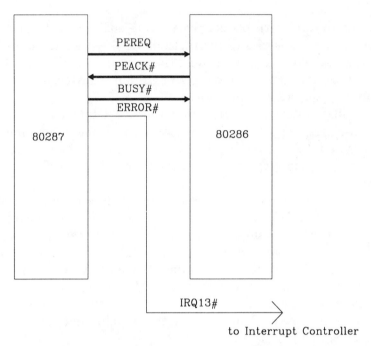

FIGURE 6-7   Relationship of the Microprocessor and the Numeric
                 Coprocessor

special type of interrupt, called an exception interrupt. In the IBM PS/2,
however, the numeric coprocessor's ERROR# output is not connected
to the ERROR# input of the microprocessor. Instead, IBM chose to
attach the ERROR# output to interrupt request level 13 (IRQ13#). In
other words, interrupts are used to report numeric coprocessor errors.

This subject is covered in more depth in Chapters 19 and 32.
Figure 6-7 illustrates the interface between the microprocessor and the
numeric coprocessor.

The Clock Line   Frequently referred to as CLK2, this is the
microprocessor's double-frequency clock input. Internally, the microprocessor then divides CLK2 by 2 to yield PCLK, the real heartbeat of
the microprocessor.

The Reset Line   The RESET input to the microprocessor is
derived from the power supply's POWERGOOD output signal. In addition, RESET also fans out and is applied to many other system components, including cards plugged into the MCA slots. When the power

supply is first turned on, its output voltages are not yet stabile. The power supply keeps the POWERGOOD signal inactive until power has stabilized. While POWERGOOD is inactive, RESET is active. When the power supply output voltages have stabilized, the POWERGOOD signal goes active and RESET goes inactive.

While RESET is active, it has two effects on the microprocessor and other system components.

1. It keeps any activity from occurring until power has stabilized.

2. It presets the microprocessor and other system devices to a known state prior to letting them begin to do their job. This ensures that the machine will always start up the same way.

Figure 6-8 illustrates the derivation of RESET from POWER-GOOD.

More information regarding RESET's affect on the microprocessor can be found in Chapter 8.

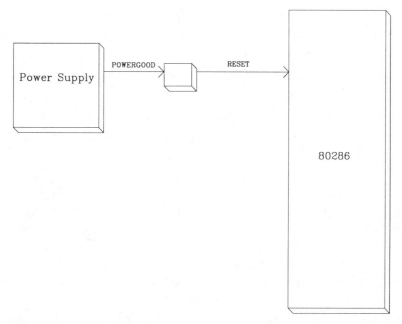

FIGURE 6-8 The Reset Logic

80286 Registers

Although not strictly required in a hardware discussion, the reader will benefit from reading this section. It describes the usage of each of the 80286 microprocessor's internal registers.

Introduction

A register can be thought of as a storage location within the microprocessor. Some registers can only be read from, some can only be written to, and others are both readable and writable. Registers are used by the programmer or the microprocessor itself for the following purposes:

- To temporarily hold values to be used in calculations.
- To receive data being read from an external memory or I/O location.
- To provide the data to be written to an external memory or I/O location.
- To hold values to be used in calculating a memory address.
- To point to the start address of an area of memory containing a specific type of information (for example, a program or the data used by a program).
- To keep track of the memory location the next instruction will be fetched from.
- To keep track of the microprocessor's current status.
- To control certain aspects of the microprocessor's operation.

   Although they are storage locations, the programmer refers to the microprocessor's registers by names (rather then by the hex addresses used to address external memory and I/O locations). Figure 6-9 illustrates what is commonly referred to as the "base architecture" register set of the 80286 microprocessor. Most of these registers are 100% backward-compatible (function identically) with the 8086/8088 microprocessor registers and can be logically divided into general registers, segment registers, and status and control registers.

   The following sections describe each of the registers in the base architecture register set.

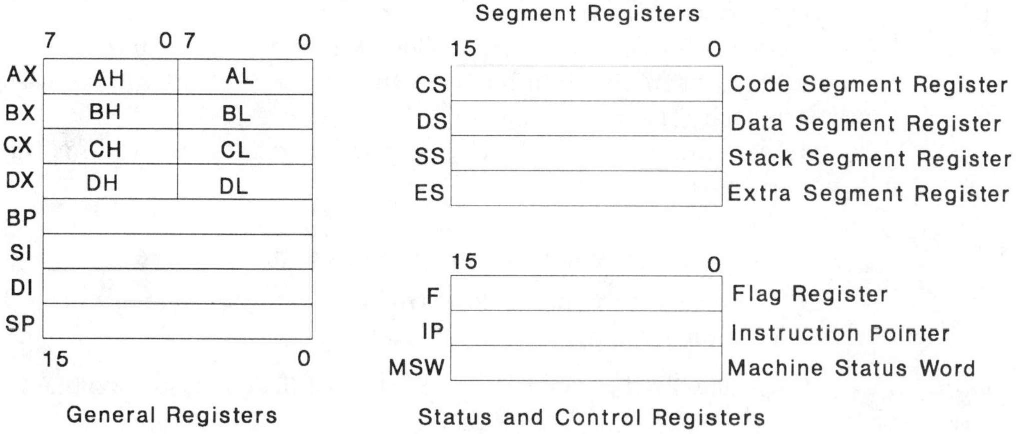

FIGURE 6-9 The 80286 Base Architecture Register Set

The General Registers

This section offers a description of each of the general registers and examples of their usage.

The AX, BX, CX, and DX Registers   Each of these four registers can hold 16-bits (two bytes) of information. As an example, the following instruction will move the value 1234_h into the AX register:

```
MOV   AX,1234    ;move the value 1234ₕ into AX
```

In addition, the programmer can individually refer to each of the 8-bit registers that make up the upper and lower half of each of these 16-bit registers. As an example, the AX register actually consists of two 8-bit registers: the AL (lower half of AX register) and AH (upper half of the AX register) registers. The same is true of the BX, CX, and DX registers.

A programmer who wants to move only 1 byte of information should use one of the 8-bit registers instead of a 16-bit register. In the following example, the programmer wants to write the value 02_h into I/O location 60_h:

```
MOV   AL,02      ;move value 02ₕ into AL
OUT   60,AL      ;write AL contents to I/O port 0060
```

In the example above, the programmer first moves the value 02_h into the 8-bit AL register and then performs an I/O write instruction to write the contents of the AL register to I/O location 60_h. This causes an I/O write bus cycle with address 000060_h on the address bus and 02_h on the lower part of the data bus (Cardinal Rule 3: 80286 always uses lower data path for data transfers with even addresses).

In general, the AX, BX, CX, and DX registers are used for the following purposes:

- To temporarily hold values to be used in calculations.
- To receive data being read from an external memory or I/O location.
- To provide the data to be written to an external memory or I/O location.
- To hold values to be used in calculating a memory address.

The BP Register   Although available for general usage by the programmer, the Base Pointer (BP) register is frequently used in forming a memory address. The programmer places the start address of a table of data items in memory (often referred to as a data structure) into the BP register. A move instruction is then executed that adds an index value to this base address to form the exact address of a data item in the table in memory. This is known as indexing into a table. The BX register can also be used in the same manner.

The Index Registers   The two Index registers are the Source Index (SI) register and the Destination Index (DI) register.

These two registers are frequently used to implement string operations. This is an operation that is performed on a string of memory locations, rather than just one. A classic example would be the move string operation where the programmer wants to perform a series of memory reads and writes to transfer a block of data from one area of memory to another. To accomplish this, the programmer would code (write) the following string of instructions:

```
    MOV    SI,XXXX    ;SI=start address of source
    MOV    DI,YYYY    ;DI=start address of destination
    MOV    CX,ZZZZ    ;CX=number bytes to move
REP MOVSB             ;move string of bytes;repeat til done
```

In this example, the programmer places the start address (XXXX) of the area of memory containing the source data into the SI register and the start address (YYYY) of the destination area in memory into the DI register. The number of bytes to move is placed into CX (ZZZZ), which acts as the Count register in this context. The programmer then executes the Repeat Move String of Bytes (REP MOVSB) instruction. When executed, this instruction performs a memory read from the memory address specified in the SI register. The byte received from this location is then written to the memory location specified in the DI register. The CX register is then decremented and the SI and DI registers are incremented. If the CX register is decremented to 0, all of the bytes have been moved and the REP MOVSB instruction has completed execution. The next instruction is then executed. If the count did not decrement to 0, however, the REP MOVSB is repeated as many times as necessary until the move is completed.

The Status and Control Registers

This section describes the Flag and Machine Status Word registers.

The Flag Register: George Bush's Personal Favorite
Figure 6-10 illustrates the Flag register. The 16 bits in the Flag register may be divided into three fields, or groups.

1. **Status flag bits**. Generally speaking, these bits reflect the result of the previously executed instruction.
2. **Control flag bits**. By setting or clearing these bits, the programmer can modify certain of the microprocessor's operations.
3. **Special bit fields**. These two bits are related to protected mode operation and are outside the scope of this book.

The status and control bits are described in Table 6-4.

The Machine Status Word (MSW) Register　　Figure 6-11 illustrates the Machine Status Word Register. The 80286 MSW register is a 16-bit register, but only 4 bits are used. They are defined in Table 6-5.

When RESET is active right after power-up, $FFF0_h$ is forced into the MSW register. This means that the microprocessor operates in real mode, no numeric coprocessor is installed, and the microprocessor will not emulate floating-point instructions. Real mode is described later in this chapter.

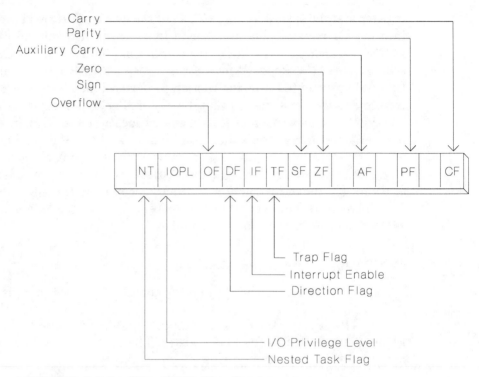

FIGURE 6-10   The 80286 Flag Register

The Segment Registers

When Intel designed the 8086/8088 microprocessor, a programming discipline commonly referred to as structured programming was becoming very popular. Programmers were paying more attention to building programs in a logical fashion.

To aid the programmer in organizing complex programs, Intel created the Segment registers. The idea was to identify a particular area (segment) of memory as holding the program, another to hold the data upon which the program acts, a "scratchpad" area of memory known as the stack and a fourth area known as the extra data segment.

In order to implement this feature, Intel included four 16-bit registers known as the Segment registers:

- Code Segment (CS) register

- Data Segment (DS) register

TABLE 6-4 The Flag Register's Status and Control Bits

Bit	Status or Control	Description
CF	Status	Carry flag. Indicates a carry or a borrow from the high-order bit in the result. Caused by an arithmetic operation.
PF	Status	Parity flag. Set to 1 if low-order 8 bits of result contains an even number of 1 bits. Cleared to 0 otherwise.
AF	Status	Auxiliary carry flag. Indicates a carry or a borrow on the low-order 4 bits of the AL. Caused by an arithmetic operation.
ZF	Status	Zero flag. Set to 1 if result is 0. Cleared to 0 otherwise.
SF	Status	Sign flag. Set equal to the high-order bit of the result. 0 = positive result, 1 = negative result.
OF	Status	Overflow flag. Set to 1 if the positive numeric result is too large (or the negative result is too small) to fit in the destination register.
TF	Control	Trap flag. Also called the single-step flag. When set to 1, causes a single-step exception interrupt after the execution of each instruction. Only used by debug programs to aid in program debugging.
IF	Control	Interrupt flag. When set to 1, the microprocessor will recognize interrupts on the INTR line. Programmer can set by executing STI instruction and clear via the CLI instruction.
DF	Control	Direction flag. When cleared to 0, causes string instructions to increment SI and DI. They are decremented when DF is set to 1.

- Stack Segment (SS) register
- Extra Segment (ES) register

Segment Register Use in Real Mode The following description provides a detailed view of how the microprocessor operates when in real mode. The "Protected Mode" section in this chapter describes how the Segment registers are used when the microprocessor is in protected mode.

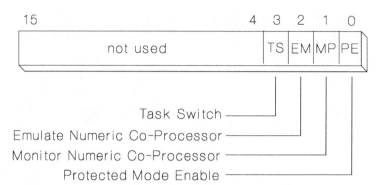

FIGURE 6-11   The 80286 Machine Status Word (MSW) Register

TABLE 6-5   The 80286 MSW Register Bits

Bit	Description
PE	Protect enable. When cleared to 0, the 80286 operates in Real Address Mode. When set to 1, microprocessor operates in Protected Virtual Address Mode.
MP	Monitor numeric coprocessor. When set to a 1, the microprocessor forwards all floating-point instructions to the 80287 numeric coprocesser for execution. This is described in detail in Chapter 32.
EM	Emulate numeric coprocessor. When set to a 1, recognition of a floating-point instruction causes an exception interrupt. The interrupt service routine that handles this exception interrupt then emulates the particular floating-point instruction that would have been executed by the numeric coprocessor if it were present. This is described in detail in Chapter 32.
TS	Task switch. This bit is related to protected mode operation and is outside the scope of this book.

When an 80286, 80386, or 80486-based system is powered up, RESET is active until the power has stabilized. The active level on RESET causes certain default values to be forced into certain of the microprocessor's internal registers. The fact that the microprocessor always starts with the same values in its registers causes it to begin execution in exactly the same way every time the system is powered up. The contents of the Machine Status Word (MSW) register is forced to

FFF0$_h$ by RESET. Bit 0 in this register is the protect enable (PE) bit. The fact that this bit always starts off cleared to 0 ensures that the microprocessor will always come up in real mode.

When in real mode, the 80286, 80386, and 80486 microprocessors operate exactly like an 8086/8088 microprocessor. In other words, although they physically have more than the 20 address lines possessed by an 8086/8088 microprocessor, they are not allowed to use these additional lines. This restricts these microprocessors to the generation of memory addresses from 00000–FFFFF$_h$. The upper address bits above A19 are always forced to 0. These microprocessors are therefore limited to the lower 1MB of memory address space.

The address placed in each of the segment registers points to the actual start address of the segments in memory. Since each segment register is only a 16-bit register, however, you can only place an address only between 0000 and FFFF$_h$ into a segment register. On the surface, this would mean that the start address of each segment must be somewhere in the first 64KB of memory address space (locations 0000–FFFF$_h$). Figure 6-12 illustrates this problem. Although the 8086/8088 microprocessors can actually address 1MB of memory address space, this means that the program, data, stack, and extra segments would be limited to the first 64KB of this space and the rest of the memory would be unavailable.

In actuality, the address the programmer places in a segment register is the high-order four digits of the address. The least-significant digit is imaginary and always considered to be zero. Placing 1000$_h$ in a segment register causes it to point to the memory segment (area) starting at address 10000$_h$ (1000 + imaginary 0). This means that a 16-bit segment register can be used to point to a start address in memory anywhere from location 00000$_h$–FFFF0$_h$. This encompasses all but the last 16 locations of the 1MB memory address range of the 8086/8088 microprocessor.

In summary, then, the segment registers tell the microprocessor the start address of the code, data, stack, and extra segments in memory. Figure 6-13 illustrates how the four segment registers are used to identify the four segments available to a programmer.

The use of each of the segment registers is defined in the following sections.

The Code Segment (CS) and Instruction Pointer (IP) Registers Instructions are frequently referred to as code. The Code Segment (CS) register is always used in conjunction with another register

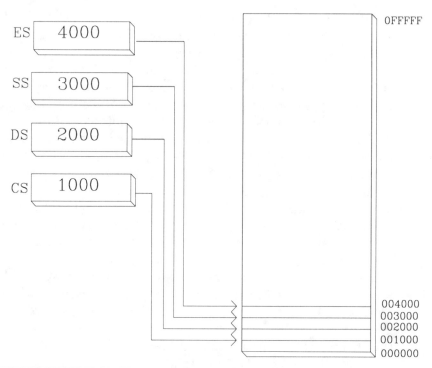

FIGURE 6-12   Result If Segment Registers Were Restricted to 16
Bits

called the Instruction Pointer (IP) register. Together, their only task is
to point to the memory location the microprocessor should fetch its next
instruction from. Figure 6-14 illustrates their usage. The CS register
points to the start address of the code segment in memory, and the 16-
bit IP register points to the exact location within the code segment
where the next instruction should be read from.

The value in the CS register supplies the SEGMENT portion of
the address, and the IP register supplies the OFFSET, or exact location,
within the segment. Intel almost always refers to memory addresses
using the SEGMENT:OFFSET format, using the colon as a separator.
For instance, if the current contents of CS and IP is 3000:0010, this
means that the next instruction will be fetched from memory location
0010_h in the code segment that starts at memory address 30000_h. The
tenth location in the segment starting at 30000_h is 30010_h. Location
30010_h is the actual memory address the microprocessor places on the
address bus to read the next instruction from. The address on the address
bus is called the physical address.

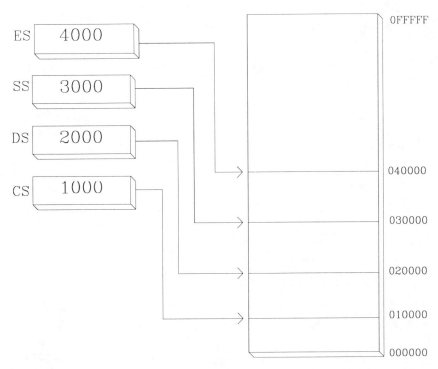

FIGURE 6-13   Segment Registers Point to Start Address of
Memory Segments

A severe limitation of the segmentation scheme used by the 8086/
8088 is tied to the width of the IP register. This register is only 16-bits
wide and is used to point to the exact location (in the Code Segment)
from which the next instruction will be fetched. The fact that it is only
16-bits wide means that it is physically impossible to point to any location within the segment greater than 64KB from the segment's start
address (the segment register value). In other words, $FFFF_h$ is the largest
value that could be placed in the IP register. As a result **segments are
limited to 64K in length**. Consequently, your entire program would
have to fit in 64KB of memory. In order to have a program bigger than
64KB, the program must occupy several 64KB blocks of memory and
the programmer must constantly be aware of which segment of memory
the next instruction to execute resides in. The start address of the memory segment must then be loaded into the CS register. The offset of the
actual instruction within the new segment is loaded into the IP register.

New values are loaded into the CS and IP registers by executing
JUMP instructions. A JUMP to a location within the same code segment

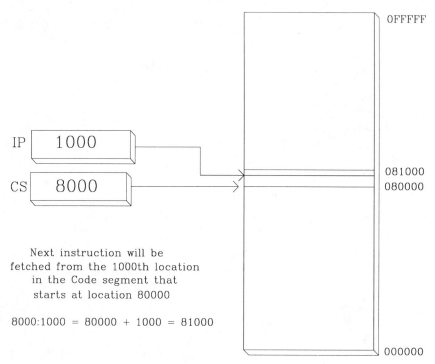

FIGURE 6-14 CS and IP Registers

loads a new value (the offset of the next instruction) into the IP register. Because the JUMP is within the same segment, this is called a NEAR JUMP.

A JUMP to a location within a different code segment loads new values into both the CS (loaded with start address of the new code segment) and IP (loaded with the offset of the instruction to jump to in the new code segment) registers. Because the JUMP is to a different code segment, this is called a FAR JUMP.

The Data Segment (DS) Register Figure 6-15 illustrates the use of the DS register to access memory. The DS register points to the area of memory that holds data associated with the program pointed to by the CS register. As an example, assume that the microprocessor executes the following instructions:

```
MOV    AX,2000    ;value 2000 into AX
MOV    DS,AX      ;contents of AX into DS
MOV    AL,[0100]  ;contents of 0100 in data segment into AL
```

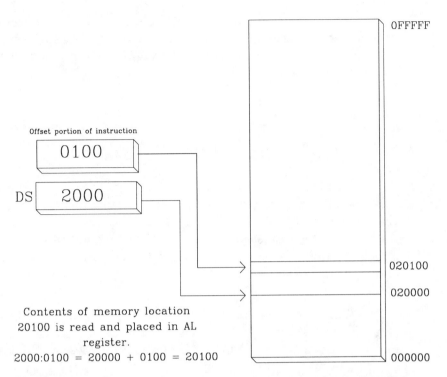

Offset portion of instruction

0100

DS 2000

OFFFFF

020100

020000

000000

Contents of memory location
20100 is read and placed in AL
register.
2000:0100 = 20000 + 0100 = 20100

FIGURE 6-15 Illustration of Location in the Data Segment

This series of instructions first places the value 2000$_h$ into the DS register. Since it is illegal to move a value directly into the DS register, it must be moved into AX first and then into DS from AX. The data segment then starts at location 20000$_h$ in memory.

The MOV AL,[0100] instruction is then interpreted as "move the contents of memory location 0100 in the data segment into the AL register." As a result, the microprocessor executes a memory read bus cycle from physical (actual) memory location 20100$_h$ (20000 + 0100) and the byte read is placed into the microprocessor's AL register. The brackets are read as "the contents of memory location."

Since the programmer did not specify what segment, the microprocessor always assumes the data segment when executing move instructions. The value placed within the brackets is the OFFSET within the segment. Just as the OFFSET portion of the address is restricted to 16-bits in the code segment (by the size of the IP register), it is in the other segments as well. It is illegal to specify an OFFSET address larger than FFFF$_h$ within the brackets.

The Extra Segment (ES) Register   The Extra Segment register is used in the same manner as the data segment register. The following series of instructions is the same as that used in the data segment example above, with one small change:

```
MOV  AX,2000      ;value 2000 into AX
MOV  ES,AX        ;contents of AX into DS
MOV  AL,ES:[0100] ;contents of 0100 in extra segment into AL
```

The ES: added just before the brackets is called a segment override. In this way, the programmer tells the microprocessor to use the ES register to supply the segment portion of the address, rather than the default DS register. The end result of executing this series of instructions would be exactly the same as the series illustrated for the data segment above.

The Stack Segment (SS) and Stack Pointer (SP) Registers   The area of memory designated as the stack is used as "scratchpad memory" by the programmer and the microprocessor. Whenever the programmer needs to save a value for a little while and get it back later, the stack is frequently used for this purpose. The programmer need not specify a memory address when writing to or reading from stack memory. This makes it a very easy method for temporarily storing information.

The Stack Segment (SS) register points to the start address of the area of memory to be used as the stack. The Stack Pointer (SP) register provides the OFFSET portion of the address and points to the exact location in the stack segment where the next item will be stored ($+2$). At the beginning of a program, the programmer places the start address of the stack segment in the SS register. The SP register starts out with a value of $FFFF_h$ when the stack is "empty." In other words, the SP starts off pointing to the "top" of the stack segment as the first place where something will be stored.

Figure 6-16 illustrates the SS and SP registers. When the programmer wants to store a value on the stack, he or she executes a PUSH instruction. For example, PUSH AX causes the contents of the AX register to be written into stack memory (via a memory write bus cycle) where SS:SP is currently pointing. Assume that the SS register contains 3000_h and the stack is empty. The SP register contains $FFFF_h$. Also assume that the AX register currently contains 1234_h and BX contains $AA55_h$. Now consider the following.

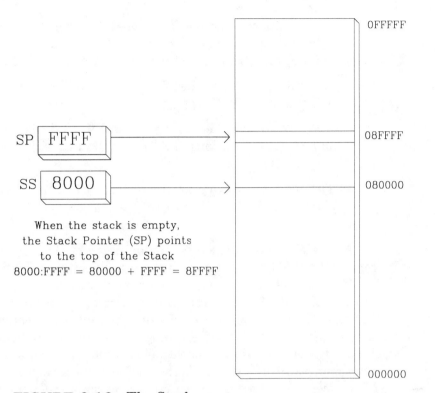

FIGURE 6-16 The Stack

1. When the PUSH AX is executed, the microprocessor first decrements the SP by 2. It then writes the 2 bytes from AX, 12 and 34, into memory starting at $3FFFD_h$ (30000 + FFFD). AX is stored in memory locations $3FFFD_h$ and $3FFFE_h$.

2. If BX is now pushed onto the stack, the SP is first decremented by 2 and the 2 bytes from BX, AA, and 55, are stored in memory starting at location $3FFFB_h$.

3. Each time the microprocessor executes a subsequent push operation, it first decrements the SP by 2 and stores the data into stack memory.

As you can see, the stack grows downward in memory from the highest memory location in the stack to the lowest.

To read data back from the stack, the programmer uses the POP instruction. When the programmer executes a POP instruction, such as POP BX, the microprocessor reads 2 bytes off the stack using the current value in SS:SP to form the memory address.

1. Continuing the example used above, a POP BX causes the microprocessor to read the 2 bytes (AA and 55) from locations $3FFFB_h$ and $3FFFC_h$ and places them into the BX register.

2. The microprocessor then increments SP by 2; SS:SP now point at 3000:FFFD.

3. A POP AX causes the microprocessor to read the 2 bytes (12 and 34) from locations $3FFFD_h$ and $3FFFE_h$ and places them into the AX register.

4. The microprocessor then increments SP by 2; SS:SP now point at 3000:FFFF, the top of the stack.

As implemented by the Intel microprocessors, the stack is a Last In, First Out (LIFO) buffer in which the last object in is the first out.

If the programmer attempts to pop more data off the stack than was pushed onto it, the microprocessor generates a special type of interrupt called a stack underflow exception interrupt to indicate that the stack is empty. Conversely, if the programmer pushes data onto the stack until the entire 64KB stack segment is full and then attempts to push one more word onto the stack, the microprocessor generates a stack overflow exception interrupt. Interrupts are covered in Chapter 19.

Definition of Extended Memory

Figure 6-17 illustrates the concept of extended memory. Simply put, extended memory is any memory that resides at addresses above 1MB (above address $0FFFFF_h$). Memory in the lower 1MB (000000–$0FFFFF_h$) is frequently referred to as conventional memory. Since the 8086/8088 microprocessors have only 20 address lines, they can address memory only in conventional memory space. This means that extended memory does not exist in machines based on these microprocessors.

In real mode, the manner in which the segment registers are used by the 80286/80386/80486 microprocessors allows the programmer to access only memory in the lower 1MB of memory address space (000000–$0FFFFF_h$). With one exception, the programmer must switch the microprocessor into protected mode in order to access extended memory. It is possible to get at extended memory when in real mode, however. The next section describes the exception.

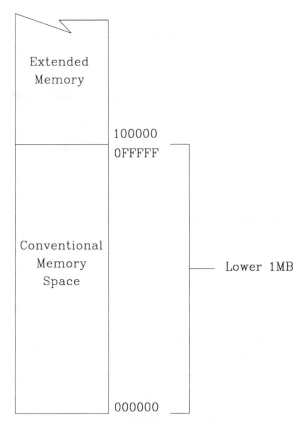

FIGURE 6-17 Extended Memory

Accessing Extended Memory in Real Mode

It is possible to access a small amount of extended memory (memory above 1MB) while in real mode. Consider the following example:

```
MOV    AX,FFFF     ;move FFFF into AX for transfer to DS
MOV    DS,AX       ;transfer FFFF to DS
MOV    AL,[0010]   ;read byte from 100000 to AL
```

In order to form the physical memory address to place on the address bus when executing the third instruction, the microprocessor places a 0 on the end of the data segment value (FFFF) to point to the start address of the data segment (FFFF0). It then adds the offset (0010) to the data segment start address to create the physical memory address:

$$DS + 0 = \text{FFFF0}_h$$
$$OFFSET = \underline{\quad 0010_h}$$

$$\text{Physical memory address} = 100000_h$$

Figure 6-18 illustrates the microprocessor placing the address on the address bus. The microprocessor performs a memory read bus cycle, driving the resultant physical memory address, 100000_h, onto the address bus. Notice that the twenty-first address bit, A20, is turned on. The microprocessor is addressing the first memory location of the second megabyte of memory address space. This is extended memory and we are accessing it in real mode!

Now consider the example on the next page:

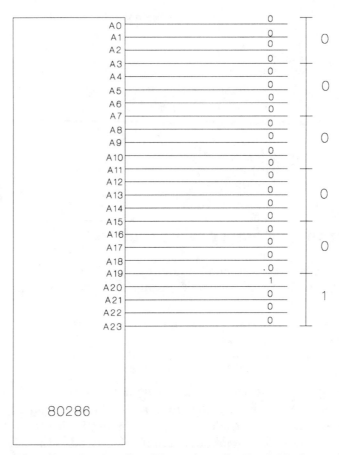

FIGURE 6-18   A20 Turned on In Real Mode

```
MOV   AX,FFFF     ;move FFFF into AX for transfer to DS
MOV   DS,AX       ;transfer FFFF to DS
MOV   AL,[FFFF]   ;read byte from 10FFEF to AL
```

Just as before, in order to form the physical memory address to place on the address bus when executing the third instruction, the microprocessor places a 0 on the end of the data segment value ($FFFF_h$) to point to the start address of the data segment (FFFF0). It then adds the offset ($FFFF_h$) to the data segment start address to create the physical memory address:

$$DS + 0 = FFFF0_h$$
$$OFFSET = \underline{\quad FFFF_h}$$
$$\text{Physical memory address} = 10FFEF_h$$

The microprocessor then performs a memory read bus cycle, thus driving the resultant physical memory address, $10FFEF_h$, onto the address bus. With the value $FFFF_h$ in the segment register and by supplying any offset in the range 0010–FFFF, it is possible to access any extended memory location from 100000–$10FFEF_h$. This is a total of 65519 extended memory locations that are accessible while still in real mode. This method is used by some PC-DOS extender programs to get at extended memory while remaining in real mode. This memory area is sometimes referred to as high memory.

Protected Mode

This section provides a description of how the 80286 microprocessor forms physical memory addresses when protected mode is enabled. This section does not provide an in-depth programmer's guide to all aspects of protected mode operation. For two reasons, that subject is outside the scope of this book.

1. It is purely a programming issue and has absolutely nothing to do with the hardware interface between the microprocessor and the rest of the system.

2. To provide an in-depth description would require a separate volume of sizable proportions. Since there are already a number of good books available on the subject, it would be an unnecessary duplication of effort.

Introduction to Protected Mode and Multitasking Operating Systems

The 80286 microprocessor's protected mode was designed to facilitate the implementation of multitasking operating systems like OS/2 and Unix. Unlike PC-DOS, which was designed to handle a single-task (applications program) at a time, a multitasking operating system is designed to run and keep track of multiple tasks.

A multitasking operating system runs an applications program (call this task A) until task A needs something it has to wait for (for example, waiting for a keystroke or the completion of a disk read operation). Since these operations take some time, it is wasteful to have the microprocessor wait for the operation to complete. Instead, the operating system stores all of the microprocessor's registers in a special segment of memory called a task state segment (TSS). There is a separate TSS for every program that the microprocessor is running. This stored information later allows the microprocessor to pick up where it had suspended task A once the requested operation has completed.

Having stored task A's state, the microprocessor can then give control to a task that was previously suspended while waiting for completion of some other operation (call this task B). The microprocessor loads all of the microprocessor's registers from the TSS belonging to task B. This TSS holds the information describing the microprocessor's state at the point when task B was suspended.

Task B then runs until it again needs something it has to wait for, at which point it is suspended and control passes to another task. A multitasking operating system can be viewed as a juggler who has to keep a number of balls in the air without dropping any.

With the help of the 80286's protected mode features, the operating system must do the following.

1. Protect application programs from each other. In other words, one application program should not play with another application program's memory segments. Any attempt on the part of one application program to access another program's areas of memory should result in an exception interrupt, which will be handled by the operating system software.

2. Protect itself from the application programs it is supervising.

3. Provide the interface between applications programs and I/O devices. It can be catastrophic if an application program manipulates an I/O device (for example, a disk) without the

operating system's knowledge. The operating system would not know data on a disk or the state of an I/O device had been altered. In order to prevent this possibility, any attempt on the part of an application program to execute an I/O read or write instruction causes an exception interrupt, which informs the operating system of the attempt.

In protected mode, segments can be described as:

1. Belonging to (accessible by) all programs. This is referred to as a global segment.
2. Belonging to a particular application program. This is referred to as a local segment because it is local to the currently running application program. Any attempt by a program other than the application program that "owns" this local segment or the operating system to access a local segment causes an exception interrupt.
3. Belonging to the operating system software. This is referred to as a system segment. Any attempt by a program other than the operating system to access a system segment causes an exception interrupt.
4. Read-only segments. Any attempt to write to a read-only segment causes an exception interrupt.
5. Execute-only code segments. Any attempt to access an execute-only segment for anything other than an instruction fetch causes an exception interrupt. Even an attempt to read the instructions as data (using MOV instructions) causes this exception. This means that another program cannot disassemble the instructions in a program's code segment to figure out what makes it tick.
6. Read/write segments. This would be a normal data segment.
7. Accessible only by programs with a privilege level equal to or greater than the segment's privilege level.

As will be seen in the next section, the operating system software maintains a group of tables in memory that describe:

1. The global segments that anyone can access. The global descriptor table (GDT) resides in memory. Each entry contains

a segment descriptor that describes a globally accessible segment.

2. The local segments which belong to a particular application program. The local descriptor table (LDT) resides in memory. Each entry contains a segment descriptor that describes a segment belonging to a particular program.

3. Interrupt service routines. The interrupt descriptor table (IDT) resides in memory. Each entry contains an interrupt descriptor that describes the location and accessibility of the interrupt service routine.

Segment Register Use in Protected Mode

The microprocessor can be placed in protected mode by turning on bit 0, the PE bit, in the MSW register. Prior to actually turning this bit on, however, the programmer must write certain tables of information into memory. Failure to do so will cause serious problems when protected mode is enabled.

With the one exception already described, it is impossible to address extended memory (memory above 1MB) while in real mode. In real mode, the segment registers can only be used to form a 5-digit address, thus limiting addresses to the range $00000-0FFFFF_h$ (the lower 1MB). Since the 80286 microprocessor actually has 24 address lines, A0:A23, it can generate memory addresses from $000000-FFFFFF_h$ (a 16MB address range). The 80286 must be switched into protected mode to do this, however.

When in protected mode, the value in the segment register is used differently than in real mode. In real mode, the value in the segment register (with the imaginary 0 on the end) was the actual start address of the respective segment (CS, DS, SS, or ES) in memory. In protected mode, however, the value placed in the segment register (usually referred to as the segment selector when in protected mode) actually contains the requestor privilege level (RPL) field, the table indicator (TI) bit, and the table index field.

Figure 6-19 illustrates the segment selector's contents. The RPL field indicates the privilege level of the program that is attempting to access the target segment. The TI bit points to either the global descriptor table (1), or the local descriptor table (0).

The index portion of the value placed in the segment register (or segment selector) provides an index into the table indicated by the Table Indicator bit.

FIGURE 6-19 The Segment Selector

In addition to the segment registers, the 80286 also has three registers known as the Global Descriptor Table Register (GDTR), the Local Descriptor Table Register (LDTR), and the Interrupt Descriptor Table Register (IDTR). The operating system programmer must load the start memory addresses of each of the three tables into these registers.

Loading a new value into a segment register causes the 80286 microprocessor to automatically generate a series of four memory read bus cycles to get the 8-byte segment descriptor from the indicated entry in the table identified by the TI bit. The microprocessor computes the start memory address of the 8-byte segment descriptor by multiplying the index by 8 (because each table entry is 8-bytes long) and adding the resulting offset to the contents of the respective Descriptor Table register (either global or local).

The 8-byte segment descriptor read from memory is loaded into a special microprocessor register known as a Descriptor Cache register. There is a corresponding cache register for each of the four segment registers. For example, when a value is loaded into the CS register, the microprocessor uses the TI bit to identify the table to access (global or local), multiplies the index by 8 and adds it to the table start address from the GDTR or LDTR. The 8-byte code segment descriptor is read into the microprocessor's Code Segment Cache register. Only when the microprocessor has the segment descriptor can it add the offset supplied by IP register to the Code Segment's actual start address and generate the bus cycle to access the desired memory location in the code segment.

This rather involved process may seem tremendously inefficient and would be if the microprocessor had to go through all of this every time it needed to access a memory location. In actuality, the microprocessor need only read a segment descriptor from memory when a new value is placed in a segment register by the programmer. All subsequent memory accesses within the same segment happen quickly because all of the segment's descriptive information is already on-board the microprocessor chip in the segment's cache register and can be used immediately in forming the actual physical memory address.

Figure 6-20 illustrates the segment descriptor's contents. A segment descriptor is 8-bytes in length and describes everything you ever wanted to know about the segment.

1. A 24-bit start address of the segment in memory. This means the programmer can specify a start memory address anywhere in the microprocessor's 16MB address range.

2. Unlike real mode, where the segment length is fixed at 64KB, the length of the segment can be specified as anywhere between 1 and 64KB.

3. Segment access rights byte. The bits in this byte allow the operating system to specify protection features associated with the segment being described.

Bytes 0 and 1, the first 2 bytes in the descriptor, specify the size of the segment being described. The next 3 bytes supply the actual start address of the segment in memory. Since this is a 24-bit value, the start address may be anywhere in the 16MB memory address space of the 80286 microprocessor. The next byte is the attribute byte and defines the following characteristics of the segment:

Not used by 80286	Byte 7
Not used by 80286	Byte 6
P | DPL | S | TYPE | A	Byte 5
Upper byte of base address	Byte 4
Middle byte of base address	Byte 3
Lower byte of base address	Byte 2
Upper byte of size	Byte 1
Lower byte of size	Byte 0

Attribute Byte

FIGURE 6-20   The Segment Descriptor

Field
Name   *Purpose*

A   Accessed bit. This bit is 0 if the segment has not been accessed.

TYPE   This 3-bit field defines the type of segment. Using this field, the segment may be defined as:

- an executable code segment (only instruction fetches can be performed from the segment). This prevents another program from reading these instructions so that they can be disassembled.

- a code segment that can be read as data or instructions. This code segment can be read by another program so that it can be disassembled.

- a readable/writable data segment.

- a read-only data segment.

S   S = 1 for a data or code segment. S = 0 for a control descriptor.

DPL   Descriptor privilege level. The program attempting to access the segment must have a Requestor Privilege Level (RPL) equal to or greater than the DPL specified here.

P   If 0, the descriptor is invalid. If 1, descriptor is valid.

An in-depth description of segment descriptors and other protected mode subjects is outside the scope of this book.

Summary

The 80286 microprocessor consists of four functional units.

1. **Bus Unit**. Handles communication with the world outside the microprocessor chip.

2. **Instruction Unit**. Decodes the instruction prior to passing it to the execution unit for execution.

3. **Execution Unit**. Handles the actual execution of the instruction.

4. **Address Unit**. When the microprocessor must address a memory location, the address unit forms the memory address that is driven out onto the address bus by the bus unit during the bus cycle.

When the microprocessor must communicate with an external device, the 80286 microprocessor's bus unit uses the address, control, and data buses to run a bus cycle. The bus cycle allows the microprocessor to transfer data between itself and external devices. Because it provides the interface between the microprocessor and all external devices, the bus unit is the focal point for many discussions in the book.

The programmer controls the microprocessor's actions by supplying a series of instructions that are executed by the microprocessor. These instructions control the microprocessor's actions by manipulating its registers.

When first powered up, the 80286 microprocessor operates in real mode, causing it to emulate an 8088 microprocessor. In order to take full advantage of the 80286's wider address bus and expanded instruction set, the programmer must switch the 80286 microprocessor into protected mode. This is accomplished by setting the protect enable (PE) bit in the MSW register to 1.

CHAPTER
7

The 80386
Microprocessor

Objectives: This chapter defines the hardware differences between the 80386 and the 80286 microprocessors. It does not cover the 80386 registers, real mode, protected mode, or any other software-related issues. The discussions of registers, real mode, and protected mode found in Chapter 6 also apply fully to the 80386.

Definition for This Chapter

• A **doubleword** is a group of four contiguous locations starting at an address that is divisible by four.

The 80386 Functional Units

As stated in Chapter 6, any microprocessor is really a system made up of a number of functional units. Each unit has a specific task and all of the units working together comprise the microprocessor. Figure 7-1 illustrates the units that make up the 80386 microprocessor.

As you can see, the 80386 microprocessor consists of five functional units.

- **Bus unit**. Handles communication with devices external to the microprocessor chip.
- **Instruction prefetcher**. Fetches instructions from memory before the microprocessor actually requests them.
- **Decode unit**. Decodes the instruction prior to passing it to the execution unit for execution.
- **Execution unit**. Handles the actual execution of the instruction.
- **Memory management unit (MMU)**. When the microprocessor must address a memory location, the MMU forms the physical memory address that is driven out onto the address bus by the bus unit during a bus cycle.

The 80386's Hardware Interface to the Outside World

This section provides a detailed description of the signal lines the 80386 microprocessor uses to communicate with the rest of the system. Many

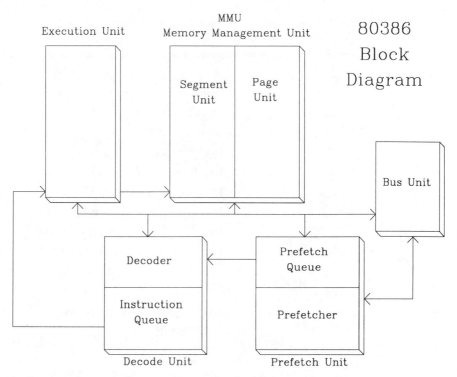

FIGURE 7-1   80386 Microprocessor Block Diagram

of these signal lines serve the same purpose as on the 80286 microprocessor. These signals are listed in Table 7-1.

The remainder of the 80386 signals have been grouped into address bus, data bus, and control bus categories. A description of each category follows.

The Address Bus

The 80386's address bus consists of 2 sets of signal lines. They are the address bus, which consists of 30 signal lines designated A2:A31, and the byte enable bus, which consists of the 4 signal lines designated BE0#:BE3#.

As demonstrated later in this chapter, the 80386 and the 80486 use the address bus, A2:A31, to identify a group of four contiguous locations, known as a **doubleword**.

The 80386 and 80486 use the byte enable lines to identify one or more of the four locations with which it actually wishes to perform

TABLE 7-1 Signals Common to the 80286 and 80386
Microprocessors

Signal Name	Description
CLK2	Double frequency clock input
M/IO#	Memory or I/O output
LOCK#	Lock output
READY#	Ready input
HOLD	Hold request input
HLDA	Hold acknowledge output
PEREQ	Processor extension request input
BUSY#	Processor extension busy input
ERROR#	Processor extension error input
INTR	Interrupt request input
NMI	Non-maskable interrupt request input
RESET	Reset input

a data transfer. Internally, the 80386 and 80486 microprocessors actually generate 32-bit addresses, giving them the ability to address any one of 4GB (4 gigabytes or 4294 megabytes) individual memory locations. When the microprocessor attempts to place a 32-bit address on the address bus, however, the two least-significant address bits, A0 and A1, get stripped off because these two address lines do not physically exist on an 80386 or 80486 microprocessor.

When designing an 80386- or 80486-based system, one should always assume that A0 and A1 are 0 whenever the microprocessor outputs an address during a bus cycle. Let's examine the result. Table 7-2 illustrates a number of addresses being output by the 80386. Remember that address bits 0 and 1 are stripped off during address output and are always assumed to be 0.

The result of always forcing A0 and A1 to 0 is that the 80386 microprocessor is capable only of outputting every fourth address. It is physically incapable of addressing any of the intervening addresses. When the 80386 outputs an address, it is really identifying a group of four locations, called a doubleword, starting at the address presented on the address bus.

TABLE 7-2 Example Addresses Output by an 80386

Address to Be Output (in hex)	Address Placed on Address Bus (in hex)
00000000	00000000
00000001	00000000
00000002	00000000
00000004	00000004
00000005	00000004
00000006	00000004
00000007	00000004
00000008	00000008
00000009	00000008
0000000A	00000008
0000000B	00000008
0000000C	0000000C
0000000D	0000000C
0000000E	0000000C
0000000F	0000000C
00000010	00000010
00000011	00000010
00000012	00000010
00000013	00000010

In addition to identifying the doubleword address on A2:A31, the microprocessor also sets one or more of the byte enable lines active to indicate which of the four locations it really wants to communicate with during the current bus cycle. Turning on a byte enable line also identifies which of the 80386's four data paths will be used to communicate with the identified location(s) in the doubleword.

The BE0# line is associated with the first location in the group of four (doubleword) and with the lowest data path, D0:D7. BE1# is associated with the second location in the doubleword and with the second data path, D8:D15. BE2# is associated with the third location in the doubleword and with the third data path, D16:D23. BE3# is associated with the fourth location in the doubleword and with the fourth data path, D24:D31. Table 7-3 illustrates this relationship.

TABLE 7-3   Relationship Between Byte Enables, Data Paths, and Locations in Doubleword

Byte Enable	Data Path Used	Location in Doubleword
BE0#	D0:D7	First
BE1#	D8:D15	Second
BE2#	D16:D23	Third
BE3#	D24:D31	Fourth

Figure 7-2 illustrates this same relationship. A2:A31 identify the doubleword. The active byte enable lines identify the location(s) within the addressed doubleword and the data path(s) to be used when communicating with them.

Table 7-4 illustrates several example addresses and a description of how they are interpreted by external logic.

In the first example, the microprocessor is identifying the doubleword starting at location 00001000_h. By also turning on the BE0# line, the microprocessor indicates its intention to communicate with the first location in the doubleword using the first data path (D0:D7).

In the second example, the microprocessor is identifying the doubleword starting at location $FA026504_h$. By also turning on the BE2# and BE3# lines, the microprocessor indicates its intention to communicate with the third and fourth locations in the doubleword using the third (D16:D23) and fourth (D24:D31) data paths.

In the third example, the microprocessor is identifying the doubleword starting at location 00000108_h. By also turning on all four of the BE lines, the microprocessor indicates its intention to communicate with all four locations in the doubleword using all four data paths.

In the fourth example, the microprocessor is identifying the doubleword starting at location $01AD0F0C_h$. By also turning on the BE1# and BE2# lines, it indicates its intention to communicate with the second and third locations in the doubleword using the second (D8:D15) and third (D16:D23) data paths.

The 80386 microprocessor is capable of performing 8-, 16-, 24-, and 32-bit transfers. When turning on multiple byte enables, it can turn on only adjacent byte enables, however. Table 7-5 illustrates the valid and invalid combinations of byte enables that can be generated during a bus cycle.

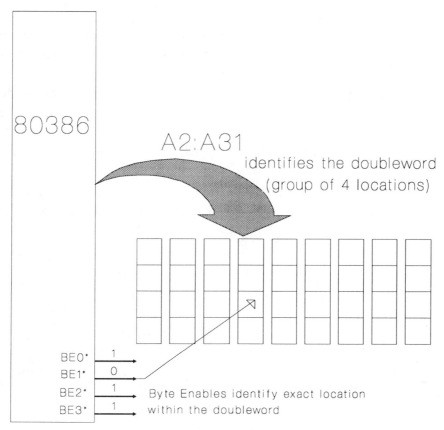

FIGURE 7-2 Address/Byte Enable Relationship

TABLE 7-4 80386 Addressing Examples

Address on A2:A31	BE3#	BE2#	BE1#	BE0#	Location(s) Addressed	Data Path Used
00001000	1	1	1	0	00001000	0
FA026504	0	0	1	1	FA026506, FA026507	2, 3
00000108	0	0	0	0	00000108-to-0000010B	0-3
01AD0F0C	1	0	0	1	01AD0F0D, 01AD0F0E	2, 3

TABLE 7-5 Byte Enable Combinations

BE3#	BE2#	BE1#	BE0#	Transfer Description
1	1	1	0	8-bit transfer with one location
1	1	0	1	8-bit transfer with one location
1	1	0	0	16-bit transfer with two locations
1	0	1	1	8-bit transfer with one location
1	0	1	0	Illegal
1	0	0	1	16-bit transfer with two locations
1	0	0	0	24-bit transfer with three locations
0	1	1	1	8-bit transfer with one location
0	1	1	0	Illegal
0	1	0	1	Illegal
0	1	0	0	Illegal
0	0	1	1	16-bit transfer with two locations
0	0	1	0	Illegal
0	0	0	1	24-bit transfer with three locations
0	0	0	0	32-bit transfer with four locations

Table 7-6 illustrates the resultant address and byte enables generated in the bus cycle caused by execution of the indicated instruction. All examples assume that the Data Segment register has 0000_h in it.

With regard to the last table entry, the EAX (Extended AX) register is the 80386's 32-bit version of the AX register.

A 24-bit transfer occurs if the programmer attempts to perform a transfer that crosses a doubleword address boundary. For example, assume the DS register contains 0000_h and the programmer attempts to execute the following instruction:

```
MOV [0101],EAX
```

This tells the 80386 (or 80486) to write the 4 bytes in the 32-bit EAX register to memory starting at location 00000101_h. To do this, the microprocessor must write the lower 3 bytes in the EAX register to locations 00000101_h–00000103_h in the doubleword starting at 00000100_h.

TABLE 7-6　Example Instructions and Resultant Addresses

Instruction	Address	BE3#	BE2#	BE1#	BE0#	Transfer Type
MOV AL,[0100]	00000100	1	1	1	0	8-bit transfer
MOV AL,[0101]	00000100	1	1	0	1	8-bit transfer
MOV BL,[0102]	00000100	1	0	1	1	8-bit transfer
MOV AH,[0103]	00000100	0	1	1	1	8-bit transfer
MOV AX,[0100]	00000100	1	1	0	0	16-bit transfer
MOV AX,[0101]	00000100	1	0	0	1	16-bit transfer
MOV AX,[0102]	00000100	0	0	1	1	16-bit transfer
MOV EAX,[0100]	00000100	0	0	0	0	32-bit transfer

It must then write the most-significant byte in the EAX register to the first location (00000104_h) in the doubleword starting at location 00000104_h. Because it cannot address two doublewords at the same time, the microprocessor must generate two back-to-back bus cycles.

During the first bus cycle, the microprocessor attempts to place address 00000101_h on the address bus, but A0 and A1 are stripped off on the way out. The resultant address placed on the address bus is 00000100_h. This identifies the doubleword starting at memory location 00000100_h. Since the programmer instructed the microprocessor to write the 4 bytes in the EAX register to memory starting at location 00000101_h, the microprocessor turns on BE1#, BE2#, and BE3# (but not BE0#) during the first bus cycle. This tells external logic that the microprocessor wants to communicate with the upper three locations in the doubleword (00000101_h–00000103_h), but not the first one (00000100_h). The least-significant 3 bytes in the EAX register are driven out onto the upper 3 data paths by the microprocessor and written into memory locations 00000101_h–00000103_h.

After the first bus cycle has completed, the microprocessor automatically initiates a second bus cycle, placing the next doubleword address, 00000104_h, on the address bus. This identifies the doubleword starting at memory location 00000104_h. Since the programmer instructed the microprocessor to write the 4 bytes in the EAX register to memory locations 00000101_h–00000104_h, the microprocessor now turns on only BE0#. This tells external logic that the microprocessor wants to communicate with the first location in the doubleword, but not the upper three. The most-significant byte in the EAX register is driven out onto the lowest data path, D0:D7, by the microprocessor and written into memory location 00000104_h. This completes the second bus cycle and also the execution of the MOV instruction.

The 80386 (or 80486) microprocessor is inefficient when attempting transfers that cross doubleword address boundaries. To obtain optimum data throughput (transfer speed), Intel therefore urges programmers to perform data transfers that do not cross doubleword address boundaries.

The Data Bus

The 80386 (and 80486) microprocessor has a 32-bit data bus. It is more correct, however, to think of it as having four 8-bit data paths:

- Data path 0 is comprised of D0:D7.
- Data path 1 is comprised of D8:D15.
- Data path 2 is comprised of D16:D23.
- Data path 3 is comprised of D24:D31.

Figure 7-3 illustrates the four data paths. Every doubleword consists of four locations and starts at an even address that is divisible by four. The microprocessor communicates with the first location over data path 0 (D0:D7), the second over data path 1 (D8:D15), the third over data path 2 (D16:D23), and the fourth over data path 3 (D24:D31).

The Control Bus

The control bus consists of all the 80386 signal lines other than the address bus, byte enables, and the data bus. These signal lines can be separated into the following subcategories:

- Bus cycle definition outputs
- Clock input
- Reset input
- Ready input
- Bus mastering lines
- Interrupt inputs

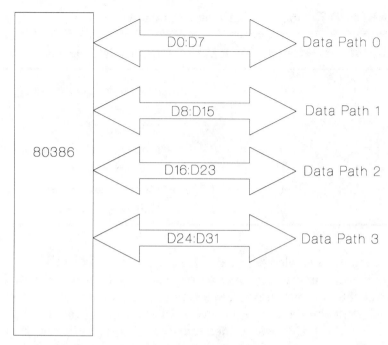

FIGURE 7-3   The 80386 Data Bus

- Processor extension lines
- Address status output
- Pipelining control input
- Bus size 16 input

The following paragraphs describe only the 80386 signal lines that differ from the 80286's control bus lines.

Bus Cycle Definition Outputs   To read data from or write data to an external location, the 80386's bus unit must run a bus cycle. During the bus cycle, the microprocessor indicates the type of bus cycle by placing the proper pattern on the bus cycle definition signal lines. Table 7-7 shows each type of bus cycle and the respective pattern that will be output onto the bus cycle definition lines.

Processor Extension Lines   With one exception, the 80386 (and 80486) microprocessor uses the same signal lines as the 80286 microprocessor to interface to the numeric coprocessor. The processor

TABLE 7-7   80386 Bus Cycle Definition

M/IO#	D/C#	W/R#	Bus Cycle Type
0	0	0	Interrupt acknowledge
0	1	0	I/O read
0	1	1	I/O write
1	0	0	Memory code (instruction) read
1	1	0	Memory data read
1	1	1	Memory data write
1	0	1	Halt or shutdown

extension acknowledge (PEACK#) signal line has been eliminated. When the 80387 numeric coprocessor requests (by turning on PEREQ) that the 80386 microprocessor run a bus cycle for it, the 80386 has no choice but to run the requested bus cycle. Intel decided that the PEACK# line used on the 80286 was unnecessary because it indicated that the microprocessor was performing a mandatory function.

Address Status Output   At the start of a bus cycle during "address time," the 80386 microprocessor places the address on the address bus and the bus cycle definition on the control bus. It also activates the address status (ADS#) output to indicate that a valid address and bus cycle definition are present on the buses.

Pipelining Control Input   See Chapter 10 for a discussion of 80286 address pipelining. The 80386 handles address pipelining differently than the 80286. The 80386 microprocessor has an input called next address (NA#). The following actions occur during a bus cycle.

1. The microprocessor outputs the address of the device it wishes to communicate with.

2. The device's address decode logic decodes the address on the address bus and chip-selects its device.

3. Logic associated with the addressed device latches the decoded chip-select and lower address bits on the address bus.

4. Since the addressed device's logic has now latched the address information, it no longer needs the address the microprocessor

is presenting on the bus. It then turns on the 80386's NA# signal, alerting the microprocessor that it can place the address for the next bus cycle onto the address bus early (during the current bus cycle). This is a variation on the address pipelining scheme used by the 80286 microprocessor. Permitting the microprocessor to place the address for the upcoming bus cycle onto the address bus early allows the next device to be addressed to see its address early. This allows the designer to use relatively slow access devices. The early decoding of the address and selection of the addressed device allows the slow device to be ready to complete the bus cycle earlier in the bus cycle than if it had not received the address for decoding until the microprocessor caused the address to be latched into the external address latch.

When addressed devices allow the microprocessor to place the next address on the bus early for a number of back-to-back bus cycles, the 80386 microprocessor is utilizing the buses to their fullest potential. These back-to-back, pipelined bus cycles provide the highest bandwidth (transfer rate) on the buses.

Bus Size 16 Input   The 80386 microprocessor has an input called Bus Size 16 (BS16#) that is used to inform the 80386 that the currently addressed device is a 16-bit device rather than a 32-bit device. If BS16# is sampled active, the 80386 performs data transfers with the addressed device using only the lower two data paths, D0:D7 and D8:D15. In cases where the 80386 requires the transfer of more than 16-bits, the microprocessor automatically generates additional bus cycles to fulfill the data transfer request if BS16# is sampled active.

For example, consider the actions caused by the execution of the following instruction (assume DS = 0000):

```
MOV EAX,[1F08]
```

Assume that the addressed device is a 16-bit device. The programmer is requesting the transfer of a doubleword (because the EAX register is 4 bytes in size) starting at memory location $00001F08_h$. At the beginning of the first bus cycle, the microprocessor places address $00001F08_h$ on the address bus and turns on all four byte enable outputs. When the currently addressed device's address decoder detects the address, it turns on BS16#. This informs the microprocessor that the currently addressed device is not capable of communicating over the upper two data paths.

The contents of location $00001F08_h$ is placed on D0:D7 and the contents of location $00001F09_h$ is placed on D8:D15 by the addressed memory. At the end of the bus cycle, when READY# is sampled active, the microprocessor will read the 2 data bytes and place them in the lower 2 bytes of the EAX register.

The microprocessor then automatically begins a second bus cycle with just BE2# and BE3# set active. The addressed 16-bit device's address decoder once again turns on BS16#, and the contents of $00001F0A_h$ and $00001F0B_h$ are transferred back to the microprocessor over the 2 lower data paths. At the end of the bus cycle, the microprocessor reads the 2 data bytes and places them into the upper 2 bytes of the EAX register, completing the overall transfer. This feature is referred to as dynamic bus sizing.

Summary

The 80386 microprocessor is extremely similar to the 80286 microprocessor. The major differences follow.

- The 80386 microprocessor has four data paths versus the 80286's two, thereby allowing double the transfer rate per bus cycle.

- The 80386 microprocessor has a larger address bus that allows up to 4GB of memory (versus 16MB maximum for the 80286).

- The 80386 microprocessor's address pipelining lead time is adjustable (versus fixed lead time for the 80286).

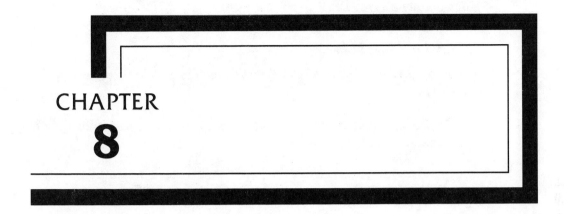

CHAPTER

8

The Power-Up Sequence

Objective: This chapter details the sequence of operations that occur immediately after a PS/2 is powered on.

Definitions for This Chapter

• **Non-volatile memory** is memory that does not lose its data when power is lost.

• **Volatile memory** is memory that does not retain stored information when power is lost.

The Power Supply: Primary Reset Source

The power supply provides the operating voltages necessary for system operation. When the power switch is first placed in the ON position, it takes some time for the power supply's output voltages to reach their proper operating levels. Erratic operation results if the system components are allowed to begin operating before the voltages have stabilized.

Figure 8-1 illustrates the derivation of RESET from POWER-GOOD. Every PC and PS/2 power supply produces an output signal commonly called POWERGOOD. On the system board, the POWER-GOOD signal produces the RESET signal. During the period required for stabilization of the output voltages, the POWERGOOD signal is kept inactive by the power supply. The RESET signal is kept active while POWERGOOD is inactive.

While RESET is active, it affects the microprocessor and other system components in two ways:

1. It keeps any activity from occurring until power has stabilized.

2. It presets the microprocessor and other system devices to a known state prior to letting them begin to do their job. This ensures that the machine will always start up the same way.

How RESET Affects the Microprocessor

Table 8-1 illustrates the values forced into the microprocessor's registers when RESET is active.

The microprocessor cannot fetch and execute instructions while RESET is active.

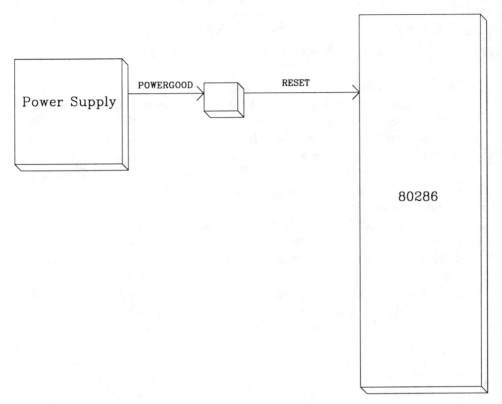

FIGURE 8-1 RESET Is Derived from POWERGOOD

TABLE 8-1 Values Preset into Microprocessor Registers by RESET

Register	Contents
FLAGS	0002_h
MSW	$FFF0_h$
IP	$FFF0_h$
CS	$F000_h$
DS	0000_h
ES	0000_h
SS	0000_h

How the Microprocessor Reacts When the Power Supply Output Voltages Have Stabilized

When the power supply output voltages have stabilized, the POWER-GOOD signal goes active and the logic on the system board responds by setting RESET inactive. The inactive level on RESET allows the microprocessor to begin functioning. When released by RESET, the microprocessor must begin fetching and executing instructions from memory. The microprocessor uses the Code Segment (CS) and Instruction Pointer (IP) register contents to point to the memory location containing the first instruction.

When RESET is active, the Machine Status Word (MSW) register had $FFF0_h$ forced into it. Since the protect enable bit, bit 0, is therefore 0, the microprocessor begins operation in real mode. The microprocessor appends an imaginary 0 on the end of the CS register contents, $F000_h$, pointing to the Code Segment start address at location $F0000_h$. It then adds the OFFSET portion of the address, $FFF0_h$, contained in the IP register, to the SEGMENT start address:

$$\begin{array}{ll} CS = & F0000 \\ IP & +FFF0 \\ \hline & FFFF0 = \text{physical memory address} \end{array}$$

The resultant memory address, $FFFF0_h$, is the power-on restart address. Since the address is formed exactly the same way every time the system is powered up, the microprocessor always fetches its first instruction from the power-on restart address.

The First Bus Cycle

The microprocessor then initiates a memory read bus cycle to fetch the first instruction from the power-on restart address in memory. The power-on restart address is always located in the boot ROM because the first instruction must be located in **non-volatile memory**.

By contrast, if the first instruction were fetched from RAM memory, the information returned is junk since RAM is **volatile memory**.

The first instruction fetched from the power-on restart address is always the first instruction of the power-on self-test, or POST. The POST program is contained in the boot ROMs and is always the first program to be run.

Additional Information Regarding RESET and POST

For additional information regarding RESET, refer to Chapter 34. For additional information regarding the POST, refer to *CBIOS for IBM PS/2 Computers and Compatibles* written by Phoenix Technologies Ltd. and published by Addison-Wesley. In the CBIOS book, POST is covered in Chapter 6 and Appendix A.

Summary

RESET is derived from the POWERGOOD signal originating in the power supply. After power-up, POWERGOOD remains inactive until the power supply output voltages have stabilized. RESET is active during this period, keeping the microprocessor and all other system components from operating. When the power has stabilized, POWERGOOD goes active, RESET goes inactive, and the microprocessor fetches its first instruction from the power-on restart address in ROM memory. This is the first instruction of the power-on self-test (POST).

The System
Board Engine

Introduction to Part II

Part II consists of Chapter 9, "The System Kernel: The Engine." This chapter describes the support logic that aids the microprocessor in performing data transfers with external devices.

The System Kernel: The Engine

Objectives: This chapter describes the support logic that helps the microprocessor perform data transfers with external devices. This logic includes the bus control logic, address latch, data bus transceivers, and data bus steering logic.

Definitions for This Chapter

• The **floppy disk controller** is the programmable device that receives commands from the microprocessor and controls one or two drive units.

• The **hi/lo byte copier** copies data between the upper and lower system data (SD) bus paths when odd-addressed information is being transferred between the microprocessor and an 8-bit device.

• The **local address bus** consists of the address bus lines connected directly to the microprocessor.

• The **local data bus** consists of the data bus lines connected directly to the microprocessor.

• The **transceiver** passes information from left-to-right, from right-to-left, or keeps the two sides separate.

• An **8-bit device (or board)** is a device that is connected only to the lower data path, D0:D7.

• A **16-bit device (or board)** is connected to both the upper (D8:D15) and the lower (D0:D7) data paths.

___

8– and 16–Bit Devices

Since it is not connected to the upper data path, any data transfer between the microprocessor and an **8-bit device** must take place over the lower data path, one byte per bus cycle.

The microprocessor can transfer 1 or 2 bytes per bus cycle when communicating with this device type. Since 2 bytes can be transferred between the microprocessor and a **16-bit device** during each bus cycle, data can be transferred twice as fast as it can with 8-bit devices.

Whenever an address decoder associated with a 16-bit device detects an address within its assigned range, it chip-selects its respective device and also sets the MCA card data size 16 signal, CD DS 16#, active. This tells the bus control logic that the microprocessor is communicating with a 16-bit device (as opposed to an 8-bit device). The necessity for this action is explained in the section on the data bus steering logic.

The Bus Control Logic

In order to perform all of the actions required to complete a bus cycle, the 80286 microprocessor requires the aid of external logic. One of the major pieces of logic involved in this process is referred to as the bus control logic. Figure 9-1 illustrates the bus control logic's relationship to the microprocessor.

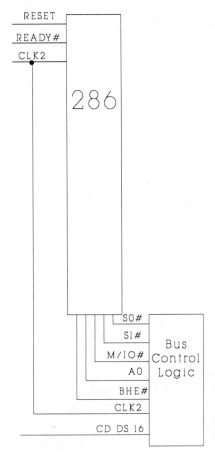

FIGURE 9-1
The Bus Control Logic

Logic external to the microprocessor can detect the beginning of a bus cycle by looking at the 80286's bus cycle definition outputs. When either S0# or S1# is detected going low, the bus cycle starts. This triggers the bus control logic's state machine that works with the microprocessor's bus unit to accomplish a data transfer during a bus cycle. The bus control logic uses CLK2, the double frequency clock, to define time slots for its state machine. At the proper points during a bus cycle, the bus control logic performs the appropriate actions to help accomplish the bus cycle.

The functions performed by the bus control logic are described in this chapter.

The Address Latch

Figure 9-2 illustrates the address latch's relationship to the microprocessor. Intel dictates that every 80286-based system must incorporate an external device known as an address latch. When the microprocessor outputs the address onto its local address bus during a bus cycle, the bus control logic signal address latch enable (ALE) commands the address latch to hold (latch) the address and remember it. Once latched, the address latch outputs the address to the system on the system address (SA) bus, SA1:SA23. Address decoders throughout the system can then examine the latched address to determine if the microprocessor is attempting to communicate with their respective device.

Notice that the address latch latches only A1:A23, but not address bit 0, A0. The reason for this is explained later. Instead of going to the address latch, A0 goes to the bus control logic, where it is allowed to pass through onto SA0 at the same time as A1:A23 are latched and presented on SA1:SA23.

The address latch must be included to support the 80286's address pipelining capability.

Address Pipelining

The 80286 microprocessor uses address pipelining when it performs back-to-back data transfers. This involves placing the address for the next bus cycle on the microprocessor's local address bus during the current bus cycle. Without the address latch, the bus cycle in progress would be disrupted. The address on the bus would change to the new address while the microprocessor was still attempting to transfer data

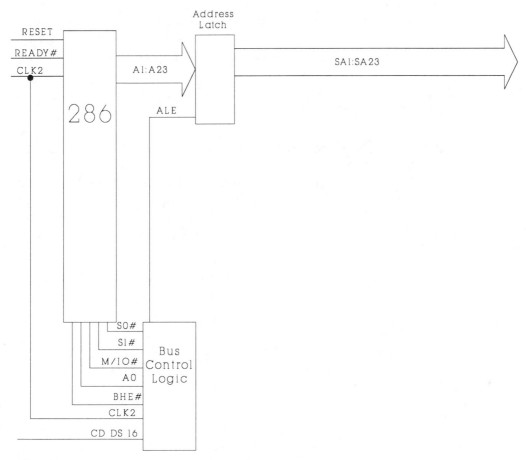

FIGURE 9-2   The Address Latch

with the device being addressed in the current bus cycle. This would then cause the address decoder currently chip-selecting its respective device to turn off the chip-select because the address had changed. Since the chip-select had been enabling the addressed device to transfer data with the microprocessor, the data transfer would be aborted in mid-bus cycle.

The incorporation of the address latch fixes this problem. Halfway through the current bus cycle (at the end of "address time"), the bus control logic pulses the address latch enable (ALE) line and commands the address latch to latch the current address. When the microprocessor starts to output the next address halfway through "data time" of the current bus cycle, the changing address on the microprocessor's local address bus does not affect the previously latched address that is being output onto the system address bus. Additional information regarding address pipelining can be found in Chapter 10.

The Data Bus Transceivers

In addition to the address latch, Intel also requires the inclusion of two devices known as transceivers.

The **transceivers** pass information from left-to-right, from right-to-left, or keep the two sides separate. As seen in Figure 9-3, each of the two data bus transceivers is connected between half of the **Local Data Bus** and the System Data (SD) bus. One transceiver is referred

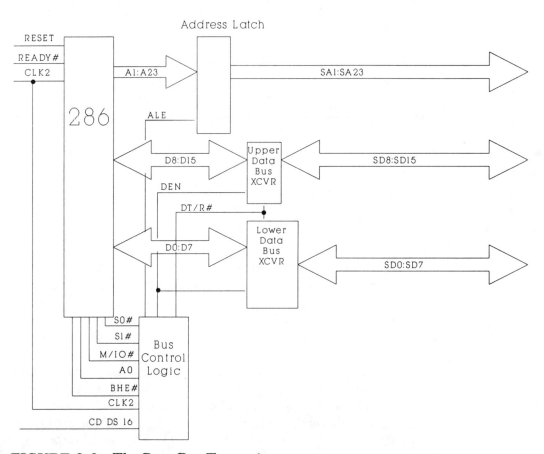

FIGURE 9-3   The Data Bus Transceivers

to as the lower data bus transceiver and the other as the upper data bus transceiver. During a read bus cycle, the bus control logic places the transceivers into receive mode to pass data from right-to-left. In this way, the data flows from the currently addressed device, over the system data bus, through the transceivers, and to the microprocessor. During a write bus cycle, the microprocessor drives data onto its local data bus. The transceivers are placed in transmit mode by the bus control logic, thereby allowing the data to flow onto the system data bus so that it can be written to the currently addressed device.

A transceiver has two control lines that allow the bus control logic to control its actions.

1. **DT/R#.** Data transmit or receive is set high to place the transceiver in transmit mode (left-to-right) during write bus cycles. It is set low during read bus cycles to place it in receive mode (right-to-left).

2. **DEN.** When set active (high), data enable enables the transceiver to actually pass the data in the direction selected by the state of the DT/R# control line.

At the proper moment during a bus cycle, the bus control logic always sets the direction line (DT/R#) to the appropriate level first, then turns on the data enable control line soon thereafter.

Data Bus Steering Logic

In order to demonstrate the circumstances requiring the use of the data bus steering logic, a series of scenarios are described in the following paragraphs. Figure 9-4 illustrates the data bus steering logic.

Scenario One: Read from an Even-Addressed Location in an 8-Bit Device.

Assume that the microprocessor executes the following instructions:

```
MOV  DX,03F4h ;Floppy Disk Controller Status address in DX
IN AL,DX      ;read Controller Status into AL
```

The first of these two instructions (MOV DX,03F4) causes the value $03F4_h$ to be placed in the microprocessor's DX register. This is the I/O address of the Floppy Disk Controller's Status register.

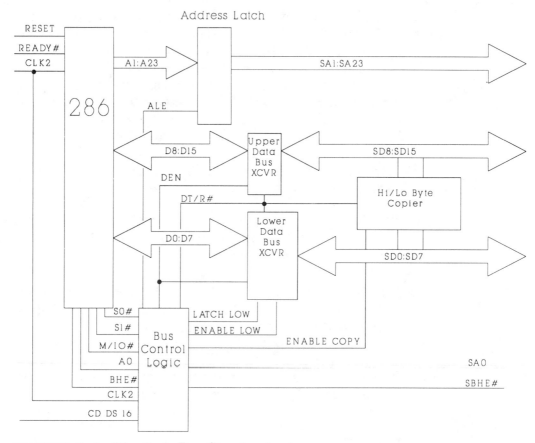

FIGURE 9-4 The Data Bus Steering Logic

The second instruction (IN AL,DX) causes the microprocessor to perform an I/O read bus cycle from the I/O address specified in the DX register (I/O location $03F4_h$). The data byte read from the Status register is placed in the microprocessor's AL register.

Upon executing the second instruction, the microprocessor initiates an I/O read bus cycle, placing address $0003F4_h$ on the address bus and setting the bus cycle definition lines to the following states:

M/IO# = 0, indicates an I/O operation

S0#   = 1, not active, so it is not a write operation

S1#   = 0, active, so it is a read operation

The bus control logic pulses the address latch enable (ALE) signal, causing the address to be latched into the address latch and presented on the system address (SA) bus. Address decoders throughout the system examine the address, but only the floppy disk controller logic is chip-selected. Since it is a read operation, the floppy disk controller status is placed onto the data bus by the **floppy disk controller**. The floppy disk controller is an 8-bit device. As a result, the byte of status information is placed on the only part of the data bus available to an 8-bit device, D0:D7.

According to Cardinal Rule Number 3, the microprocessor expects data read from even-addressed locations to come back over the lower data path. The bus control logic senses that the microprocessor is communicating with an 8-bit device because CD DS 16# does not go active. Since the data from the Floppy Disk Controller Status register is already on the proper path (D0:D7), the bus control logic sets the lower data bus transceiver to receive mode (DT/R# = 0) and enables it to pass the data through (DEN = 1) to the microprocessor. The byte flows through the lower data bus transceiver onto the lower data path on the microprocessor's local data bus.

At the end of data time, READY# is sampled active by the microprocessor. The microprocessor reads the data byte off the lower data path and the bus cycle ends. The status byte is placed in the microprocessor's AL register, thereby completing the execution of the IN instruction.

In this example, everything worked correctly and no additional logic was required to complete the data transfer.

Scenario Two: 8-Bit Read from an Odd-Addressed Location in an 8-Bit Device.

Assume that the microprocessor executes the following instruction:

```
IN  AL,61  ;read contents of I/O Port 61 into AL
```

I/O port (address) 61 is an 8-bit I/O address that the programmer reads to ascertain the cause of a non-maskable interrupt (NMI). The microprocessor begins an I/O read bus cycle, placing address 000061_h on the address bus and setting the bus cycle definition lines to the following states:

M/IO# = 0, indicates an I/O operation

S0#   = 1, not active, so it is not a write operation

S1#   = 0, active, so it is a read operation

The bus control logic pulses the address latch enable (ALE) signal, which causes the address to be latched into the address latch and presented on the system address (SA) bus. Address decoders throughout the system will look at the address. Only the port 61_h logic will be chip-selected. Since port 61_h is an 8-bit device, the byte of information being read will be placed on the only part of data bus available to an 8-bit device, D0:D7.

According to Cardinal Rule Number 3, the microprocessor expects data read from odd-addressed locations to come back over the upper data path. The bus control logic will realize that the microprocessor is communicating with an 8-bit device because CD DS 16# does not go active. Since the data coming from port 61 is on the wrong path, something must be done. To fix the problem, simply copy the data to the proper data path. Another transceiver is added in between the upper and lower system data bus paths. This is referred to as the **hi/lo byte copier**.

The bus control logic sets the upper path data bus transceiver to receive mode (DT/R# = 0) and enables it to pass the data through (DEN = 1) to the microprocessor. The low on DT/R# also sets up the hi/lo byte copier to pass data from the lower data path to the upper. The bus control logic then activates the ENABLE COPY line. This enables the hi/lo byte copier to pass the data byte to the upper system data bus path, SD8:SD15.

The byte will flow through the upper data bus transceiver onto the upper data path on the microprocessor's local data bus. At the end of data time, READY# is sampled active by the microprocessor. The microprocessor reads the data byte off the upper data path and the bus cycle ends. The byte is placed in the AL microprocessor's register, thereby completing the execution of the IN instruction. In this example, the additional logic referred to as the data bus steering logic was required to complete the data transfer. The data bus steering logic consists of several items.

1. Logic in the bus control logic that senses the state of CD DS 16# so that it can tell if the microprocessor is communicating with an 8- or 16-bit device.

2. Logic in the bus control logic that observes the A0 and BHE# outputs of the microprocessor to determine what kind of transfer the microprocessor is attempting to perform (8-bit transfer with an even address, 8-bit transfer with an odd address, or 16-bit transfer starting at an even address).

3. Hi/lo byte copier.

Scenario Three: 8-Bit Write to an Odd-Addressed Location in an 8-Bit Device.

The microprocessor outputs the byte to be written to the odd address on the upper path of the local data bus (Cardinal Rule Number 3). The bus control logic sets the DT/R# control line high, placing the data bus transceivers into transmit (left-to-right) mode and activates the DEN signal to enable the data bus transceivers. The byte flows from the upper path of the local data bus to the upper path of the system data (SD) bus. The bus control logic activates the ENABLE COPY signal.

Because DT/R# is set to transmit mode during write operations, the hi/lo copier copies the byte being output by the microprocessor on SD8:SD15 down to SD0:SD7 on the system data bus. This allows the data byte to get to the currently addressed 8-bit device, which will place the byte into the odd-addressed location.

Scenario Four: 16-Bit Write to an 8-Bit Device.

The data bus steering logic recognizes that the current bus cycle is a 16-bit transfer by the low on address bit 0 and BHE#. As far as the microprocessor is concerned, a 16-bit write transfer will be executed using both halves of the data bus. Transparent to the microprocessor, however, the data bus steering logic first allows the byte destined for the even address to flow over SD0:SD7 to the 8-bit device. This byte is then written into the location addressed by the even address currently on the address bus.

The bus control logic then blocks the microprocessor's A0 and forces SA0 to a 1. Although the microprocessor is still outputting the even address, the next sequential odd address is seen on the system address bus. The data bus steering logic now turns on the ENABLE COPY signal and the byte destined for the odd-addressed location is routed down to SD0:SD7 so that it can get to the 8-bit device. The byte is written into the odd location and the bus cycle is terminated.

Although it may appear that this was two bus cycles, it was really one prolonged bus cycle that was stretched out by setting READY# inactive until the operations were completed.

Scenario Five: 16-Bit Read from an 8-Bit Device.

The system board data bus steering logic recognizes that the current bus cycle is a 16-bit transfer by the low on address bit 0, A0, and BHE#.

As far as the microprocessor is concerned, a 16-bit read transfer will be executed. Transparent to the microprocessor, however, the data bus steering logic first executes an 8-bit read from the even address being output by the microprocessor. The 8-bit device sends the resultant byte back to the system board over SD0:SD7.

The system board's lower data bus transceiver is actually a combined latch and transceiver. The bus control logic turns on the LATCH LOW signal, causing the lower data bus transceiver to latch and hold the byte from the even address temporarily. This is done because the microprocessor thinks it is talking to a 16-bit device and expects both bytes to come back simultaneously.

The data bus steering logic then performs an 8-bit read from the next sequential odd address. This is accomplished by forcing bit 0 on the system address bus (SA0) to a 1 (transparent to the microprocessor). The byte read from the odd address is then sent back to the system board over SD0:SD7 (the only data path available to an 8-bit device). The bus control logic activates the ENABLE COPY signal. The hi/lo copier then copies this byte from the lower part of the system data bus (SD0:SD7) to the upper part of the system data bus (SD8:SD15).

The byte is then transferred to the microprocessor's local data bus on D8:D15 when DEN is activated, while the byte previously read from the even address is simultaneously transferred to the microprocessor over D0:D7 by turning on the ENABLE LOW line to the lower data bus transceiver.

Scenario Six: 8-bit Read from a 16-Bit Device

No intervention required by the data bus steering logic.

Scenario Seven: 16-Bit Read from a 16-Bit Device

No intervention required by the data bus steering logic.

Scenario Eight: 8-Bit Write to a 16-Bit Device

No intervention required by the data bus steering logic.

Scenario Nine: 16-Bit Write to a 16-Bit Device

No intervention required by the data bus steering logic.

Summary

Intel microprocessors require the aid of additional logic in order to communicate properly with external devices. These devices include the address latch, data bus transceivers, bus control logic, and the data bus steering logic. This logic ensures that the data being transferred during a bus cycle arrives at its destination on the proper path(s).

PART

III

The Bus Cycle

Introduction to Part III

Part III consists of Chapters 10 and 11. Chapter 10 provides a detailed description of the bus cycle, while Chapter 11 provides a detailed description of the logic that generates the READY# signal.

CHAPTER
10

Detailed View of the Bus Cycle

Objective: Previous chapters provided an introduction to the bus cycle. Using timing diagrams, this chapter provides a detailed analysis of the bus cycle.

"Address and Data Time" Revisited

The concept of the bus cycle was introduced in Chapter 4. As you recall, the microprocessor performs a bus cycle in order to transfer information between itself and a memory or I/O location. The microprocessor's bus unit uses the address, data, and control buses to address a device, tell it the type of transaction in progress, and transfer the data between the microprocessor and the currently addressed location. The microprocessor uses the bus cycle definition lines to indicate the type of transaction. The possible types of bus cycles are shown in Table 10-1.

This chapter provides a detailed description of each bus cycle type, except the interrupt acknowledge bus cycle which is described in Chapter 19.

To perform a bus cycle, the microprocessor's bus unit leaves the idle state and enters the state we refer to as address time. During this "tick" of PCLK, the microprocessor places the address and bus cycle definition on the buses. Address decoders throughout the system start decoding the address during this time slot. For this reason, it has been nicknamed "address time" by the author. The address time state is always followed by the data time state. During this state, the microprocessor expects the data to be transferred between itself and the currently addressed device. For this reason, it has been nicknamed "data time" by the author.

TABLE 10-1   80286 Bus Cycle Definition

M/IO#	S1#	S0#	Bus Cycle Type
0	0	0	Interrupt acknowledge
0	0	1	I/O read
0	1	0	I/O write
1	0	0	Halt or shutdown
1	0	1	Memory read
1	1	0	Memory write

Table 10-2 lists both the nicknames used in this book and the state names used by Intel.

The various actions that must take place during a bus cycle (for example, address latching, passage of data through the data bus transceivers, and so on) have been described in previous chapters. This chapter provides an in-depth look at the sequence and exact timing of these actions in relation to each other.

The Read Bus Cycle

With the exception of the bus cycle definition output, I/O and memory read bus cycles are identical. This section describes the exact timing of the actions performed during a read bus cycle. Figure 10-1 is a timing diagram illustrating a series of typical 80286 read bus cycles.

PCLK has been placed across the top of the timing diagram as a point of reference. Remember that each cycle of PCLK defines the duration of one bus unit state. Vertical dotted lines have been superimposed on the diagram to define each cycle of PCLK (and, therefore, each state). In addition, the name of each state is written across the top of the diagram.

A general idea of the information presented can be derived from the state names across the top. In this example, the sequence of states is as follows:

T_c	Data time
T_s	Address time
T_c	Data time
T_s	Address time
T_c	Data time
T_c	Data time
T_s	Address time

TABLE 10-2   80286 and 80386 Bus Cycle State Names

Nickname	80286 Name	80386 Name
Address time	T_s	T_1
Data time	T_c	T_2

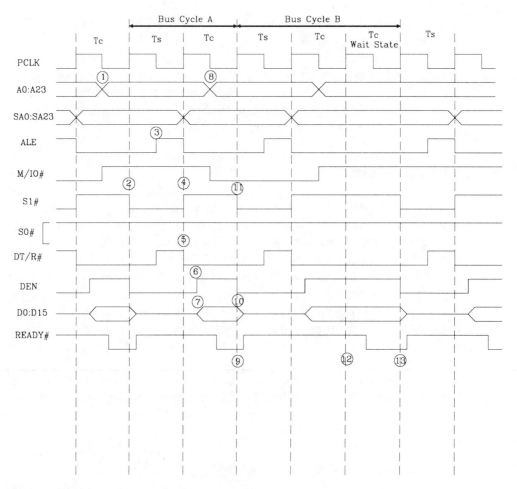

FIGURE 10-1 The Read Bus Cycle

Every bus cycle consists of at least an address time and data time pair. An additional data time (wait state) will be inserted in the bus cycle if the microprocessor samples its READY# input inactive at the end of data time. Based on these rules, the states illustrated on the diagram can be interpreted as follows:

T_c	Data time	End of previous bus cycle
T_s	Address time	Start of bus cycle A
T_c	Data time	Second half of bus cycle A
T_s	Address time	Start of bus cycle B

T_c	Data time	Second half of bus cycle B
T_c	Data time	Wait state inserted in bus cycle B
T_s	Address time	Start of next bus cycle

Thus, the diagram illustrates the end of a bus cycle followed by a 0-wait state bus cycle (bus cycle A), a 1-wait state bus cycle (bus cycle B), and the start of another bus cycle.

When reading a timing diagram, one scans from left-to-right (from earlier in time to later in time) looking for the signals that change first, second, and so on. Since PCLK is always pulsing (changing), it is not necessary to note that it changes.

Bus Cycle A

Bus cycle A starts at reference point 2, the beginning of the T_s time slot (address time). Scanning from left-to-right, however, we see something changing state prior to the start of bus cycle A. Halfway through T_c time in the previous bus cycle (at reference point 1), the microprocessor starts to output the address for the upcoming bus cycle (bus cycle A) before the actual start of bus cycle A. The address change is illustrated by the crossover point at reference point 1, the crossover indicating that the address starts to change to the new address at this point. This early address output is caused by the 80286's address pipelining capability. Figure 10-2 illustrates the address latch.

Since the address for the current bus cycle has already been latched into the address latch, the microprocessor can safely output a new address onto its local address bus during the current bus cycle without interfering with the current bus cycle. Its address is already latched and being presented to the rest of the system on the system address (SA) bus for examination.

In addition to outputting the address for the upcoming bus cycle early, the microprocessor also sets the M/IO# line (reference point 1) to the appropriate state for the upcoming bus cycle. This will be a 1 for a memory operation or a 0 for an I/O operation.

At reference point 2, bus cycle A actually begins. The 80286 outputs the remainder of the bus cycle definition on S0# and S1#. In the case of a read bus cycle, S1# is set active (low) and S0# stays high.

At reference point 3 (in the second half of T_s), the bus control logic sets address latch enable (ALE) active and keeps it active until the end of T_s. The address latch latches the address on the falling edge of

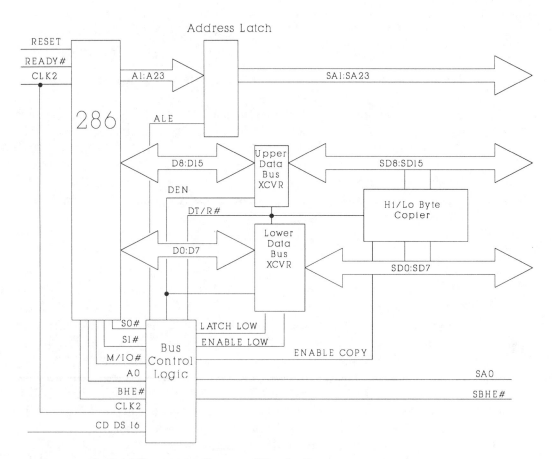

FIGURE 10-2 The 80286 System "Engine"

ALE (when it goes low again). Once latched, the address is presented on the system address (SA) bus where it can be examined by address decoders throughout the system. At this point, the microprocessor can safely output the address for the next bus cycle without having any effect on the latched address. If the microprocessor has another bus cycle to perform, it starts to output the address halfway through T_c (at reference point 8). In this example, the microprocessor is, in fact, performing back-to-back bus cycles. You can see the address changing at reference point 8.

At reference point 4, the microprocessor removes the active level from the S1# line. Logic associated with the currently addressed device should have decoded the bus cycle definition lines by now to ascertain the type of bus cycle (read).

At reference point 5, the bus control logic sets the DT/R# line (data transmit or receive) line low because this is a receive (read) operation. This pre-conditions the data bus transceivers to pass the data being read from the currently addressed device from right-to-left through the data bus transceivers to the microprocessor. Shortly after setting the DT/R# line low (at reference point 6), the bus control logic sets data enable (DEN) active (high), enabling the data bus transceivers to actually pass the data. At this point (reference point 7), the data coming from the currently addressed device might begin to show up on the microprocessor's local data bus.

The microprocessor expects the currently addressed device to complete the data transfer during T_c. At the end of T_c, in bus cycle A, the microprocessor samples its READY# input active (low) at reference point 9. This tells the microprocessor that the currently addressed device is ready to end the bus cycle. Since this is a read operation, the microprocessor reads the data the device is supplying (at reference point 10) and ends the bus cycle, thus completing bus cycle A.

Bus Cycle B

Even though its address and M/IO# setting are output during bus cycle A (at reference point 8, due to pipelining), bus cycle B actually begins at reference point 11 with the output of S0# and S1#. Since this is another read bus cycle, S1# is active (low) and S0# inactive (high).

Bus cycle B proceeds the same way as bus cycle A until the end of T_c time (reference point 12). When the 80286 microprocessor samples READY# at this point, the currently addressed device has not yet set it active to indicate its readiness to end the bus cycle. Sampling READY# inactive tells the microprocessor to "stretch" the bus cycle by inserting another T_c time (wait state).

The microprocessor leaves all signals exactly the same as they were, waiting until the end of this extra T_c to sample READY# again. At the trailing edge (the end) of the extra T_c (reference point 13), the microprocessor samples READY# again. This time it is sampled active (low), telling the microprocessor that it can safely read the data from its local data bus and end the bus cycle.

Since another T_s time slot follows this bus cycle, another bus cycle begins.

The Write Bus Cycle

I/O and memory write bus cycles are identical (except for the bus cycle definition output). This section describes the exact timing of the actions performed during a write bus cycle. Figure 10-3 is a timing diagram illustrating a typical 80286 write bus cycle.

A general idea of the information presented can be derived from the state names across the top. In this example, the sequence of states is as follows:

T_c	"Data time"	End of previous bus cycle
T_s	"Address time"	Start of bus cycle
T_c	"Data time"	End of bus cycle
T_s	"Address time"	Start of next bus cycle

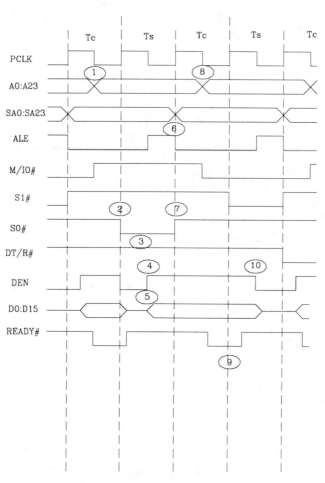

FIGURE 10-3   The Write Bus Cycle

This timing diagram illustrates one 0-wait state bus cycle bracketed by the end of the previous bus cycle and the start of the next bus cycle.

The address and M/IO# setting for the bus cycle is pipelined out early at reference point 1. At the start of the bus cycle (reference point 2), the microprocessor outputs the remainder of the bus cycle definition on S0# and S1#. S0# is active (low) to indicate a write operation and S1# is set inactive.

Because this is a transmit (write) operation, the bus control logic sets data transmit or receive (DT/R#) high at reference point 3. Since the quiescent (idle) state for the DT/R# line is high, no change is actually seen on this line, but it is nonetheless important that it is high at this point. This pre-conditions the data bus transceivers to pass the data being output by the microprocessor (on the local data bus) to the system data bus. Immediately after setting DT/R# high, the bus control logic sets data enable (DEN) active (high) to enable the data bus transceivers to pass the data onto the system data bus (reference point 4). At the same time, the microprocessor begins outputting the data to be written to the device (reference point 5).

Address latch enable (ALE) is pulsed by the bus control logic at reference point 6, causing the address to be latched into the address latch (at the trailing edge of ALE). The latched address is now presented on the system address (SA) bus for examination by all address decoders in the system.

At reference point 7, the microprocessor removes the active level from the S0# line. Logic associated with the currently addressed device should have decoded the bus cycle definition lines by now to ascertain the type of bus cycle (write). If the microprocessor is going to run another bus cycle immediately after this one, it pipelines the next address out at reference point 8.

At the trailing edge of T_c (reference point 9), the microprocessor samples its READY# input to determine if the currently addressed device has accepted the data yet. In this example, READY# is sensed active (low), and the microprocessor ends the bus cycle.

Note that the bus control logic continues to keep DEN active, and the microprocessor continues to drive the data onto the local data bus for half a PCLK tick longer. The microprocessor placed the data on the data bus early (reference point 5) and keeps it there after the actual end of the bus cycle (reference point 10) for the reason described in the following paragraphs.

In order to guarantee that the information is received correctly by the device being written to, every digital device capable of receiving data requires that a manufacturer-specified setup time and hold time be observed. In other words, the data must be present on its inputs for at least the specified setup time before the latch point and must remain present for at least the specified hold time after the latch point to ensure that the device receives the data correctly. Since the microprocessor does not know the setup and hold times for the individual device types it may be writing to, Intel's design takes worst-case setup and hold times into account by placing the data out very early in the bus cycle and keeping it there as long as possible after the actual end of the bus cycle.

Continuing to drive the data onto the data bus for half of a PCLK tick into the next bus cycle does not disturb the next bus cycle. It takes time for an address decoder to detect an address and chip-select the next device. The fact that the data from the previous write bus cycle is still present on the data bus cannot affect a device that has not yet been chip-selected.

The Halt or Shutdown Bus Cycle

When the microprocessor executes a HALT instruction, it initiates a halt or shutdown bus cycle and ceases fetching and executing instructions. The microprocessor indicates it is running a halt or shutdown bus cycle by placing the following values on the bus cycle definition lines and address bit 1.

- S1# and S0# are set low.
- M/IO# is set high.
- Address bit 1 is set high.

It should be noted that S0# and S1# are low only during the bus cycle itself. After the microprocessor has halted, the halt condition can be recognized externally by the following signs.

- S1# and S0# are high.
- M/IO# is high.
- Address bit 1 is high.

All of these conditions are static (constant), and therefore easily recognizable.

Shutdown

When the microprocessor enters the shutdown condition, it initiates a halt or shutdown bus cycle and ceases operations. This occurs if multiple protection exceptions are incurred while attempting to execute one instruction. An exception is a special type of internal interrupt that occurs automatically if one of a number of types of unrecoverable software conditions is detected. A shutdown can be easily detected by the same signs as those for a halt, except that address bit 1 is low.

During a halt or shutdown, the 80286 may service Processor Extension Request or HOLD requests. For further information on these two subjects, refer to Chapter 20 and Chapter 32.

Either non-maskable interrupt request (NMI) or RESET forces the 80286 out of either a halt or a shutdown. If interrupts are enabled, a maskable interrupt request (INTR) also forces the microprocessor out of a halt. For information on these subjects, refer to Part V.

Summary

This chapter provided a detailed look at the timing and the sequence of events that occur during a bus cycle. The execution of a bus cycle is handled jointly by the microprocessor and the bus control logic. The bus control logic detects the start of a bus cycle by watching two of the three bus cycle definition lines, S0# and S1#. When the microprocessor sets either of these signals active, the bus control logic's state machine is triggered. This state machine is built around the same three states as the microprocessor's bus unit state machine: idle, T_s, and T_c. The two state machines move through the same states in tandem, controlling the actions of the address latch, data bus transceivers, and data bus steering logic.

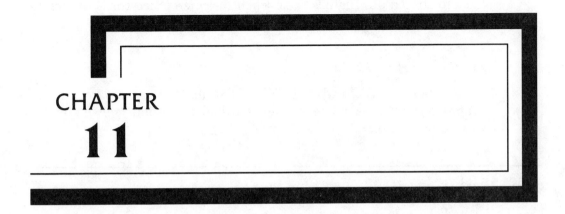

CHAPTER
11

The Ready Logic

Objective: This chapter describes the method used in the PS/2 product line to stretch out the bus cycle when the microprocessor is talking to a relatively slow device.

Definition for This Chapter

• **Access time** is defined as the amount of time that elapses from device chip-select until the device is ready to complete the data transfer (either a read or a write).

Access Time

Figure 11-1 illustrates the concept of **access time**.

The **access time** for a device is device- and manufacturer-dependent. Consequently, the access time for different types of RAM, ROM, and I/O devices differs. Although you might expect each device type to have a READY# output pin that goes active when the device is ready to complete a data transfer, no such pin exists.

Stretching the Transfer Time

When you begin to access a slow access device, the microprocessor's bus cycle must be stretched out to match the device's access time. The

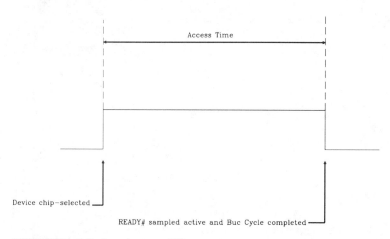

FIGURE 11-1 Access Time

READY# input on the microprocessor serves this purpose. Since there is no ready output from I/O or memory devices, IBM had to provide some other method for turning off the READY# signal until the currently addressed device is ready to complete the bus cycle.

Ready Timers

A very simple way to implement this is to provide a timer associated with each type of device. When the device is chip-selected by its respective address decoder (when it is first addressed), its timer is triggered simultaneously. When triggered, the timer takes a predefined amount of time to expire. This expiration period is equal to the access time for the particular device. During that period of time, the timer keeps the READY# line inactive (high). When the timer expires, the microprocessor's READY# line is allowed to go active again, thereby telling the microprocessor that the bus cycle can now be completed.

The Default Ready Timers

IBM provided a series of default timers for the different type of devices. These default timers are located on the system board. There is a separate timer associated with each of the following types of devices:

- RAM mounted on the system board
- RAM mounted on an MCA card
- I/O devices
- ROM memory mounted on the system board

Table 11-1 illustrates the number of wait states that are inserted into a bus cycle by the default timers when accessing each of the four device groups listed above.

Some of the entries for system board RAM list 0, 1, or 2 wait states per bus cycle. The variance is due to the use of page mode or static column RAM (SCRAM). When using this type of RAM memory, the access time for a given bus cycle is dependent on the bus cycle that occurred immediately before the bus cycle in question. This subject is covered in Chapter 21.

TABLE 11-1   Number of Wait States Inserted by the Default
Ready Timers

PS/2 Model	50Z	60	70-16MHz	70-20MHz	80-16MHz	80-20MHz
System board RAM	0	1	0/1/2	0/1/2	1	0/1/2
System board ROM	1	1	1	1	1	1
I/O	1	1	2	2	2	2
MCA RAM	0	0	2	2	2	2

Custom Ready Timers

When, on the other hand, an engineer is designing a card to be inserted in a micro channel slot, the access time for this device may be longer than the ready timeout provided by its respective default timer. IBM provided a way for the designer to override the default timer and stretch out the bus cycle by the required number of wait states to match the access time of the device. This is implemented with the card channel ready (CD CHRDY) signal on the MCA connector. Figure 11-2 illustrates the relationship of the CD CHRDY signal to the READY# logic on the system board.

When the address decoder on an MCA card decodes an address assigned to its respective device, it chip-selects the device and also triggers the custom ready timer on the card. When triggered, the timer forces the normally active CD CHRDY signal inactive. When the default timer logic on the system board sees CD CHRDY go inactive, the default timer is overridden and READY# is not sent to the microprocessor until the CD CHRDY signal is seen going active again. When the access time for the card-mounted device has elapsed, the custom timer then allows CD CHRDY to go active again. The default ready timer logic on the system board then immediately sets READY# active, thus informing the microprocessor that it can end the bus cycle. In this way, the designer of an add-in card can insert any number of wait states into a bus cycle when a particular device is addressed.

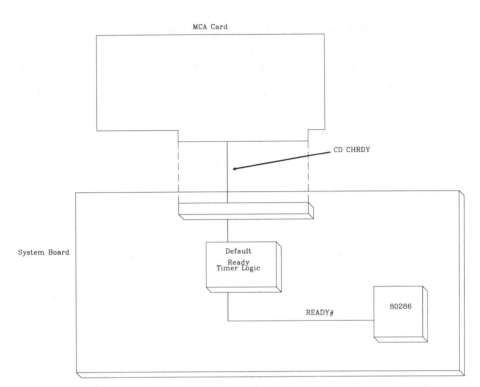

FIGURE 11-2 Custom Ready Timer Logic

Summary

The microprocessor cannot end a bus cycle until READY# is sampled active at the end of data time. The amount of time necessary to complete a bus cycle is dependent on the access time of the device currently being accessed.

Each device that the microprocessor can address has an associated ready timer that is triggered when the device is first chip-selected. The timeout value of the timer is equal to the access time for the device. When the timer is triggered, it turns READY# off and keeps it off until the access time has elapsed. It then allows READY# to go active and the bus cycle to end.

Every MCA card that requires more than the default number of wait states also has its own ready timer. This timer is triggered by the card's address decoder and turns off card channel ready (CD CHRDY) until the access time for the card has elapsed. Turning off CD CHRDY causes the READY# signal to be turned off, thereby preventing the bus cycle from completing until the access time for the card has expired. When the card's ready timer has expired, the CD CHRDY signal goes active again, which allows READY# to go active and the bus cycle to complete.

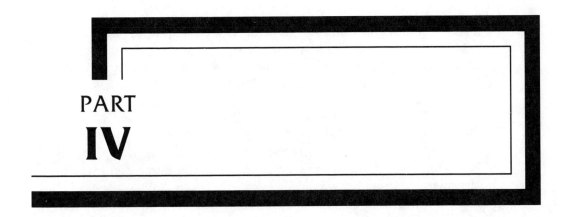

PART
IV

The Micro Channel Architecture (MCA)

Introduction to Part IV

Part IV consists of Chapters 12 through 18. The purpose of this section is to provide a detailed understanding of all aspects of the micro channel architecture (MCA). Each chapter builds upon the information contained in the previous chapters. The following is a synopsis of each chapter.

Chapter 12: This chapter introduces the concept of the micro channel architecture, bus masters, and bus arbitration.

Chapter 13: This chapter provides a detailed explanation of bus arbitration, the process wherein bus masters compete for the use of the micro channel buses.

Chapter 14: This chapter describes the POS registers that replaced the DIP switches used in previous products to resolve conflicts between boards installed in a PC. Chapter 15 continues this discussion to its logical conclusion.

Chapter 15: The previous chapter provided a detailed description of the POS registers. These registers allow automatic configuration of the unit every time it is powered up by placing each card into setup mode and writing the appropriate values to their respective POS registers. This chapter continues the discussion by describing the configuration program and automatic system configuration.

Chapter 16: This chapter describes the different types of bus cycles that bus masters can run when granted the buses. The newer bus cycle types, known as "streaming data procedures," are described in Chapter 18.

Chapter 17: This chapter defines the purpose of every signal on the 16-bit MCA connectors, the video extension to the 16-bit MCA connectors, the 32-bit MCA connectors, and the matched memory extension connector.

Chapter 18: This chapter defines the hardware and software enhancements to the micro channel that were announced by IBM in October of 1989.

Introduction to the Micro Channel Architecture (MCA)

Objectives: This chapter introduces the concept of the MCA, bus masters, and bus arbitration.

The Concept

If asked to physically identify the MCA in a PS/2, it would be most correct to point to the slots used to install MCA adapter cards. The signals provided on each of these slots can be divided into four basic categories:

- The address bus group
- The control bus group
- The data bus group
- The bus arbitration group

Three of these four signal groups are present on the expansion slots found in IBM PC/XT/AT products and compatible computers. In the micro channel, the bus arbitration group has been added. The micro channel architecture, this collection of buses, is frequently referred to as "the channel." As an example, a bus master will request the use of the channel to communicate with another device. Although "buses" can be substituted for "channel," the latter was chosen because it suggests the channel of communication that exists between the bus master and a device.

MCA defines both the signals found on the MCA connectors as well as the permissible bus cycle types that can be run by bus masters and the software protocol that bus masters must use when communicating with each other. It also defines the support logic that resides on the system board and MCA cards that is necessary to support all of the micro channel capabilities. Some examples are the central arbitration control point (CACP), translation logic, and the data bus steering logic, all of which are discussed in subsequent chapters.

The IBM PC/XT/AT and compatible products were essentially meant to be single-processor systems. They have one microprocessor located on the system board that uses the address, control, and data buses to communicate with the various memory and I/O devices found in a system.

The microprocessor on the system board is the bus master most of the time in a PC/XT/AT. It uses the buses to fetch instructions and to communicate with memory and I/O devices when instructed to do so by the currently executing instruction. Upon occasion, however, devices other than the microprocessor need the buses to communicate with other devices in the system. These devices are the DMA controller and the RAM refresh logic. The DMA controller uses the buses to transfer data between I/O devices and memory and the refresh logic uses the buses periodically to refresh the information stored in RAM memory.

When a device other than the microprocessor (such as the DMA controller or the refresh logic) requires the use of the buses, it must force the microprocessor to give up control of the buses. This is accomplished by turning on the Intel microprocessor's hold request (HOLD) input. Upon detecting HOLD active, the microprocessor electrically disconnects itself from the address, control, and data buses so that the requesting device can use them to communicate with other devices. This is called "floating the buses." The microprocessor then turns on its hold acknowledge (HLDA) output to inform the requesting device that it has yielded the buses to it, thereby making it the new bus master. The device remains bus master as long as it keeps the microprocessor's HOLD input active.

When a bus master other than the microprocessor on the system board has finished using the buses, it should turn off the microprocessor's HOLD input, thus allowing the microprocessor to re-connect itself to the buses and become bus master again.

It is also possible for a card inserted into an IBM PC/XT/AT expansion slot to become bus master, but there is a major drawback. When a card becomes bus master in a PC/XT/AT, it can remain bus master as long as it keeps the microprocessor's HOLD line active. There are no safety mechanisms built into a PC/XT/AT to prevent a bus master card from monopolizing the use of the buses to the exclusion of the microprocessor on the system board, the RAM refresh logic, and potential bus master cards inserted into other expansion slots.

If, due to poor design or a failure, a card should lock up the buses for an inordinate amount of time, the system board microprocessor cannot continue to fetch and execute instructions. This could have serious consequences. In addition, the refresh logic would be unable to become bus master on a timely basis, and data in RAM memory could be lost. Finally, other bus master cards inserted in expansion slots would be unable to become bus master and transfer data. To summarize, severe problems can be incurred when bus master cards are used in a PC/XT/AT.

IBM fixed this problem when designing the MCA by including the bus arbitration signals and a central arbitration control point (CACP). The CACP provides a method for resolving situations where multiple bus masters are competing for the use of the buses. As explained in Chapter 13, no device is allowed to monopolize bus usage in a PS/2.

By establishing a method for resolving bus conflicts, IBM created a system that can safely support multiple bus masters. This means that PS/2 products support use of the buses by:

- The microprocessor on the system board
- The DMA controller on the system board
- The refresh logic on the system board
- Bus master cards inserted into MCA slots

Typically, a bus master card is quite intelligent and incorporates a microprocessor and its own local ROM, RAM, and I/O devices. An example is a disk controller card built around an 80386 microprocessor, which executes its own software from its local (on-board) ROM memory. It stores data received from other bus masters in its local RAM memory prior to writing it to disk. It can read large amounts of data from disk, store it in its local RAM memory, and forward it to another device, such as memory on the system board, when necessary. It controls an array (group) of eight disk drives.

Other bus masters can issue high-level commands or requests to the example disk controller. An example is a request sent to the disk controller card to search for a database file called "TOM.DBF" on the eight disk drives it controls. If the file is found, it reads a particular record and sends it back to the requesting bus master. After issuing the request to the disk controller card, the requesting bus master can continue other processing until the disk controller card responds. Upon completing the search, the disk controller card can become bus master and transfer the requested data into system memory for the other bus master to use.

A PS/2 system can safely incorporate a number of intelligent bus master cards, each essentially running on its own. When required, they can communicate with each other and transfer data between themselves. IBM has created a system designed to support multi-processing, through its multiple processors, each handling a portion of the overall task. Properly implemented, the parallel processing accomplished in this type of system is extremely efficient and fast.

Summary

The micro channel architecture, a collection of buses, is frequently referred to as the channel. A bus master requests the use of the channel to communicate with another device. The term channel was chosen because it suggests the channel of communication between the bus master and a device.

The MCA defines both the signals found on the MCA connectors as well as the permissible bus cycle types that can be run by bus masters and the software protocol that bus masters must use when communicating with each other. It also defines support logic residing on the system board and MCA cards that is necessary to support all of the micro channel capabilities. Some examples are the central arbitration control point (CACP), translation logic, and the data bus steering logic, all of which are discussed in subsequent chapters.

By establishing a method for resolving bus conflicts, IBM created a system that can safely support multiple bus masters.

Bus Arbitration

Objective: This chapter provides a detailed explanation of bus arbitration, the process wherein bus masters compete for the use of the micro channel buses.

Types of Bus Masters

The PS/2 supports the following types of bus masters:

1. **The system board CPU.** This is the default bus master. The system board microprocessor is bus master when no other bus master requires the use of the buses.

2. **The refresh logic** on the system board. The refresh logic requests the use of the buses and becomes bus master once every 15 microseconds (millionths of a second). Upon becoming bus master, the refresh logic uses the buses to run one memory read bus cycle, thus refreshing one row of memory in dynamic RAM throughout the system. This subject is covered in Chapter 21.

3. **The DMA controller** on the system board. When instructed to do so, the DMA controller requests the use of the buses and, upon becoming bus master, runs a series of bus cycles to transfer a block of data between an I/O device and memory.

4. **Bus master** cards installed in MCA slots. Most of these cards are intelligent (incorporate their own microprocessor), operate on their own most of the time, and become bus master only when they need to transfer data with another device in the system.

Bus Arbitration

Figure 13-1 illustrates the system board arbitration logic. The device known as the central arbitration control point (CACP) resides on the system board. When multiple devices require the use of the buses simultaneously, the CACP initiates the process of deciding which will be granted the use of the buses (in other words, which will become bus master).

When the DRAM refresh logic on the system board requires the use of the buses to refresh DRAM memory, it turns on the REFRESH

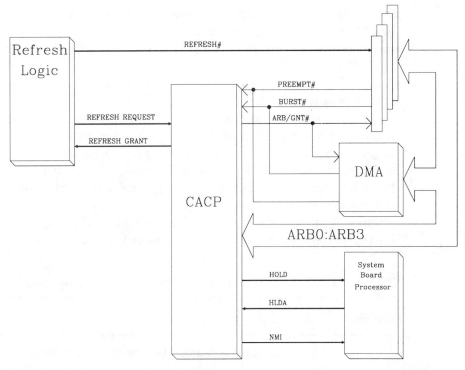

FIGURE 13-1 The System Board Bus Arbitration Logic

REQUEST input to the CACP. When the DMA controller or a bus master card in an MCA slot requires the use of the buses, it turns on the CACP's PREEMPT# input. The following sections describe the decision making process the CACP uses to decide which of the competing devices will become bus master.

The System Board Microprocessor: Low Man on the Totem Pole

When no devices are currently requesting the use of the buses (when PREEMPT# and REFRESH REQUEST are turned off), the CACP keeps the hold request (HOLD) line to the microprocessor inactive, thus allowing the system board microprocessor to remain bus master. The microprocessor can continue to fetch and execute instructions. When a device other than the system board microprocessor requires the use of the buses (when PREEMPT# and/or REFRESH REQUEST is active), the CACP turns on the HOLD line to the system board microprocessor, forcing the microprocessor to surrender the address, control, and data buses. After floating (disconnecting from) the buses, the microprocessor turns on hold acknowledge (HLDA) to tell the CACP that it has surrendered the buses. The CACP is then free to grant the buses to another device. The process the CACP uses to decide which device becomes bus master is described in the following sections.

The system board microprocessor is low man on the totem pole and must give up control of the buses whenever any other device wants to use them. If HOLD goes active, the microprocessor must yield ownership of the buses. Table 13-1 lists the arbitration priority code assigned to each potential bus master type by the CACP. Although the microprocessor is shown as having the lowest priority code, F_h, it does not actually have a priority code. That is just IBM's way of saying the microprocessor loses if anyone else wants the buses.

TABLE 13-1   The Arbitration Priority Code Assignment

Arbitration Code	Assigned To
−2	Memory refresh logic
−1	Non-maskable interrupt (NMI)
0	DMA channel 0 (programmable to any priority code)
1	DMA channel 1
2	DMA channel 2
3	DMA channel 3
4	DMA channel 4 (programmable to any priority code)
5	DMA channel 5
6	DMA channel 6
7	DMA channel 7
8	Available for assignment to a bus master card
9	Available for assignment to a bus master card
A	Available for assignment to a bus master card
B	Available for assignment to a bus master card
C	Available for assignment to a bus master card
D	Available for assignment to a bus master card
E	Available for assignment to a bus master card
F	System board microprocessor

The Refresh Logic: Top Dog

The refresh logic must become bus master once every 15 microseconds to refresh the information stored in the next row of DRAM memory locations. When 15 microseconds has elapsed since the last refresh bus cycle, the refresh logic turns on the REFRESH REQUEST input to the CACP, thereby indicating its desire to become bus master.

The following events occur when the microprocessor on the system board is the bus master.

1. The CACP responds to REFRESH REQUEST by turning on HOLD to tell the system board microprocessor to yield the buses. When the microprocessor responds with HLDA, the CACP grants the buses to the highest priority device currently requesting the use of the buses.

2. In Table 13-1, refresh is shown with the highest priority code, −2. Priority code −2 is an artificial value and is IBM's way of saying that the refresh logic wins if REFRESH REQUEST is active.

3. The CACP uses a special output signal, REFRESH GRANT, to inform the refresh logic that is bus master. The refresh logic can then use the buses to run one memory read bus cycle to refresh a row of storage locations in DRAM memory.

4. The CACP observes the refresh bus cycle and, when completed, the refresh logic loses ownership of the buses. If no other request for the buses is pending, the CACP then turns off the HOLD signal, thereby allowing the system board microprocessor to become bus master again. The microprocessor reattaches itself to the buses and turns off HLDA to indicate that it has resumed control of the buses.

If a device other than the microprocessor on the system board is bus master and is running a bus cycle when the REFRESH REQUEST signal is set active, the CACP allows the current bus master's bus cycle to complete before granting the buses to the refresh logic. Prior to granting the buses to the refresh logic, however, the CACP also drives and keeps the ARB/GNT# (Arbitrate/Grant) line high to prevent other bus masters from using the buses during this period.

The DMA Controller and Bus Master Cards

When the DMA controller on the system board or a bus master card installed in an MCA slot requires the use of the buses, it turns on the PREEMPT# signal to the CACP. The PREEMPT# signal is active when low. Multiple devices can safely place a low on this line simultaneously because they need not drive any voltage onto the line to activate it. Each simply provides a path to ground for the PREEMPT# line, thus placing a 0 on the line.

The following paragraphs describe the actions taken by the CACP if the microprocessor on the system board is currently the bus master when PREEMPT# is set active.

When the CACP sees PREEMPT# go active, it responds by turning on HOLD to tell the system board microprocessor to yield the buses. When the microprocessor responds with HLDA, the CACP grants the buses to the highest priority device currently requesting the use of the buses.

When the CACP sees the PREEMPT# line go active, it knows that one or more potential bus masters are requesting the use of the buses. The arbitration (judgment) scheme used by the CACP can be likened to the following scenario.

> The CACP fires a pistol in the air and all of the contestants have 300 nanoseconds (billionths of a second) to battle it out. At the end of the 300ns, the CACP drops the flag. The one contestant left standing is the winner, and the buses are granted to this device.

This may seem like a silly analogy, but it is an accurate portrayal of the arbitration scheme. The following sequence explains the process in more technical terms.

1. The PREEMPT# line is set active by one or more devices that require the use of the buses.

2. The CACP makes the normally low arbitrate/grant (ARB/ GNT#) line go high (places it in the arbitrate state).

3. During the 300ns arbitration cycle, each potential bus master drives its respective 4-bit arbitration priority code onto the arbitration bus (ARB0:ARB3) and compares its code to the composite priority code on the arbitration bus. If the device sees that any other device is driving a priority code higher

than its own onto the arbitration bus, it ceases to drive its priority code onto the bus. Essentially, it has dropped out of the race. It continues to drive PREEMPT# active, however, because it has not yet gotten to use the buses. The exact method used by a competing device to decide whether to stay in the competition or drop out is described in the next section.

4. By the end of the 300ns arbitration cycle, all competing devices except the one with the highest code should have dropped out of the race (ceased to drive its priority code onto the arbitration bus).

5. At the end of the 300ns arbitration cycle, the CACP drops the ARB/GNT# line low to grant the buses to the winner. Only the device with the highest priority code will be left driving its arbitration priority code onto the arbitration bus. When the bus master that is still driving its priority code onto the bus sees the ARB/GNT# line go the Grant state (low), it realizes that it has been granted the use of the buses.

6. The winning device ceases to drive a low onto the PREEMPT# line because it has won the use of the buses.

7. The winning bus master can now use the buses to run one bus cycle. When the CACP sees the bus cycle end, it takes the buses away from the device and either returns them to the system board microprocessor (if no other requests are pending) or begins another competition to see which device gets the buses next.

When the device that was just granted the buses has completed the bus cycle and wishes to run another, it must turn on PREEMPT# and compete for the buses again.

Setting bit 5 in the arbitration register at I/O port 0090_h extends the arbitration cycle time from 300ns to 600ns. This feature can be used for devices that require a longer arbitration cycle.

Local Bus Arbiters

Figure 13-2 illustrates the local bus arbiter logic. Each bus master incorporates a local bus arbiter. During an arbitration cycle, the arbiter performs the following tasks.

1. Drives the device's priority code onto the arbitration bus.

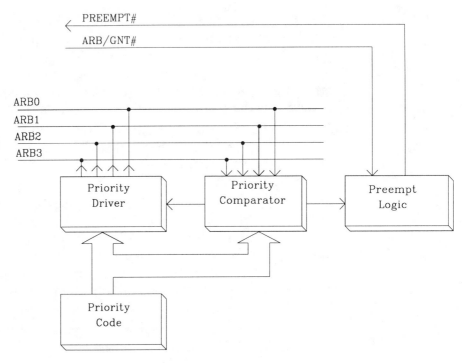

FIGURE 13-2 The Local Bus Arbiter

2. Compares the device's priority code to the composite priority code being driven onto the arbitration bus by all of the competing bus masters.

3. If the arbiter detects that another competing bus master is driving a higher priority code onto the bus than its own, the arbiter ceases to drive its priority code onto the bus and drops out of the competition. The device continues to drive PREEMPT# active, though, because it has not yet used the buses.

4. If it is still driving its priority code onto the arbitration bus when the ARB/GNT# line is driven low by the CACP, the local bus arbiter recognizes that it has been granted the use of the buses and ceases to drive PREEMPT# active.

Beginning with the most-significant bit, ARB3, each bit of the device's priority code is compared to its respective bit on the arbitration bus, ARB0:ARB3. When the competing local bus arbiter detects a mismatch on one of the bits, it should immediately cease driving all of its lower-order bits low. If the local bus arbiter subsequently detects a match on that bit, it continues to drive the lower-order bits until another mismatch occurs.

It should be noted that all four arbitration bus signal lines, ARB0:ARB3, have pull-up resisters on them. Figure 13-3 illustrates the arbitration bus. This causes each of these lines to remain high unless a device places a low on the line by grounding it.

It should further be noted that when a local bus arbiter drives its priority code onto the arbitration bus, it does not drive all 4 bits of its priority code onto the four arbitration bus lines. Only the bits in its code that are 0 are driven onto their respective arbitration bus lines. For example, assume that two devices with priority codes of A_h (1010_b) and 5_h (0101_b) compete for the buses and that the buses are currently idle. The following sequence of events would occur.

1. Both devices drive the PREEMPT# line active to alert the CACP that they want use of the buses.

2. The CACP drives a high onto ARB/GNT# to signal the beginning of the arbitration cycle. The low-to-high transition on ARB/GNT# triggers the local bus arbiters on both devices.

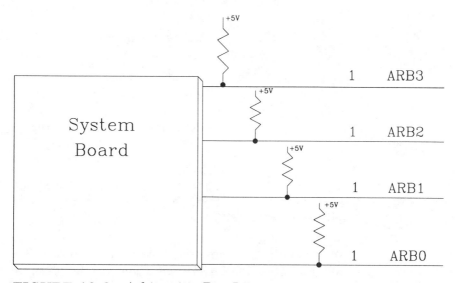

FIGURE 13-3 Arbitration Bus Lines

3. Because only bits 0 and 2 of its priority code, 1010_b, are 0's, the first device's local bus arbiter drives ARB0 and ARB2 low. The second device simultaneously drives ARB1 and ARB3 low because only bits 1 and 3 of its priority code, 0101_b, are low. As a result, the composite code on the arbitration bus is 0000_b.

4. The first device immediately sees a mismatch between bit 3 of its arbitration priority code (1010_b) and ARB3 of the composite code currently on the arbitration bus (0000_b). As a result, the first device ceases driving its lower bits, ARB0 and ARB2, low. This means it is no longer driving any lows onto the arbitration bus.

5. Simultaneously, the second device detects a mismatch between bit 2 of its priority code (0101_b) and ARB2 of the composite code currently on the arbitration bus (0000_b) and ceases driving ARB1 low. The resulting composite code on the arbitration bus is a 0111_b.

6. The first device still refrains from driving ARB0 and ARB2 low because of the mismatch on ARB3. The second device, however, now has a match on ARB2 and again drives a low onto ARB1. This results in a 0101_b on the arbitration bus.

7. At this point, device one is not driving any bits low because of the continued mismatch on ARB3. Device two continues to drive ARB3 and ARB1 low. Since device one's local bus arbiter now has a solid miscompare and device two's local bus arbiter has a solid compare on all bits, all bit changing ceases for the remainder of the arbitration cycle.

8. At the end of the arbitration cycle, the CACP drives ARB/GNT# low to grant the buses to the winner. Device two knows that it is the winner because it has a compare on all four arbitration bits and ARB/GNT# is now in the grant state (low).

Table 13-1 lists the arbitration priority codes assigned to the bus master types found in a PS/2. As previously explained, refresh and NMI have the highest priorities and this is indicated by their artificially high codes in the table.

Priority codes 0_h-7_h are assigned to DMA channels 0-7. Refer to Chapter 20 for additional information. Priority codes 8_h-E_h are reserved for use by bus master cards installed in MCA slots. The designer of a bus master card must set aside an I/O address that the programmer can write its 4-bit priority code to during the automatic configuration that occurs during the power-up sequence. Refer to Chapter 15 for more information regarding configuration. The configuration program ensures that no two bus master cards have the same priority codes.

The priority codes for DMA channels 0 and 4 are programmable. This allows the programmer to reassign the priority of either DMA channel, thereby freeing up its original priority code for use by a bus master card that requires very high priority.

Bursting Bus Masters

If an engineer is designing a bus master card that must transfer blocks of data by running multiple bus cycles, it should be implemented as a bursting bus master.

When a card requires the use of the buses to run a series, or burst, of bus cycles, it should turn on PREEMPT# and arbitrate for the use of the buses as described in the previous section. Upon being granted the buses, the bus master should then turn on the BURST# signal to the CACP and keep it on until the last bus cycle in the burst has been initiated.

The CACP interprets an active level on BURST# to mean that the requesting device does not wish to arbitrate for each individual bus cycle that it must perform in order to transfer the block of data. The CACP allows the bursting bus master to retain the use of the buses for multiple bus cycles until one of two events occurs:

1. The bursting bus master completes its series of bus cycles and turns off BURST# to indicate completion.
2. Upon winning the buses, the bursting bus master must watch the PREEMPT# line to see if it goes active before the bus master has completed its series of bus cycles. If sensed active, this means that another bus master wishes to use the buses.

If any other potential bus master wishes to use the buses during the period while the current bus master is bursting, it should turn on PREEMPT#. When the current bursting bus master senses PREEMPT# or REFRESH REQUEST active, it is preempted. In other words, it must give up the buses prior to completing its overall data transfer.

The bursting bus master should respond to the preemption by yielding the buses within 7.8 microseconds. It indicates that it is surrendering the buses by turning off the BURST# signal. When the CACP senses BURST# has been turned off, it begins a new competition to decide the next bus master.

The Fairness Option: The Meek Shall Inherit the Bus

All bursting bus masters should implement the fairness option. If the fairness option is enabled and the bursting bus master is preempted, it will not compete in another arbitration cycle until the PREEMPT# line is sensed inactive. In other words, the bursting bus master is not allowed to compete for the buses again until all other devices with pending bus requests have had a chance to use the buses in order of priority and have ceased to drive PREEMPT# active. This feature prevents a high priority bursting bus master from locking out low priority devices.

Bus Timeout Error: Someone's Being a Hog

Refer to Figure 13-1. When preempted, the bursting bus master indicates that it is yielding control of the buses by turning off the BURST# signal. If the bus master does not indicate release of the buses (by turning off BURST#) within 7.8 microseconds after PREEMPT# is sensed active, it is considered to be an error condition.

The CACP immediately takes the following steps.

1. Drives the ARB/GNT# line to the arbitrate state (high) to force the offending bus master to yield the buses.

2. Turns off HOLD to give the buses back to the system board microprocessor so that it can service interrupts.

3. Generates a non-maskable interrupt (NMI) to the system board microprocessor.

4. In the NMI interrupt service routine, the programmer must write a 0 to bit 6 of the arbitration register at I/O port 0090_h to force the CACP to let the ARB/GNT# line go low again. Not to do so prevents the CACP from granting the buses to any other devices and can result in data transfers not occurring when they should.

5. The programmer then reads the arbitration register at I/O port 0090_h to find out the arbitration priority code of the last device that was granted the use of the buses. This allows the

programmer to identify the bus master that refused to yield the buses.

CACP *Programmability*

The arbitration register at I/O port 0090_h may be used to control certain operational characteristics of the CACP. Table 13-2 provides its bit assignment.

TABLE 13-2 The Arbitration Register, I/O Port 0090_h

Bit	Function
7	Enable system board microprocessor cycle.
	1 = Enables the microprocessor to run bus cycles during the CACP's arbitration cycle.
	0 = The microprocessor is not allowed to run bus cycles during the CACP's arbitration cycle.
	This bit is set to 0 by a system reset. It may also be read to determine its current state.
6	Arbitration mask bit.
	0 = CACP is allowed to arbitrate normally.
	1 = The ARB/GNT# line is set high, forcing all bus masters to disconnect from the buses. The microprocessor is given control of the buses (by turning its HOLD input off) while this bit is high.
	This bit is normally low and is set low by a system reset. The CACP automatically sets this bit active (high) if an NMI is sensed so that the buses can be given back to the microprocessor. The microprocessor can then service the interrupt.
5	When a 1 is written to the Enable Extended Arbitration bit, the arbitration cycle time is extended from 300ns to 600ns, thereby allowing more time for bus arbitration. When this bit is read, it returns the state of the Bus Timeout bit. A 1 indicates that a bus timeout has occurred because the current bus master refused to give up the buses within 7.8 microseconds after preempted by another bus master requesting the use of the buses.
4-0	These bits are undefined for a write and should always be set to 0. When read, these bits contain the arbitration priority code of the bus master that was granted the buses last. When a bus timeout causes an NMI, these bits are read to determine the faulty bus master.

Summary

Machines based on the micro channel provide support for multiple bus masters. When required, any or all of the bus masters can request the use of the buses to communicate with another device in the system. The central arbitration control point (CACP) initiates the process to decide which bus master should be granted the use of the buses next. Safeguards are included to ensure that no bus master is able to monopolize the use of the micro channel buses to the exclusion of other bus masters that require their use.

The configuration program assigns arbitration priority codes to bus masters and ensures that no two will have the same priority. The system board microprocessor has the lowest priority of all. When any other bus master requires the use of the buses, the CACP activates the microprocessor's HOLD input, forcing the microprocessor to yield the buses. The buses may then be granted to another bus master. The refresh logic has the highest priority, followed by the DMA channels, bus master cards installed in MCA slots, and the system board microprocessor. Every bus master card incorporates a device known as a local bus arbiter that allows the card to take part in the competition for the buses.

A bursting bus master requires the use of buses to perform a series, or burst, of bus cycles rather than just a single bus cycle. Bursting bus master cards should implement a fairness feature. Essentially, this means that the card yields the buses to other bus masters that request the buses while the bursting bus master is in the midst of a burst of bus cycles. This is known as preempting the bursting bus master. After the other bus masters have used the buses, the bursting bus master can request the use of the buses again and resume bursting until either the burst completes or is preempted again. If a bursting bus master does not yield the buses within 7.8 microseconds after it is preempted by another bus master, a bus timeout occurs. A bus timeout causes NMI to be generated.

CHAPTER
14

Programmable
Option Select (POS)

Objective: This chapter describes the POS registers that replaced the DIP switches used in previous products to resolve conflicts between boards installed in a PC. Chapter 15 continues this discussion.

Definition for This Chapter

• **Shadow RAM** is the RAM memory that the entire system ROM is copied to during the POST, thus relocating the BIOS and interrupt service routines to faster, RAM memory.

Introduction: DIP Switches and Pseudo DIP Switches

Many add-in boards designed to be installed in IBM PC/XT/AT expansion slots have dual in-line package (DIP) switches located on them. Figure 14-1 illustrates a typical set of DIP switches. Many system boards also have DIP switches located on them.

DIP switches are included on these boards to permit the following types of selection:

• Alteration of the address range detected by the board's address decode logic.

• Selection of a particular interrupt request line to be used by the board.

• Selection of a particular DMA channel to be used by the board.

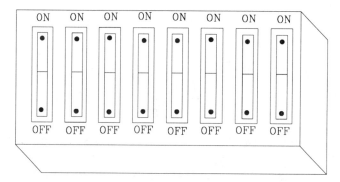

FIGURE 14-1 Illustration of DIP Switches

These switches allow the user to resolve conflicts between boards to be installed in the same machine. Problems arise if two boards either respond to the same address range or attempt to use the same interrupt request line or DMA channel. The user changes the switch settings to resolve the conflict.

Typically, when a DIP switch is off, it places a 1 on the signal line to which it is connected. Turning the switch on places a low on the respective signal line. For example, changing the setting of a particular DIP switch may alter the way the board's address decoder works and cause it to detect a different address range.

The DIP switches frequently are manufactured in packages containing a bank of eight DIP switches. By flipping the switches, the user selects a particular pattern of 1's and 0's. The position of each switch selects a particular operational characteristic of the board.

When designing the PS/2, IBM was determined to eliminate the DIP switches and allow automatic configuration of each board without removing the machine's covers or the cards. They accomplished this by substituting one or more special I/O locations in place of the banks of DIP switches. Each I/O location contains 8 bits of information (Cardinal Rule Number 1). When writing a byte to one of these locations, each bit can be set to either a 0 or a 1. In other words, each individual bit in the I/O locations can select a particular operational characteristic of the board. By writing the correct information to these locations, MCA adapter cards can be automatically configured.

All MCA cards installed in a PS/2 are automatically configured by programming each card's configuration I/O locations every time the unit is powered on. This is accomplished as part of the power-on self-test (POST).

The Programmable Option Select (POS) Registers

In order to implement these special configuration registers, IBM set aside I/O addresses 0100_h–0107_h. They are referred to as the programmable option select (POS) registers. At least a subset of the POS registers must be implemented on every MCA card. The I/O locations at these I/O addresses are referred to as POS registers 0–7. For example, POS register 6 is at I/O location 0106_h.

Some POS registers are reserved for special purposes by IBM; the remainder are reserved for board designers to use when implementing the pseudo-DIP switch banks that configure a board. Table 14-1 list the POS registers and their specified use.

POS registers 0 and 1 are reserved for the adapter ID, a 16-bit card-specific number assigned by IBM. When an engineer designs a new MCA card, a special, card-specific ID number must be obtained from IBM. The card should be designed so that this 16-bit adapter ID can be read from POS registers 0 and 1. Whenever a PS/2 is powered up, the power-on self-test (POST) reads the ID from the card in each MCA slot and compares it to the configuration information stored in battery backed-up CMOS RAM memory. This allows the POST to confirm that each card is inserted in the same slot whenever the unit is powered up.

When the unit is first powered up, the adapter ID provided by an MCA adapter can be 0000_h for up to one second to indicate that the card is not ready yet. The ID is considered defective if it remains 0000_h for more than one second.

Pre-Defined POS Register Bits

Refer to Table 14-2. Bit 0 in POS register 2 is defined by IBM as the card enable bit. When this bit is set to 0, the adapter is disabled, thereby allowing only its POS registers to be accessed. The card is then reset. Any attempts to read from or write to other addresses on the card will have no effect. Setting this bit to a 1 enables the card to respond normally.

TABLE 14-1   The POS Registers

POS Register	I/O Address	Purpose
0	0100_h	Least-significant byte of adapter ID
1	0101_h	Most-significant byte of adapter ID
2	0102_h	Option select data byte 1
3	0103_h	Option select data byte 2
4	0104_h	Option select data byte 3
5	0105_h	Option select data byte 4
6	0106_h	Least-significant byte of subaddress extension
7	0107_h	Most-significant byte of subaddress extension

TABLE 14-2   Pre-Defined POS Register Bits

POS Register	Bit	Function
2	0	Card enable bit.
5	7	Channel check active indicator bit.
5	6	Channel check status indicator.

The remainder of the bits in POS register 2 are available to the designer for use as option switches.

Two bits in POS register 5 have also been defined.

Bit 7 in POS register 5 is the channel check active indicator bit. This bit is set to 0 by the card if it is currently generating channel check (a signal on the MCA connector) to report a hardware failure. When a card generates channel check, it causes an NMI to the system board microprocessor. In the NMI interrupt service routine, the programmer can read port 0061_h and check bit 6 to determine if channel check is the cause of the NMI.

If it is, the programmer can then check bit 7 of each MCA card's POS register 5 to determine which card is generating the channel check. If software determines that the cause of the channel check is correctable, the card designer can provide a method to turn off the channel check active indicator bit.

Bit 6 in POS register 5 is the channel check status indicator bit. This bit is set to 0 by the card currently generating channel check if additional status information is available regarding the cause of the channel check. The additional channel check status information can be read from POS registers 6 and 7.

With the exception of bit 0 of POS register 2 and bits 6 and 7 of POS register 5, POS registers 2–5 are available for implementation of card-specific option select switches.

The Subaddress Extension: POS Register 6 and 7

POS registers 6 and 7 are also referred to as the Subaddress Extension registers. If a card requires more space than is available in POS registers 2–5 for option switches, POS registers 6 and 7 can be used to access a larger area of option switches located on the card.

When the card is first powered up or reset, an address counter is reset on the card. This counter is used to address a series of additional

POS registers on the card and initially points to the first location in the extension POS locations. The first time a write is performed to POS register 6 and 7, the information is stored in the extension POS location currently addressed by the address counter (initially, location 0). The counter is then automatically incremented to point to the next extended POS location. Each subsequent write to POS registers 6 and 7 stores data in the next sequential extended POS location. In this way, the designer is able to implement the necessary number of POS registers to allow full configuration of the card.

Why the POS Register Addresses Do Not Conflict

It may be obvious by now that there is an apparent problem inherent in IBM's method of implementing the POS registers. Every card designer must implement the POS registers at I/O locations 0100_h–0107_h. Take the case where two adapter cards are installed in the PS/2's MCA slots. If the programmer performs a read from POS register 0 to get the lower part of the card ID, will the data read be the card ID from the first card or the second?

In fact, before the programmer can actually access a card's POS registers, the card must be placed into setup mode. Each card has two basic modes of operation:

1. **Enable Mode**. When in enable mode, the card's POS registers at I/O locations 0100_h–0107_h cannot be accessed. All of the addresses normally used to control the card can be accessed, however.

2. **Setup Mode**. When in setup mode, the card's POS registers at I/O locations 0100_h–0107_h can be accessed, but the addresses normally used to control the card cannot be accessed.

In order to place an adapter card into setup mode, the programmer must write the correct information to the Adapter Enable/Setup register at I/O address 0096_h. Table 14-3 illustrates the value that must be written to the Adapter Enable/Setup register in order to place a particular card into setup mode.

Only one adapter card can be placed into setup mode at a time. After placing the card into setup mode, the card enable bit, bit 0 in POS register 2, should be set to 0. This disables all card functions except the POS registers. Once placed into setup mode, any subsequent access to

TABLE 14-3   Placing a Card into Setup Mode

Card Slot to Be Placed in Setup Mode	Value to Be Written to I/O Port 0096_h
1	08_h
2	09_h
3	$0A_h$
4	$0B_h$
5	$0C_h$
6	$0D_h$
7	$0E_h$
8	$0F_h$

I/O ports 0100_h–0107_h causes the respective card setup for slot n (CD SETUP(n)) signal line to go active. This disables the normal logic on an adapter card and enables its POS register logic so that the respective POS register can be accessed. When the programmer has completed programming the card's POS registers, the following actions must be taken.

1. The card enable bit, bit 0 in POS register 2, should be set to 1. This enables all of the card's functions except its POS registers.

2. A 00_h should be written to the Adapter Enable/Setup register. This disables the CD SETUP logic on the system board and places the card back into enable mode.

The bit assignment (how each bit is used) for the Adapter Enable/Setup register is illustrated in Table 14-4.

Writing a 1 to bit 7 of the Adapter Enable/Setup register causes the channel reset (CHRESET) signal to be set active. While active, this signal applies reset to all of the MCA adapter cards. **This bit must be 0 to communicate with the adapter cards' POS registers.**

Writing a 1 to bit 3 of the Adapter Enable/Setup register allows the logic on the system board to use bits 0–2 to select a card to be placed into setup mode whenever a POS register access is performed.

TABLE 14-4   The Adapter Enable/Setup Register (I/O Port 0096$_h$)

Bit	Description
7	Channel reset
6	Reserved. Should always be 0.
5	Reserved. Should always be 0.
4	Reserved. Should always be 0.
3	Allow card setup
2	Card select bit 2
1	Card select bit 1
0	Card select bit 0

Required POS Register Option Switches

Certain types of MCA cards require the implementation of specific POS register option switches. These option switches can be implemented in any of the available POS registers (POS registers 2-5). The following list describes the instances requiring their implementation.

1. **Fairness Enable Bit.** All bursting bus master cards should implement the fairness enable bit in one of the available POS register bits. Unless specifically turned off by the programmer, this bit should always be a 1, forcing the Bus Master card to exhibit fairness.

2. **Arbitration Code.** All bus master cards must implement a 4-bit arbitration code field in one of the available POS registers. During the configuration phase of the POST, the arbitration priority code for the card will be written to the respective POS register.

3. **Device ROM Segment Address.** All I/O cards that include a ROM containing information such as the BIOS routine for the card must permit the start address of the ROM to be changed during the configuration phase of the POST. This allows resolution of possible addressing conflicts with other cards. This field may be up to 4 bits in length and will be implemented in one of the available POS registers (POS registers 2-5).

4. **I/O Device Address**. Any I/O card that can reside in a system with other cards of the same type must provide a method of resolving addressing conflicts with the other card(s). This field will be implemented in one of the available POS registers (POS registers 2–5).

System Board POS Registers

Just as expansion boards for the PC/XT/AT had configuration switches, so did the system boards. They were used to select the amount of memory installed on the system board and indicated the presence of a numeric coprocessor and so on. In the PS/2, these switches have been replaced by POS registers.

Each PS/2 system board incorporates option switches (POS registers) that are used to set up the system board. Each time the system is powered up, the system board and each adapter card must be placed into setup mode and their POS registers programmed.

WARNING! Caution must be exercised regarding setup mode. Placing two devices in setup mode at the same time results in improper operation and possible hardware damage. Although it is not possible to place two MCA adapter cards into setup mode simultaneously, it is possible with an adapter card and the system board logic. If two devices are in setup mode and the programmer attempts to read from any of the POS registers, the POS register address will be recognized by both devices' address decode logic. As a result, the same POS register in both devices will drive data onto the data bus at the same time. This results in garbled data and possible hardware damage. If both POS registers are trying to drive a 1 onto the same data bus signal line simultaneously, the two output drivers can damage each other.

Placing the System Board into Setup Mode To place the system board into setup mode, the System Board Enable/Setup register at I/O port 0094_h must be programmed with the proper information. Table 14-5 details the bit assignment for this register.

To place the system board devices other than VGA (RAM memory, floppy disk interface, serial port, and parallel port) into setup mode, write $7F_h$ to the System Board Enable/Setup register at I/O port 0094_h ($0111\ 1111_b$). This places these four system board devices into setup mode.

Once these devices have been placed into setup mode, they can be configured by performing a write to system board POS register 2 (I/O

TABLE 14-5   The System Board Enable/Setup Register, Port
                 0094_h

Bit	Function
7	0 = Allow setup of system board devices other than VGA.
	1 = Place system board devices other than VGA in enable mode.
6	Reserved
5	0 = Allow setup of VGA.
	1 = Place VGA in enable mode.
4	Reserved
3	Reserved
2	Reserved
1	Reserved
0	Reserved

Note: The bits marked "Reserved" should always be set to ones.

port 0102_h). System board POS register 3 (I/O port 0103_h) can be read
from (and, on some models, written to). These are the only POS registers
implemented for these devices.

Setting Up the System Board Devices (Other than VGA)
Table 14-6 details the bit assignment for system board POS register 2.
    To set up the floppy disk interface, parallel port, and serial port
exactly as POST does, perform the following steps.

1. Write $7F_h$ (0111 1111$_b$) to I/O port 0094_h, the system board
   Enable/Setup register. This places these system board devices
   into setup mode. The $7F_h$ has the effects indicated in Table
   14-7.

2. Write 17_h (0001 0111$_b$) to system board POS register 2 at I/O
   port 0102_h. This sets up the floppy disk interface, serial port,
   and parallel port as indicated in Table 14-8.

3. Place the system board back into enable mode by writing an
   FF_h to the system board enable/setup register at I/O port
   0094_h.

TABLE 14-6 System Board POS Register 2, Port 0102_h

Bit	Function
7	0 = Disable parallel port extended mode. This is the setting used by POST. Port is output-only.
	1 = Enable parallel port extended mode (bi-directional operation).
6-5	Parallel port select.
	00 = Parallel port 1 (default used by POST)
	01 = Parallel port 2
	11 = Parallel port 3
4	Enable parallel port.
	0 = Disable parallel port
	1 = Enable parallel port (default used by POST)
3	Serial port select.
	0 = Serial port 1 (default used by POST)
	1 = Serial port 2
2	Serial port enable.
	0 = Disable serial port
	1 = Enable serial port (default used by POST)
1	Enable floppy disk interface.
	0 = Disable floppy disk interface
	1 = Enable floppy disk interface (default used by POST)
0	Enable system board.
	0 = Disable system board devices other than VGA
	1 = Enable system board devices other than VGA (default used by POST)

Verifying the Presence and Type of Installed System Board RAM Memory   After the system board RAM memory has been placed into setup mode, the presence and type of system board RAM memory can be checked by reading from system board POS register 3 at I/O port 0103_h. On the Model 50 and 60, POS register 3 can be written to enable or disable the system board memory address decoder.

Table 14-9 defines the bit assignment for system board POS register 3 as implemented in the Model 50 and 60.

TABLE 14-7   The System Board Enable/Setup Register After $7F_h$ Written to It

Bit	Value	Function
7	0	Places the system board devices other than VGA into setup mode.
6	1	Reserved
5	1	Leave the VGA in enable mode.
4	1	Reserved
3	1	Reserved
2	1	Reserved
1	1	Reserved
0	1	Reserved

TABLE 14-8   System Board POS Register 2 After 17_h Written to It

Bit	Value	Function
7	0	Disable parallel port's extended mode. In other words, the parallel port will be output only.
6-5	00	The parallel port responds to the I/O ports assigned to parallel port 1.
4	1	Enable the parallel port's address decoder.
3	0	The serial port responds to the I/O ports assigned to serial port 1.
2	1	Enable the serial port's address decoder.
1	1	Enable the floppy disk interface's address decoder.
0	1	Enable the system board devices other VGA. Turning on this bit allows bits 1, 2, and 4 to control the floppy disk interface, the serial port, and the parallel port.

Table 14-10 defines the bit assignment for system board POS register 3 as implemented in the Model 70. It is a read-only register that can be accessed only while the system board is in setup mode. It contains information regarding the presence and type of memory card installed in each of the three system board memory connectors.

TABLE 14-9 System Board POS Register 3, Port 0103_h, in Models 50 and 60

Bit	Function
7	Reserved
6	Reserved
5	Reserved
4	Reserved
3	Reserved
2	Reserved
1	Reserved
0	Enable system board RAM
	0 = Disable system board RAM's address decoder
	1 = Enable system board RAM's address decoder

Table 14-11 defines the bit assignment for system board POS register 3 as implemented in the Model 80. It is a read-only register that can be accessed only while the system board is in setup mode. It contains information regarding the presence and type of memory card installed in each of the two system board memory connectors.

The Model 80 memory card type and presence bits have the meaning indicated in Table 14-12.

Configuring the System Board RAM and ROM Memory (Model 70 and 80)   While the system board RAM memory is in setup mode, the system board RAM address decode logic can be programmed. This allows the programmer to tailor the distribution of the installed RAM memory to suit the user's particular needs.

As described in the previous section, the programmer can determine the presence and type of system board memory cards by reading from system board POS register 3.

Two additional registers are then used to configure the system board RAM address decoder so that the installed system board memory cards respond to the desired address ranges. These two registers are referred to as Memory Encoding registers 1 and 2. In some literature, IBM refers to Memory Encoding register 2 as the Split Address register. These two registers are located at I/O locations $00E1_h$ and $00E0_h$, respectively.

TABLE 14-10   System Board POS Register 3, Port 0103$_h$, in Model 70

Bit	Function
7	Reserved.
6	Type of memory card installed in memory connector 3.
	0 = 1MB card installed
	1 = 2MB card installed
5	Memory card present in memory connector 3.
	0 = Card present
	1 = Card not present
4	Reserved.
3	Type of memory card installed in memory connector 2.
	0 = 1MB card installed
	1 = 2MB card installed
2	Memory card present in memory connector 2.
	0 = Card present
	1 = Card not present
1	Type of memory card installed in memory connector 1.
	0 = 1MB card installed
	1 = 2MB card installed
0	Memory card present in memory connector 1.
	0 = Card present
	1 = Card not present

The values written to these two registers allow the programmer to:

- Enable or disable the boot ROM.

- Enable or disable the split memory block feature.

- Set the address at which the first megabyte of system board RAM is split.

- Set the start address of the split memory block.

TABLE 14-11   System Board POS Register 3, Port 0103$_h$, in Model 80

Bit	Function
7	Reserved
6	Reserved
5	Reserved
4	Reserved
3	Type of memory card installed in memory connector 2.
2	Memory card present in memory connector 2.
1	Type of memory card installed in memory connector 1.
0	Memory card present in memory connector 1.

TABLE 14-12   Model 80 POS Register 3 Memory Card Type and Card Present Bits

System Board Type	Type	Present	Meaning
Type 1*	0	0	1MB memory card present.
	0	1	Reserved
	1	0	Reserved
	1	1	Card not present.
Type 2*	0	0	Reserved
	0	1	Reserved
	1	0	2MB memory card present.
	1	1	Card not present.**

*Note: The Model 80 Type 1 system board is based on the 80386 microprocessor running at 16MHz. The Type 1 system board is based on the 80386 microprocessor running at 20MHz.
**Note: At least 1MB must be installed in connector 1 of the Model 80 Type 2 system board. Therefore, an 11 pattern is invalid in bits 0 and 1 of the Type 2 system board's POS register 3.

- Selectively enable or disable each installed system board memory card.

- Enable or disable system board RAM parity checking.

In order to describe the function of these two registers, some terms must first be discussed. The PS/2 Model 70 and 80 are based on the Intel 80386 microprocessor and both incorporate a feature called **shadow RAM**. Among other things, the following paragraphs describe this feature.

The system (or boot) ROM contains:

- the complete power-on self-test (POST)
- the BIOS routines
- the interrupt service routines for the standard devices shipped with a system
- the BASIC language interpreter

The BIOS routines are a collection of routines written by IBM software engineers. The system ROM contains a BIOS routine for each standard device shipped with a system. Including them in ROM means that applications programmers need not be familiar with the intricacies of how each type of I/O device is controlled. Issuing a command to an I/O device requires only that the programmer place a number representing the request type in the AH register and call (jump to) the device's BIOS routine.

If an applications program depends heavily on the BIOS routines in ROM, the instructions that make up the BIOS routines must be fetched from system ROM frequently. Since ROM memory has a notoriously slow access time relative to that of RAM memory, the instructions could be read more quickly and the BIOS routine therefore executed more quickly if the BIOS routines were located in RAM rather than ROM.

The memory address decode logic on the system board is designed in such a way that the memory address range from $000E0000_h$–$000FFFFF_h$ is assigned to two devices: the 128KB System ROM and the top 128KB of the first 1MB of system board RAM.

Two devices occupying the same address space is a unique situation. When the ROM memory address decoder is enabled (as explained later), any memory read within the ROM's assigned address range accesses the System ROM; any memory write within the same range accesses the top 128KB of the first 1MB of RAM (the shadow RAM).

After POST has verified that RAM is working correctly, the complete contents of the 128KB system ROM is copied to RAM memory. This is accomplished by performing a read from each location in the

000E0000$_h$–000FFFFF$_h$ address range followed immediately by a write to the same location. In this manner, the data is read from the ROM location and written to the RAM location with the same address. Reading and writing every address in the range places a complete copy of the system ROM in the shadow RAM.

After the copy has been completed, the programmer uses Memory Encoding register 1 to disable the ROM address decoder and make the shadow RAM read-only (as if it were ROM). Any subsequent calls to the BIOS routines will now access the shadow RAM rather than the ROMs. The substantially faster RAM access time and the fact that the RAM is a 32-bit device will cause the BIOS routines to be executed more quickly from this point forward, resulting in substantial speed increases when running applications programs that call the BIOS routines frequently.

Figure 14-2 illustrates the manner in which the first 1MB of memory address space is allocated by IBM. The first 640KB of space, from addresses 00000000$_h$–0009FFFF$_h$, is reserved for system board RAM. The 128KB block from 000A0000$_h$–000BFFFF$_h$ is allocated to the VGA's video RAM memory. The range from 000C0000$_h$–000DFFFF$_h$ is set aside for additional BIOS ROMs that may be located on MCA adapter cards. Finally, 000E0000$_h$–000FFFFF$_h$ is allocated to the system ROM and the shadow RAM.

This means that the first 1MB of installed system board RAM memory cannot occupy the entire first megabyte of memory space. It must be split between the first 1MB of memory space and some other area of memory space. Up to 640KB of it can be mapped into the first 1MB of space. Of the remaining 384KB, 128KB is allocated to the shadow RAM space from 000E0000$_h$–000FFFFF$_h$.

The values written into the Memory Encoding registers during setup allow the first 1MB of system board RAM memory to be addressed in a number of ways. Table 14-13 illustrates the allocation choices available.

The following paragraphs explain each of these choices.

Figure 14-3 illustrates the first choice. In the first configuration choice, 512KB of the first 1MB of system board RAM responds to the addresses from 00000000$_h$–0007FFFF$_h$. The top 128KB is used as the shadow RAM and responds to the system ROM address range. The remaining 384KB of the first 1MB of system board RAM is not used when this configuration is chosen.

Figure 14-4 illustrates the second choice. In the second configuration choice, 640KB of the first 1MB of system board RAM responds

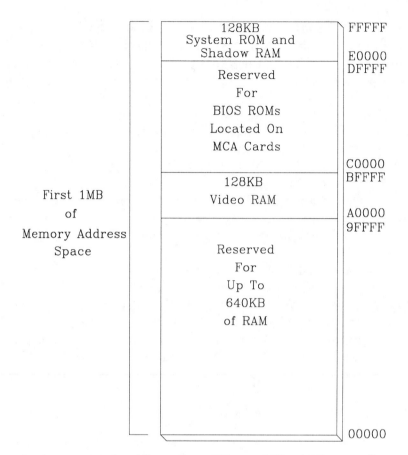

FIGURE 14-2   Allocation of First 1MB of Memory Space

to the addresses from 00000000$_h$–0009FFFF$_h$. The top 128KB is used as the shadow RAM and responds to the system ROM address range. The remaining 256KB of the first 1MB of system board RAM is not used when this configuration is chosen.

Figure 14-5 illustrates the third choice. In the third configuration choice, 512KB of the first 1MB of system board RAM responds to the addresses from 00000000$_h$–0007FFFF$_h$. The top 128KB is used as the shadow RAM and responds to the system ROM address range. The remaining 384KB of the first 1MB of system board RAM is called the split memory block and can be allocated at any 1MB address boundary above the first 1MB.

Figure 14-6 illustrates the fourth choice. In the fourth configuration choice, 640KB of the first 1MB of system board RAM responds

TABLE 14-13   Possible Choices for First 1MB (1024KB) System
Board RAM Distribution

Total Memory RAM Used	RAM Starting At 00000000	Shadow RAM	RAM Not Used	Split Block
1024KB	512KB (00000000-0007FFFF)	128KB	384KB	0KB
1024KB	640KB (00000000-0009FFFF)	128KB	256KB	0KB
1024KB	512KB (00000000-0007FFFF)	128KB	0KB	384KB
1024KB	640KB (00000000-0009FFFF)	128KB	0KB	256KB

1st 1MB of RAM   is allocated like this

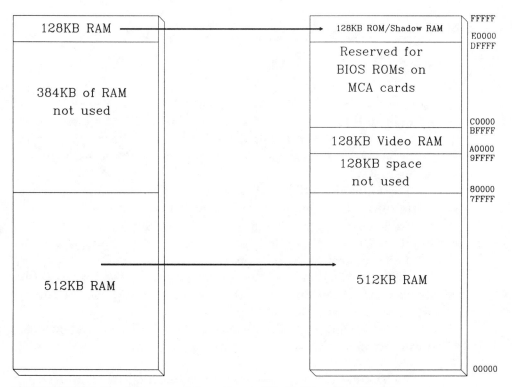

FIGURE 14-3   Memory Allocation with Split and 640 off

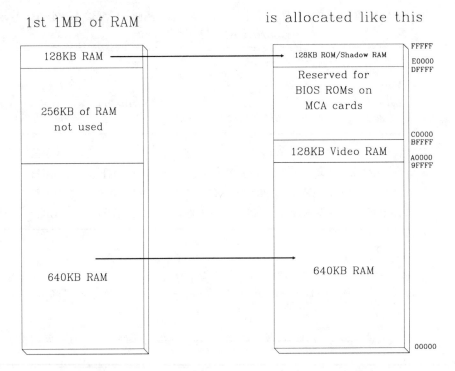

FIGURE 14-4   Memory Allocation with Split off and 640 on

to the addresses from 00000000_h–to $0009FFFF_h$. The top 128KB is used as the shadow RAM and responds to the system ROM address range. The remaining 256KB of the first 1MB of system board RAM is the split memory block and can be allocated at any 1MB address boundary above the first 1MB.

The following tables and paragraphs define the purpose of each bit written into the Memory Encoding registers.

Table 14-14 describes the bit assignment for Memory Encoding register 1 at I/O location $00E1_h$ as defined for the Model 70 and the Type 2 (20MHz version) Model 80.

Table 14-15 describes the bit assignment for Memory Encoding register 2 at I/O location $00E0_h$ as defined for the Model 70 and the Type 2 (20MHz version) Model 80.

The following procedure sets up the Model 70's system board RAM as described:

1. Writing a 00_h to Memory Encoding register 1 at I/O port $00E1_h$ has the effect indicated in Table 14-16.

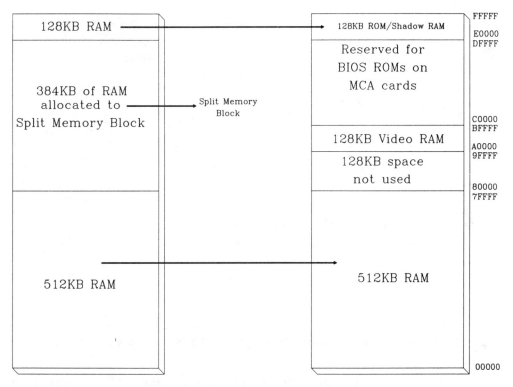

FIGURE 14-5　Memory Allocation with Split on and 640 off

2. Writing a C6$_h$ to Memory Encoding register 2 at I/O port 00E0$_h$ has the effect indicated in Table 14-17.

The overall effect is as follows:

1. The first 640KB of the first 1MB of system board RAM is located in the 00000000$_h$–0009FFFF$_h$ range.

2. The upper 128KB of the first 1MB of system board RAM is allocated to shadow RAM in the range 000E0000$_h$–000FFFFF$_h$.

3. The system ROM is enabled. Any reads from its address range access the system ROM and writes access the shadow RAM.

4. All 6MB of system board RAM is enabled. The first 1MB is allocated as described above. The other 5MB of system board

1st 1MB of RAM   is allocated like this

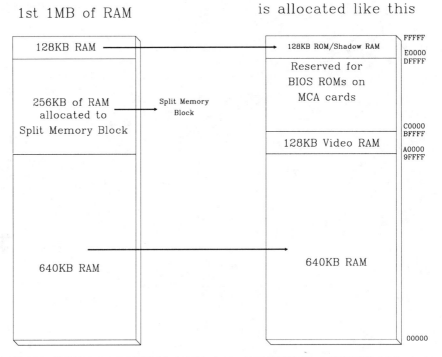

FIGURE 14-6   Memory Allocation with Split and 640 on

RAM occupies addresses from 00100000$_h$, the start address of the second megabyte of memory address space, to 005FFFFF$_h$.

5. The 256KB split memory block starts at memory address 00600000$_h$.

The Model 80 Type 1 (16MHz version) implements the first 1MB of system board RAM in a slightly different fashion than the Model 70 and the Model 80 Type 2. In order to use the upper 128KB of the first 1MB of system board RAM as shadow RAM, the split memory block option must be disabled. In other words, shadow RAM and the split memory block are mutually exclusive. When enabled, the split memory block may be set to either 384KB or 512KB in size.

Memory Encoding register 1 has exactly the same bit assignment as the Model 70 and the Model 80 Type 2, but is interpreted a little differently. These differences are outlined below:

1. If the split memory block is enabled, shadow RAM must be disabled (the ROM enable bit must be active).

TABLE 14-14   Model 70/80 (Type 2) Memory Encoding Register 1
Bit Assignment

Bit	Function
7	0 = Enable system board memory card 2's second 1MB block.
	1 = Disable it.
	This bit is reserved in the Model 80 and should always be a 1.
6	0 = Enable system board memory card 2's first 1MB block.
	1 = Disable it.
	This bit is reserved in the Model 80 and should always be a 1.
5	0 = Enable system board memory card 1's second 1MB block.
	1 = Disable it.
4	0 = Enable system board memory card 1's first 1MB block.
	1 = Disable it.
3	Split memory block enable bit.
	0 = Enable split memory block.
	1 = Disable it.
2	640KB bit. If split memory block is enabled by bit 3:
	0 = 640KB RAM in lower 1MB.
	1 = 512KB RAM in lower 1MB.
1	Shadow RAM enable bit.
	1 = Shadow RAM disabled. ROM address decoder enabled and shadow RAM is write-only.
	0 = Shadow RAM enabled. ROM address decoder disabled and shadow RAM is read-only.
0	0 = Enable system board RAM parity check.
	1 = Disable system board RAM parity check.

2. When the split memory block is enabled, its size is determined
by the state of the 640KB bit:

640KB bit = 0, split memory block size is 384KB
(640KB + 384KB = 1024KB, or 1MB).
640KB bit = 1, split memory block size is 512KB
(512KB + 512KB = 1024KB, or 1MB).

No memory is allocated to shadow RAM when the split memory block is enabled.

TABLE 14-15   Model 70/80 (Type 2) Memory Encoding Register 2 Bit Assignment

Bit	Function
7	Reserved (should be 1).
6	Reserved (should be 1).
5	0 = Enable system board memory card 3's second 1MB block.
	1 = Disable it.
	In the Type 2 Model 80, bits 4 and 5 control card 2 rather than card 3.
4	0 = Enable system board memory card 3's first 1MB block.
	1 = Disable it.
3-0	When the split memory block is enabled (see bit 3 in Memory Encoding register 1), these four bits define the starting address of the split memory block.

3 2 1 0

0 0 0 0 Invalid

0 0 0 1 Starts at memory address 00100000

0 0 1 0 Starts at memory address 00200000

0 0 1 1 Starts at memory address 00300000

0 1 0 0 Starts at memory address 00400000

0 1 0 1 Starts at memory address 00500000

0 1 1 0 Starts at memory address 00600000

0 1 1 1 Starts at memory address 00700000

1 0 0 0 Starts at memory address 00800000

1 0 0 1 Starts at memory address 00900000

1 0 1 0 Starts at memory address 00A00000

1 0 1 1 Starts at memory address 00B00000

1 1 0 0 Starts at memory address 00C00000

1 1 0 1 Starts at memory address 00D00000

1 1 1 0 Starts at memory address 00E00000

1 1 1 1 Starts at memory address 00F00000

TABLE 14-16   Effect of Writing 00_h to Memory Encoding Register 1

Bit	Value	Function
7 =	0	Enables the second 1MB block of the system board memory card in connector 2.
6 =	0	Enables the first 1MB block of the system board memory card in connector 2.
5 =	0	Enables the second 1MB block of the system board memory card in connector 1.
4 =	0	Enables the first 1MB block of the system board memory card in connector 1.
3 =	0	Split memory block is enabled. Its start address is defined by the value written to bits 0-3 of Memory Encoding register 2.
2 =	0	640KB of system board RAM in first 1MB of memory address space.
1 =	0	System ROM address decoder is enabled. Reads performed in the $000E0000_h$–$000FFFFF_h$ range access the ROM. Writes to this address range access the shadow RAM.
0 =	0	Enables system board RAM parity checking.

3. If shadow RAM is enabled and the split memory block disabled, 128KB of what would have been allocated to the split memory block is allocated to shadow RAM and the remainder of the split memory block is disabled. The amount of disabled memory is determined by the state of the 640KB bit:

   640KB bit = 0, 256KB RAM disabled.
   640KB bit = 1, 384KB RAM disabled.

4. Since the Model 80 Type 1 accepts only 1MB memory modules, bits 7-6 and 5-4 in Memory Encoding register 1 are interpreted as indicated in Tables 14-18 and 14-19.

5. Since the Model 80 Type 1 only has two system board memory connectors, bits 7-4 in Memory Encoding register 2 are reserved and should always be 1.

TABLE 14-17 Effect of Writing C6$_h$ to Memory Encoding
Register 2

Bit	Value	
7 =	1	Not used
6 =	1	Not used
5 =	0	Enables the second 1MB block of the system board memory card in connector 3.
4 =	0	Enables the first 1MB block of the system board memory card in connector 3.
3-0 =	0110	The 256KB split memory block starts at memory location 00600000$_h$.

TABLE 14-18 Interpretation of Bite 7 and 6 in Memory Encoding
Register 1

Bits	
7 6	Function
0 0	Invalid
0 1	Invalid
1 0	1MB card enabled in connector 2.
1 1	Card in connector 2 disabled.

Setting Up the VGA on the System Board   To place the
VGA into setup mode, bit 5 of the system board Enable/Setup register
(Port 0094$_h$) must be 0. Having placed the VGA into setup mode, the
programmer may access the VGA's only POS register, POS register 2 at
I/O port 0102$_h$. Bit 0 is the only bit used in this register and will enable
the VGA's address decoder when set to a 1. If set to a 0 while the VGA
is displaying data, the VGA will continue to generate video output, but
is inaccessible to reads and writes.

   After the VGA has been enabled, it should be placed back in
enable mode by setting bit 5 of the system board Enable/Setup register
(port 0094$_h$) to a 1.

TABLE 14-19   Interpretation of Bite 5 and 4 in Memory Encoding Register 1

Bits	
5 4	Function.
0 0	Invalid.
0 1	Invalid.
1 0	1MB card enabled in connector 1.
1 1	Card in connector 1 disabled.

TABLE 14-20   Card Selected Feedback Register Bit Assignment

Bit	Function
7-1	Not used.
0	Card selected feedback bit.
	0 = Not selected.
	1 = Selected.

The Card Selected Feedback Register

The PS/2 design allows the programmer to verify that a system board I/O device or an MCA card is responding when it is addressed. Each of these devices has an output known as its feedback signal.

Whenever an I/O device on the system board or an MCA card is addressed, its address decoder should set its respective feedback signal line active. This will set the card selected feedback bit active in the Card Selected Feedback register at I/O port 0091_h. This register's bit assignment is defined in Table 14-20.

This register may be read after a device is addressed to determine if its address decoder detected the address. Reading this register resets bit 0 to 0. This capability is used by diagnostics programs and the configuration program to determine that a device occupies a particular address range and is responding.

Each MCA card slot has a separate card selected feedback signal (CD SFDBK (n)) that is output to the system board logic so that it can be detected by the Card Selected Feedback register.

Summary

This chapter explored the history, implementation, and use of the POS registers. POS registers replace the old DIP switches found on PC/XT/ AT cards and system boards. They allow automatic configuration of the unit every time it is powered up by placing each card into setup mode and writing the appropriate values to their respective POS registers.

Provision is made for up to four "banks" of programmable DIP switches on each MCA card in the form of POS registers 2–5. In addition, each card has two POS registers, 0 and 1, from which the adapter ID can be read. Finally, an MCA card can also utilize the Subaddress Extension registers, POS registers 6 and 7, to implement additional POS registers if four registers are not enough.

CHAPTER
15

Automatic System Configuration

Objectives: The previous chapter provided a detailed description of the POS registers. These registers allow automatic configuration of the unit every time it is powered up by placing each card into setup mode and writing the appropriate values to their respective POS registers.

This chapter continues the discussion by describing the configuration program and automatic system configuration.

The Reference Diskette and Automatic Configuration

A reference diskette is delivered with every PS/2 product. It contains the system configuration utility program files and files describing the setup of the system board and some adapter cards.

Every MCA adapter card is accompanied by a diskette containing a file describing its setup. These files are known as adapter description files, or ADFs. The reference diskette contains an ADF for the system board and some MCA adapter cards.

Figure 15-1 illustrates the ADFs being merged onto the backup reference diskette. The reference diskette is permanently write-protected. Its contents must be copied to a backup diskette that is not write-protected. Each of the ADF files for adapter cards must then be copied onto the backup reference diskette using the "Copy an Option Utility" program on the backup reference diskette. Once this process has been completed, the backup reference diskette will contain the ADFs for the system board and all of the MCA adapter cards that are to be installed in the system.

The ADF identifies a card's POS registers and how the bits in each register control various aspects of the card's operation. When the configuration program is run, the following information regarding each card is stored in the unit's battery backed-up CMOS RAM:

- The MCA slot the card is installed in.
- The Adapter ID.
- The address of the implemented POS registers.
- The data that must be written to each of the card's POS registers when the unit is powered up to configure it for proper operation.

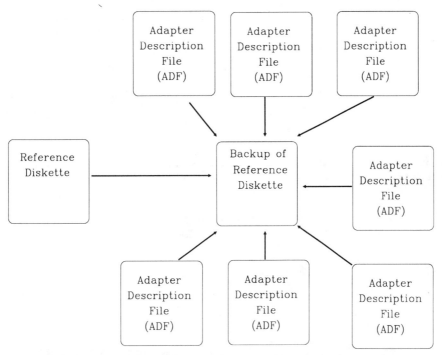

FIGURE 15-1   All ADFs Are Merged onto Backup Reference
Diskette

Each time the unit is powered up, the configuration portion of
the POST automatically takes inventory of the installed cards and configures them. POST confirms that the proper card is inserted in each
MCA slot and configures them as follows.

1. The card in MCA slot 1 is placed into setup mode by writing
   a 08_h to the Adapter Enable/Setup register at I/O port 0096_h.

2. The card is disabled by clearing the card enable bit (bit 0 of
   POS register 2) to 0.

3. The card's adapter ID is read from POS registers 0 and 1 and
   compared to the adapter ID stored in CMOS RAM. If the ID
   is incorrect, POST indicates a configuration error and the
   configuration program must be run again.

4. If the card's ID is correct, POST writes the POS data stored
   in CMOS RAM to the card's POS registers that are defined in
   CMOS RAM. This automatically configures the card.

5. The card is then enabled by setting its card enable bit (bit 0 of POS register 2) to 1.

6. The card is taken out of setup mode by writing a 00_h to the Adapter Enable/Setup register at I/O port 0096_h.

7. The same procedure is executed for each MCA card slot in succession until all of the installed cards have been checked and configured.

The ADF File Format

ADF files can be created using any word processor capable of producing a file in ASCII text format. The file name must adhere to the following format:

```
@cardid.adf
```

where the "at" sign is followed by the 16-bit card ID (in hex), a period, and the filename extension "adf."

Each file consists of the following elements.

1. The card ID.

2. The card name.

3. The number of POS registers implemented on the card.

4. A description of system resources, such as a particular interrupt request line, that the card must utilize for proper operation. This is known as a fixed resource, meaning no variability is allowed (for example, interrupt request 3, IRQ3, must be used and no other interrupt request line can be substituted).

5. When a card can use any one of a number of system resources, the allowable choices must be described. Examples are cards that can use one of a number of interrupt request lines, DMA channels, memory, or I/O address ranges.

6. For each system resource that allows two or more choices, some helpful text describing the choices must be supplied.

The following is a sample ADF file. Lines starting with a semicolon are comments included for explanatory purposes. Each comment has been numbered and additional numbered explanations follow the sample file.

; 1. The following line provides the card's 16-bit adapter ID

```
AdapterId 0CCFFh
```

; 2. The following line provides the name of the MCA card

```
AdapterName "Sample MCA Adapter Card"
```

; 3. The following line indicates the number of the highest POS
; Register used, – 1. For example, if POS register 5 is the highest
; POS register used, NumBytes must be set to 4.

```
NumBytes 2
```

; 4. The following line indicates that the card requires the use of
; interrupt request 5 (IRQ5) and that bits 3 and 2 of POS register
; 2 must be set to 01_b to enable this function.

```
FixedResources POS[0]=XXXX01XXb int 5
```

; 5. The named item block that follows consists of the nameditem
; statement, the prompt message, the available choices, and the
; help text to be displayed during configuration.

```
NamedItem

Prompt "Arbitration Priority Code"
   choice "Code 8"   pos[1]=XXXX1000b  arb 8
   choice "Code 9"   pos[1]=XXXX1001b  arb 9
   choice "Code 10"  pos[1]=XXXX1010b  arb 10
   choice "Code 11"  pos[1]=XXXX1011b  arb 11
   choice "Code 12"  pos[1]=XXXX1100b  arb 12
   choice "Code 13"  pos[1]=XXXX1101b  arb 13
   choice "Code 14"  pos[1]=XXXX1110b  arb 14

Help

   "Only change arbitration priority code if a conflict
   exists. Conflicts are indicated with an asterisk (*). Use
   F5=Previous and F6=Next keys to change arbitration
   priority code assignments. 0 is the highest priority."
```

; 6. The named item block that follows consists of the nameditem
; statement, the prompt message, the available choices, and the
; help text to be displayed during configuration.

```
NamedItem
```

```
Prompt "ROM start address assignment"

   choice "C0000" pos[1]=1100XXXXᵦ mem C0000—C07FF
   choice "D0000" pos[1]=1101XXXXᵦ mem D0000—D07FF

Help

  "This card contains a BIOS ROM that can start at memory
   address C0000ₕ or D0000ₕ. Use
   F5=Previous and F6=Next keys to alter selection."
```

The following keywords in the sample file are necessary to indicate the type of statement:

AdapterId

AdapterName

NumBytes

FixedResources

NamedItem

Prompt

Choice

Help

Sample ADF file explanations follow.

1. The **AdapterID** statement indicates that the card's Adapter ID is CCFF$_h$. It may be read from the card's POS register 0 and 1.

2. The **AdapterName** statement indicates that the card name is "Sample MCA Adapter Card."

3. The **NumBytes** statement indicates that POS register 3 $(3 - 1 = 2)$ is the highest POS register implemented on this card.

4. The **FixedResources** statement is fully explained in comment number 4 above.

5. The **first NamedItem** statement begins a named item block that lists the possible choices for the arbitration priority code to be assigned to this card.

The choice statements indicate that any code between 8 and 14 can be assigned to the card.

The POS statements on each line indicate that bits 0-3 of POS register 3 (POS register 2 is referred to as pos[0], POS register 3 as POS[1], etc.) are used to select the priority code.

The help block immediately after the choices contains helpful text that will be displayed on the screen during configuration. The user is presented with the choices and the help text is displayed to aid in making a selection.

6. The **second NamedItem** statement begins a named item block that lists the possible choices for the start memory address to be assigned to the BIOS ROM located on this card.

The choice statements indicate that the start memory address may be either C0000$_h$ or D0000$_h$.

The POS statements on each line indicate that bits 4-7 of POS register 3 are used to select the start memory address.

The choices are followed by help text to be displayed during configuration.

Automatic Configuration

Under the following circumstances, a complete configuration procedure must be executed.

1. Initial installation of the unit.

2. A dead battery causes all information in the CMOS RAM to be lost (including the configuration information).

3. The POST detects a bad checksum when testing the CMOS RAM. This indicates that corrupted information is stored in CMOS RAM. A complete explanation of the checksum error can be found in Chapter 26.

In any of these cases, no valid information is stored in CMOS RAM. The automatic configuration program must be run.

The system board is configured first by the automatic configuration program, and the program then sequentially configures MCA adapter cards starting with the card in MCA slot 1. This card is placed into setup mode and its adapter ID is read from POS registers 0 and 1.

It is then compared to the ID portion of the ADF file names found on the reference diskette. When a match is found, the first non-conflicting choice from each NamedItem list is chosen and the resultant POS register addresses and data are stored in CMOS RAM.

The program then proceeds to the next card. It will not backtrack in an attempt to resolve resource conflicts. If a conflict cannot be resolved automatically, the user must select Change Configuration from the menu and attempt to resolve the conflict by manually making choices.

If a card requires the use of an interrupt request line and does not specify which one, the configuration program selects the line least used by other adapters.

Once all resource conflicts have been resolved, either automatically or manually, the resultant POS register addresses and data are stored in CMOS RAM. Any adapter with a resource conflict that cannot be resolved is disabled by setting the card enable bit, bit 0, in POS register 2 to a 0 in CMOS RAM.

Each adapter slot is allocated 2 bytes for ID storage and 4 bytes for POS register storage in CMOS RAM, for a total of 6 bytes of CMOS RAM per adapter slot. In systems (such as the Model 50) with only 64 bytes of CMOS RAM, the configuration information is stored in these locations. In systems that have 2KB of CMOS RAM (such as the Model 60) in addition to the 64 location CMOS chip, the configuration information is stored in the 2KB CMOS RAM chip rather than the 64 location chip. For additional information, refer to Chapter 26.

POST Configuration Error Checking

Each time the unit is powered on, POST verifies that each card occupies the proper slot and then configures and enables it. If a battery failure or a corrupted CMOS RAM is indicated, one of the following error codes is displayed and a full re-configuration must be run.

- Dead battery: POST Error Code 161
- Corrupted CMOS RAM data: POST Error Code 162

If POST detects an error indicating that the configuration of the unit has been altered (rather than a dead battery or corrupted CMOS

RAM), one of the following error codes is displayed and the Change Configuration program must be run.

- Memory configuration change detected: POST Error Code 164
- Adapter card configuration change detected: POST Error Code 165

Summary

When a PS/2 is first set up, the battery backed-up RAM is empty. The reference diskette delivered with the system contains the configuration program. Each add-in MCA card to be installed in the system is delivered with a diskette containing an adapter description file (ADF). After the configuration program is copied onto a diskette that is not write-protected, all of the ADFs are copied onto the diskette as well.

The automatic configuration program is then run. The system board is configured first by the automatic configuration program, and the program then sequentially configures MCA adapter cards starting with the card in MCA slot 1. This card is placed into setup mode and its adapter ID is read from POS registers 0 and 1. It is then compared to the ID portion of the ADF file names found on the reference diskette. When a match is found, the first non-conflicting choice from each NamedItem list is chosen and the resultant POS register addresses and data are stored in CMOS RAM.

The program then proceeds to the next card. It does not backtrack in an attempt to resolve resource conflicts. If a conflict cannot be resolved automatically, the user must select Change Configuration from the menu and attempt to resolve the conflict by manually making choices.

CHAPTER
16

The Basic Types of MCA Data Transfers

Objective: This chapter describes the different types of bus cycles bus masters are permitted to run when granted the channel. The newer bus cycle types, known as "streaming data procedures," are described in Chapter 18.

Enhanced Bus Cycle Types

When the PS/2 was introduced, IBM defined the types of bus cycles that a bus master can run when communicating with another device over the micro channel. In October of 1989, IBM announced plans to support additional bus cycle types to improve the speed at which data can be transferred over the micro channel. These are known as the "streaming data procedures" and have already been partially implemented in IBM's new RISC System/6000 product line, which uses the micro channel. The new data transfer types are discussed in Chapter 18.

The Standard Bus Cycle Types

The fastest bus cycle run by the Intel 80286 and 80386 microprocessors is a 0-wait state bus cycle, with a duration of two PCLK cycles (address time (Ts) + data time (Tc)). The PS/2 Model 50Z is based on the 80286 microprocessor running with a PCLK speed of 10MHz. This means that each tick, or cycle, of PCLK is 100ns in duration. The Model 50Z can therefore run a 0-wait state bus cycle in 200ns, transferring 2 bytes per bus cycle using its two 8-bit data paths. At this rate, it can perform 5 million (1 second divided by 200ns) 2 byte data transfers per second, yielding a transfer rate of 10MB/second.

In defining the type of bus cycle that a bus master can use when performing a data transfer with a device on the micro channel, IBM used the Model 50Z bus cycle as a standard. In other words, every bus master must use bus cycles no faster than an 80286 10MHz bus cycle when communicating over the micro channel. Virtually all MCA cards on the market are therefore designed to generate and understand a bus cycle that runs no faster than 10MHz. A bus master card that communicates at a faster rate will be unable to talk to anyone who can understand it.

If the current bus master is a 32-bit device performing data transfers with another 32-bit device, it can transfer 4 bytes of data during every bus cycle. When communicating over the micro channel at 10MHz, it therefore has a data transfer rate of 20MB/second (5 million 200ns transfers/second at 4 bytes/transfer = 20MB/second). For example, assume that the current bus master is based on an 80386 running at 20MHz. This means that its address time (T_1) and data time (T_2) are each 50ns in duration, twice as fast as the Model 50Z. It is thus capable of performing a 0-wait state bus cycle in 100ns. When communicating over the micro channel, however, this bus master must run a 10MHz rather than a 20MHz bus cycle in order to conform to IBM's MCA standard. If the bus cycle is allowed to run at the processor's full speed, the addressed device has only half the normal amount of time to decode the address and only half the normal amount of time to transfer the data. In other words, the device is not able to respond in time and the data transfer is faulty.

As another example, the 25MHz Model 70 is based on a 25MHz 80386 microprocessor capable of performing a 0-wait state bus cycle in 80ns (as opposed to 200ns for the Model 50Z). It can access the devices located on the system board at this speed (if they can respond fast enough) but not cards installed in the MCA slots. The bus control logic in the Model 70 slows down its bus cycle as it appears on the micro channel by stretching out its address (T_1) and data time (T_2) slots to simulate a 10MHz 80286 bus cycle. The READY# input to the 80386 microprocessor is deactivated until the slow MCA bus cycle has been completed, thus causing wait states to be inserted in the microprocessor's bus cycle.

There are three versions of the 10MHz 80286 bus cycle that are considered valid by MCA devices:

- The default bus cycle
- The synchronous extended bus cycle
- The asynchronous extended bus cycle

The following sections describe each of the three standard MCA bus cycle types.

The Default Bus Cycle

The default bus cycle is the fastest type of bus cycle that bus masters in the current PS/2 models are permitted to run on the channel. Simply put, the default bus cycle is nothing more than a 10MHz 80286 0-wait state bus cycle. Figure 16-1 illustrates the default bus cycle.

Address time (Ts) and data time (Tc) are each 100ns in duration. The bus cycle is a 0-wait state bus cycle (relative to a 10MHz clock rate) because the addressed card's ready signal, card channel ready for MCA slot n (CD CHRDY(n)), went active prior to the beginning of the data transfer period. This allows the bus cycle to complete at the end of data time (Tc) with no wait states inserted.

A description of the sequence of events that occur during a default bus cycle follows. The step numbers are identical to the reference numbers from Figure 16-1.

1. When the current bus master is using address pipelining, the address for the upcoming bus cycle is actually output before

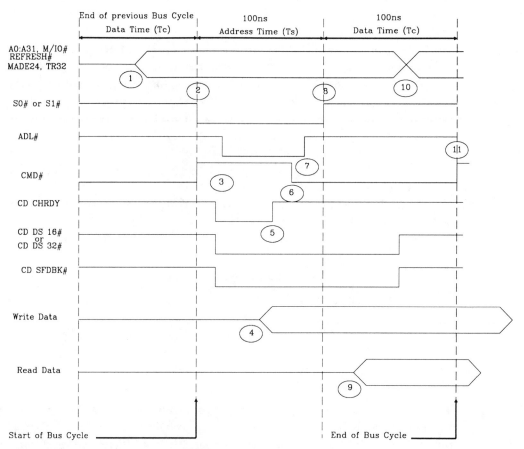

FIGURE 16-1   The Default Bus Cycle

the start of the bus cycle. At this time, the bus master also outputs M/IO#, part of the bus cycle definition.

REFRESH# is generated if the current bus master is the Refresh logic on the system board. An active level on REFRESH# informs memory cards everywhere that a refresh bus cycle is in progress and they should use the row address being output by the bus master to refresh the next row of RAM memory. Additional explanation of refresh can be found in Chapter 21.

The bus master sets MADE24 (memory address enable 24) active if it is generating a memory address in the lower 16MB address range (00000000_h to $00FFFFFF_h$). If a 32-bit bus master is generating an address greater than 16MB ($00FFFFFF_h$), it sets MADE24 inactive. Additional information regarding the MADE24 signal can be found in Chapter 17.

If the current bus master is a 16-bit bus master, it leaves TR32 (translate address to address understood by 32-bit slaves) active. Only 32-bit bus masters set TR32 inactive. Additional information regarding the TR32 signal can be found in Chapter 17.

2. The actual start of the bus cycle is signaled by the bus master setting either S0# or S1# active. Along with M/IO#, the S0# and S1# signals make up the bus cycle definition.

If the current bus cycle was preceded by another bus cycle, the CMD# line goes inactive at this point. The CMD# signal is active until the end of a bus cycle and indicates the data transfer period.

3. The address decode latch (ADL#) signal goes active. The currently addressed slave can latch the decoded address on either the leading or trailing edge of ADL#.

The currently addressed device should have decoded its address by this point and is chip-selected. This begins the actual access to the device and its ready timer should begin to run, setting the card's CD CHRDY# (n) signal inactive until the access time for the device has elapsed.

The addressed slave's address decoder should turn on either CD DS 16 (n)# or CD DS 32 (n)# (card data size 16 or 32 for slot n), unless its is an 8-bit device.

The addressed slave's address decoder should turn on the CD SFDBK (n)# signal to show that it has recognized an address within its assigned range.

4. If a write bus cycle is in progress, the bus master starts to output the data onto the data bus halfway through address time.

5. When the access time for the addressed device has elapsed, the CD CHRDY# (n) signal is allowed to go active again. If this occurs prior to the leading edge of the CMD# signal, this is considered to be a default bus cycle and terminates at the end of data time (Tc).

6. The bus master sets CMD# active to signal the beginning of the data transfer period.

7. The bus master allows the ADL# signal to go inactive. As stated earlier, the slave can latch the decoded address on either the leading or trailing edge of the ADL# signal.

8. The bus master allows the S0# or S1# line to go inactive. The slave should have decoded the bus cycle type by now, so the bus master need not drive either of these lines active.

   This is the start of data time (Tc), the second half of the bus cycle.

9. If a read bus cycle is in progress, the slave begins to drive the data back to the bus master somewhere during this time period.

10. If another bus cycle follows the current one and the bus master is using pipelining, the address for the upcoming bus cycle begins to appear (along with M/IO#, REFRESH#, MADE24, and TR32).

    When the address changes, the card data size line (16 or 32) and the card selected feedback lines will go inactive because the slave's address decoder no longer sees an address within its assigned range.

11. Since this a default bus cycle, the bus cycle ends at the end of data time (Tc). The trailing edge of the CMD# signal marks the end. If a read bus cycle is in progress, the bus master should read the data from the data bus at this time. If a write bus cycle is in progress, the slave has the data and the bus cycle can end.

During a write bus cycle, the bus master puts the data out very early and leaves it on the data bus for a long time (actually past the end of the bus cycle) to ensure that the slave gets the data correctly.

The Synchronous Extended Bus Cycle

The synchronous extended bus cycle is a special case. It occurs when the addressed card's ready signal, CD CHRDY(n), goes active in synchronism with (at the same time as) the leading edge (start) of data time (Tc). In this case, one wait state is inserted in the bus cycle, extending it to 300ns (address time (Ts) + data time (Tc) + data time (Tc)). Figure 16-2 illustrates the synchronous extended bus cycle.

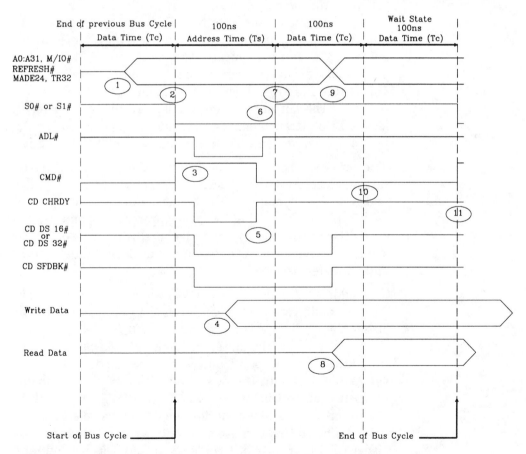

FIGURE 16-2   The Synchronous Extended Bus Cycle

A description of the sequence of events that occur during a synchronous extended bus cycle follows. The step numbers are identical to the reference numbers from Figure 16-2.

1. When the current bus master is using address pipelining, the address for the upcoming bus cycle is actually output before the start of the bus cycle. At this time, the bus master also outputs M/IO#, part of the bus cycle definition.

    REFRESH# is generated if the current bus master is the refresh logic on the system board. An active level on REFRESH# informs memory cards everywhere that a refresh bus cycle is in progress and that they should use the row address being output by the bus master to refresh the next row of RAM memory.

    The bus master sets MADE24 (memory address enable 24) active if it is generating a memory address in the lower 16MB address range (00000000_h to $00FFFFFF_h$). If a 32-bit bus master is generating an address greater than 16MB ($00FFFFFF_h$), it sets MADE24 inactive.

    If the current bus master is a 16-bit bus master, it leaves TR32 (translate address to address understood by 32-bit slaves) active. Only 32-bit bus masters set TR32 inactive.

2. The actual start of the bus cycle is signaled by the bus master setting either S0# or S1# active. Along with M/IO#, the S0# and S1# signals make up the bus cycle definition.

    If the current bus cycle was preceded by another bus cycle, the CMD# line goes inactive at this point. The CMD# signal is active until the end of a bus cycle and indicates the data transfer period.

3. The address decode latch (ADL#) signal goes active. The currently addressed slave can latch the decoded address on either the leading or trailing edge of ADL#.

    The currently addressed device should have decoded its address by this point and is chip-selected. This begins the actual access to the device and its ready timer should begin to run, setting the card's CD CHRDY# (n) signal inactive until the access time for the device has elapsed.

    The addressed slave's address decoder should turn on either CD DS 16 (n)# or CD DS 32 (n)#, unless it is an 8-bit device. The addressed slave's address decoder should turn on the CD SFDBK (n)# signal to show that it has recognized an address within its assigned range.

4. If a write bus cycle is in progress, the bus master starts to output the data onto the data bus halfway through address time.

5. When the access time for the addressed device has elapsed, the CD CHRDY# (n) signal is allowed to go active again. If this occurs synchronous to (at the same time as) the trailing edge of the CMD# signal, it is considered to be a synchronous extended bus cycle and terminates at the end of the second data time (Tc). In other words, one wait state is inserted into the bus cycle.

    The bus master sets CMD# active to signal the beginning of the data transfer period.

6. The bus master allows the ADL# signal to go inactive. As stated earlier, the slave can latch the decoded address on either the leading or trailing edge of the ADL# signal.

7. The bus master allows the S0# or S1# line to go inactive. The slave should have decoded the bus cycle type by now and the bus master need not drive either of these lines active. This is the start of data time (Tc), the second half of the bus cycle.

8. If a read bus cycle is in progress, the slave begins to drive the data back to the bus master somewhere during this time period.

9. If another bus cycle follows the current one and the bus master is using pipelining, the address for the upcoming bus cycle begins to appear (along with M/IO#, REFRESH#, MADE24, and TR32). When the address changes, the card data size line (16 or 32) and the card selected feedback lines go inactive because the slave's address decoder no longer sees an address within its assigned range.

10. Since this is a synchronous extended bus cycle, the bus master does not end it at the end of data time (Tc). Instead, the bus master waits one more data time (Tc) for the data transfer to complete. This is a wait state.

11. The bus cycle ends at the end of the second data time (Tc) (the wait state). The trailing edge of the CMD# signal marks

the end. If a read bus cycle is in progress, the bus master should read the data from the data bus at this time. If a write bus cycle is in progress, the slave has the data and the bus cycle can end.

During a write bus cycle, the bus master puts the data out very early and leaves it on the data bus for a long time (actually past the end of the bus cycle) to ensure that the slave gets the data correctly.

The Asynchronous Extended Bus Cycle

The asynchronous extended bus cycle is more common than the synchronous extended bus cycle. It occurs when the addressed card's ready signal, CD CHRDY(n), goes active at some time after the leading edge (start) of data time (Tc). Figure 16-3 illustrates the asynchronous extended bus cycle.

The exact duration of the bus cycle is dependent on when the addressed device lets its ready signal, CD CHRDY(n), go active. Since each additional wait state adds 100ns to the duration of the bus cycle, the bus cycle duration is 300ns or more, with each wait state adding 100ns (for example, 400ns, 500ns, 600ns, and so on) to the total duration of the bus cycle.

A description of the sequence of events that occur during an asynchronous extended bus cycle follows. The step numbers are identical to the reference numbers from Figure 16-3.

1. When the current bus master is using address pipelining, the address for the upcoming bus cycle is actually output before the start of the bus cycle. At this time, the bus master also outputs M/IO#, part of the bus cycle definition.

   REFRESH# is generated if the current bus master is the refresh logic on the system board. An active level on REFRESH# informs memory cards everywhere that a refresh bus cycle is in progress and that they should use the row address being output by the bus master to refresh the next row of RAM memory.

   The bus master sets MADE24 (memory address enable 24) active if it is generating a memory address in the lower 16MB address range (00000000_h–$00FFFFFF_h$). If a 32-bit bus master is generating an address greater than 16MB ($00FFFFFF_h$), it sets MADE24 inactive.

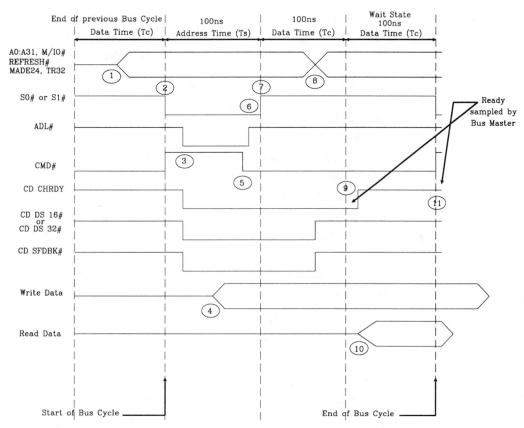

FIGURE 16-3 The Asynchronous Extended Bus Cycle

If the current bus master is a 16-bit bus master, it leaves TR32 (translate address to address understood by 32-bit slaves) active. Only 32-bit bus masters set TR32 inactive.

2. The actual start of the bus cycle is signaled by the bus master setting either S0# or S1# active. Along with M/IO#, the S0# and S1# signals make up the bus cycle definition.

   If the current bus cycle was preceded by another bus cycle, the CMD# line goes inactive at this point. The CMD# signal is active until the end of a bus cycle and indicates the data transfer period.

3. The ADL# (address decode latch) signal goes active. The currently addressed slave can latch the decoded address on either the leading or trailing edge of ADL#.

The currently addressed device should have decoded its address by this point and is chip-selected. This begins the actual access to the device and its ready timer should begin to run, setting the card's CD CHRDY# (n) signal inactive until the access time for the device has elapsed.

The addressed slave's address decoder should turn on either CD DS 16 (n)# or CD DS 32 (n)# (card data size 16 or 32 for slot n), unless it is an 8-bit device.

The addressed slave's address decoder should turn on CD SFDBK (n)# to show that it has recognized an address within its assigned range.

4. If a write bus cycle is in progress, the bus master starts to output the data onto the data bus halfway through address time.

5. The bus master sets CMD# active to signal the beginning of the data transfer period.

6. The bus master allows ADL# to go inactive. As stated earlier, the slave can latch the decoded address on either the leading or trailing edge of the ADL# signal.

7. The bus master allows the S0# or S1# line to go inactive. The slave should have decoded the bus cycle type by now, and the bus master need not drive either of these lines active. This is the start of data time (Tc), the second half of the bus cycle.

8. If another bus cycle will follow the current one and the bus master is using pipelining, the address for the upcoming bus cycle begins to appear (along with M/IO#, REFRESH#, MADE24 and TR32).

When the address changes, the card data size line (16 or 32) and the card selected feedback lines go inactive because the slave's address decoder no longer sees an address within its assigned range.

9. Since this is an asynchronous extended bus cycle, the bus master samples the CD CHRDY (n) signal at the end of data time (Tc) to see if the addressed slave is ready to end the bus cycle. In this case, the slave is not ready yet, and the bus master waits one more data time (Tc) (a wait state) before checking the CD CHRDY (n) line again.

10. If a read bus cycle is in progress, the slave begins to drive the data back to the bus master somewhere during this time period.

11. The bus cycle ends at the end of the third (or a subsequent) data time (Tc) (wait state) if the $^{CD\,CHRDY}$ (n) line is sampled active. The trailing edge of the CMD# signal marks the end. If a read bus cycle is in progress, the bus master should read the data from the data bus at this time. If a write bus cycle is in progress, the slave has the data and the bus cycle can end.

    During a write bus cycle, the bus master puts the data out very early and leaves it on the data bus for a long time (actually past the end of the bus cycle) to ensure that the slave gets the data correctly.

The Matched Memory Bus Cycle

IBM produces a memory card known as a matched memory card. Although it works when installed in any version of the Model 70 or 80, its full advantage is realized only in the Model 80 Type 1 (the 16MHz version).

Figure 16-4 illustrates the matched memory bus cycle. When the 80386 microprocessor on the Model 80 Type 1 system board begins a bus cycle, the system board logic turns on the matched memory cycle (MMC#) signal line. This is the system board's way of saying, "I talk fast. Do you?" If the card currently being addressed is a matched memory card, its address decoder turns on the matched memory cycle request (MMCR#) signal line. This is the matched memory card's way of saying, "I talk fast, too. Let's talk fast together!" Having agreed to talk fast together, the system board logic runs a matched memory cycle rather than a default bus cycle.

The matched memory cycle is essentially a default bus cycle with a twist. The twist is that it last 187.5ns instead of the default bus cycle time of 200ns. Address time (Ts) and data time (Tc) are each only 93.75ns in duration (rather than 100ns). This means that the system board microprocessor can perform 5,347,593 transfers per second, yielding a transfer rate of 21.39MB/second when communicating with a 32-bit matched memory card. This is a 6.95% increase over the maximum transferred rate achievable when running default bus cycles.

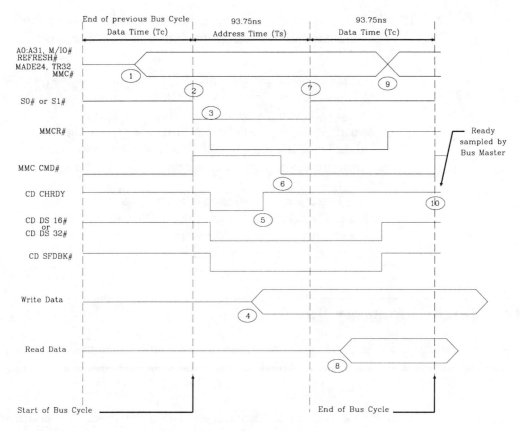

FIGURE 16-4   The Matched Memory Bus Cycle

Additional information regarding the matched memory cycle can be found in Chapter 17 in the section entitled "The 32-Bit MCA Matched Memory Cycle Extension."

A description of the sequence of events that occur during a matched memory bus cycle follows. The step numbers are identical to the reference numbers from Figure 16-4.

1. When the current bus master is using address pipelining, the address for the upcoming bus cycle is actually output before the start of the bus cycle. At this time, the bus master also outputs M/IO#, part of the bus cycle definition. The system board microprocessor sets matched memory cycle (MMC#) active to indicate that it can support matched memory bus cycles.

REFRESH# is generated if the current bus master is the refresh logic on the system board. An active level on REFRESH# informs memory cards everywhere that a refresh bus cycle is in progress and that they should use the row address being output by the bus master to refresh the next row of RAM memory.

The bus master sets MADE24 (memory address enable 24) active if it is generating a memory address in the lower 16MB address range (00000000_h–$00FFFFFF_h$). If a 32-bit bus master is generating an address greater than 16MB ($00FFFFFF_h$), it sets MADE24 inactive.

If the current bus master is a 16-bit bus master, it leaves TR32 (translate address to address understood by 32-bit slaves) active. Only 32-bit bus masters set TR32 inactive.

2. The actual start of the bus cycle is signaled by the bus master setting either S0# or S1# active. Along with M/IO#, the S0# and S1# signals make up the bus cycle definition. If the current bus cycle was preceded by another matched memory bus cycle, the MMC CMD# line goes inactive at this point. The MMC CMD# signal is active until the end of a bus cycle and indicates the data transfer period.

3. The currently addressed device should have decoded its address by this point and is chip-selected. This begins the actual access to the device and its ready timer should begin to run, setting the card's CD CHRDY# (n) signal inactive until the access time for the device has elapsed.

If the addressed slave supports matched memory bus cycles, it should activate the (MMCR#) signal at this point. This informs the system board logic that matched memory bus cycle timing should be used. The system board will not generate ADL# or CMD#.

The addressed slave's address decoder should turn on either CD DS 16 (n)# or CD DS 32 (n)# (card data size 16 or 32 for slot n), unless it is an 8-bit device. The addressed slave's address decoder should turn on CD SFDBK (n)# to show that it has recognized an address within its assigned range.

4. If a write bus cycle is in progress, the bus master starts to output the data onto the data bus halfway through address time.

5. When the access time for the addressed device has elapsed, the CD CHRDY# (n) signal is allowed to go active again.

6. The system board sets MMC CMD# active to signal the beginning of the data transfer period.

7. The bus master allows the S0# or S1# line to go inactive. The slave should have decoded the bus cycle type by now, and the bus master need not drive either of these lines active. This is the start of data time (Tc), the second half of the bus cycle.

8. If a read bus cycle is in progress, the slave begins to drive the data back to the bus master somewhere during this time period.

9. If another bus cycle will follow the current one and the bus master is using pipelining, the address for the upcoming bus cycle begins to appear (along with M/IO#, REFRESH#, MADE24, MMC# and TR32).

   When the address changes, the card data size line (16 or 32) and the card selected feedback lines go inactive because the slave's address decoder no longer sees an address within its assigned range.

10. The system board microprocessor samples the *CD CHRDY* (n) line at the end of data time (Tc). If the currently addressed slave is ready to end the bus cycle and a read bus cycle is in progress, the bus master should read the data from the data bus at this time. If a write bus cycle is in progress, the slave has the data and the bus cycle can end.

    If the *CD CHRDY* (n) line is sampled inactive at the end of data time, the system board microprocessor waits one more data time before again checking to see if the slave is ready to end the bus cycle. This would be a wait state. The longer the access time of the slave, the more wait states get inserted in the bus cycle.

    During a write bus cycle, the bus master puts the data out very early and leaves it on the data bus for a long time (actually past the end of the bus cycle) to ensure that the slave gets the data correctly.

Summary

As implemented in the current PS/2 products on the market, the Micro Channel supports three different bus master bus cycle types: the default bus cycle, the synchronous extended bus cycle, and the asynchronous extended bus cycle. The default bus cycle takes 200ns and provides a data transfer rate of 20MB/second. The synchronous extended bus cycle takes 300ns, and the asynchronous extended bus cycle takes 300ns or longer.

The matched memory bus cycle is only supported by the Model 80, Type 1 (16 MHz). It provides a data transfer rate of 21.39 MB/second. Some of the latest PS/2 models and the entire RISC System/6000 support faster bus cycle types known as "streaming data procedures." They are described in Chapter 18.

The MCA Connectors

Objectives: This chapter defines the purpose of every signal on the 16-bit MCA connectors, the video extension to the 16-bit MCA connectors, the 32-bit MCA connectors, and the matched memory extension connector.

Definitions for This Chapter

• The **slave** is the device being addressed by the current bus master.

• An **8-bit slave** is a slave installed in a 16-bit MCA slot that is connected to and can use only the lowest data path, D0:D7.

• A **16-bit bus master** is installed in a 16-bit MCA slot and can therefore only use the lower two data paths, D0:D7 and D8:D15, during data transfers.

• A **16-bit slave** is a slave installed in a 16-bit MCA slot that is connected to and can use the lower 2 data paths, D0:D7 and D8:D15.

• A **32-bit bus master** is a bus master that is installed in a 32-bit MCA slot and can use all 4 data paths during data transfers.

• A **32-bit slave** is a slave installed in a 32-bit MCA slot that is connected to and can use all 4 data paths.

The 16-Bit MCA Slots

A 16-bit MCA slot includes the lower 16 data bus lines, D0:D15. As illustrated in Figure 17-1, it consists of 8- and 16-bit sections, with an optional video extension connector (described at the end of this chapter).

Figure 17-2 illustrates all of the signals found on the 16-bit MCA connector. They have been grouped by function and are described in the following sections. Refer to Figures 17-1 and 17-2 throughout the discussion of the signals on the 16-bit MCA slot.

Address Bus

Figure 17-3 illustrates the address-related signals on the 16-bit MCA connector. When the current bus master initiates a bus cycle, it places the address on the address bus during address time (T_s), consisting of

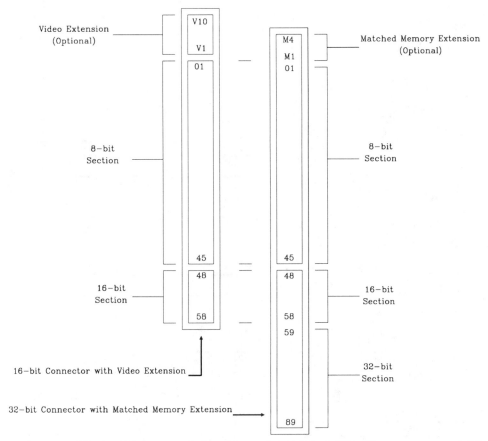

FIGURE 17-1 Diagram of the 16- and 32-/bit MCA Connectors and Their Optional Extensions

A0:A23 and SBHE#. The address is placed on A0:A23 and the bus master will turn on SBHE# if it intends to use the upper data path, D8:D15, during the transfer. Activating SBHE# is another way of saying that the bus master intends to communicate with an odd address (Cardinal Rule Number 3). The address is visible to all installed MCA cards and to the logic on the system board. In other words, the current bus master can communicate with any slave in the system. A 24-bit address bus provides the capability to address up to 16MB of memory.

The memory address enable 24 (MADE24) signal is set active by the current bus master whenever a memory address within the first 16MB of address space is on the address bus. MADE24 should be used as an enable by the address decoders on memory cards installed in 16-bit MCA slots.

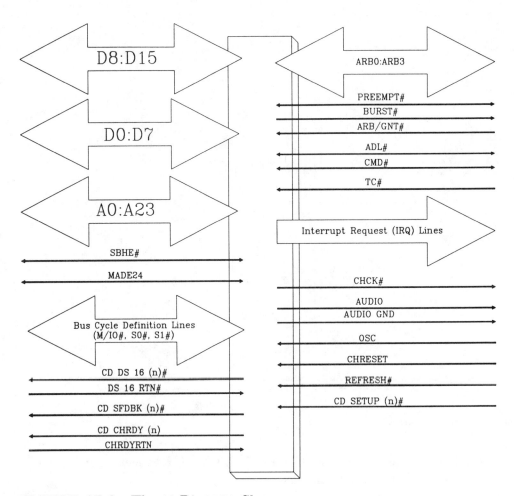

FIGURE 17-2 The 16-Bit MCA Slot

If a memory bus cycle is in progress and MADE24 is inactive, it means that the current bus master is reading from or writing to a memory address greater than 16MB. All memory cards installed in 16-bit MCA slots should therefore ignore the address. This prevents 16-bit memory cards from incorrectly responding to addresses greater than 16MB that are addressing memory cards installed in 32-bit MCA slots.

Data Bus

Refer to Figure 17-4. The data to be transferred during a bus cycle's data time (T_c) is transferred over the data bus. The data bus consists of two 8-bit data paths, D0:D7 and D8:D15.

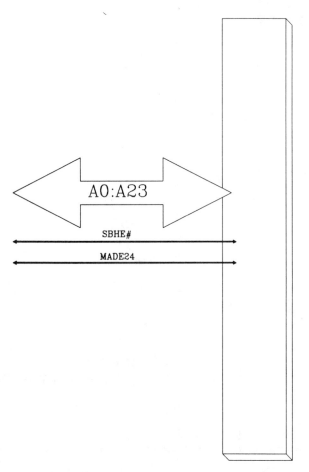

FIGURE 17-3   The 16-Bit MCA Address Bus

The lower path, D0:D7, is used during data transfers with even addresses. The upper path, D8:D15, is used during data transfers with odd addresses.

Bus Cycle Definition

When the current bus master initiates a bus cycle, it places the bus cycle definition on the bus cycle definition lines during address time (T_s). The state of these lines must be decoded by the addressed slave to determine the type of bus cycle in progress. Table 17-1 defines the types of bus cycles.

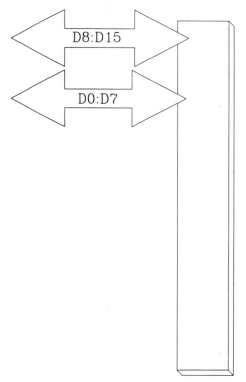

FIGURE 17-4
The 16-Bit MCA Data Bus

TABLE 17-1   Bus Cycle Definition Interpretation

M/IO#	S0#	S1#	Bus Cycle Type
0	0	0	Interrupt acknowledge
0	0	1	I/O write
0	1	0	I/O read
1	0	0	Halt or shutdown
1	0	1	Memory write
1	1	0	Memory read

Bus Cycle Timing

The signals described in Table 17-2 provide points of reference for both
the bus master and the slave during a bus cycle on the micro channel.

TABLE 17-2 Bus Cycle Timing Signals

Signal	Function
ADL#	Address decode latch. The current bus master sets ADL# active during address time (T_s) to indicate that a valid address and bus cycle definition are present on the micro channel. The currently addressed slave may latch the address on either the leading or trailing edge of ADL#. ADL# is not active during matched memory bus cycles.
CD CHRDY (n)	Card channel ready signal for MCA slot 'n'. The currently addressed slave sets this normally active signal inactive when it first detects that it is being addressed. It is kept inactive until the slave is ready to end the bus cycle. If a read bus cycle is in progress, CD CHRDY (n) is kept inactive until the addressed slave has placed the data on the data bus for the bus master to read. If a write bus cycle is in progress, CD CHRDY (n) is kept inactive until the addressed slave has accepted the data on the data bus.
CHRDYRTN	Channel ready return. In addition to being routed to the system board microprocessor, the CD CHRDY (n) signal is turned around on the system board and sent out over this line so that the current bus master, no matter where it is physically located, can see ready and know when to end the bus cycle.
CMD#	The command signal is set active by the current bus master to indicate that it is data time (T_c) (time to transfer the data). The trailing edge (end) of CMD# indicates the end of the bus cycle. CMD# is not active during matched memory bus cycles.

Device Size

Figure 17-5 illustrates the 16-bit size lines. When a **16-bit slave**'s address decoder detects an address in its assigned range, it should both activate the slave's chip-select line and activate CD DS 16 (n)#, the card data size 16 signal line. The address decoder informs the current bus master that it is communicating with a slave that is connected to both of the 8-bit data paths, D0:D7 and D8:D15.

If this signal (or CD DS 32 (n)#)does not go active during a bus cycle, the bus master is communicating with an **8-bit slave** and all

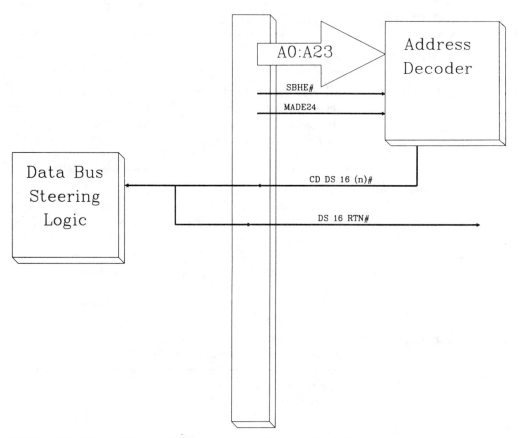

FIGURE 17-5 The 16-Bit MCA Size Lines, CD DS 16 (n)#

communications must take place over the lower data path, D0:D7. In this case, the system board's data bus steering logic may be automatically activated to route the data over the correct data path.

In addition to being routed to the system board's data bus steering logic, the CD DS 16 (n)# signal is also turned around on the system board and routed to all of the MCA slots on the data size 16 return (DS 16 RTN#) signal line. In this way, the current bus master, wherever it is physically located, is informed that all communications will take place over the lower data path, D0:D7, when DS 16 RTN# is inactive.

For additional information, refer to the section in this chapter entitled "The System Board's Data Bus Steering and Translation Logic."

Bus Arbitration

Figure 17-6 illustrates the MCA bus arbitration signals. A detailed description of the MCA bus arbitration signals can be found in Chapter 13. The MCA bus arbitration signals are listed with a brief description in Table 17-3.

Reset

Figure 17-7 illustrates the channel reset logic. When the unit is first powered up, the RESET signal remains active until the power supply voltages have stabilized. During this period of time, the CHRESET (channel reset) signal is also active. When active, CHRESET has two effects on the installed MCA cards.

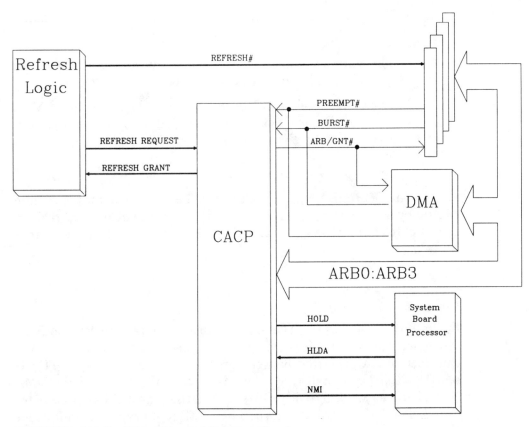

FIGURE 17-6 The Bus Arbitration Logic

TABLE 17-3   The Bus Arbitration Signals

Signal	Function
ARB0:ARB3	This is the 4-bit arbitration bus that competing bus masters place their arbitration priority codes on during an arbitration cycle.
ARB/GNT#	The arbitrate/grant line identifies the start and end of an arbitration cycle for competing bus masters.
PREEMPT#	The preempt line is used by the DMA controller and competing bus masters to request the use of the buses.
BURST#	Bursting bus masters use the burst line to inform the central arbitration control point (CACP) that they require the use of the buses to run multiple bus cycles, rather than just a single bus cycle.

1. The cards are prevented from doing anything until the power has stabilized and CHRESET has become inactive.

2. The active level on CHRESET forces all of the installed MCA cards to a known default state so that they always begin operating exactly the same way every time the unit is powered up.

The CHRESET signal line can also be set active under program control by writing the proper value to the adapter enable/setup register at I/O port 0096_h. CHRESET is activated when bit 7 of the register is set to a 1.

DMA

Figure 17-8 illustrates the TC# signal. During a DMA transfer, the DMA controller sets the transfer complete (TC#) signal active when all of the data has been transferred between an I/O slave and memory. TC# is sent to all of the installed MCA cards so that the I/O card the DMA controller was working with can see that the transfer has been completed. The I/O card should respond by setting its respective interrupt request (IRQ) output active, thereby informing the microprocessor that the transfer has been completed.

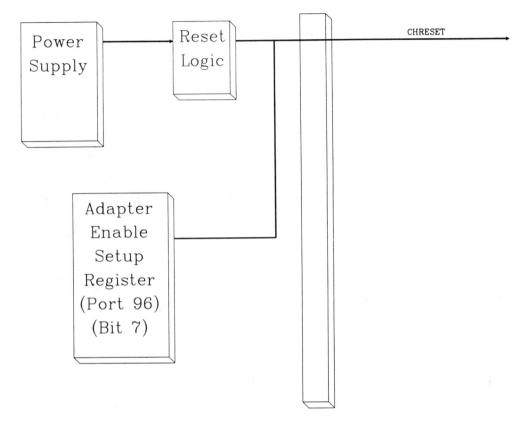

FIGURE 17-7 The Channel Reset Logic

Interrupts

Figure 17-9 illustrates the interrupt logic. The two Intel 8259 programmable interrupt controllers (PICs) are located on the system board. When a device on the micro channel requires servicing by the system board microprocessor, it should activate its respective interrupt request (IRQ) line to inform the system board microprocessor. A detailed description of interrupts can be found in Chapter 19.

Table 17-4 lists the MCA interrupt request lines and the devices that normally use them.

Configuration

Figure 17-10 illustrates the card enable/setup lines. In order to access an MCA card's POS registers, the card must first be placed into setup mode. This is accomplished in the following fashion.

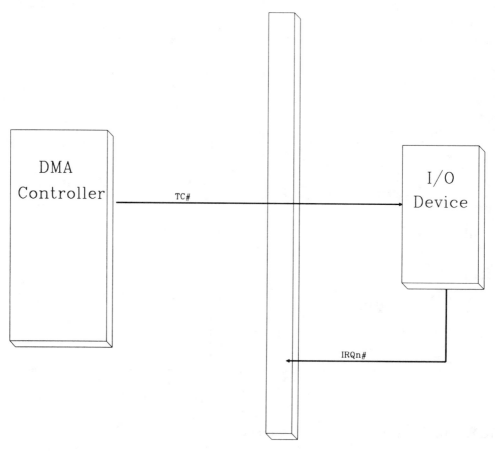

FIGURE 17-8 The Transfer Complete (TC#) Logic

1. The proper value must be written to the adapter enable/setup register at I/O port 0096_h to place the desired MCA card slot into setup mode.

2. Any subsequent access in the POS register address range, 0100_h to 0107_h, causes the CD SETUP (n)# (card setup line for MCA slot 'n') signal to go active, thereby placing the card into setup mode and enabling its POS registers so that they can be read from or written to.

   A detailed description of the POS registers can be found in Chapter 14.

MCA
Connector

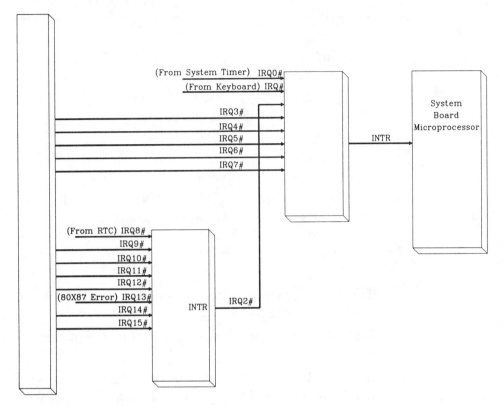

FIGURE 17-9 The MCA Interrupt Logic

Error Reporting

Figure 17-11 illustrates the MCA error reporting logic. When an MCA card experiences a hardware failure, it activates the channel check (CHCK#) signal to report the error to the system board microprocessor. This causes the following actions to take place.

1. The CACP sets the ARB/GNT# line high to force the current bus master to disconnect from the buses so that the microprocessor can use them.

2. If active, the CACP deactivates HOLD to give the buses back to the microprocessor so that it can handle the error.

TABLE 17-4 Interrupt Request Line Assignment

Interrupt Line	Device usually assigned to
IRQ3#	Serial port 2
IRQ4#	Serial port 1
IRQ5#	Parallel port 2
IRQ6#	Floppy disk interface
IRQ7#	Parallel port 1
IRQ9#	VGA
IRQ10#	none
IRQ11#	none
IRQ12#	Mouse interface
IRQ14#	Hard disk interface
IRQ15#	none

3. The CACP then activates non-maskable interrupt request (NMI) to inform the microprocessor of the error.

4. The microprocessor jumps to the NMI interrupt service routine and executes it.

5. In the NMI interrupt service routine, the programmer reads the contents of system control port B at I/O port 0061_h to determine the NMI source. Bit 6 will be a 1 if channel check caused the NMI.

6. Upon determining that channel check caused the NMI, the programmer sequentially places each installed MCA card into setup mode and checks bit 7 of POS register 5 at I/O port 0105_h to determine if the respective card caused the NMI.

7. The exact action taken when the NMI source is found is card-dependent.

Channel check's ability to cause an NMI can be enabled or disabled by writing the desired value to system control port B at I/O port 0061_h. Writing a 0 to bit 3 enables channel check, while setting it to a 1 disables it. The current status of this bit can be checked by reading from port 0061_h and checking the state of bit 3.

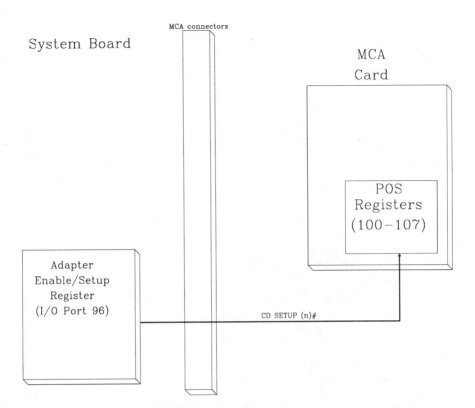

FIGURE 17-10   Card Setup Logic

Audio

Figure 17-12 illustrates the MCA audio signals. Timer 2 on the system board is a programmable frequency source that normally supplies the input frequency to the speaker driver. Under certain circumstances, an MCA card may need to generate audio output using the system board speaker logic. In this case, the MCA card places the desired frequency on the AUDIO signal line. On the system board, the AUDIO signal is also tied to the speaker driver input and causes audio output from the speaker. The AUDIO GND line provides the MCA card a common ground reference for the speaker driver so that it will interpret the input voltages correctly.

DRAM Refresh

When the refresh logic on the system board becomes bus master and is running a memory read bus cycle to refresh a row of dynamic RAM

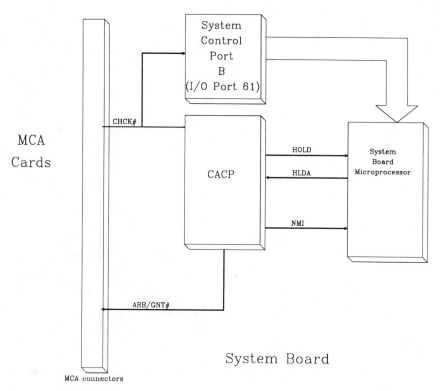

FIGURE 17-11   MCA Error Reporting

memory, the REFRESH# signal is set active. This informs each installed memory card that a refresh bus cycle is in progress and that the address bus contains a row address to be sent to every bank of RAM memory simultaneously. For additional information regarding dynamic RAM refresh, refer to Chapter 21.

Miscellaneous

Table 17-5 defines the purpose of the remaining 16-bit MCA signals.

The 32-Bit MCA Slots

Figure 17-1 illustrates the 32-bit MCA extension. A 32-bit MCA slot is defined as one that includes all 32 data bus lines, D0:D31, and the full 32-bit address bus. It is comprised of a 16-bit MCA slot with the ad-

MCA Connectors

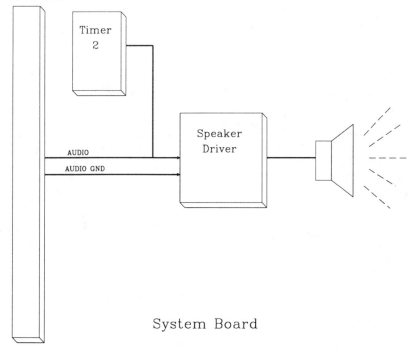

FIGURE 17-12 The Speaker Logic

TABLE 17-5 Miscellaneous 16-Bit MCA Signals

Signal	Function
OSC	The oscillator signal is a free-running 14.31818MHz signal generated on the system board and made available to MCA cards for general use. As an example, it is used by the CGA (color graphics adapter) card in the PC/XT/AT as the source for the display's color burst signal.
CD SFDBK(n)#	Figure 17-13 illustrates the MCA feedback logic. Card selected feedback for MCA slot 'n' goes active whenever the address decoder on the MCA card installed in slot 'n' detects an address within its assigned range. Feedback is described in Chapter 14.

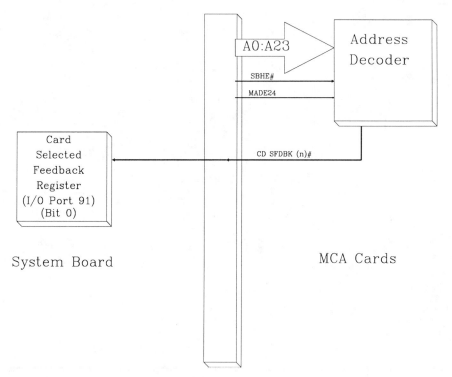

FIGURE 17-13   The Feedback Logic

ditional signals appended that are necessary to provide support for the expanded address and data buses. These additional signals are the 32-bit extensions to the micro channel. The optional matched memory cycle extension is discussed immediately after this section.

The following sections define all of the signals located on the 32-bit extension. They have been grouped by function. Refer to Figure 17-14 throughout the discussion of the signals on the 32-bit MCA extension.

Address Bus

Figure 17-15 illustrates the address-related signals on the 32-bit MCA extension. The address bus is extended to a full 32-bits, which provides the capability to address up to 4GB (4,294MB) of memory. This extension is provided by A24:A31. A0:A23 are found on the 16-bit portion of the connector.

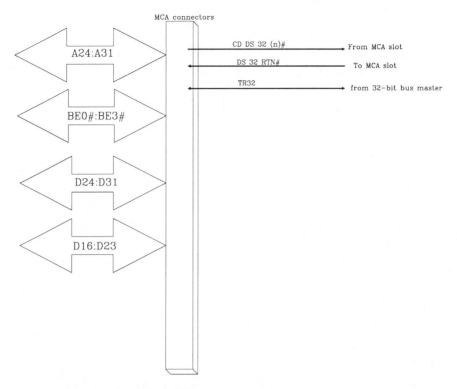

FIGURE 17-14   The 32-Bit MCA Extension

When the Intel 80386 or 80486 microprocessor places an address on the address bus, it uses A2:A31 to identify a group of four locations (known as a doubleword). In addition to the address, the microprocessor also uses four byte enable lines, BE0#:BE3#, to identify exactly which of the four locations within the addressed doubleword it really wishes to communicate with. The active byte enable line also identifies which of the 4 data paths will be used to communicate with the location.

The microprocessor may turn on anywhere from 1 to all 4 of the byte enables, thereby allowing it to identify up to 4 bytes to be transferred during a bus cycle. For additional information regarding the addressing technique used by the 80386 microprocessor, refer to Chapter 7.

Data Bus

Figure 17-16 illustrates the data lines on the 32-bit MCA extension. The data bus is extended by adding 2 additional data paths, D16:D23 and

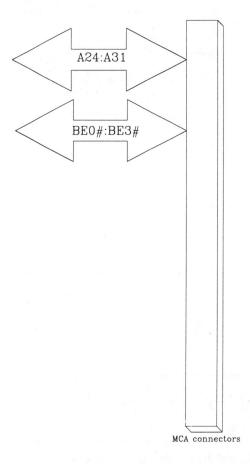

MCA connectors

FIGURE 17-15
The 32-Bit MCA Address Bus

D24:D31. D0:D7 and D8:D15 are found on the 16-bit portion of the connector.

The System Board's Data Bus Steering and Translation Logic

Problems occur in the following situations.

1. When a **32-bit bus master** attempts to communicate with a 16-bit slave.

2. When a 32-bit bus master attempts to communicate with an 8-bit slave.

3. When a **16-bit bus master** attempts to communicate with a **32-bit slave**.

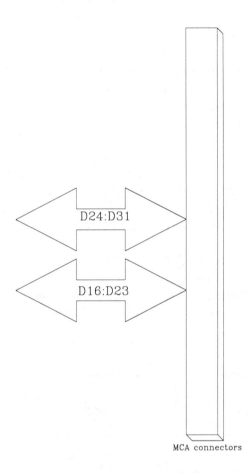

MCA connectors

FIGURE 17-16
The 32-Bit MCA Data Bus

4. When a 16-bit bus master attempt to communicate with an 8-bit slave.

When a 32-bit slave is addressed, it responds by setting the signal CD DS 32 (N)# (card data size 32 for slot N) active. This informs the system board data bus steering and translation logic that the addressed device is capable of communicating over all four data paths. On the system board, CD DS 32 (N)# is then turned around and sent out to all of the 32-bit MCA slots on the CD DS 32 RTN# signal line to inform the 32-bit bus master, wherever it is physically located, that the addressed device can communicate over all four data paths.

The following sections describe the problems incurred in each of these circumstances and how they are rectified.

32-Bit Bus Master Communicating with 16-Bit Slaves
When a 32-bit bus master reads data from or writes data to a 16-bit

slave, it sometimes requires help from system board support logic known as the data bus steering and translation logic.

TR32 is a normally active signal only driven inactive when a 32-bit bus master is running a bus cycle. An inactive level informs the system board's translation logic that the bus master will be generating A2:A31 and the proper byte enable lines.

Table 17-6 lists the circumstances when data bus steering is necessary. Remember that the byte enable lines are active when low (0). Data path 0 consists of D0:D7, path 1 of D8:D15, path 2 of D16:D23, and path 3 of D24:D31. Figure 17-17 illustrates the system board's data bus steering and translation logic.

The example described in the following paragraphs illustrates the process.

Example. In this example, the 32-bit bus master is performing a read data transfer with a 16-bit slave. During address time, the bus master places the doubleword memory address 00000100_h on A2:A31

TABLE 17-6   32-Bit Bus Master Communicating with 16-Bit Slaves

Operation Type	Byte Enables 3 2 1 0	Copy From Path	Copy To Path
Read	0 0 0 0	0 and 1	2 and 3
Read	0 0 0 1	0 and 1	2 and 3
Read	0 0 1 1	0 and 1	2 and 3
Read	0 1 1 1	1	3
Read	1 0 0 0	0	2
Read	1 0 0 1	0	2
Read	1 0 1 1	0	2
Write	0 0 0 0	3 and 2	1 and 0
Write	0 0 0 1	3 and 2	1 and 0
Write	0 0 1 1	3 and 2	1 and 0
Write	0 1 1 1	3	1
Write	1 0 0 0	2	0
Write	1 0 0 1	2	0
Write	1 0 1 1	2	0

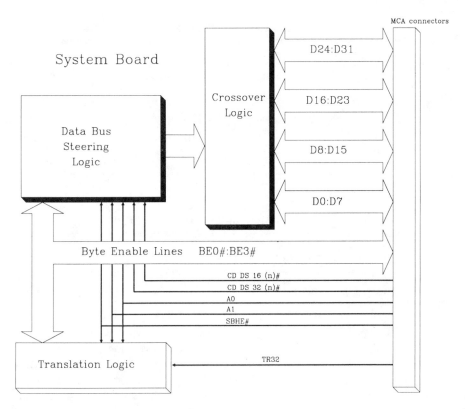

FIGURE 17-17   The System Board Data Bus Steering and
Translation Logic

and activates all 4 byte enable lines. In other words, the bus master is
identifying the doubleword starting at memory address 00000100_h and
intends to transfer all 4 bytes from memory locations 00000100_h,
00000101_h, 00000102_h, and 00000103_h. It expects the 4 bytes to be transferred over the data paths indicated in Table 17-7.

The system board data bus steering logic interprets its inputs
as indicated in Table 17-8.

During the example data transfer, the following sequence of
events takes place.

1. Since 16-bit slaves are not connected to the byte enable lines,
   the translation logic must convert the byte enables to A0, A1,
   and SBHE#, signals understood by 16-bit slaves. This is done
   in two stages. First, the active level on BE0# and BE1# are
   converted to A0 = 0, A1 = 0, and SBHE# = 0.

TABLE 17-7   Data Paths Used in 32/16 Example

Byte Enable	Identifies Location	Identifies Data Path
0	00000100_h	0 (D0:D7)
1	00000101_h	1 (D8:D15)
2	00000102_h	2 (D16:D23)
3	00000103_h	3 (D24:D31)

TABLE 17-8   32-Bit Bus Master Communicating with 16-Bit Slave

Steering Logic's Inputs	Interpreted as
Any BE line active	32-bit bus master running bus cycle
Read in progress	Data coming from slave to master
CD DS 16 (n)# = 0	Communicating with a 16-bit slave. Data must be routed from slave's lower 2 data paths to master's 4 data paths. In addition, the system board translation logic must create A0, A1 and SBHE# from the byte enable lines being generated by the 32-bit bus master.
BE2# or BE3# active	Indicates master expects data on one or both of the upper 2 paths. System board data bus steering logic must copy the data from lower paths to upper paths.
TR32 = 0	Bus master is generating the byte enables and A2:A31.

2. The 16-bit slave now sees address 00000100_h on the address bus and SBHE# active. This is interpreted as the bus master requesting the contents of the even address on the address bus, 00000100_h, and the contents of the next sequential odd address (SBHE# = 0), 00000101_h. Since it is a read, the slave places the byte read from the even address (00000100_h) onto the lower data path (path 0, D0:D7) and the byte read from the odd address (00000101_h) onto the second data path (path 1, D8:D15).

3. Since the bus master has turned on all 4 byte enables to indicate that it expects all 4 bytes to be received at the same time, the steering logic latches and holds the 2 bytes just read from the 16-bit slave.

4. The second stage now begins and is a continuation of the same bus cycle. The steering logic now converts the active levels on BE2# and BE3# to A0 = 0, A1 = 1, and SBHE# = 0.

5. As a result, the 16-bit slave now sees address 00000102_h on the address bus and SBHE# active. This is interpreted as the bus master requesting the contents of the even address on the address bus, 00000102_h, and the contents of the next sequential odd address (SBHE# = 0), 00000103_h. Since it is still a read, the slave places the byte read from the even address (00000102_h) onto the lower data path (path 0, D0:D7) and the byte read from the odd address (00000103_h) onto the second data path (path 1, D8:D15).

6. Since the bus master is expecting these 2 bytes to come back over the upper two data paths, the steering logic now activates the crossover logic, copying the byte on path 0 (D0:D7) to path 2 (D16:D23) and the byte on path 1 (D8:D15) to path 3 (D24:D31).

7. The steering logic now allows the 2 previously latched bytes onto the lower 2 data paths and the bus master is presented with all 4 requested bytes simultaneously.

8. Up until now, the steering logic has kept the channel ready return (CHRDYRTN) line from going active, thereby preventing the bus master from completing the bus cycle. This has caused the bus master to insert wait states in the bus cycle while it awaits completion of the data transfer. The steering logic now allows CHRDYRTN to go active. At the end of the current data time, the bus master samples ready active, reads the 4 bytes of data, and ends the bus cycle.

32-Bit Bus Masters Communicating with 8-Bit Slaves
When a 32-bit bus master reads data from or writes data to an 8-bit slave, it sometimes requires help from the system board data bus steering and translation logic.

TR32 is a normally active signal only driven inactive when a 32-bit bus master is running a bus cycle. An inactive level informs the system board's translation logic that the bus master will be generating A2:A31 and the proper byte enable lines.

Table 17-9 list the circumstances when data bus steering is necessary. Also refer to Figure 17-17.

The example described in the following paragraphs illustrates the process.

Example. In this example, the 32-bit bus master is performing a write data transfer with an 8-bit slave. During address time, the bus master places the doubleword address 00000100_h on A2:A31 and activates BE1# and BE2#. In other words, the bus master is identifying the doubleword starting at memory address 00000100_h and intends to transfer 2 bytes to locations 00000101_h and 00000102_h. It expects the 2 bytes

TABLE 17-9   32-Bit Bus Master Communicating with 16-Bit
Slaves

Operation Type	Byte Enables 3 2 1 0	Copy From Path	To Path(s)
Read	1 1 0 1	0	1
Read	1 0 1 1	0	2
Read	0 1 1 1	0	3
Read	1 1 0 0	0	1
Read	1 0 0 1	0	1,2
Read	0 0 1 1	0	2,3
Read	1 0 0 0	0	1,2
Read	0 0 0 1	0	1,2,3
Read	0 0 0 0	0	1,2,3
Write	1 1 0 1	1	0
Write	1 0 1 1	2	0
Write	0 1 1 1	3	0
Write	1 1 0 0	1	0
Write	1 0 0 1	1,2	0
Write	0 0 1 1	2,3	0
Write	1 0 0 0	1,2	0
Write	0 0 0 1	1,2,3	0
Write	0 0 0 0	1,2,3	0

to be transferred to the slave over the data paths indicated in Table 17-10.

The system board data bus steering logic interprets its inputs as indicated in Table 17-11.

During the example data transfer, the following sequence of events takes place.

1. Since 8-bit slaves are not connected to the byte enable lines, the translation logic must convert the byte enables to A0 and A1, signals understood by 8-bit slaves. This is done in two stages. First, the active level on BE1# is converted to A0 = 1, A1 = 0.

TABLE 17-10 Data Paths Used in 32/8 Example

Byte Enable	Identifies Location	Identifies Data Path
1	00000101_h	1 (D8:D15)
2	00000102_h	2 (D16:D23)

TABLE 17-11 32-Bit Bus Master Communicating with 8-Bit Slave

Steering Logic's Inputs	Interpreted as
Any BE line active	32-bit bus master running bus cycle
Write in progress	Data going from master to slave
CD DS 16 (n)# = 1 and CD DS 32 (n)# = 1	Communicating with an 8-bit slave. Data may have to be routed from master's upper 3 data paths to slave's only path (D0:D7).
BE1#, BE2# or BE3# active	Indicates the master is writing data over one or more of its upper 3 data paths. Since the 8-bit slave is only connected to the lowest path, data must be copied to D0:D7.
TR32 = 0	The bus master is generating the byte enables and A2:A31. This means they must be translated to A0 and A1, signals understood by the 8-bit slave.

2. The 8-bit slave now sees address 00000101_h on the address bus. The bus master has placed the byte to be written to odd address 00000101_h onto path 1, D8:D15.

3. Since the slave is connected only to path 0, D0:D7, the steering logic activates the crossover logic to copy the data byte from path 1 to path 0 so that it can get to the slave. The byte is written into location 00000101_h.

4. The second stage now begins and is a continuation of the same bus cycle. The translation logic now converts the active level on BE2# to A0 = 0, A1 = 1.

5. As a result, the 8-bit slave now sees address 00000102_h on the address bus. The bus master has placed the byte to be written to even address 00000102_h onto path 2, D16:D23.

6. Since the slave is connected only to path 0, D0:D7, the steering logic activates the crossover logic to copy the data byte from path 2 to path 0 so that it can get to the slave. The byte is written into location 00000102_h.

7. Up until now, the steering logic has kept the CHRDYRTN (channel ready return) line from going active, thereby preventing the bus master from completing the bus cycle. This has caused the bus master to insert wait states in the bus cycle while it awaits completion of the data transfer. The steering logic now allows CHRDYRTN to go active. At the end of the current data time, the bus master samples ready active and ends the bus cycle.

16-Bit Bus Masters Communicating with 32-Bit Slaves
When a 16-bit bus master reads data from or writes data to an 32-bit slave, it sometimes requires help from the system board data bus steering and translation logic.

When a 16-bit bus master is in control, TR32 is left active, informing the translation logic on the system board that it must convert A0, A1, and SBHE# to the proper combination of byte enable lines, which allows the 16-bit bus master to properly address 32-bit slaves.

The lower address lines generated by a 16-bit bus master are A0, A1 and SBHE#. 32-bit slaves, however, do not understand these signals and require the activation of one or more of the byte enable lines. Table 17-12 defines the manner in which the 16-bit bus master's address outputs are translated to the proper pattern on the byte enable lines.

TABLE 17-12   Translation of 16-Bit Bus Master Address Outputs
to the Proper Byte Enables

16-Bit Bus Master Address Outputs			Are Translated to				Copy Necessary?
SBHE#	A1	A0	BE3#	BE2#	BE1#	BE0#	
1	0	0	1	1	1	0	No
0	0	1	1	1	0	1	No
1	1	0	1	0	1	1	Yes
0	1	1	0	1	1	1	Yes
0	0	0	1	1	0	0	No
0	1	0	0	0	1	1	Yes

Figure 17-17 illustrates the system board's data bus steering and translation logic. The data must be copied between paths in any case where either BE2# or BE3# is activated. This is because the 16-bit bus master is connected only to the lower two data paths and cannot communicate directly with a 32-bit slave's upper two paths.

The example described in the following paragraphs illustrates the process.

Example. In this example, the 16-bit bus master is performing a read from location 00000102_h on a 32-bit slave. During address time, the bus master places address 00000102_h on the address bus and sets SBHE# high because it is not addressing an odd address. The system board data bus steering logic interprets its inputs as indicated in Table 17-13.

During the example data transfer, the following sequence of events takes place.

1. The 16-bit bus master places address 00000102_h on the address bus and sets SBHE# high. The system board's translation logic converts SBHE#, A1, and A0 to an active level on BE2#.

2. The 32-bit slave sees that the doubleword address on A2:A31 is 00000100_h because it cannot see address bits A0 and A1 and always assumes they are 00. In addition, it sees BE2# active and identifies 00000102_h as the address within the doubleword that the bus master wishes to communicate with.

TABLE 17-13   16-Bit Bus Master Communicating with 32-Bit Slave

Steering Logic's Inputs	Interpreted as
No BE line active	16-bit bus master running bus cycle
Read in progress	Data coming from slave to master
CD DS 16 (n)# = 1 and CD DS 32 (n)# = 0	Communicating with a 32-bit slave, data may have to be routed from slave's upper two paths (D15:D23 and D23:D31) to master's two paths (D0:D7 or D8:D15).
TR32 = 1	An active TR32 indicates that the current bus master is a 16-bit bus master and is not generating the byte enables. When communicating with a 32-bit slave, A0, A1, and SBHE# must then be translated to the proper byte enables so that the slave will understand the address.

3. The 32-bit slave reads the byte from 00000102_h and places it on data path 2 (D16:D23) to send back to the bus master.

4. The steering logic knows that a 16-bit bus master is running the bus cycle because it did not set any of the byte enable lines active at the start of the bus cycle. Realizing this and knowing that the requested data is coming back over data path 2 (which is not connected to the 16-bit master), the steering logic instructs the crossover logic to copy the data byte from data path 2 to data path 0 so that it can get to the bus master.

5. Up until now, the steering logic has kept the channel ready return (CHRDYRTN) line from going active, thereby preventing the bus master from completing the bus cycle. This has caused the bus master to insert wait states in the bus cycle while it awaits completion of the data transfer. The steering logic now allows CHRDYRTN to go active. At the end of the current data time, the bus master samples ready active, reads the byte of data, and ends the bus cycle.

16-Bit Bus Masters Communicating with 8-Bit Slaves
When a 16-bit bus master reads data from or writes data to an 8-bit

slave, it sometimes requires help from the system board data bus steering logic. Table 17-14 list the circumstances when data bus steering is necessary. Also refer to Figure 17-17.

In the second table entry, the 16-bit bus master is addressing an odd address. Since the bus master transfers data between itself and odd addresses over path 1, D8:D15, and the 8-bit device is only connected to data path 0, D0:D7, copying must take place during the bus cycle in order for the data to get where it is going.

In the third table entry, the 16-bit bus master is addressing an even address (A0 = 0), but has also activated SBHE#, indicating that it also intends to use its upper data path, D8:D15, to transfer data between itself and the next sequential odd address.

The example described in the following paragraphs illustrates the process.

Example. In this example, the 16-bit bus master is performing a write data transfer with an 8-bit slave. During address time, the 16-bit bus master places address 00000101_h on the address bus and activates SBHE#. In other words, the bus master intends to write a byte to location 00000101_h over its upper data path, D8:D15. The system board data bus steering logic interprets its inputs as indicated in Table 17-15.

During the example data transfer, the following sequence of events takes place.

1. During address time, the bus master places address 00000101_h on the address bus and activates SBHE#. The bus cycle definition is also output by the bus master.

2. The 16-bit bus master writes the data byte over its upper data path, D8:D15.

3. By monitoring A0 and SBHE#, the steering logic senses that the bus master is sending the byte over the upper path. The

TABLE 17-14   16-Bit Bus Master Communicating with 8-Bit Slaves

SBHE#	A0	Copy Necessary?
1	0	No
0	1	Yes
0	0	Yes

TABLE 17-15   16-Bit Bus Master Communicating with 8-Bit Slave

Steering Logic's Inputs	Interpreted as
No BE lines active	16-bit bus master running bus cycle
Write in progress	Data going from master to slave
CD DS 16 (n)# = 1 and CD DS 32 (n)# = 1	Communicating with an 8-bit slave. Data may have to be routed from master's upper data path to slave's only path (D0:D7).

fact that neither CD DS 16 (n)# nor CD DS 32 (n)# is active tells the steering logic that the slave is an 8-bit device.

4. The steering logic activates the crossover logic to copy the data byte from the upper data path to the lower one so that it can get to the 8-bit slave.

5. The data byte is written into the odd location, 00000101_h on the slave.

6. Up until now, the steering logic has kept the CHRDYRTN line from going active, thereby preventing the bus master from completing the bus cycle. This has caused the bus master to insert wait states in the bus cycle while it awaits completion of the data transfer. The steering logic now allows CHRDYRTN to go active. At the end of the current data time, the bus master samples ready active and ends the bus cycle.

The 32-Bit MCA Matched Memory Cycle Extension

Refer to Figure 17-1. The three signals on this connector are provided to support a special type of IBM memory card known as a matched memory card. These three signals allow a card that supports matched memory cycles (described in the previous chapter) to use slightly faster bus cycle timing when a system board that also supports matched memory cycles (the 16 MHz Type 1 Model 80) is communicating with it. The following paragraphs provide a review of the information covered in the previous chapter.

When the 80386 microprocessor on the Model 80 Type 1 (16MHz) system board begins a bus cycle, the system board logic turns on the MMC# (matched memory cycle) signal line. This is the system board's way of saying, "I talk fast. Do you?" If the card currently being addressed is a matched memory card, its address decoder will turn on the matched memory cycle request (MMCR#) signal line. This is the matched memory card's way of saying, "I talk fast, too. Let's talk fast together!" Having agreed to talk fast together, the system board logic runs a matched memory cycle rather than a default bus cycle.

The matched memory cycle is essentially a default bus cycle with a twist. The twist is that it last 187.5ns instead of the default bus cycle time of 200ns. Address time and data time are each only 93.75ns in duration (rather than 100ns). This means that the system board microprocessor can perform 5,347,593 transfers per second, yielding a transfer rate of 21.39MB/second when communicating with a 32-bit matched memory card. This is a 6.95% increase over the maximum transferred rate achievable when running default bus cycles.

Since the duration of the address time and data time periods are shorter than normal, the system board does not generate ADL# or CMD# during a matched memory cycle. The system board supplies the signal MMC CMD# in place of CMD#. The duration of MMC CMD# reflects the shortened nature of the data time period.

The Video Extension

Every IBM PS/2 incorporates a display interface called the video graphics array, or VGA. It consists of the VGA chip, or gate array, on the system board, the Video RAM Memory, and the digital-to-analog converter, or DAC.

Figure 17-18 illustrates the video logic on the system board. The 256KB of video RAM memory is mounted on the system board and resides within the memory address range from A0000$_h$ to BFFFF$_h$. Information to be displayed on the screen is written into video RAM memory by the programmer. Each character to be displayed on the screen must then be converted to a series of dots by the VGA and the information regarding the color and intensity of each dot is then sent to the DAC (digital-to-analog converter) over the 8-bit palette bus. Each display dot on the screen is known as a PEL, or picture element, and actually consists of a red, green, and blue phosphor dot.

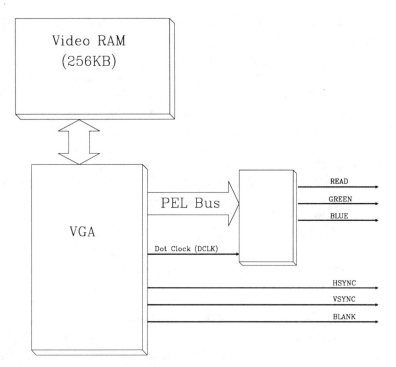

FIGURE 17-18   Block Diagram of the PS/2 Video Logic

The DAC, in turn, converts the VGA's information regarding a dot into the correct voltage levels for its three display gun outputs. The VGA's dot clock output tells the DAC when to actually turn on the three electron gun outputs to irradiate a dot.

The VGA also supplies two synchronization signals, HSYNC and VSYNC, to the display to tell it when the electron beam gets to the end of a line and to the bottom of the screen. A third synchronization signal, BLANK, tells the DAC to turn off the three electron gun outputs during the horizontal and vertical retrace periods.

HSYNC, or horizontal sync, tells the display to reposition the electron beam to the start of the next horizontal scan line on the left side of the screen. VSYNC, or vertical sync, tells the display to reposition the electron beam to the top left corner of the screen in preparation for the next screen output.

Internally, the DAC actually consists of three separate DACs, one for each display gun (red, green, and blue). The information sent to the DAC by the VGA tells it the voltage levels to place on each of the three gun outputs the next time a dot is to be written. Every time the dot clock signal goes active, it is time to turn on the guns and write another dot on the screen.

What If the VGA Output Isn't Good Enough?

IBM has provided a way to easily upgrade the PS/2 with a new, higher-resolution display interface if the VGA does not supply high enough resolution or enough colors for your application. The IBM 8514/A video interface is an example of a VGA substitute that can be installed in the PS/2.

Refer to Figure 17-1. In every PS/2, one of the 16-bit MCA connectors is a little longer than the others. The additional signals supplied on this extension to the normal 16-bit MCA connector is known as the video extension.

Figure 17-19 illustrates the video extension connector. The following three signals on the video extension are normally high: ESYNC, EDCLK, and EVIDEO. The normally active states on these three signals allows the VGA to perform as described above. When an advanced video card is installed in the MCA slot that includes the video extension, however, it grounds these three signals and sets them inactive. This yields the effects described in Table 17-16.

In other words, the VGA is effectively cut out of the circuit just by inserting the advanced video card into the 16-bit MCA slot with the video extension. The advanced video card then acts as the video interface, supplying dot information to the DAC on the system board and synchronization information to the display. The same system board display connector can still be used to connect the display unit to the system unit.

Summary

The 16-bit MCA connectors provide all of the signals necessary for 16-bit bus masters to communicate with 8- and 16-bit slaves. In every PS/2, one of the 16-bit MCA connectors is physically longer than the others. This extension to the connector, referred to as the video extension, provides the capability to install an advanced video card that electrically replaces the VGA interface that is located on the system board, thus providing a higher-resolution display than the VGA affords.

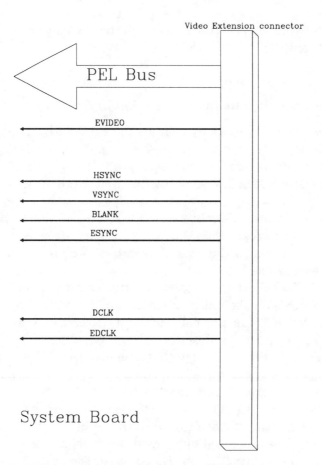

FIGURE 17-19   The Video Extension

The 32-bit MCA connectors actually consist of a 16-bit MCA connector with an extension referred to as the 32-bit MCA extension. The 32-bit connector provides all the signals necessary for 32-bit bus masters to communicate with 8-, 16-, and 32-bit slaves.

TABLE 17-16   The Video Extension Enable Signals

Signal	Function
EDCLK	When set low (grounded), this normally active signal causes the VGA to electrically disconnect itself from dot clock line to the DAC so that the advanced video card can provide dot clock instead.
EVIDEO	When set low (grounded), this normally active signal causes the VGA to electrically disconnect itself from the palette bus going to the DAC. This allows the 8514/A advanced video card, rather than the VGA, to provide palette register addresses and data to the DAC.
ESYNC	When set low (grounded), this normally active signal causes the VGA to electrically disconnect itself from the three synchronization signals. This allows the 8514/A advanced video card, rather than the VGA, to provide the synchronization signals to the DAC and display.

CHAPTER

18

MCA Enhancements, Present and Future

Objective: This chapter defines the hardware and software enhancements to the micro channel that were announced by IBM in October of 1989.

Overview of the MCA Enhancements

In October of 1989, IBM announced that future machines using the micro channel would incorporate several enhancements:

- Streaming data procedures, or SDP
- Data and address integrity checking
- The subsystem control block, or SCB, architecture
- DMA improvements
- Synchronous channel check

The new IBM RISC System/6000 workstation uses the micro channel and supports several of the new features. As of the printing of this book, the following PS/2 models also provide support for some of the following new features:

- Model 65 (061 and 121)
- Model 70 (A21, B21, A61, and B61)
- Model 80 (A21 and A31)

Present PS/2 models other than those mentioned above do not provide support for the new features and cannot be upgraded unless the entire system board is replaced.

If MCA cards that implement the new transfer types are installed in these older PS/2 models, they will use the default bus cycle when performing data transfers and will thus be limited to a 20MB/second transfer rate.

The following sections describe the enhancements to the micro channel.

New Transfer (Bus Cycle) Types

The streaming data procedures, or SDP, announced by IBM are actually three new types of bus cycles. The following sections describe these new bus cycle types.

The 32-Bit Streaming Data Procedure (SDP)

The 32-bit SDP is identical to the Intel 80486 microprocessor's burst transfer type. It is called the 32-bit SDP mode because 4 bytes (32 bits) of data are transferred during each 100ns data time period. Just as with the default bus cycle type, the duration of address time and data time are still 100ns each.

Figure 18-1 is a timing diagram of the 32-bit SDP. The following discussion assumes a 32-bit bus master performing a 16-byte data transfer (4 doublewords) with a 32-bit slave. The overall transfer proceeds in the following fashion.

1. During the 100ns allotted to address time, the bus master places the address and bus cycle definition on the buses.

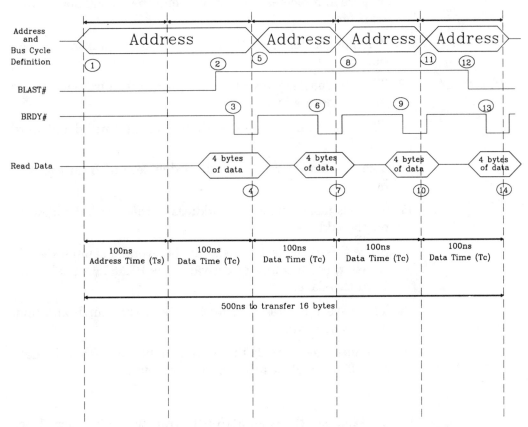

FIGURE 18-1   The 32-Bit Streaming Data Procedure (SDP)

2. The bus master signals its requirement to run a series (or burst) of transfers rather than just a single transfer, by turning off the burst last (BLAST#) signal. This occurs because the bus master wants to switch into 32-bit SDP mode.

3. The slave indicates its ability to support the 32-bit SDP (burst mode) by setting burst ready (BRDY#) active. This means that each subsequent data transfer in the series (or burst) will take only one tick of the clock, or 100ns (rather than address time (100ns) + data time (100ns), or 200ns).

4. The first doubleword (4 bytes) of data is transferred between the bus master and the slave on the data bus.

5. The bus master places the address of the second doubleword on the address bus.

6. The slave indicates it is ready to end the second doubleword transfer.

7. The bus master reads the second doubleword from the data bus.

8. The bus master places the address of the third doubleword on the address bus.

9. The slave indicates it is ready to end the third doubleword transfer.

10. The bus master reads the third doubleword from the data bus.

11. The bus master places the address of the fourth doubleword on the address bus.

12. Since this is the last transfer in the overall example 16-byte transfer, the bus master activates the BLAST# signal to inform the slave.

13. The slave indicates it is ready to end the fourth and final doubleword transfer.

14. The bus master reads the fourth doubleword from the data bus. This concludes the 16-byte transfer.

In this example, the overall 16-byte transfer took 500ns: 1 address time + 4 data times. If the same transfer had been performed using the default bus cycle, each doubleword transfer would have taken 200ns (address + data time), and the overall transfer would therefore have taken 800ns.

Once the bus master and the slave switch into 32-bit SDP mode, 4 bytes of data can be transferred every 100ns. This means that the transfer rate when using 32-bit SDP mode is 40MB/second (as opposed to 20MB/second for a 32-bit bus master using the default bus cycle).

The 64-Bit Streaming Data Procedure (SDP)

The 64-bit SDP mode uses both the data and address buses to transfer data. The starting address for the transfer is sent to the slave during address time. This is the only address the slave will receive from the master and it is the slave's responsibility to latch the start address and automatically increment the address for each doubleword transferred during the overall transfer. Just as with the default bus cycle type, the duration of address time and data time are still 100ns each.

Figure 18-2 is a timing diagram of the 64-bit SDP. The following discussion assumes a 32-bit bus master performing a 16-byte data transfer (4 doublewords) with a 32-bit slave. The overall transfer proceeds in the following fashion.

1. During the 100ns allotted to address time, the bus master places the address and bus cycle definition on the buses. The slave latches the address and treats it as a start address for the data transfer.

2. The bus master signals its requirement to run a series of transfers rather than just a single transfer.

3. The slave indicates its ability to support the 64-bit SDP. This means that each subsequent data transfer in the series will only take one tick of the clock, or 100ns (rather than address time (100ns) + data time (100ns), or 200ns).

4. The address bus and the data bus are each used to transfer 4 bytes of data.

5. The slave indicates that it is ready to end the transfer and the first 8 bytes of data are transferred.

6. The address bus and the data bus are each used to transfer 4 bytes of data.

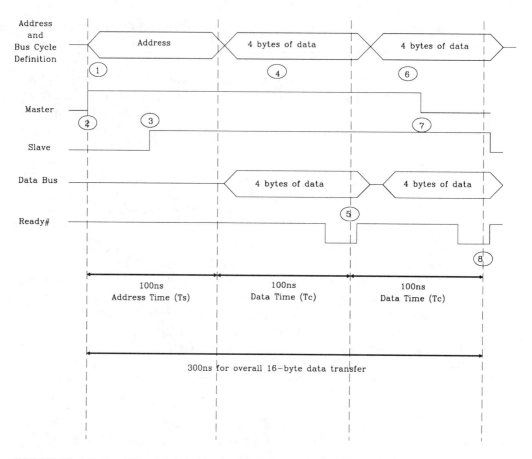

FIGURE 18-2 The 64-Bit Streaming Data Procedure (SDP)

7. The bus master indicates signals that this is the last data transfer in the series.

8. The slave indicates that it is ready to end the transfer and the second 8 bytes of data are transferred. This completes the overall 16-byte example data transfer.

In this example, the overall 16-byte transfer took 300ns: 1 address time + 2 data times. If the same transfer had been performed using the default bus cycle, each doubleword transfer would have taken 200ns (address + data time), and the overall transfer would therefore have taken 800ns.

Once the bus master and the slave switch into 64-bit SDP mode, 8 bytes of data can be transferred every 100ns. This means that the transfer rate when using 64-bit SDP mode is 80MB/second (as opposed to 20MB/second for a 32-bit bus master using the default bus cycle).

The Enhanced 64-Bit Streaming Data Procedure (SDP)

The enhanced 64-bit SDP mode is identical to the 64-bit SDP mode with one exception. The duration of the address and data time periods is shortened to 50ns (rather than 100ns). Figure 18-3 is a timing diagram of the enhanced 64-bit SDP.

This means that 8 bytes of data can be transferred every 50ns. The transfer rate when using 64-bit SDP mode is therefore 160MB/second (as opposed to 20MB/second for a 32-bit bus master using the default bus cycle).

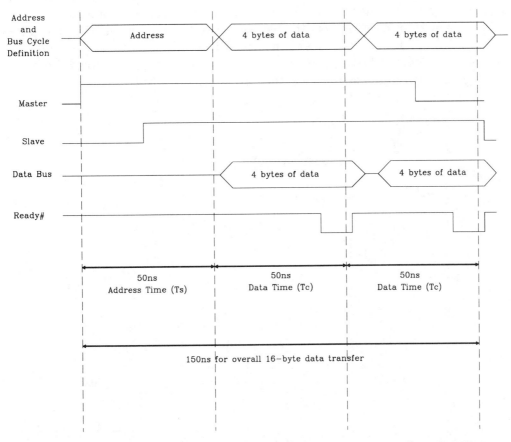

FIGURE 18-3 The Enhanced 64-Bit Streaming Data Procedure (SDP)

Data and Address Integrity Checking

Another of the announced improvements was the addition of parity checking to the information passed over the data and address buses. Basically, this means that information passed over the buses can be automatically checked for accuracy when it gets to its destination. This change brings the addition of parity generation logic to bus masters and parity checking logic to slaves. An explanation of the concept of parity follows.

Figure 18-4 illustrates the parity logic. This discussion assumes even parity (this concept will be explained shortly). In future machines, every 8-bit path on the data bus and the address bus will have an additional signal line that carries its parity bit.

When a bus master places a byte of information on a path (8 adjacent data or address lines) of the address bus or data bus, the parity generator associated with that path counts the number of 1 bits in the byte and sets the path's parity bit to 1 in order to force an even number of 1 bits in the overall 9-bit pattern. If the 8-bit pattern already contains an even number of 1 bits, the parity bit is set to 0.

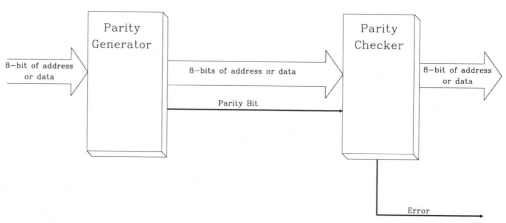

FIGURE 18-4 Parity Check Logic

On the slave (the receiving) end, the parity checker associated with this path examines the 9-bit pattern to ensure that it still contains an even number of 1 bits. If it does not, the information (data or address) has been corrupted while in route (by electrical noise, perhaps), and the parity checker generates an error (probably a channel check). If the parity is still even, no error is generated and the information is used.

This method is good at finding single bit failures. Although not foolproof, it is better than nothing. The same method is used to generate and check the integrity of data written into and read from system board RAM memory.

If an even number of 1 bits get dropped from the 9-bit pattern while in transit, the parity checker misses the failure. For example, assume that a BD_h ($1011\ 1101_b$) is being transferred over a data path. The bus master's parity generator for this data path determines that the 8-bit pattern already has an even number of 1 bits, and it sets the parity bit to 0. Assume that data bits 2 and 3 on the data path have a problem and these bits are 0 when they arrive on the slave end ($1011\ 0001_b$). The path's parity checker counts the bits and finds 4 one bits in the pattern. Since this is an even number of 1 bits, no error is generated.

Synchronous Channel Check

This feature was added so that a slave can generate an error while transferring a block of data using one of the new SDP data transfer modes. The alternative would be to wait until the entire transfer was over before generating the error.

DMA Improvements

IBM also announced their intention to improve upon the DMA controller that is currently used in the entire PS/2 product line.

Figure 18-5 illustrates the DMA controller used in the current PS/2. The current DMA controller is attached only to A0:A23 on the address bus. It therefore cannot generate addresses greater than $00FFFFFF_h$ and can handle only data transfers between I/O devices and memory within the lower 16MB of memory address space.

In addition, the current DMA controller is attached only to the lower two data paths, D0:D7 and D8:D15. This limits it to transferring

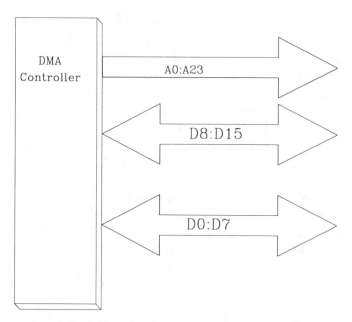

FIGURE 18-5   The Current DMA Controller

2 bytes per transfer. Even the Model 70 and 80, built around the 32-bit 80386 microprocessor, can transfer only 2 bytes per transfer.

Figure 18-6 illustrates the proposed DMA controller. Future DMA controllers will be attached to the entire 32-bit address bus, A0:A31, and will therefore be able to generate any memory address up to FFFFFFFF$_h$. As a result, they will be able to handle data transfers between I/O devices and memory anywhere in the 4GB address range of 32-bit microprocessors.

The future DMA controller will also be attached to all 4 data paths in models based on 32-bit microprocessors. This will allow it to transfer up to 4 bytes per transfer versus the current 2 bytes.

Subsystem Control Block (SCB) Architecture

PS/2 systems support multiple bus masters. No method was provided, however, to define which bus master is using particular parts of memory at a given moment. In addition, there was no definition of command structures that could be left in memory and picked up and interpreted correctly by other bus masters. Since no standard was introduced to define the format of messages passed between bus masters, the potential for a "Tower of Babel" scenario is real.

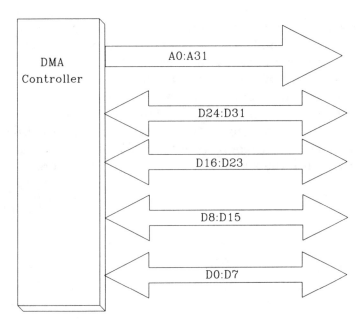

FIGURE 18-6 Proposed DMA Controller

IBM rectified this situation by implementing the software definition known as the subsystem control block (SCB) architecture, which provides a complete definition of inter-master communication in the micro channel environment. As of this printing, the specification was unavailable for an in-depth look.

Summary

In October 1989, IBM announced its intention to enhance the micro channel to provide support for faster data transfer rates, data and address integrity checking, DMA improvements, and additional error reporting capability. The faster data transfer rates are achieved with the new streaming data procedures (SDPs), which allows bus masters to run three new types of bus cycles on the micro channel. Some newer PS/2 products support some of these transfer types, as do the entire RISC System/6000 product line. Older PS/2s do not support them.

Parity checking will be added to both the data and address buses to ensure that information is transferred over the buses without error.

Proposed versions of the DMA controller will connect the DMA controller to the entire 32-bit address bus, thereby permitting the DMA controller to transfer data anywhere in the 4GB address range of 32-bit microprocessors. It will also use all 4 data paths.

The new subsystem control block (SCB) architecture provides concrete guidelines for inter-master communication.

The synchronous channel check capability will be added in future products to allow error reporting in the midst of a SDP transfer rather than waiting until the end of the transfer to report errors.

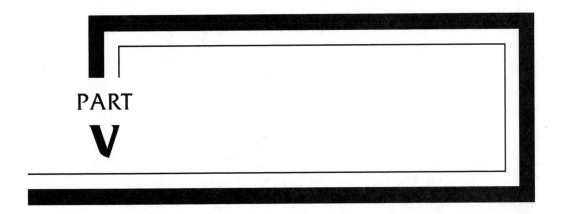

PART

V

The Interrupt
Subsystem

19

The Interrupt Subsystem

Objective: This chapter provides a detailed explanation of both hardware and software interrupts. Both the non-shareable method used in the PC/XT/AT and the shareable method used in the PS/2 product line are covered.

Definitions for This Chapter

• A **BIOS routine** is a routine supplied by the system manufacturer, usually in system ROM. The BIOS routine is designed to interact with a specific I/O device, causing it to perform specified functions upon request. The applications programmer can control, sense the status of, or channel data to or from a specific I/O device by placing a request number in the AH register and calling the device-specific BIOS routine. The BIOS routine interprets the request number, instructs the I/O device to perform the requested function, and returns the results to the caller.

• The **cascade bus** is used by the master interrupt controller to command the slave interrupt controller to send the interrupt slot number to the microprocessor.

• An **exception interrupt** is generated when the execution of an instruction results in an error. The interrupt causes the microprocessor to jump to the interrupt service routine written to handle the particular type of error condition.

• An **interrupt** is a condition internal or external to the microprocessor that causes execution of the current program to be temporarily interrupted. The microprocessor is then forced to execute another program to service the interrupting device or internal condition. At the completion of the interrupt servicing, the microprocessor then returns to its original program flow.

• Intel microprocessors automatically generate two back-to-back **interrupt acknowledge** bus cycles to request the interrupt slot number from the Intel 8259 Programmable Interrupt Controller. At the trailing edge of the second interrupt acknowledge bus cycle, the microprocessor reads the slot number from the lower data path, D0:D7.

• The **interrupt controller** prioritizes concurrent interrupt requests and forwards them to the microprocessor one at a time, in order of priority.

- The **interrupt instruction (INT)** allows the programmer to call a routine without knowing its start memory address. The number specified after the INT instruction is the slot number in the interrupt table. When executed, the INT instruction causes the microprocessor to react as if an interrupt request had been sensed on the INTR line. The only difference is that the interrupt slot number is supplied by the INT instruction rather than by the 8259 interrupt controller.

- The **interrupt request** signal line is used by an I/O device to inform the microprocessor that it requires service.

- The **interrupt return (IRET)** instruction must be the last instruction in every interrupt service routine (ISR). When executed, it causes the microprocessor to reload the CS, IP, and Flag registers from stack memory, which causes the microprocessor to resume execution of the interrupted program at the point where it was interrupted.

- The **interrupt service routine (ISR)** is a special program written to handle the servicing of interrupt requests from a specific device type.

- The **interrupt slot number** is the 8-bit number sent to the microprocessor to identify the ISR that must be run to service the current interrupt request. It identifies a slot, or entry, in the interrupt table in RAM memory. It is also referred to as the interrupt vector, interrupt ID, or interrupt type code.

- The **interrupt table** is located in RAM memory and contains pointers to as many as 256 ISRs. In real mode, each table entry consists of 4 bytes of information—a 2 byte CS value and a 2 byte IP value.

- The **maskable interrupt request (INTR)** is an input that informs the microprocessor when an external hardware device requires servicing.

- **Non-maskable interrupt (NMI)** is an input that causes the microprocessor to jump to the NMI interrupt service routine. Slot 2 in the interrupt table is dedicated to NMI. In a PS/2, NMI is used to report hardware failures (such as a RAM parity error) to the microprocessor.

- A **phantom, or ghost interrupt** can occur in the PC/XT/AT product line when a noise spike on an interrupt request line registers as a pending interrupt request. This problem has been eliminated in the PS/2 product line (with MCA) by making the interrupt request lines active low and placing pull-up resistors on them.

• A **POP operation** causes the microprocessor to read 2 bytes from memory starting at the location pointed to by the Stack Pointer (SP) register. These 2 bytes are then placed in the target register, and the SP register is incremented by 2 to point to the next data item stored in stack memory.

• A **PUSH operation** causes the microprocessor to decrement the Stack Pointer (SP) register by 2 to point to the next available location in stack memory. The microprocessor then performs a memory write bus cycle to write the contents of the specified register into stack memory.

• PS/2 products with the micro channel have **shareable interrupts**. This means that multiple I/O devices can be attached to the same interrupt request signal line without causing damage to each other.

• The **stack** is an area of RAM memory set aside as scratchpad memory. One way the microprocessor uses stack memory is to store the Flag, CS, and IP register contents when servicing an interrupt. CS and IP are saved so the microprocessor knows the memory address at which to resume execution of the interrupted program.

What Is an Interrupt?

At various times, an I/O device within a PC system may require help, or servicing, by the microprocessor. The I/O device uses an **interrupt request** signal line to request the microprocessor's help.

The exact type of servicing a device requires is defined by the type of device and its current condition. For example, a parallel port connected to a printer may generate an **interrupt** request to ask the microprocessor that the next character be sent to the printer. In this case, the microprocessor responds by performing an I/O write bus cycle to send the character to the parallel port.

A second example is the interrupt request generated by a hard disk controller to tell the microprocessor that a data transfer to or from memory has been completed. If this is a disk read operation, the microprocessor responds to the interrupt request by using the data that the disk controller just loaded into memory.

As a third and final example, the keyboard interface generates an interrupt request to inform the microprocessor that a key has been pressed. The microprocessor should respond by performing an I/O read from the keyboard interface to get the keyboard character.

In each of these cases, the microprocessor responds to an interrupt request by executing a special program known as an **interrupt service routine (ISR)**. The interrupt service routine's task is to service the request. Since different types of interrupt requests require different types of servicing on the part of the microprocessor, there must be a separate interrupt service routine for each type of interrupt request that can be generated by the various hardware devices found in a PS/2 system.

An interrupt causes the microprocessor to temporarily suspend execution of the current program and forces it to jump to another program, known as an interrupt service routine, or ISR. At the conclusion of the ISR, the microprocessor must then return to the original, interrupted program flow.

How the Microprocessor Responds to an Interrupt Request

This section provides a detailed explanation of how an Intel microprocessor services an interrupt request. Figure 19-1 flowcharts the series of actions that must take place.

The Intel microprocessors have one interrupt request input that detects requests from I/O devices. The interrupt request lines from the various I/O devices are not connected directly to the microprocessor's single interrupt request input, however. Instead, they are connected to a device known as an **interrupt controller**. The device universally used in the PS/2- and PC-compatible machines is the Intel 8259 Programmable Interrupt Controller, or PIC. Up to eight interrupt request lines can be tied to one 8259 interrupt controller.

Figure 19-2 illustrates the Intel 8259 Programmable Interrupt Controller. At any given moment in time, one or more of the PIC's interrupt request inputs may be active. The PIC uses a priority scheme to decide which of the pending interrupt requests is the most important. It will then pass that interrupt request along to the microprocessor by setting the microprocessor's interrupt request, or INTR, input active.

The INTR input to the microprocessor is the **maskable interrupt request** line. While executing a particular series of instructions,

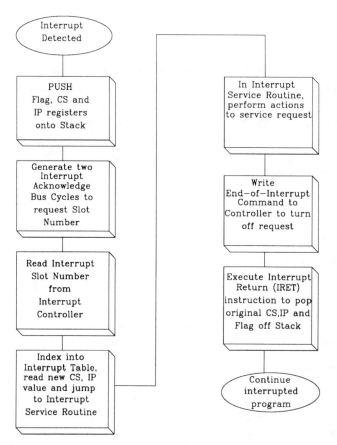

FIGURE 19-1   Flowchart of Interrupt Servicing

the programmer can turn off recognition of external interrupt requests by executing a clear interrupt enable (CLI) instruction. The programmer is then ensured that subsequent instructions will not be interrupted. As soon as the critical series of instructions has been executed, the programmer re-enables recognition of external interrupt requests by executing a set interrupt enable (STI) instruction. Any interrupt request pending on the INTR line will now be recognized by the microprocessor. To avoid problems, the programmer should take care, however, to ensure that interrupt recognition is not disabled for a long time.

For example, the serial port may be generating an interrupt request because it has a character to place in memory. If the microprocessor does not read the character from it on a timely basis, it may be written over by the next character received over the communications line.

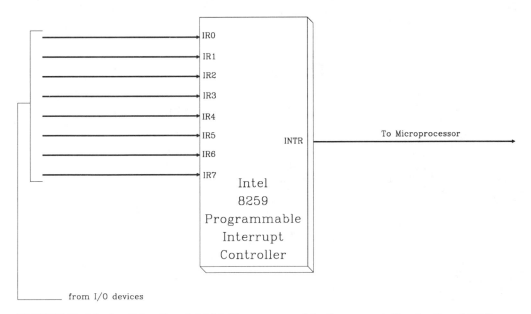

FIGURE 19-2   The Intel 8259 Programmable Interrupt Controller (PIC)

The microprocessor is engaged in fetching instructions from memory right up until the interrupt request is recognized. The only purpose of the microprocessor's Code Segment (CS) and Instruction Pointer (IP) registers is to point to the location in memory from where the next instruction should be fetched. At this point, the microprocessor had just completed the execution of an instruction and was about to fetch the next instruction from memory when the interrupt request was sensed. The CS and IP registers now point to where the microprocessor would have fetched its next instruction from if it had not been interrupted. If the microprocessor is to successfully pick up where it left off after servicing the request, it must save the contents of these two registers. (In other words, the microprocessor must save a bookmark.)

Figure 19-3 illustrates the **stack**; the microprocessor's immediate response to an interrupt request is to store the contents of the CS and IP registers in stack memory.

Assume that the stack is currently empty (contains no data). In the figure, the Stack Segment register, SS, contains 5000_h, indicating that the stack segment starts at memory location 50000_h. The Stack Pointer register, SP, contains $FFFE_h$. In response to an interrupt request, the microprocessor automatically performs three **PUSH** operations:

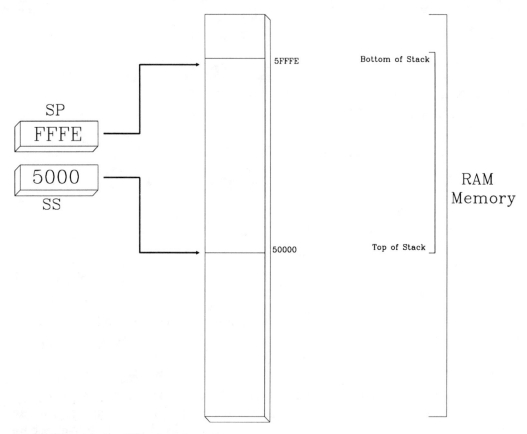

FIGURE 19-3   The Stack

1. The microprocessor first pushes the contents of the Flag register onto the stack. To do this, the microprocessor decrements SP by 2 ($FFFE_h - 2 = FFFC_h$), then performs a memory write to the address specified by SS:SP ($5000:FFFC_h$). Figure 19-4 illustrates the stack's contents after the contents of the Flag register have been pushed into stack locations $5FFFC_h$ and $5FFFD_h$.

2. The microprocessor then pushes the contents of the CS register onto the stack. To do this, the microprocessor decrements SP by 2, then performs a memory write to the address specified by SS:SP ($5000:FFFA_h$). Figure 19-5 illustrates the stack's contents after the contents of the CS register has been pushed into stack locations $5FFFA_h$ and $5FFFB_h$.

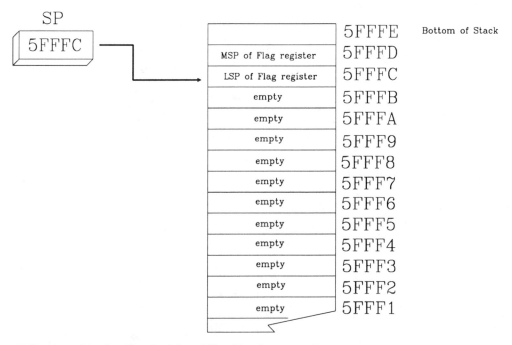

FIGURE 19-4   Stack After Flag Register PUSH

3. The microprocessor then pushes the contents of the IP register onto the stack. To do this, the microprocessor decrements SP by 2, then performs a memory write to the address specified by SS:SP (5000:FFF8$_h$). Figure 19-6 illustrates the stack's contents after the contents of the IP register has been pushed into stack locations 5FFF8$_h$ and 5FFF9$_h$.

The microprocessor saves the contents of the Flag register because it is quite possible that the instruction that would have been executed next (if the microprocessor had not been interrupted) would have checked the Flag bits to determine the result of the previously executed instruction.

To summarize, the microprocessor's immediate response to an interrupt request is to push the contents of the CS, IP, and the Flag registers into stack memory. This is done so that the microprocessor can resume its original program flow after the interrupt request servicing has been completed.

Having saved its bookmark (CS and IP) and the Flag register on the stack, the next logical action is to find out what device initiated

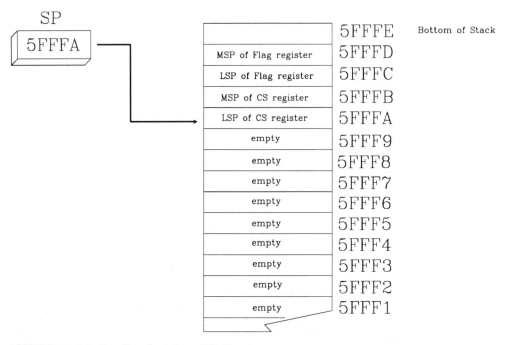

FIGURE 19-5 Stack After CS Register PUSH

the request. The microprocessor performs this inquiry by executing two back-to-back **interrupt acknowledge** bus cycles. Logic external to the microprocessor converts the bus cycles into two pulses on the PIC's Interrupt Acknowledge input. When the PIC senses these two interrupt acknowledges, it realizes that the microprocessor wants to know what device it should service.

The microprocessor needs to know the requesting device so that it can jump to the proper interrupt service routine (ISR). As with any other program, each ISR must reside in memory. In order to execute an ISR, the microprocessor must know the start memory address of each ISR. When the microprocessor is in real mode, Intel sets aside the first 1024 memory locations, from 00000_h–$003FF_h$, as the **interrupt table**. In protected mode, the interrupt table may be located anywhere in the memory space. This discussion focuses on real mode operation. Refer to Figure 19-7.

The interrupt table is subdivided into 256 individual entries or slots, each containing 4 bytes of information (256 divided into 1024 equals 4 locations per slot or entry). The system ROMs that are shipped with the PS/2 contain (among other things):

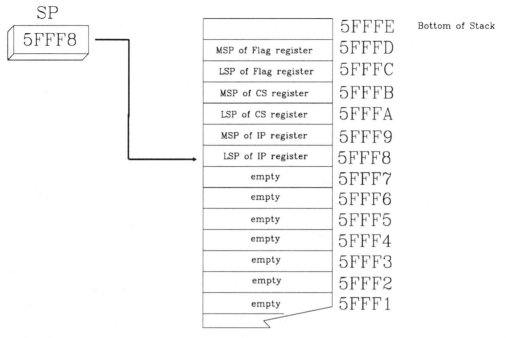

FIGURE 19-6 Stack After IP Register PUSH

- The power-on self-test (POST).

- The interrupt service routines (ISRs) for the standard I/O devices that are shipped with the system.

- The BIOS routines for the standard I/O devices that are shipped with the system (discussed later).

- The BASIC language interpreter.

In other words, the programmers who write the system ROM code know the start memory address of each of the ISRs for the standard I/O devices that are shipped with the system. During the execution of the POST, then, the programmer copies the start memory address of each of these ISRs into the proper slots in the interrupt table. At the completion of the POST, the interrupt table slots associated with each of the standard I/O devices have been automatically filled in with the start memory address of their respective ISRs in ROM memory.

When the microprocessor generates two interrupt acknowledge bus cycles to request the interrupt type from the PIC, the PIC responds

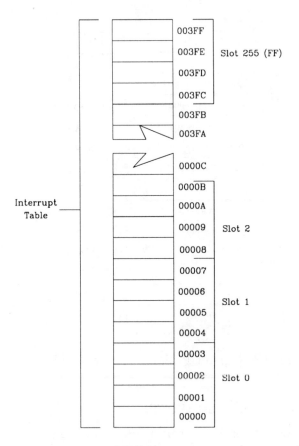

RAM Memory

FIGURE 19-7 The Interrupt Table (Real Mode)

by placing an 8-bit number on the lower data path, D0:D7. This number is commonly referred to by the following names:

- Interrupt type code
- Interrupt ID
- Interrupt vector
- **Interrupt slot number**

Note: The term interrupt slot number is used in this chapter because it is the most correct of the four.

At the trailing edge of the second interrupt acknowledge bus cycle, the microprocessor reads the interrupt slot number from the lower data path. The interrupt slot number must then be converted into the actual start memory address of the respective slot, or entry, in the interrupt table. Since each entry in the interrupt table consists of four locations, the microprocessor indexes into the interrupt table by multiplying the slot number from the PIC by the number 4. This will produce the actual start memory address of the desired interrupt slot. This slot contains the start memory address of the target ISR in the form of a new CS and IP value.

The microprocessor then automatically performs one or two memory read bus cycles (the 80386 and 80486 perform one bus cycle; the 80286 must perform two) to read the 4 bytes of information from the interrupt slot. The first 2 bytes of information are placed into the IP register and the second 2 bytes into the CS register. The microprocessor then resumes normal operation. In other words, the microprocessor looks at the CS and IP registers to determine the memory location to read the next instruction from. Since these two registers have just been loaded from the interrupt slot in the interrupt table, they now point to the first instruction of the appropriate ISR.

In this way, the microprocessor begins to fetch and execute the instructions that make up the ISR. For example, the keyboard interface uses the IRQ1 input to the master interrupt controller to generate an interrupt request when a key is pressed. The interrupt slot number assigned to this input is 09_h. This means that slot 9 in the interrupt table contains the 4-byte start address of the keyboard interrupt service routine in memory.

The microprocessor calculates the actual start memory address of slot 9 in the interrupt table by multiplying the interrupt slot number, 09_h in this case, by a factor of 4. Since 9 times 4 equals 36 in decimal, 24_h, this means that the start memory address of slot 9 in the interrupt table is 00024_h.

The start address of the keyboard interrupt service routine is contained in memory addresses 00024_h through 0027_h. The microprocessor executes the following steps.

1. Reads the contents of locations 00024_h and 00025_h and places it into the IP register.

2. Reads the contents of locations 00026_h and 00027_h and places it into the CS register.

3. Looks at the CS and IP registers to determine the memory location to fetch its next instruction from.

It then initiates a memory read bus cycle, reading the first instruction from the keyboard interrupt service routine.

In the interrupt service routine, the programmer performs the actions necessary in order to service the request that was issued by the I/O device. For example, if this were the keyboard interrupt service routine, the microprocessor should perform an I/O read from the keyboard data port at I/O address 0060_h to get the keyboard scan code (the character pressed on the keyboard).

After servicing the request, but before the end of the interrupt service routine, the microprocessor must write an EOI (End-of-Interrupt) command to the interrupt controller. This forces the controller to turn off the current interrupt request so that it will not be double-serviced.

Each interrupt service routine must end with an **interrupt return (IRET)** instruction. When the microprocessor executes the IRET instruction, it automatically performs three **POP**s to read the original IP, CS, and Flag register contents from the stack.

1. Refer to Figure 19-8. Executing the first POP, the microprocessor performs a read from memory locations $5FFF8_h$ and $5FFF9_h$. The 2 bytes read are placed in the IP register. The SP register is then incremented by 2 to point to $5FFFA_h$.

2. Refer to Figure 19-9. Executing the second POP, the microprocessor performs a read from memory locations $5FFFA_h$ and $5FFFB_h$. The 2 bytes read are placed in the CS register. The SP register is then incremented by 2 to point to $5FFFC_h$.

3. Refer to Figure 19-10. Executing the third POP, the microprocessor performs a read from memory locations $5FFFC_h$ and $5FFFD_h$. The 2 bytes read are placed in the Flag register. The SP register is then incremented by 2 to point to $5FFFE_h$. The stack is now empty again.

At this point, the CS, IP, and Flag registers have been automatically reloaded with the values that were present when the interrupt occurred. The microprocessor now resumes normal operation. In other words, the microprocessor looks at the CS and IP registers to determine the memory location to read the next instruction from. In this way, the microprocessor has automatically returned to its original program flow after completing servicing of the interrupt.

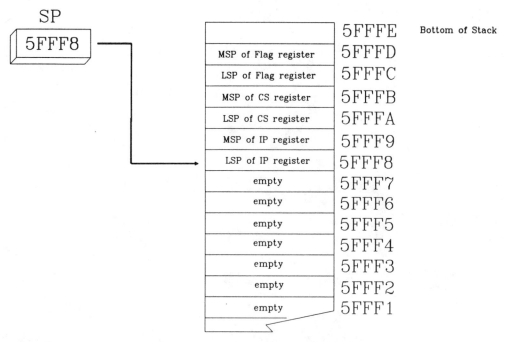

FIGURE 19-8   Stack Prior to POP to Load IP Register

What If One 8259 Interrupt Controller Is Not Enough?

The PC and XT had only one 8259 programmable interrupt controller. This imposed a limit of eight interrupt request lines available for usage by I/O devices. In order to provide an expanded number of usable I/O interrupt request lines, the designers of the AT provided a second 8259 interrupt controller. The same configuration has been used in the PS/2 product line, as well.

Figure 19-11 illustrates the two interrupt controller chips in a master/slave configuration. The 8259 PIC connected directly to the microprocessor is the master interrupt controller; the additional PIC is the slave interrupt controller. The interrupt request output of the slave interrupt controller is connected to one of the interrupt request inputs of the master interrupt controller (IRQ2#). This is referred to as cascading one interrupt controller through another.

Each of these highly programmable PIC chips contains a series of registers. By programming (writing values to) these registers during

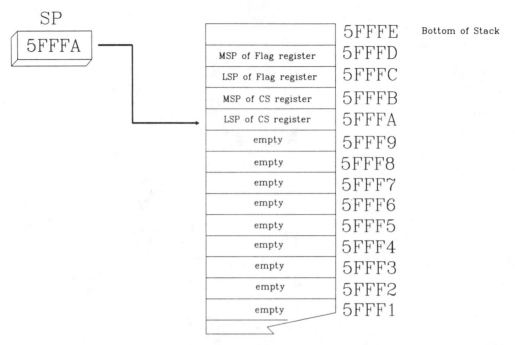

FIGURE 19-9   Stack Prior to POP to Load CS Register

the POST, the programmer can specify the operational characteristics of each of the chips.

During the POST, a special 8-bit register in the master interrupt controller is programmed with a value indicating that the Interrupt Request Level Two (IR2) input of the master interrupt controller is connected to the slave interrupt controller rather than an I/O device. All of the other interrupt request inputs of the master interrupt controller are designated as I/O interrupt request inputs to be handled in the fashion described earlier.

The slave interrupt controller contains a register known as the Slave ID register. During the POST, this register is programmed with the value 02_h. This is its slave ID number and corresponds to the input on the master it is connected to.

In addition, during the POST both of the interrupt controllers are programmed to utilize a fixed priority scheme. This means that on each of the interrupt controllers, the interrupt request level 0 (IR0) input has the highest priority, and the interrupt request level 7 (IR7) input has the lowest priority. If all of the interrupt request lines go active at

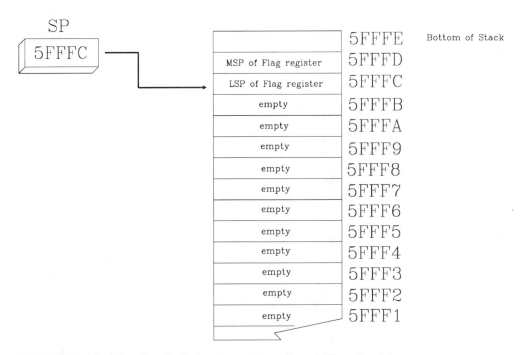

FIGURE 19-10   Stack Prior to POP to Load Flag Register

the same time, the interrupt request level 0 input is serviced first, followed by the others in decreasing order of priority.

Up until now, the terms interrupt request levels 0 through interrupt request level 7 have been used to identify the individual interrupt request inputs to the interrupt controller chip. The actual signal lines connected to the these inputs are designated as shown in Figure 19-11. The signal names given to these lines are interrupt request level 0 (IRQ0#) through IRQ15#.

IRQ0# through IRQ7# are connected to the master interrupt controller, and IRQ8# through IRQ15# are connected to the slave interrupt controller. With the exception of IRQ2#, each of these interrupt request lines is available to be connected to the interrupt request output of an I/O device.

The fact that both controllers are programmed for fixed priority yields the following overall priority. IRQ0# is the highest priority, followed immediately by IRQ1#. Since IRQ2# is really the interrupt request output of the slave interrupt controller, the slave's eight inputs, IRQ8# through IRQ15#, come next in the priority sequence. Finally, IRQ3# through IRQ7# are the lowest five in the priority sequence.

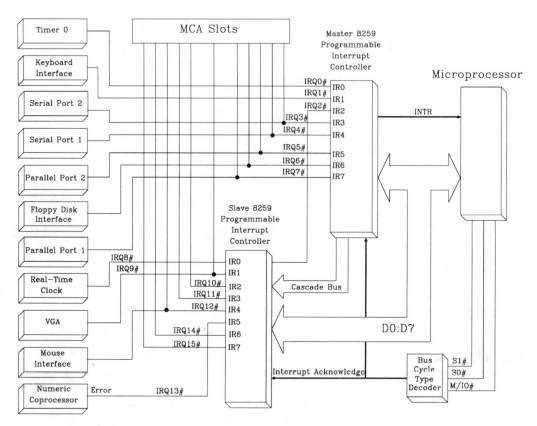

FIGURE 19-11 Cascaded Interrupt Controllers

Refer to Figure 19-11 again. Some of the interrupt request lines are dedicated to special I/O devices that reside on the system board.

- IRQ0# is connected to the output of Timer 0, frequently called the System Timer. This timer and other timers are discussed in detail in Chapter 33.

- IRQ1# is connected to the keyboard interrupt request line coming from the keyboard interface.

- IRQ2# is connected to the interrupt request output of the slave interrupt controller rather than to an I/O device.

- IRQ8# is connected to the alarm output of the Real Time Clock And Configuration RAM chip. This subject is covered in more detail in Chapter 26.

- The IRQ13# input to the slave interrupt controller is connected to the ERROR output of the numeric coprocessor.

The remainder of the interrupt request lines are attached to the 16-bit MCA connectors and are available for use by MCA cards. Although available for general usage, the following MCA interrupt request lines are typically used by the indicated devices.

- IRQ3# is attached to the 16-bit MCA connectors and is typically used as the interrupt request line for serial port 2.

- IRQ4# is attached to the 16-bit MCA connectors and is typically used by the interrupt request output of serial port 1.

- IRQ5# is attached to the 16-bit MCA connectors and is typically used by parallel port 2.

- IRQ6# is attached to the 16-bit MCA connectors and is used by the floppy disk controller on the system board.

- IRQ7#, the last interrupt request line on the master interrupt controller, is attached to the 16-bit MCA connectors and is typically used by parallel port 1.

- IRQ9# is attached to the 16-bit MCA connectors and is used by the VGA interface on the system board.

- IRQ10# is attached to the 16-bit MCA connectors and is available for use by MCA cards.

- The IRQ11# input to the slave interrupt controller is attached to the 16-bit MCA connectors and is available for use by MCA cards.

- The IRQ12# input to the slave interrupt controller is attached to the 16-bit MCA connectors and is used by the mouse interface in the PS/2.

- IRQ14# is attached to the 16-bit MCA connectors and is available for use by MCA cards. It is typically used by hard disk controllers.

- IRQ15# is attached to the 16-bit MCA connectors and is available for use by MCA cards.

Servicing of Requests to the Slave Interrupt Controller

When the slave interrupt controller detects an interrupt request on one of its inputs, it generates an interrupt request to what it thinks is the microprocessor but is, in fact, the master interrupt controller. The master interrupt controller senses the IRQ2# input active and, in turn, generates an interrupt request to the microprocessor.

The microprocessor requests the interrupt slot number by generating two interrupt acknowledge bus cycles. When the master interrupt controller sees the double interrupt acknowledge, it interprets this as the microprocessor's request for the interrupt slot number. Since it is servicing IRQ2#, the output of the slave interrupt controller, the master interrupt controller does not know exactly which device requires service. The slave interrupt controller is the device that knows the answer to the question.

To pass the interrupt slot number request along to the slave interrupt controller, the master interrupt controller places the slave ID, a 2 (010_b), onto a 3-bit bus (the **cascade bus**) connected to the slave interrupt controller. The slave interrupt controller compares the slave ID it sees on the cascade bus to its slave ID (programmed in during the POST) and responds by placing the proper interrupt slot number onto D0:D7 on the data bus.

At the trailing edge of the second interrupt acknowledge bus cycle, the microprocessor reads the interrupt slot number from the lower data path. The microprocessor multiplies it by 4 to produce the actual start memory address of the slot in the interrupt table and reads the 4 bytes of information from the slot. These 4 bytes are placed in the CS and IP registers.

The microprocessor then uses the contents of the CS and IP registers to identify the memory location to read the next instruction from.

The Interrupt Slot Number Assignments

During the POST, the two interrupt controllers are each programmed with the interrupt slot numbers for each of the interrupt requests inputs. Table 19-1 defines the slot number assignments.

TABLE 19-1 Interrupt Slot Number Assignment

IRQ Line	Assigned Interrupt Slot Number
0	08_h
1	09_h
2	$0A_h$
3	$0B_h$
4	$0C_h$
5	$0D_h$
6	$0E_h$
7	$0F_h$
8	70_h
9	71_h
10	72_h
11	73_h
12	74_h
13	75_h
14	76_h
15	77_h

Shareable Interrupts

The Intel 8259 programmable interrupt controller chip's interrupt request inputs can be programmed to recognize either a positive-going pulse or a static (unchanging) low level as a valid interrupt request. The programmer may select either of these recognition modes for all eight inputs at once. There is no provision for the selection of either type on an input-by-input basis.

PC/XT/AT Interrupt Request Recognition and Handling

On the PC, XT, and the AT, the interrupt controller is programmed to recognize a positive-going pulse as a valid interrupt request on an input. There are two problems inherent in this method and they are described in the following paragraphs.

In the PC/XT/AT, any unused interrupt request line is connected to the 8259 on one end and the expansion connectors on the other. An interrupt request (IRQ) line that is unused by any expansion cards acts as an antenna and is prone to pick up noise. This means that a noise spike (a low to high transition) could be interpreted as a valid interrupt request by the 8259.

The 8259 would then generate an interrupt request to the microprocessor. The microprocessor responds by requesting the interrupt slot number from the 8259. Since the noise spike has dissipated by now, the 8259 no longer sees an interrupt request pending on the respective IRQ line. Nonetheless, the 8259 must respond with an interrupt slot number.

Under these conditions, the 8259 is designed to respond with the interrupt slot number of the respective interrupt controller's IR7 (interrupt request level 7) input. Refer to Figure 19-11 again. Depending upon the whether the **ghost**, or **phantom**, **interrupt** was detected by the master or slave interrupt controller, the microprocessor jumps to either the IRQ7 or IRQ15 interrupt service routine.

At the beginning of each of these routines, the programmer should perform an I/O read from the respective 8259's In Service Register (IRS). If bit 7 in the ISR is set to a 1, then the IRQ7# or the IRQ15# is real and the programmer should continue on to service the request. If, on the other hand, bit 7 in the ISR is not set to a 1, the request was a phantom, or ghost, interrupt and should be ignored. The programmer just executes an interrupt return (IRET) instruction to return to the original, interrupted, program flow.

The second problem when using positive-edge triggered interrupts is that the interrupt request lines cannot be shared by multiple devices. If two devices are tied to the same interrupt request line and they both generate an interrupt request simultaneously, hardware damage could result because two separate current sources would be attempting to drive 5 volts onto the same signal line at the same time.

PS/2 Interrupt Request Recognition and Handling

In the IBM PS/2, the 8259 has been altered to recognize only a static, unchanging low as a valid interrupt request. The ability to program the 8259 for positive-edge triggered interrupt request recognition has been eliminated. This means that the interrupt controller need only sense a low level on an interrupt request input to register an interrupt request. When implemented this way, interrupt request lines may be shared by two or more devices. The following paragraphs define how this works.

PS/2 products with the micro channel have **shareable interrupts**. This means that multiple I/O devices can be attached to the same interrupt request signal line without causing damage to each other.

Each shareable interrupt request line has a pull-up resistor attached to it on the system board. When no requests are being generated, or when no I/O devices are physically connected to the line, the line is pulled up to a good, high level. This provides a good deal of noise immunity on the line, thereby preventing phantom interrupt requests.

Figure 19-12 illustrates two devices sharing an interrupt request line. An I/O device that places a low on an interrupt request line when it generates a request may share the line with other devices that use it the same way. The following example describes the interaction of two devices sharing the same IRQ line.

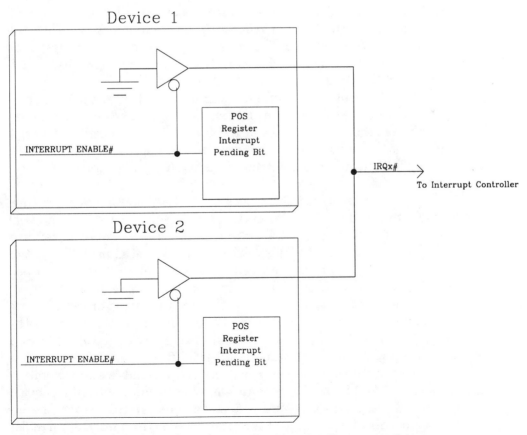

FIGURE 19-12 Two I/O Devices Sharing the Same IRQ Line

When device 1 must generate an interrupt request, it sets its INTERRUPT ENABLE# (triangular device) signal active. This enables the open-collector driver, thereby creating a path to ground ($\equiv$) on the IRQx# line (x = any IRQ number) to the interrupt controller. In addition to setting IRQx# active (low), device 1 sets the interrupt pending bit in one of its POS registers active.

Assuming device 2 must generate an interrupt request at the same time, it sets its INTERRUPT ENABLE# signal active. This enables the open-collector driver, creating another path to ground on the IRQx# line to the interrupt controller. In addition to setting IRQx# active (low), device 2 sets the interrupt pending bit in one of its POS registers active.

The two devices both placing an active level on the IRQx# line does not cause any hardware damage because neither is driving current onto the IRQx# signal line. Both devices are providing a path to ground, and IRQx# ends up active (low).

When the 8259 interrupt controller senses a low on the IRQx# line, it generates an interrupt request to the microprocessor. When the microprocessor requests the interrupt slot number, the 8259 responds with the interrupt slot number for IRQx#. The microprocessor then jumps to the IRQx interrupt handler routine.

In this routine, the programmer must first determine which of the various devices sharing this line currently requires servicing. To do this, the programmer reads from the proper POS register on device 1 and tests to see if its interrupt pending bit is set active. In this example, device 1 is generating an interrupt request, so its interrupt pending bit is set.

Having identified the requesting device, the programmer then services the request from device 1. Assuming that device 1 is a serial port requesting the next character to transmit, the programmer services the request by writing the next character to the serial port. The act of servicing the request causes device 1's interrupt pending bit to be turned off, preventing double servicing of the request. Device 1 also turns off its interrupt enable signal, causing the open-collector driver to cease providing a path to ground for the IRQx# signal line. Execution of the IRET instruction at the end of the interrupt service routine causes a return to the original, interrupted, program flow.

Since device 2 has not been serviced yet and is still generating IRQx#, the 8259 immediately senses another pending interrupt request on IRQx# and proceeds as outlined above. This time, however, the interrupt pending bit for device 1 is not active. The IRQx interrupt handler routine then reads from device 2's POS register and checks its interrupt pending bit to see if it is active. Since it is, the programmer then jumps to the appropriate interrupt service routine to handle the request from device 2. Just as with device 1, the act of servicing the request causes device 2's interrupt pending bit to be turned off, preventing double servicing of the request. Device 2 also turns off its interrupt enable signal, causing the open-collector driver to cease providing a path to ground for the IRQx# signal line. Execution of the IRET instruction at the end of the interrupt service routine causes a return to the original, interrupted, program flow.

Since both device 1 and device 2 have been serviced, neither is providing a path to ground on the IRQx# signal line. All interrupts pending on this line have now been serviced and IRQx# is pulled high again by its pull-up resistor.

Interrupt Latency

Since the interrupt handler routine must read from a POS register on each device sharing the interrupt request line until a device with an active interrupt pending bit is found, it stands to reason that the lower down on the list the device is the more time it will take to detect and service the request (if other devices, further up the list, are also generating requests). This latency, or delay, can cause problems ranging from slow servicing of a device right up to overflow conditions and missing characters. The problem can be solved in one of two ways.

- Move some devices to other request lines.
- During the configuration process install the devices requiring the fastest servicing first and the others later in the process.

Non-Maskable Interrupt Requests (NMI)

In addition to the maskable interrupt request input INTR, the Intel microprocessors have an additional interrupt request input known as **non-maskable interrupt** (NMI) input. Unlike the maskable interrupt request input, the non-maskable interrupt request input (NMI) cannot be masked out by the programmer. In other words, if the NMI input goes active, the microprocessor must immediately service that interrupt request. In a PS/2, the NMI line is typically used to report serious or fatal hardware failures to the microprocessor.

A classic example is a memory parity error. When the microprocessor senses an active signal on the NMI input, it responds by first pushing the Flag, CS, and IP registers onto the stack.

Rather than request the interrupt slot number from the interrupt controller, the microprocessor automatically uses slot 2 in the interrupt table. This slot is dedicated to the NMI interrupt. During the POST, the programmer writes the start address of the NMI interrupt service routine (located in ROM memory) into slot number 2 of the interrupt table.

After saving the three registers on the stack, the microprocessor then jumps to the NMI interrupt service routine by loading CS and IP from slot 2. In the NMI interrupt service routine, the programmer reads the contents of the following I/O ports to determine the cause of the NMI:

- System control port B at I/O port 0061_h.
- System control port A at I/O port 0092_h.
- Arbitration register at I/O port 0090_h.

The error is then reported on the screen.

Tables 19-2 through 19-4 define the bit assignment of these three ports and identifies the bits related to NMI with an asterisk.

As illustrated in these three tables, there are four possible causes for an NMI:

TABLE 19-2 System Control Port B at I/O Port 0061_h

Bit	Function
* 7	System board RAM parity check
* 6	Channel check
5	Timer 2 output
4	Refresh request
3	Channel check enabled
2	Parity check enabled
1	Speaker data enabled
0	Timer 2 gate to speaker

TABLE 19-3   System Control Port A at I/O Port 0092ₕ

Bit	Function
7	Fixed disk activity LED
6	Fixed disk activity LED
5	Reserved
* 4	Watchdog timer status
3	Security lock latch
2	Reserved
1	Alternate gate A20
0	Alternate hot reset

TABLE Table 19-4   The Arbitration Register at I/O Port 0090ₕ

Bit	Function
7	Enable system microprocessor cycle
6	Arbitration masked by NMI
* 5	Bus timeout
4	Reserved
3-0	Arbitration priority code of last bus master

- **System board RAM parity check**. Chapter 21 contains a detailed description of the system board RAM parity check logic.

- **Channel check**. Chapter 17 provides a detailed description of the channel check logic.

- **Watchdog timer status**. Chapter 33 provides a detailed description of the watchdog timer.

- **Bus timeout**. Chapter 13 provides a detailed description of bus timeout.

The programmer can selectively enable or disable the ability of external logic to generate an NMI. This is accomplished by writing the desired value to the Real-Time Clock Address register at I/O port 0070ₕ.

A 1 written to bit 7 disables the NMI logic's ability to generate an NMI; a 0 enables it.

Software Interrupts

Exception interrupts and software interrupts generated by the interrupt (INT) instruction are the two types of software conditions that can cause an interrupt to an Intel microprocessor. Both types of software interrupts are discussed in the following section.

The Exception Interrupts

Generally speaking, an exception interrupt results when the microprocessor attempts to execute an instruction and incurs an error while during so. A classic example would be an attempt to divide a number by 0. When an Intel microprocessor attempts to execute an instruction that would cause a divide-by-zero condition, the microprocessor immediately generates a divide-by-zero exception interrupt. Slot 0 in the interrupt table is dedicated to this condition and points to the start address of the divide-by-zero interrupt service routine supplied by the programmer.

Various other types of illegal software conditions can cause exception interrupts as well. A number of slots in the lowermost part of the interrupt table are reserved by Intel to point to the interrupt service routines for various software error conditions. Table 19-5 defines the conditions and their respective slots. Due to the hardware-orientation of this book, a detailed description of each of these conditions is not included. This information may be found in the Intel processor reference manuals.

The Software Interrupt Instruction

The **interrupt instruction (INT)** allows the programmer to call (jump to) a routine without knowing its start memory address. The number specified after the INT instruction is the slot number in the interrupt table. When executed, the INT instruction causes the microprocessor to react as if an interrupt request had been sensed on the INTR line. The only difference is that the interrupt slot number is supplied by the INT instruction rather than by the 8259 interrupt controller.

TABLE 19-5   Exception Interrupt Slot Assignment

Slot Number	Assigned to
0	Divide-by-zero exception
1	Single step, or trap, interrupt
2	NMI
3	Breakpoint
4	Interrupt on overflow
5	BOUND range exceeded
6	Invalid opcode
7	Processor extension not available
8	Double exception detected
9	Processor extension segment overrun
A	Invalid task state segment
B	Segment not present
C	Stack segment overrun or not present
D	General protection

The interrupt instruction allows the program to simulate a hardware interrupt request. This instruction take the following format:

```
INT   13
```

When the microprocessor executes the example instruction shown above, it reacts very much as it would to a hardware interrupt request received on the maskable interrupt request line, INTR.

It first saves the contents of the Flag, CS, and IP registers on the stack. At this time, CS and IP point to the instruction immediately after the INT instruction. Since the interrupt was not actually caused by a hardware interrupt request on the INTR line, however, the microprocessor does not issue two interrupt acknowledge bus cycles to request the interrupt slot number from the 8259 programmable interrupt controller. The interrupt slot number is supplied by the hexadecimal number to the right of the INT instruction.

In the example above, the programmer has designated slot number 13_h (a decimal 19). The microprocessor multiplies this number by

4 (13_h x 4 = $4C_h$) to yield the start memory address of slot 13_h in the interrupt table.

Just as it would for a hardware request, the microprocessor then reads the four bytes of information starting at this memory address and places them into the CS and IP registers. The CS and IP registers now point to the start address of the INT 13_h interrupt service routine in memory. The microprocessor begins to fetch and execute the instructions that make up this routine. At the conclusion of the routine, execution of the interrupt return (IRET) instruction pops the original Flags, CS and IP off the stack, thus causing the microprocessor to resume executing the original program at the instruction immediately after the INT instruction. The true value of the INT instruction lies in the fact that a programmer can call (jump to) a routine without knowing where it actually resides in memory. All the programmer needs to know is the slot number that contains its start address.

When Microsoft introduced the disk operating system (DOS) for the IBM PC, it was identified as version 1.0. An operating system such as PC-DOS is really nothing more than a collection of useful routines that the programmer can call (jump to) to perform various commonly used functions. The PC-DOS routines allow the programmer to control the various devices in the system without having an intimate knowledge of the operations required to control them.

One direction that Microsoft could have taken would have been to publish a list of the start memory addresses of the various routines that make up PC-DOS. A programmer could then jump to the start memory address of the appropriate routine to get a particular job done. This method would have caused tremendous compatibility problems, however.

Consider this. Not too long after version 1.0 of PC-DOS was released, IBM released version 1.1. This was followed rather closely by various other versions leading up to the version currently on the market. Now consider the fact that as the various versions of PC-DOS were issued, the size, functionality, and placement of the various routines that make up PC-DOS were altered. This means that the list of start memory addresses for the various routines specified in version 1.0 is no longer valid for any of the other versions. In fact, it would require a separate list of start memory addresses for the routines in each and every version of PC-DOS on the market.

If the designers of an applications program had used the DOS routines by actually jumping to the start memory addresses of the various routines embedded in version of 1.0 of PC-DOS, that version of the applications program would run correctly only with version 1.0 of PC-DOS. They would have had to issue a separate version of the applications program for every version of PC-DOS. It would also mean that the end-user would have to know the version of PC-DOS that they are running in order to buy the correct version of the application program they want to run. The end-user could never upgrade PC-DOS without relegating virtually all of his or her application's programs to the scrap heap. This obviously would have been an untenable solution to the problem.

As PC-DOS is loaded into memory when the machine is powered up, the PC-DOS load procedure includes the automatic placement of the start memory addresses for the various PC-DOS routines into pre-defined slots in the interrupt table. IBM guaranteed applications program developers that the pointers to the various PC-DOS routines would always reside in the same slots in the interrupt table, irrespective of the PC-DOS version. This means that an application program developer does not need to know the actual start memory address of a PC-DOS routine that he or she wants to use. To call the routine, the programmer simply specifies the correct slot number in an interrupt instruction. The Microsoft and IBM technical reference guides contain information detailing the routines called by each interrupt slot.

PC-DOS routines are not the only ones that can be called using the interrupt instruction. The basic input/output system (BIOS) routines are a collection of useful routines written by IBM and embedded in the system ROMs. There is one routine for each standard I/O device shipped with the system. Some examples are the keyboard, floppy disk, and hard disk **BIOS routines**.

Rather than expecting each application's programmer to understand the proper sequence of I/O writes and reads required in order to control and sense the status of various I/O devices, IBM supplies the BIOS routines. All the application's programmer need know is how to call the appropriate routine to talk to the target device. During the POST, the start memory address of each of the BIOS routines is stored in predefined slots in the interrupt table. IBM supplies a list of the interrupt slots assigned to each BIOS routine. This list is available in the IBM publication *The IBM Personal System/2 and Personal Computer BIOS Interface Technical Reference*.

Summary

To summarize, the Intel microprocessors recognize two classes of interrupts: hardware interrupts and software interrupts. Hardware interrupts can be divided into two categories: maskable interrupts and non-maskable interrupts (NMI).

Maskable interrupt requests are originated by I/O devices in the system when they require servicing. In the PS/2 products that incorporate the micro channel architecture, more than one device may share an interrupt request line. NMI requests are originated by error detection logic within the system.

Software interrupts can be divided into two categories: exception interrupts and interrupt instructions.

The exception interrupt is generated as a result of a software error condition. The interrupt instruction (INT) allows the programmer to call a routine without knowing its start memory address. It is used to call PC-DOS and BIOS routines.

PART
VI

Direct Memory
Access (DMA)

Direct Memory Access (DMA)

Objective: Every PS/2 incorporates direct memory access (DMA) logic. The DMA logic allows an I/O device to have direct access to system memory without the intervention of the microprocessor. This chapter describes the interaction between the microprocessor, the DMA controller, and the I/O device. It provides a detailed description of the DMA data transfer initiation, the data transfer itself, and the completion and termination of the data transfer.

Definitions for This Chapter

• A **DMA channel** is the hardware interface between I/O devices and memory.

• The **DMA controller, (DMAC)**, gives an I/O device the ability to directly access memory without the intervention of the microprocessor.

• **Serial DMA** is the transfer methodology utilized by the PS/2 DMA controller. The DMA controller must actually perform two bus cycles in sequence (or serially) in order to transfer a byte or a word between an I/O device and memory.

How Block Data Transfers Were Performed Before the Advent of DMA

The primary purpose of DMA logic is to facilitate the transfer of large blocks of data between an I/O device and system memory. Prior to the invention of DMA logic, every aspect of a block data transfer had to be handled by the microprocessor itself.

The following list identifies the basics steps involved in initiating a disk read operation to transfer a block of data into system memory without the aid of DMA.

1. The microprocessor must first determine the number of bytes of information to be transferred into memory and the start address in memory where the data will be placed as it is received from the disk controller.

2. The microprocessor issues the proper commands to the disk controller to initiate the disk read operation.

3. Having initiated the disk read operation, the microprocessor must wait for the disk controller to confirm availability of the first data byte.

4. The microprocessor then performs an I/O read from the disk controller to get the data byte and then a memory write bus cycle to write the data byte into the designated start memory address.

5. The microprocessor decrements the number of bytes remaining to be transferred and checks to see if the transfer count has been exhausted yet.

6. If the transfer count is not exhausted, the microprocessor increments the memory address to point to the memory location where the next data byte will be placed when it becomes available.

7. The microprocessor returns to monitoring the disk controller for the availability of the next data byte (step 3).

The microprocessor continues in this loop until the byte transfer count has been exhausted (the completion of the block data transfer into memory).

The microprocessor is involved in every aspect of the data transfer and is therefore unavailable to perform any other functions.

The DMA Controller (DMAC)

When using the **DMA controller (DMAC)**, the microprocessor must still initiate the block data transfer between the I/O device and memory, but the actual data transfer and its termination are handled solely by the DMA controller. This frees up the microprocessor to continue with other productive activities while the data transfer is taking place. Once a DMA block data transfer has been initiated, the DMA controller and the I/O device do not disturb the microprocessor again until the entire block of data has been transferred.

Upon completion of the data transfer, the I/O device interrupts the microprocessor to indicate completion. In response, the microprocessor temporarily suspends its current task and performs an I/O read from the I/O device to check the completion status of the transfer. The microprocessor continues processing if the I/O device indicates that no errors were encountered.

How DMA Is Implemented in the PS/2 Product Line

Figure 20-1 illustrates the DMA controller. The DMA controller used in the IBM PS/2 product line can handle data transfers between system memory and up to eight I/O devices.

The eight **DMA channels** are referred to as DMA channels 0 through 7. Each DMA channel within the DMA controller has its own set of I/O registers that the programmer uses to set up the data transfer. The set of I/O registers associated with a particular DMA channel allows the programmer to specify:

- the transfer count

- the start memory address

- the direction of transfer with reference to memory

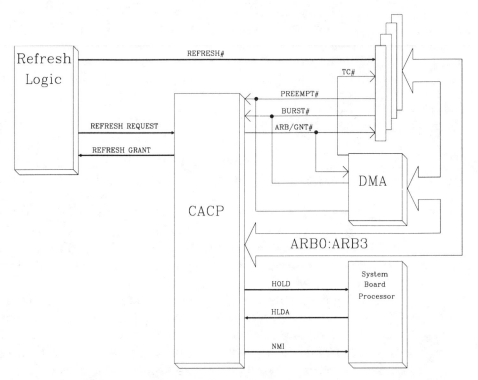

FIGURE 20-1 The PS/2 DMA Logic

- the amount of information to be moved between memory and the I/O device during each individual transfer (8 or 16 bits)
- the address of the I/O device's data port.

If the I/O device associated with the particular DMA channel is an 8-bit I/O device, the DMA channel is programmed for 1 byte (8 bits) per transfer. If, on the other hand, the I/O device associated with the specified DMA channel is a 16-bit I/O device, the respective DMA channel will be programmed to transfer 1 word (16 bits) per transfer. Please note that the DMA controller currently used in the PS/2 product line cannot perform 32-bit (doubleword) transfers.

After the DMA channel has been set up by the programmer, the I/O device should be programmed to initiate the overall block data transfer. For example, the programmer would issue the proper series of I/O write commands to a hard disk controller to initiate a disk write operation.

Having set up the respective DMA channel and issued the proper commands to the I/O device (in this case, the hard disk controller), the microprocessor can then go on to another task. The entire data transfer and its termination is handled by the I/O device and its respective DMA channel.

When performing a hard disk transfer, the programmer can perform data transfers only in multiples of the sector size. When running PC-DOS, a sector on a floppy or hard disk contains 512 bytes of information. This is the smallest data transfer possible, then, when transferring information between a disk drive and memory. The following list describes an example data transfer between system memory and a hard disk controller.

1. In the example of a write operation to a hard disk controller, some time will elapse before the disk controller has positioned the target disk drive's read/write heads over the appropriate point on the disk and the target sector has rotated under the head.

2. When the heads have been positioned and the data transfer can begin, the hard disk controller must then request the first data item (a byte or a word) from its associated DMA channel. In this example, assume that the hard disk controller is a 16-bit device (that is, it is connected to the lower 2 data paths, D0:D7 and D8:D15). In order to request the

transfer of the first word of information from memory to the hard disk controller, the hard disk controller must first become bus master. In order to do this, it issues PREEMPT# to the central arbitration control point (CACP) on the system board.

3. When the CACP senses PREEMPT# active, it initiates an arbitration cycle to allow the hard disk controller to compete for ownership of the buses. The process of bus arbitration is covered in Chapter 13.

4. The hard disk controller has the same arbitration priority code as the DMA channel assigned to it. In this example, assume that DMA channel 3 is assigned to handle transfers between this hard disk controller and system memory. This means that both DMA channel 3 and the hard disk controller both use arbitration priority code 3.

5. At the end of the arbitration cycle, DMA channel 3 detects that the arbitration priority code of the winning bus master is 3, the code assigned to itself and the hard disk controller. DMA channel 3 is now bus master.

6. DMA channel 3 then performs a memory read bus cycle to read a word of information from the start memory address previously specified by the programmer. The word is held in a temporary holding register inside the DMA controller.

7. DMA channel 3 then automatically initiates an I/O write bus cycle to send the data word to the hard disk controller. Using a pair of I/O memory bus cycles to transfer an object is referred to as **serial DMA**.

8. Having read the first word from memory and sent it to the hard disk controller, DMA channel 3 decrements (subtracts 1 from) its word transfer count. If the transfer count is exhausted (that is, the count goes to -1), the DMA controller generates the signal terminal count achieved (TC#) to inform the hard disk controller that the transfer has been completed. Proceed to step 9.

   If the transfer count has not been exhausted, the DMA controller gives up the buses after the data word has been transferred. The hard disk controller will not request the use of the buses again until it is ready for the next data word to be transferred from system memory. At that time, it turns on PREEMPT# again. Proceed to step 2.

9. Figure 20-2 illustrates the Transfer Complete logic. Upon sensing TC# active, the hard disk controller sets its interrupt request line active to inform the microprocessor of transfer completion.

10. The microprocessor then performs an I/O read from the hard disk controller status register to determine the status completion (that is, whether or not the transfer completed with errors).

The hard disk controller therefore engages in bus arbitration for each individual word transfer that must be performed. This continues until the word transfer count has been exhausted by the DMA channel.

Memory Addressing Limit

Figure 20-3 illustrates the DMA controller's connection to the address and data buses. The DMA controller is connected to bits 0 through 23 on the address bus. Even in PS/2 products that incorporate 32-bit slots (with a full 32-bit address bus), the DMA controller is capable of generating memory addresses only up to 24-bits wide. This places a limitation on DMA transfers in that data can be transferred only to or from the lower 16MB of system memory. If a PS/2 incorporating 32-bit slots

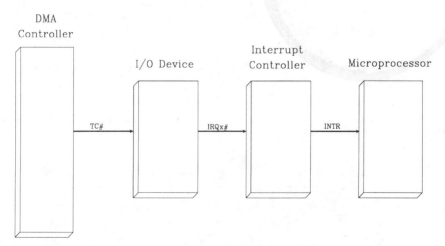

FIGURE 20-2   The DMA Transfer Complete Logic

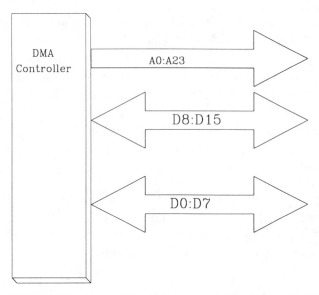

FIGURE 20-3 The PS/2 DMA Controller's Interface to the Address and Data Buses

has more than 16MB of memory installed, the DMA controller cannot transfer data into or out of memory above 16MB.

Data Size Limit

Refer to Figure 20-3 again. The DMA controller currently used in the PS/2 product line is capable of transferring data only over the lower 2 data paths, D0:D7 and D8:D15. This means that the models that incorporate 32-bit 80386 microprocessors can transfer only 2 bytes per DMA transfer even though they have a 32-bit data bus.

DMA Transfer Rate

The default bus cycle is the fastest type of bus cycle run by the DMA controller to transfer data between main memory and an I/O device. In the PS/2 Model 50Z, both the 286 microprocessor and the DMA controller use a 10MHz clock. Since one cycle of a 10MHz clock is 100 nanoseconds in duration, a default bus cycle takes 200 nanoseconds (address time + data time).

The PS/2 Model 70 and 80 are based on the 386 microprocessor and are available with a PCLK speed of 16MHz, 20MHz, or 25MHz. In the 16MHz versions of these machines, however, the clock used by the DMA controller is one-half the speed of the microprocessor's PCLK (16MHz divided by 2, or 8MHz).

This means that one cycle of the DMA clock is 125 nanoseconds in duration. Since the default bus cycle takes two cycles of the DMA clock, the default bus cycle run by the DMA controller in the 16MHz machine is 250 nanoseconds in duration, yielding a slower transfer rate than that produced by the same DMA controller utilized in the PS/2 Model 50 and Model 60.

In the 20MHz versions of the Model 70 and 80, the clock supplied to the DMA controller is, once again, one-half the microprocessor speed, or 10MHz. As with Model 50Z, the DMA controller requires 200 nanoseconds to complete a default bus cycle.

The following factors affect the maximum achievable data transfer rates when performing DMA data transfers in a PS/2:

- DMA clock speed

- Duration of the fastest possible DMA I/O access. This factor varies from model to model.

- Duration of the DMA memory access. This factor varies from model to model and may be different when accessing memory on the system board versus memory on an MCA card (referred to as channel memory).

- Number of bytes transferred per DMA transfer. Maximum is 16 bits (2 bytes) per DMA transfer.

Table 20-1 illustrates the DMA data transfer rates achievable in various PS/2 units.

The Model 50Z Type 1 and 2 system boards differ only in component layout and memory. The Type 2 supports 120ns or 85ns DRAM memory. The Model 70 Type 1 and 2 differ in CPU speed, component layout, and memory. The Type 1 is based on an Intel 80386 microprocessor running at 16MHz, and the Type 2 is based on an Intel 80386 microprocessor running at 20MHz. The Model 80 Type 1 and 2 differ in CPU speed, component layout, and memory. The Type 1 is based on an Intel 80386 microprocessor running at 16MHz, and the Type 2 is based on an Intel 80386 microprocessor running at 20MHz.

TABLE 20-1 DMA Transfer Rates

Model	Type	I/O Access	Channel Memory Access	System Memory Access	Total Access	DMA Transfer Rate	Notes
50Z	1	300ns	200ns	—	500ns	4.00MB/s	
50Z	1	300ns	—	300ns	600ns	3.33MB/s	
50Z	2	300ns	200ns	—	500ns	4.00MB/s	
50Z	2	300ns	—	200ns	500ns	4.00MB/s	85ns DRAM
50Z	2	300ns	—	300ns	600ns	3.33MB/s	120ns DRAM
60	n/a	300ns	200ns		500ns	4.00MB/s	
60	n/a	300ns	—	300ns	600ns	3.33MB/s	
70	1	250ns	250ns		500ns	4.00MB/s	
70	1	250ns	—	375ns	625ns	3.20MB/s	
70	2	200ns	200ns		400ns	5.00MB/s	
70	2	200ns	—	300ns	500ns	4.00MB/s	
80	1	250ns	250ns		500ns	4.00MB/s	
80	1	250ns	—	375ns	625ns	3.20MB/s	
80	2	200ns	200ns		400ns	5.00MB/s	
80	2	200ns	—	300ns	500ns	4.00MB/s	

Note: MB/s = megabytes per second

The following examples demonstrate how the table is used. Assume that the current DMA transfer transfers data between an I/O device and RAM memory installed on an MCA card in the Model 70, Type 1. If neither the I/O device nor the memory card inserts wait states in the bus cycles, the data transfer rate is 4MB/s (MB per second). The I/O device is accessed using a default bus cycle 250ns in duration because the DMA controller uses an 8MHz clock. This yields a clock cycle time of 125ns. Since a default bus cycle takes two cycles, it is 250ns in duration. The channel memory access is also 250ns in duration.

On the same unit, a data transfer between an I/O device and system board memory takes place at the rate of 3.20MB/s. The transfer rate is diminished relative to the previous example because the Model 70 Type 1 inserts one wait state (an additional 125ns) in the bus cycle when the DMA controller accesses system board memory.

Summary

The DMA controller handles the transfer of blocks of data between an I/O device and memory. In order to initiate a DMA transfer, the programmer must set up both the DMA controller and the I/O device. The DMA controller is programmed with the start memory address, the transfer count, the direction of transfer with reference to memory, the individual transfer size (8- or 16-bits) and the address of the I/O device's data port.

In addition, the I/O device must be issued a command that causes it to initiate the data transfer. When the I/O device is ready to begin the transfer, it arbitrates for the use of the buses. When the DMA channel associated with the I/O device senses that the I/O device has won the use of the buses, the DMA controller uses the buses to perform a read bus cycle from the source device (either the I/O device or memory). The data read is latched by the DMA controller and a write bus cycle is initiated to write the data item to the destination device (either the I/O device or memory).

The DMA channel then increments the start memory address and decrements the transfer count. If the transfer count goes from 0 to -1, the transfer has been completed; if it does not, additional data transfers remain. The DMA controller surrenders the buses and waits for the I/O device to initiate another transfer. This continues until the transfer count goes to -1.

When the overall block transfer has been completed, the DMA controller turns on its TC# output to inform the I/O device that the transfer has been completed. The I/O device, in turn, turns on its interrupt request output to inform the microprocessor that the transfer has been completed.

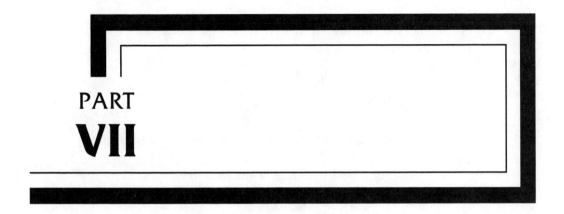

Memory

Introduction to Part VII

The memory incorporated into a PS/2 product can be divided into two basic categories:

- System Board Memory
- Channel Memory

The system board memory can be subdivided into four areas:

- System board dynamic RAM memory
- The cache memory subsystem
- System board ROM memory
- The real-time clock and configuration RAM

Special memory connectors are provided on the system board for the installation of dynamic RAM memory. The amount of memory that may be installed in these memory slots is system-specific. Some of the 80386- and 80486-based systems also incorporate cache memory subsystems on the system board to improve system performance.

The user can also install additional memory, referred to as channel memory, on MCA cards.

Part VII describes the memory subsystems utilized in the PS/2 product line. The following is a synopsis of each chapter:

Chapter 21: RAM Memory: Theory of Operation. This chapter provides a detailed description of internal DRAM layout, the DRAM addressing logic, and the DRAM addressing sequence. It defines access time, RAS/CAS delay, pre-charge delay and cycle time. DRAM refresh is fully described, as are memory banks and parity. Page mode, static column (SCRAM) and static RAM (SRAM) are also described. Lastly, the structure and advantages of interleaved memory architecture are discussed.

Chapter 22: System Board DRAM Memory. This chapter provides a description of the various DRAM memory configurations found on PS/2 system boards.

Chapter 23: Cache Memory: Theory of Operation. This chapter provides a detailed description of how a cache memory subsystem performs. The Intel 82385 cache memory controller is used as the example. The PS/2 models incorporating cache memory are identified.

Chapter 24: Channel Memory. This chapter discusses memory cards installed in MCA slots.

Chapter 25: ROM Memory on the System Board and MCA Cards. This chapter describes the ROMs on the system board and the device ROMs that can reside on MCA cards.

Chapter 26: The Real-Time Clock and Configuration RAM. This chapter describes the Motorola and Dallas semiconductor versions of the real-time clock and configuration RAM chip as well as the additional CMOS battery backed-up RAM found in some PS/2 models.

RAM Memory: Theory of Operation

Objectives: This chapter provides a detailed description of internal DRAM layout, the DRAM addressing logic, and the DRAM addressing sequence. It defines access time, RAS/CAS delay, pre-charge delay, and cycle time. DRAM refresh is fully described, as well as memory banks and parity. Page mode, static column (SCRAM) and static RAM (SRAM) are also described. Lastly, the structure and advantages of interleaved memory architecture are discussed.

Definitions for This Chapter

• **Bit cell** is the name given to the logic in a memory device that stores a 1 or a 0.

• The **column address decoder** is the device in a DRAM chip that interprets the column address latched into the DRAM's column latch and activates the proper column line within the DRAM.

• The **column address latch** is the device in a DRAM chip that latches the column address presented on the memory address bus when CAS# goes active.

• The **column address strobe (CAS)** is the signal the DRAM addressing logic generates to latch the column address into the DRAM chips.

• **Cycle time** is the combination of a DRAM's RAS access time and its pre-charge delay. It defines how frequently a DRAM may be accessed.

• **Dynamic RAM (DRAM)** memory is so named because it must be refreshed on a dynamic, ongoing basis or it loses the information stored in it.

• DRAM **access time** is the period of time from the activation of the RAS# line until the DRAM chip is ready to complete the data transfer. The DRAM access time is also referred to as the RAS access time.

• **DRAM addressing logic**. This logic translates the address output by the current bus master to the row and column addresses expected by DRAM memory chips. It presents the row and column address to the DRAM chips in the proper sequence.

• Under control of the DRAM addressing logic, the **DRAM address multiplexer (MUX)** selects either the row portion or the column portion of the current bus master's address to route to the DRAM chips.

• A **DRAM bank** is created by addressing the same location within a series of DRAM chips simultaneously. This enables the current bus master to transfer one or more bytes during a single bus cycle.

• **Interleaved memory architecture** is used to speed up access to sequential DRAM memory locations. What would ordinarily be one bank of DRAM memory is split up into two banks. Support logic within the interleaved memory logic keeps track of which bank was accessed last. Using address pipelining, the memory subsystem can detect that the upcoming access is to the same bank or the other bank. If to the other bank, the memory logic need not allow for the pre-charge delay and can let the microprocessor access it immediately.

• The **memory address bus** supplies the row and column address to the DRAM chips. These addresses are derived from the address being output by the current bus master and are routed onto the memory address bus by the MUX under the control of the DRAM addressing logic.

• Sequential **page mode DRAM** locations are laid out or distributed sequentially along a row. When the current bus master performs a series of bus cycles to access locations within the same row, the page mode DRAM requires only the column portion of the address. Since the RAS/CAS delay can therefore be skipped, the access time is substantially reduced. The CAS# line must be activated for each new column address presented to the page mode DRAM chips.

• When a byte of information is written into RAM memory, an additional **parity** bit is appended to it by the parity generation logic. If necessary, the parity bit is set to a 1, forcing the number of 1 bits in the 9-bit pattern to an even number. When a RAM memory location is read from, the byte of data is sent back to the requesting bus master and is also applied to the parity checking logic with the parity bit from memory. If an odd number of 1 bits is detected, the parity logic generates a RAM parity check error, thereby causing an NMI to the system board microprocessor.

• The **pre-charge delay** is the length of time it takes a DRAM to charge up after it has been read from. If the DRAM is accessed during this period of time, faulty data may be returned.

• The **RAS/CAS delay** is the delay between activation of RAS# and activation of CAS#. It is necessary to ensure proper operation of the DRAM chip.

• DRAM storage locations require **refresh** on a periodic basis in order to retain the information stored in them. A row of locations within a DRAM memory chip is refreshed by setting the DRAM's R/W# pin to the read state and latching the row address into the DRAM's row latch with RAS#.

• The **refresh row counter** contains the address of the next row to be refreshed within the DRAM memory chips. It is located on the system board and outputs a new row address onto the address bus every 15 microseconds. When the last row address has been refreshed, the refresh row counter rolls over to Row 0 and starts over again.

• The **refresh timer** is located on the system board and outputs an active signal every 15 microseconds to request the buses to run a refresh bus cycle. This timer is not programmable in the PS/2 product line.

• The **row address decoder** is located inside the DRAM chips and selects the row line to be activated during a bus cycle.

• The DRAM addressing logic uses the **row address strobe (RAS)** signal to latch the row address into the DRAM chips.

• The **row comparator** is found in DRAM memory systems utilizing page mode or static column (SCRAM) DRAM memory chips. Using address pipelining, it compares the row to be addressed in the upcoming bus cycle to the row already latched into the DRAM chips. If they are equal, this is a row, or page, hit and it is only necessary to present the new column address to the DRAM chips.

• Page mode and static column (SCRAM) DRAM memory subsystems also include an external **row latch** used to hold the row address currently latched into the DRAM chips. The row comparator compares this row address to the row to be addressed in the upcoming bus cycle. Also see row comparator definition.

• Every DRAM chip contains an internal **row address latch** used to hold the row address currently being accessed.

• Sequential **static column RAM (SCRAM)** locations are laid out or distributed sequentially along a row. When the current bus master performs a series of bus cycles to access locations within the same row, the SCRAM requires only the column portion of the address. Since the RAS/

CAS delay can therefor be skipped, the access time is substantially reduced. The CAS# line is kept active (static) for each new column address presented to the SCRAM chips.

• Unlike DRAM, **Static RAM (SRAM)** memory does not require refreshing at regular intervals in order to maintain the information stored in memory. This is because SCRAM uses single-bit latches known as D-flip flops, unlike DRAM which uses capacitors to store information. In addition, SRAM chips have very fast access times because they do not require that the address be split into a row and column and presented in sequence.

Dynamic RAM (DRAM) Memory

A **dynamic RAM (DRAM)** memory chip contains many storage locations. Depending on the manufacturer and the chip type, a DRAM memory chip may contain 64K, 256K, 1M, 4M, or more storage locations. Internally, the storage locations are laid out in rows and columns.

In order to identify the specific location with which the current bus master wants to communicate, the DRAM chip must receive the address in two steps, the row address first, then the column address.

The intersection of the row and column defines the exact location with which the current bus master wants to communicate. The state of the DRAM's read/write pin, high or low, defines the type of memory operation. The data bus is connected to the DRAM chip so that the data can be transferred from the DRAM chip to the microprocessor during a read or from the microprocessor to the DRAM chip during a write.

Overview of the DRAM Addressing Sequence

The following steps describe the exact sequence of events that must occur when addressing a DRAM memory location. Figure 21-1 illustrates the internal construction of a DRAM chip.

1. The row address must be routed to the DRAM's address pins.

2. The **row address strobe (RAS#)** line must be set active by the DRAM addressing logic. This causes the row address present on the DRAM's address inputs to be latched into the **row address latch** inside the DRAM.

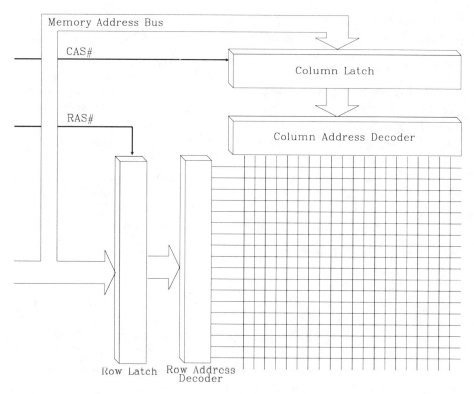

FIGURE 21-1   Block Diagram of a DRAM Memory Chip

3. The **DRAM addressing logic** delays a fixed amount of time before giving the column address to the DRAM chip. This is called the **RAS/CAS delay** and is described later in this chapter.

4. After the RAS/CAS delay has elapsed, the DRAM addressing logic routes the column portion of the address to the DRAM's address inputs and sets **column address strobe (CAS#)** active. This causes the column address to be latched into the **column address latch** inside the DRAM chip.

5. The DRAM chip now has all the information it needs to identify the location with which the current bus master is attempting to communicate. The DRAM's internal **row address decoder** selects and activates the specified row line. The DRAM's internal **column address decoder** selects and activates the specified column line.

   The point at which the row and the column lines intersect identifies the storage location with which the current bus master is attempting to communicate.

6. The state of the DRAM's read/write input pin indicates whether the current bus master is attempting to read the information stored in the specified storage location or write information into that location.

If a read operation is in progress, the contents of the indicated location is placed on the data bus by the DRAM so that it can be read by the current bus master. If a write operation is in progress, the information that the current bus master is presenting on the data bus is written into the specified storage location, thereby completing the bus cycle.

The Source of the Row and Column Addresses

The fact that the DRAM expects to see the address presented in two steps, row and column, presents a special problem because this form does not correspond to the address output by the current bus master. As a result, some type of logic is needed to translate the address being output by the current bus master into a row and column address. This address translation logic is commonly referred to as the DRAM addressing logic.

Bus masters always output 24-bit (the 80286 microprocessor) or 32-bit (the 80386 and 80486 microprocessors) addresses onto the address bus. From the DRAM addressing logic's perspective, the address is treated as three packets of information. Figure 21-2 illustrates this concept.

- The uppermost bits on the address bus are used by the DRAM address decoder to determine if the address currently on the bus is within the address range assigned to the DRAM.

- The row address is taken from the lower portion of the address.

- The column address is also taken from the lower portion of the address (the row and column addresses are of equal size).

The DRAM Addressing Logic

As stated earlier, the steps involved in addressing DRAM must occur in an exact sequence and at specified intervals. A time delay device included

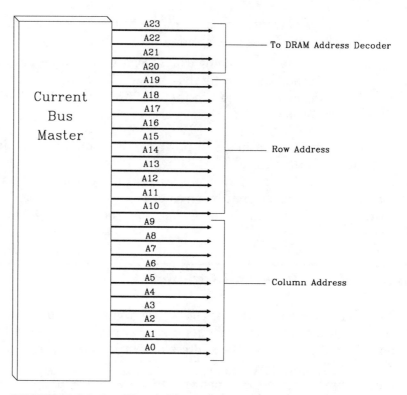

FIGURE 21-2   The Address Output by the Current Bus Master

in the DRAM addressing logic properly sequences the actions of the DRAM addressing logic.

The time delay device has one input called a trigger and a series of outputs. Once triggered by an active level on its trigger input, the time delay device sequentially turns on each of its outputs at precise intervals. For example, the time delay device shown in Figure 21-3 has a 10 nanosecond (10ns) resolution. 10ns after it is triggered its first output goes active; 10ns later the second output goes active, and so on. By tapping off selected outputs of the time delay device, the designer can choose the exact moment in time (relative to the trigger point) for a specific event to occur.

The major components of the DRAM addressing logic are

- the DRAM address decoder
- the time delay
- the **DRAM addressing multiplexer (MUX)**
- the RAS/CAS generation logic

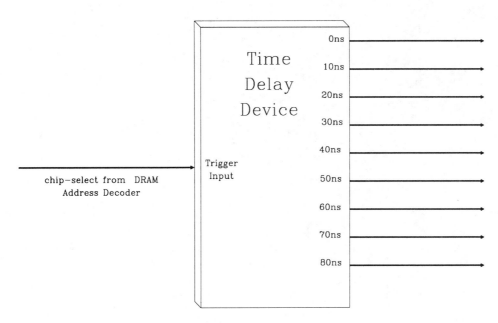

FIGURE 21-3 The Time Delay Device

  Figure 21-4 illustrates the DRAM addressing logic. The MUX has two sets of inputs and one set of outputs. It has only one control line, the select line, that controls its function. This line can be either high or a low. A low selects the "A" set of inputs to be gated through (routed through) to the MUX's outputs. When the select line is high, the "B" set of inputs is selected and gated through to the MUX's outputs. As you can see, a MUX is nothing more than a two-position switch that can select one of two groups of input signals to gate through to its output lines.

  The uppermost bits on the address bus are connected to the DRAM address decoder so that it can determine if the address currently on the bus falls within the range of addresses assigned to this DRAM. The lower bits on the address bus are connected to the MUX. One half of these bits are connected to the MUX's "A" set of inputs, and the other half to its "B" set of inputs. Initially, the select line on the MUX is set to 0, which selects the "A" set of inputs to be gated through to the MUX's outputs. The outputs of the MUX are connected to the memory address bus, which is attached to the address inputs of the DRAMs.

Detailed Description of The DRAM Addressing Sequence

The following list describes the sequence of events during addressing of a DRAM memory location. Refer to the DRAM addressing logic block

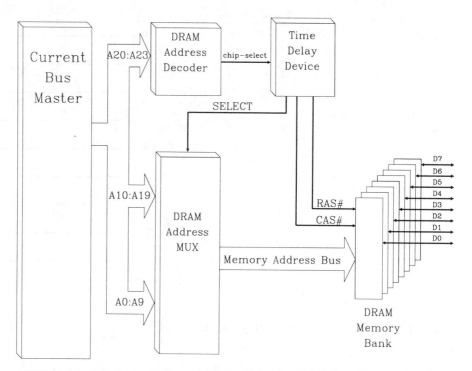

FIGURE 21-4   Block Diagram of DRAM Addressing Logic

diagram in Figure 21-4 again and the related timing diagram illustrated in Figure 21-5.

1. **DRAM address decode**. At the beginning of the bus cycle, the current bus master places the address on the address bus, and the bus cycle definition on the bus cycle definition lines. The DRAM address decoder determines that it is a memory address by the high on the M/IO# line and decodes the uppermost bits on the address bus to determine if the address is within the range of addresses assigned to the DRAM. If it is, the DRAM address decoder's chip-select output is set active, thereby providing a trigger to the time delay device.

2. **The row address**. When initially triggered, the time delay outputs are all low, which causes the MUX's select input to be low. This selects the MUX's "A" set of inputs, address bits A0:A9, to be gated onto the **memory address bus**. This

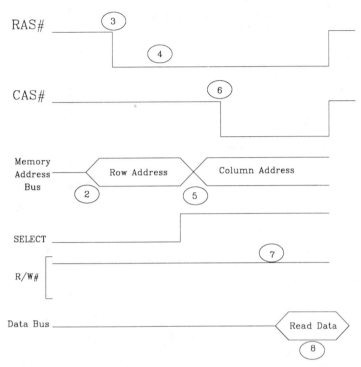

FIGURE 21-5 Simplified DRAM Addressing Timing Diagram

portion of the address provides the row address to the DRAM memory.

3. **Row Address Strobe (RAS#).** In the example DRAM addressing logic (Figure 21-4), 10ns is allowed to pass to allow the row address to settle on the memory address bus prior to latching it into the DRAM chip. 10ns after the time delay is triggered by the chip-select, the first output of the time delay goes active (high), causing RAS# to be set active. The high-to-low transition on the RAS# line causes the DRAM's internal row address latch to latch the row address presented to it on the memory address bus.

4. **RAS/CAS delay.** For correct operation, the designer must delay a specific amount of time prior to presenting the column address to the DRAM chips. If the column address is presented too soon, the DRAM chips will not function correctly. This delay between the presentation of the row address and the column address is known as the RAS/CAS delay. Figure 21-6 illustrates access time, RAS/CAS delay, and CAS access time.

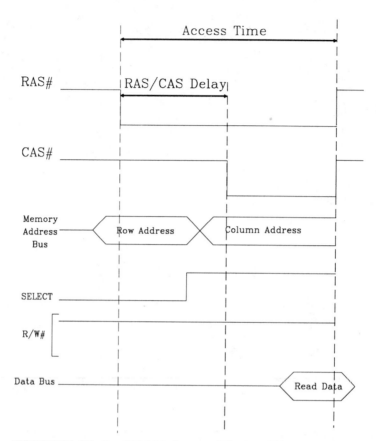

FIGURE 21-6   DRAM Access Timing Diagram

The exact duration of the delay is specific to the type of DRAM chips being used.

5. **The column address**. In the example DRAM addressing logic, the time delay's second output goes active 20ns after the trigger, setting the MUX's select line to a 1. This selects the MUX's "B" set of inputs, A10:A19, to be gated onto the memory address bus. This portion of the address provides the column address to the DRAM memory.

6. **Column Address Strobe (CAS#)**. In the example logic, 10ns is allowed to pass to allow the column address to settle on the memory address bus prior to latching it into the DRAM chip. The time delay's third output goes active 10ns later, which causes CAS# to go active (low). The high-to-low transition on CAS# causes the DRAM chip's internal column address latch

to latch the column address being presented to it on the memory address bus. The column address is then presented to the **column address decoder** in the DRAM chip.

7. **Read or write?** Internally, the DRAM chip has now latched the row and column addresses and activates one row and one column line. The point at which they intersect defines the location the current bus master is attempting to access. The DRAM addressing logic uses the S0# and S1# bus cycle definition lines to determine if a read or write operation is in progress. The read/write control input of the DRAM chip is set accordingly.

8. **The data transfer**. Assuming a read operation is in progress, the contents of the addressed DRAM storage location is placed on the data bus so that it can be read by the current bus master. If it is a write operation, the data sent to the DRAM by the current bus master is written into the addressed storage location.

How Data Is Stored in a DRAM Chip

A typical DRAM location can store only 1 bit of information, a 1 or a 0. This 1 bit storage location is called a **bit cell** and consists mainly of a capacitor. As an example, an electrical charge is placed on the capacitor to store a 1, while the capacitor is discharged to store a 0 in the location.

The most important operational characteristic of a capacitor is its tendency to lose a charge over a period of time. When a bit is stored in a DRAM bit cell by placing a charge on its capacitor, the capacitor discharges in a relatively short period of time and loses the bit stored in it.

DRAM Refresh

To ensure that information stored in DRAM memory is not lost, the bit cells containing charges must periodically be recharged, or **refreshed**, to a high level.

Storage locations in a typical DRAM chip are refreshed by activation of the row line. When a row line is activated with the DRAM's read/write pin in the read state, every bit cell (every storage location) that contains a charge along the row is automatically recharged to a high level.

DRAM refresh is handled by the refresh logic, which is separate from the microprocessor. In a PS/2, the refresh logic consists mainly of a **refresh row counter** and timer #1, the **refresh timer**. Figure 21-7 illustrates the refresh logic. When the system is first powered up, the system's RESET signal is active until the power has come up and stabilized. The active level on reset causes the refresh row counter to be preset to a count of 0 (Row 0). The refresh timer is designed to output an active signal, REFRESH REQUEST, once every 15 microseconds.

When the power has stabilized and RESET goes inactive, the system begins to run and the microprocessor begins to fetch and execute instructions. The refresh timer outputs the REFRESH TRIGGER signal 15 microseconds after the system begins to run.

In order to refresh a row of DRAM memory, the refresh logic must send a row address to the DRAM and set the DRAM's read/write

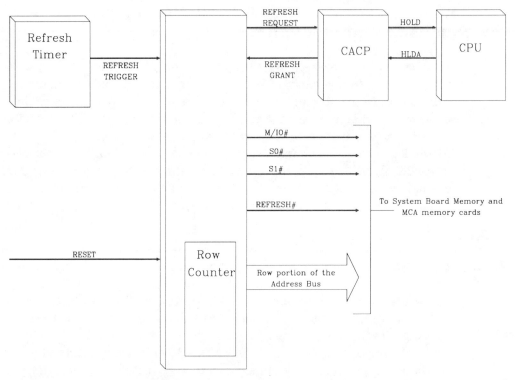

FIGURE 21-7   The Refresh Logic

control line to the read state. To do this, the refresh logic must run a special memory read bus cycle. In other words, the refresh logic must become bus master before running the refresh bus cycle.

The refresh logic has the highest arbitration priority code. When the central arbitration control point, or CACP, detects REFRESH RE-QUEST, the following actions take place.

1. The CACP turns on hold request (HOLD) to command the microprocessor to give up the buses. If the microprocessor has a bus cycle in progress when HOLD goes active, it completes the bus cycle and disconnects itself from the address, data, and control buses so that another device can use the buses.

2. After disconnecting itself from the three buses, the microprocessor turns on hold acknowledge (HLDA) to inform the CACP that the buses are available.

3. The CACP turns on REFRESH GRANT to inform the refresh logic that it is now bus master.

4. The refresh logic turns on the REFRESH# signal (on the micro channel connectors) so that DRAM memory cards throughout the system will know that a refresh bus cycle is in progress.

5. The refresh logic sets the bus cycle definition lines (M/IO#, S0#, and S1#) to indicate that a memory read bus cycle is in progress.

6. The refresh row counter outputs its current row number (initially, Row 0) onto the portion of the address bus that supplies the row portion of the address to DRAM memory. At the same time, the row counter is internally incremented by 1 (to Row 1).

7. The REFRESH# signal informs every memory card in the system that a refresh bus cycle is in progress. Consequently, on every memory card the row address from the refresh row counter is applied to the "A" set of inputs of the card's DRAM address MUX. The row address, currently row 0, is gated through every memory card's MUX onto its memory address bus. The card's DRAM addressing logic then sets RAS# active to latch the row address into every DRAM chip in the system simultaneously.

8. Since the bus cycle definition lines are set to indicate that a memory read bus cycle is in progress, the read/write pin on every DRAM chip will be set to the read state.

9. This set of actions causes the exact same row line (initially, row 0) within every DRAM chip in the system to be activated at the same time, thereby refreshing every location along that row in every DRAM chip.

10. After completion of the refresh bus cycle, the CACP returns bus ownership to the system board microprocessor by turning off HOLD.

11. The microprocessor connects itself to the buses and turns off HLDA to indicate that it is bus master again. Normal program execution resumes and continues until another 15 microseconds has elapsed. At that time, the refresh timer outputs REFRESH REQUEST again to request another refresh bus cycle.

12. When the refresh logic has once again been granted bus mastership, it again outputs the contents of the refresh row counter (incremented by 1 during the previous refresh bus cycle) onto the portion of the address bus that supplies the row address to the DRAMs.

In this way, the next sequential row in every DRAM chip in the system is refreshed. This action continues once every 15 microseconds as long as the system is powered on. When the last row within the DRAM chips has been refreshed, the row counter rolls over to all 0's again and the process starts over at the first row in the DRAM chips.

The PS/2 Refresh Timer

In the PC/XT/AT, the refresh interval of timer #1, the refresh timer, was programmable, thereby allowing a programmer to change the refresh interval to something other than 15 microseconds. This practice is dangerous, however, because alteration of the refresh interval raises the possibility that some DRAM memory locations will have entirely discharged by the time the refresh logic gets around to refreshing their respective rows again. If this happens, data in DRAM memory may be lost. To prevent this possibility in the PS/2 series, IBM removed the ability to program the refresh timer and built it to operate at a fixed frequency of a REFRESH REQUEST once every 15 microseconds.

Destructive Read: Pre-Charge Delay and Cycle Time

When a DRAM location is read, the DRAM must have some way of determining if the location contains a charge (that is, if it contains a 1 or a 0). The only way it can ascertain the presence of a charge is to discharge the bit cell's capacitor. This is a destructive read process because it discharges the capacitor used to store a bit in order to determine if there was in fact a bit stored in that location. However, since a storage device that can be read only one time would be useless, every DRAM chip contains logic that recharges a DRAM location back to a good level after the destructive read takes place. The location is recharged only if it is determined that it originally held a charge. It takes some time to recharge a DRAM location back to a good level again. This period of time is the **pre-charge delay**.

Figure 21-8 illustrates pre-charge delay and **cycle time**. This timing diagram illustrates the pre-charge delay immediately following after the access time. If a bus master immediately attempts to read data from the same memory location again, the data received is likely to be garbage because the storage location may not have been charged back to a good level yet.

To ensure that the data read from the DRAM is good data, the hardware should not allow a bus master to access the DRAM again until the pre-charge delay has elapsed. The bus master can be held off by keeping its READY# line inactive until both the **access time** and pre-charge delay has elapsed. When READY# is then set active, the microprocessor is allowed to complete the first transfer and can immediately and safely initiate a subsequent transfer.

When a DRAM chip manufacturer specifies the access time on a DRAM (for example, 80ns, 100ns, or 120ns access time), it does not paint an entirely accurate picture. Although the first access to a 100ns DRAM chip can be safely made in 100ns, the hardware must delay initiation of a subsequent access until the DRAM's pre-charge delay has elapsed. Since the pre-charge delay is usually equal to the access time for the DRAM, the access time should be doubled to ascertain how often the DRAM chip may be safely accessed. For example, a DRAM chip with a rated access time of 100ns could only be accessed safely once every 200ns (100ns Access Time + 100ns Pre-Charge delay). The overall period of time consisting of the access time and the pre-charge delay is known as the **cycle time**, and this factor should be considered the true access time for the DRAM chips.

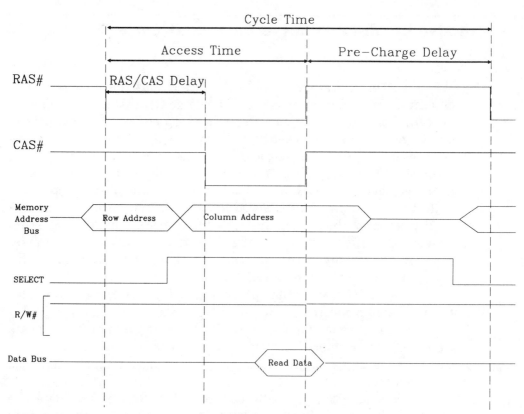

FIGURE 21-8 Pre-Charge Delay and Cycle Time

The DRAM Bank

Figure 21-9 depicts the **DRAM bank**. The typical DRAM chip utilized
in personal computers stores 1 bit of information per location. Since
the microprocessor expects to be able to read or write at least 1 byte of
information at a time, the ability to store and retrieve 1 bit per location
appears relatively useless.

To create a usable design, the engineer combines a series of 8
DRAM chips so that, taken collectively, they can store 1 byte of information per location. This is referred to as a bank of DRAM. The designer
connects the memory address bus in parallel to all 8 DRAM chips. The
RAS# and CAS# lines are also connected to all 8 DRAM chips and to
the read/write control line. This enables the microprocessor to address
the exact same location in all 8 DRAM chips simultaneously.

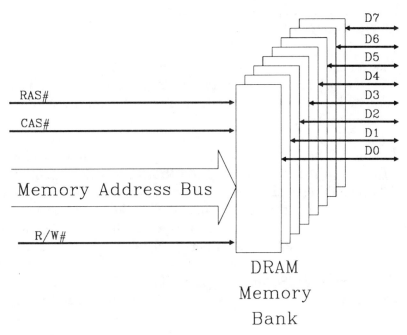

FIGURE 21-9   The DRAM Bank

The designer connects each individual data bus line to the data input/output pin on a DRAM chip within the bank of DRAM.

When the microprocessor performs a memory write operation and places the address on the address bus, the DRAM addressing logic performs the necessary breakdown of the address into the row and column addresses and selects the exact same row and column within each of the 8 DRAM chips within the bank. The read/write pin on the DRAM chips is set to the write state and each of the 8 data bits that make up the byte to be written into the memory location is presented to its respective DRAM chip within the bank. The 8 data bits bits are then written into exactly the same location within the 8 individual DRAM chips.

When the microprocessor performs a memory read operation to read a byte of information from DRAM, it simultaneously addresses precisely the same row and column location within each of the 8 DRAM chips. The bit stored in that location within each of the 8 DRAM chips is driven onto the respective data bus line by the individual DRAM chip. From the microprocessor's perspective, it is communicating with DRAM memory that can store 1 byte of information per location.

Width of DRAM Bank

The original IBM PC and XT were based on the Intel 8088 microprocessor, which had an 8-bit data bus. A bank of DRAM in those machines consisted of 8 DRAM chips plus a **parity** bit (parity is discussed later in this chapter).

Figure 21-10 illustrates a 16-bit DRAM bank. The IBM PC/AT (or any PC based on the 80286 microprocessor) has a 16-bit data bus, so a bank of DRAM consists of 16 DRAM chips, divided into two halves. All even-addressed locations are located in the lower half (connected to the lower data path, D0:D7), and all odd-addressed locations are in the upper half (connected to the upper data path, D8:D15). Each half consists of 8 data DRAMs and a parity DRAM.

Figure 21-11 illustrates a 32-bit DRAM bank. Systems based on the 80386 or 80486 microprocessor have a 32-bit data bus, and each bank of DRAM consists of 32 data DRAM chips plus 4 parity DRAMs.

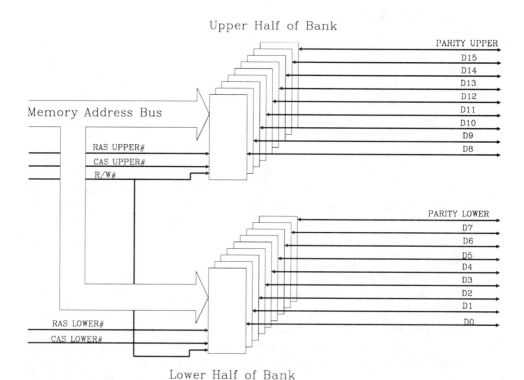

FIGURE 21-10   16-Bit DRAM Bank

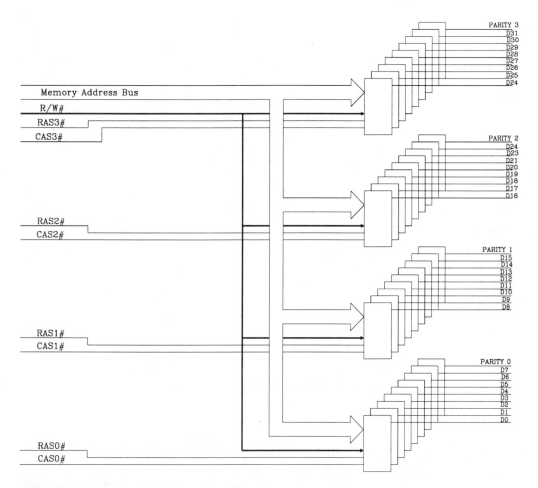

FIGURE 21-11 32-Bit DRAM Bank

Thus a bank of DRAM is sized to match the width of the data bus so that the microprocessor can transfer the maximum amount of information per bus cycle.

DRAM Parity

The DRAM memory subsystem used in the PC/XT/AT and the PS/2 products incorporates parity generation and checking logic. Consider the DRAM bank pictured in Figure 21-12. This bank of DRAM consists of 8 DRAM chips and an additional ninth DRAM chip referred to as the parity DRAM. All of the address lines, as well as the RAS# and CAS#

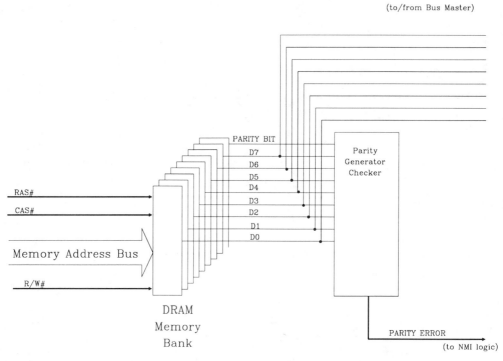

FIGURE 21-12   The System Board DRAM Parity Logic

lines and the read/write control line, are connected in parallel to all 9 DRAM chips. The 8 data lines are connected to the 8 data DRAM chips. The data bus is connected not only to the data DRAM chips, but also to the parity generater/checker chip.

When the microprocessor writes a byte of information to the DRAM chips, it is presented to both the DRAM chips and to the parity generator/checker. During a memory write operation, parity is generated and written into the parity DRAM chip. Parity is checked for correctness during memory reads (as described further on), but not during memory write operations.

When the data byte is presented to the parity generator/checker chip during a write operation, it checks for an even number of 1 bits in the data byte. If the number is even, the parity generator places a 0 on the PARITY line going to the parity DRAM chip. The parity bit and the data byte are simultaneously written into the same address within the parity DRAM and the data DRAM. That means that a total of 9 bits of information is written into the addressed memory location during a write operation. If the parity generator does not detect an even number of 1 bits in the data byte being written to the data DRAM, it places a

1 on the PARITY line to the parity DRAM. The total number of 1 bits in the 9-bit pattern written into the addressed memory location is therefore always an even number of 1 bits. Thus, the parity generator's job is to force the 9-bit pattern written into memory to always consist of an even number of 1 bits.

When the data is later read back from memory, the 9 bits of information are driven out onto the data bus and the parity line by the data and parity DRAMs. The data byte is sent back to the microprocessor over the data bus and is also presented to the parity generator/checker, now acting as a parity checker, rather than a parity generator. In addition to the 8 data bits being presented to the parity checker, the parity bit is also being presented to it. The parity checker examines the 9-bit pattern and tests it to see if it contains the necessary even number of 1 bits.

If it does not contain an even number of 1 bits, an error has occurred and the parity check logic generates a parity error. The parity error causes a non-maskable interrupt (NMI) request to the microprocessor, and the microprocessor is forced to jump to the NMI interrupt service routine. In this routine, the programmer performs an I/O read from System Control B at I/O address 0061_h to ascertain the cause of the NMI. If bit 7 in the return byte is set to a 1, a parity check was encountered while reading from system board DRAM memory. The NMI routine then reports a DRAM parity error on the screen.

Page Mode and Static Column (SCRAM) DRAM

The Model 70 Types 1 (16MHz) and 2 (20MHz) and the Model 80 Type 2 (20MHz) incorporate either **page mode** or **static column (SCRAM)** system board memory. Although this is not explicitly stated in the IBM PS/2 Technical Reference Guide, the access times quoted in the Specifications section of the Model 70 and 80 Technical Reference Guide show quite clearly that this is the case. Table 21-1 illustrates these specifications.

During the following discussion, it will become clear that either page mode or SCRAM memory is utilized in these systems. The terminology and access times quoted in Table 21-1 are explained.

Page Mode DRAM

Page Mode DRAM is just a variation on standard DRAM memory. In most respects its operation is identical. Sequential page mode DRAM

TABLE 21-1 Model 70/80 Memory Access Times

Model	Memory Read (Page Hit)	Memory Read (Page Miss)	Memory Write (Page Hit)	Memory Write (Page Miss)
70-1	125ns	250ns	187.5ns	250ns
70-2	100ns	200ns	150ns	200ns
80-2	100ns	200ns	150ns	200ns

locations are laid out or distributed sequentially along a row. Location 0 in a page mode DRAM chip is located in row 0, column 0; location 1 is located in row 0, column 1; location 2 at row 0, column 2, and so on.

Sequential locations within a row are accessed if the currently executing program is performing sequential memory read operations. Since most program execution is sequential in nature (in-line code fetches), program execution very often proceeds along a row of memory. At the end of a row in a page mode DRAM chip, the next sequential location is in column 0 at the beginning of the next row. Subsequent locations are located along that row. For example, a 1Mbit (1 megabit) page mode DRAM chip consists of a 1,024 by 1,024 row/column matrix. This means that each row contains 1,024 locations. The microprocessor can perform 1,024 memory accesses within the row before having to cross over into the next row. The original designers of page mode DRAM called it by that name because they considered one row of RAM memory to be a page of DRAM memory.

In a standard DRAM chip, a memory location is addressed in the following fashion.

1. The row address is placed on the memory address bus.
2. The RAS# line is activated.
3. RAS/CAS delay ensures proper operation.
4. The column address is placed on the memory address bus.
5. The CAS# line is activated.

At this point, the DRAM chip has the row and the column address and can therefore identify the addressed memory location. The data transfer can be performed.

Figure 21-13 illustrates the DRAM addressing logic. To take full advantage of the operational characteristics of page mode DRAM chips,

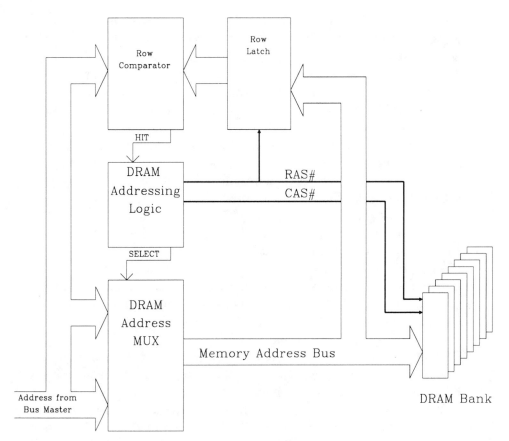

FIGURE 21-13 Page Mode DRAM Support Logic

some external support logic is necessary. This support consists of a **row latch** and a **row comparator**.

The first access to a page mode DRAM is identical to that for a standard DRAM. The row address is placed on the memory address bus and RAS# is activated. When RAS# is activated in a page mode DRAM system, the DRAM chips latch the row address and the row address is also latched into the row latch that is external to the DRAM chips.

The output of the row latch is applied to one side of the row comparator. After the RAS/CAS delay has elapsed, the DRAM addressing logic places the column address on the memory address bus and activates CAS#. This causes the column address to be latched by the DRAM. Up until this point, the page mode DRAM addressing scheme is identical to that for standard DRAM.

One other ingredient that is necessary for the page mode DRAM architecture to work correctly is the address pipelining capability of the

80286 and 80386 microprocessors. Both the 80286 and the 80386 microprocessors can place the address for the upcoming bus cycle on the address bus during the current bus cycle.

The row comparator compares the row address currently held by the row latch to the portion of the address bus that contains the row address for the upcoming DRAM access. If they are equal, it means that the upcoming DRAM access will be within the same row (or page) within the page mode DRAM chips. This is a page hit (see Table 21-1). When the row comparator detects that they are equal, it informs the DRAM addressing logic. The DRAM addressing logic responds by keeping RAS# active at the end of the current bus cycle.

The continued activation of RAS# tells the page mode DRAM chips to remember the previously latched row address because the upcoming access to going to be within the same row. Since the page mode DRAM chip already has the row address, the new column address can immediately be gated through the DRAM addressing multiplexer (MUX) onto the memory address bus and CAS# activated. This commands the DRAM chips to latch the new column address.

When sequential accesses fall within the same row of page mode DRAM memory, it is unnecessary to wait for the RAS/CAS delay to elapse before giving the DRAM chip the next column address. Since the RAS/CAS delay is approximately 50 percent of the overall access time for the DRAM chips, the access time can effectively be cut in half by eliminating this delay. For example, page mode DRAM chips rated at 100ns per access require 100ns for the first access, but subsequent sequential accesses within the same row can be performed in approximately 50ns. As long as subsequent, back-to-back memory reads are within the same row, the RAS# line stays active throughout multiple accesses. New column addresses appear on the memory address bus and CAS# is set active once for each new column address.

When the row comparator detects that the upcoming bus cycle will access a row other than the one internally latched within the DRAM chips, it must instruct the page mode DRAM chips to forget the currently latched row address. This is accomplished by letting RAS# go inactive and is called a page miss (see Table 21-1).

The next access is exactly the same as a standard DRAM access. The new row address must be sent to the DRAMs and latched, followed by the RAS/CAS delay and the latching of the column address. If, however, subsequent accesses past that point are within the same row, the memory logic can cut the access time in half by again doing away with RAS# and the RAS/CAS delay.

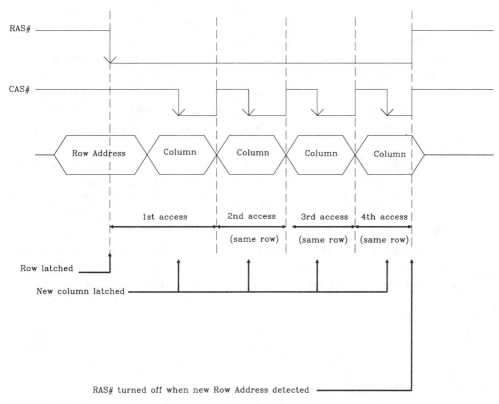

FIGURE 21-14   Page Mode DRAM RAS/CAS Timing

Page mode DRAM takes advantage of one very important characteristic of any microprocessor, namely its continual fetching of instructions. Since the majority of program execution is sequential in nature (in-line code fetches), program execution very often proceeds along a row of memory. A series of memory reads from locations located within the same row can take place quickly because the DRAM access time is cut approximately in half by eliminating RAS# and the RAS/CAS delay.

Anything that can be done to increase the rate at which instructions are sent to the microprocessor has a substantial impact on the overall performance of application programs. Any application program that tends to read large blocks of data from page mode DRAM memory sequentially also takes advantage of this architecture.

Static Column RAM (SCRAM)

Static Column RAM (SCRAM) probably has one of the most misleading names in the industry. Many people believe that static column RAM is a form of **static RAM**, but it is not. (Static RAM is discussed later in this chapter.) Actually, static column RAM is another form of DRAM memory that is so similar to page mode DRAM that the two are frequently confused in trade articles. Just like page mode DRAM, SCRAM is structured with sequential memory locations distributed along a row and requires the same external support logic as page mode RAM (that is, it requires a row latch and a row comparator and takes advantage of address pipelining).

The only difference between the two technologies lies in how SCRAM recognizes that a new column address has been presented to it. Whereas page mode DRAM requires that CAS# be activated each time a new column address is presented to it, SCRAM is slightly more intelligent.

Figure 21-15 illustrates SCRAM address timing. When the SCRAM chip detects RAS# remaining active from one access to another, it recognizes that it will not be receiving a new row address, only a

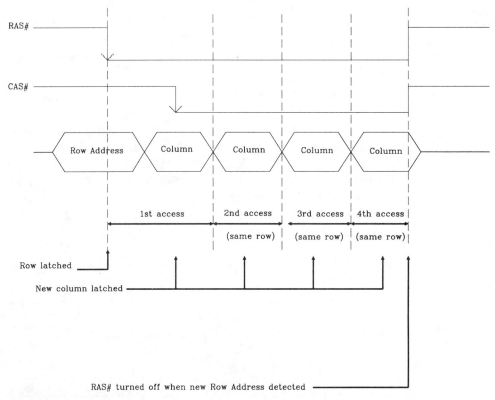

FIGURE 21-15 SCRAM Access Timing

column address. It then observes the memory address bus. When it sees the value on the address lines begin to change, it interprets this as a new column address appearing and waits a predetermined length of time for the column address to stabilize. It then generates its own CAS internally, latching the column address.

It is possible to design a memory subsystem that accommodates either SCRAM or page mode DRAM chips. Although the SCRAM chip does not need to have CAS# activated each time a new column address is presented to it, it still operates properly if CAS# is activated. As a result, a memory subsystem designed for page mode DRAM may also work with SCRAM.

Static RAM (SRAM)

Unlike DRAM, which uses capacitors to store information, static RAM (SRAM) uses single-bit latches (D-flip flops). Consequently, SRAM memory does not require refreshing at regular intervals to maintain the information stored in memory.

Once a bit of information has been written into one of these flip-flops, the SRAM chip continues to hold the data as long as power is applied to the SRAM chip. The information does not degrade over a period of time as it does with DRAM. SRAM is called static because the information written into it remains static without being refreshed at regular intervals.

Another important characteristic of SRAM is its relatively short access time. This is mainly due to the fact that the SRAM receives the entire address at once rather than requiring the address in two steps (as with DRAMs). Once chip-selected, the SRAM uses the address on its address inputs to identify the addressed memory location and the data transfer takes place.

Although SRAM is typically much faster than DRAM memory, it is cost-prohibitive to populate an entire system with it. SRAM chips typically cost ten times more than DRAMs, are physically larger, consume more power, and generate more heat. All of these factors, taken collectively, add substantially to the overall cost of a system. In the faster 80386- and 80486-based systems, limited amounts of high-speed SRAM are used as cache memory to improve the microprocessor's overall transfer rate when addressing memory. This subject is covered in Chapter 23.

Interleaved Memory Architecture

Interleaved memory architecture is another method that takes advantage of the sequential nature of program execution. The problem addressed by the interleaved memory architecture is the period of time the microprocessor is forced to wait when performing back-to-back accesses to the same DRAM chip. This wait is necessary because the DRAM chip is charging back up again after a destructive read. This is referred to as the pre-charge delay.

When an interleaved memory architecture is used, what would ordinarily be one bank of DRAM memory is split up into two banks. This is illustrated in Figure 21-16. In an 80386-based system, the microprocessor can fetch a doubleword (4 bytes) per bus cycle. The memory designer arranges the memory so that the doubleword consisting of the first four memory locations, locations 00000000_h through 00000003_h, is

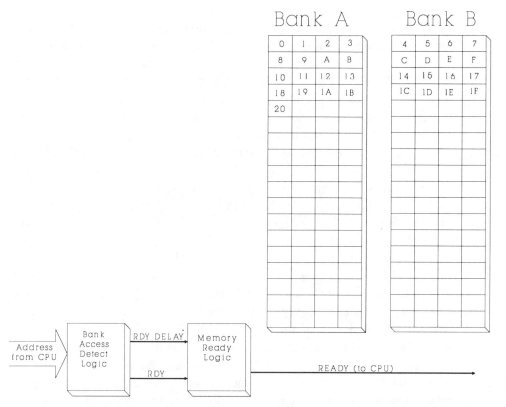

FIGURE 21-16   Interleaved Memory Architecture

physically located in DRAM Bank A. The second doubleword, consisting of locations 00000004_h through 00000007_h, is physically located in DRAM Bank B. The next doubleword is physically located in DRAM Bank A and consists of locations 00000008_h through $0000000B_h$. The following doubleword is physically located in DRAM Bank B and consists of locations $0000000C_h$ through $0000000F_h$, and so on.

Assume that the 80386 microprocessor has just fetched an instruction from the doubleword starting at location 00000000_h in DRAM Bank A. That means that the microprocessor will more than likely fetch the next instruction from the doubleword starting at memory address 00000004_h in DRAM Bank B. While the microprocessor is performing the second instruction prefetch from the doubleword in Bank B, the DRAMs that make up Bank A are going through pre-charge delay and charging back up again.

When the microprocessor completes the fetch from the doubleword in Bank B, the next instruction fetch is more than likely going to be from the next doubleword in Bank A starting at location 00000008_h. While the microprocessor is fetching the third doubleword from Bank A, the DRAMs that make up Bank B will be charging back up again.

The microprocessor is able to perform back-to-back read operations (in this case, instruction fetches) without waiting for the pre-charge delay. The only times that the microprocessor must wait for the pre-charge delay to elapse is when the next memory access is within the same bank as the previous access. This occurs when a jump instruction instructs the microprocessor to fetch its next instruction from a location residing in the same bank from which the previous instruction was read. It also occurs when the currently executing instruction instructs the microprocessor to read data from a memory location within the same bank as the previous access.

Figure 21-16 illustrates the interleaved memory architecture support logic. Support logic within the interleaved memory logic keeps track of which bank was accessed last. Using address pipelining, this logic can detect that the upcoming access is from the same bank or the other bank. If it is from the other bank, the memory logic need not allow for the pre-charge delay and can let the microprocessor access it immediately. On the other hand, if the upcoming access is within the same bank, the memory logic keeps the READY line inactive until the pre-charge delay has elapsed. The memory logic then sets READY active, lets the current bus cycle end, and enables the microprocessor to safely begin the next bus cycle within the same bank.

Summary

The RAM memory used in the PS/2 product line consists of two basic types: Dynamic RAM (DRAM) and Static RAM (SRAM). All of the PS/2 products utilize DRAM memory to populate up to 16MB of main memory. In addition, some of the 80386- and 80486-based PS/2 products utilize a relatively small amount of SRAM memory to provide fast access cache memory for the system board microprocessor. Cache memory is described in detail in Chapter 23.

DRAM memory has relatively slow access time due to its requirement that the address be provided in two segments, row and column, separated by a delay. Some types of DRAM memory, namely page mode and SCRAM, allow faster access when the current bus master is accessing sequential memory locations.

DRAM memory requires the inclusion of special support logic that handles the translation of the current bus master's address to the row/column format expected by the DRAMs. Dynamic RAM must be refreshed on a periodic basis or it begins to lose information. PS/2 products incorporate logic that automatically refresh DRAM memory. DRAMs are organized in banks so that the current bus master can read or write one byte or multiple bytes during each bus cycle. The PS/2 products also incorporate parity checking logic that verifies the correctness of the data read from DRAM memory.

SRAM memory provides faster access times because it requires neither the division of the address into a row and column nor the intervening RAS/CAS delay.

Interleaved memory architecture is used to speed up access to sequential DRAM memory locations. What would ordinarily be one bank of DRAM memory is split up into two banks. Support logic within the interleaved memory logic keeps track of which bank was accessed last. Using address pipelining, the logic can detect that the upcoming access is from the same bank or the other bank. If it is from the other bank, the memory logic need not allow for the pre-charge delay and can let the microprocessor access it immediately.

System Board
RAM Memory

Objective: This chapter provides a description of the various DRAM memory configurations found on PS/2 system boards.

Model 50 Series

The Model 50 and the 50Z differ only in the speed and width of the DRAM memory utilized on the system board. The following two sections describe the differences between the two.

Model 50

The Model 50 system board DRAM memory subsystem is quite inefficient for two reasons.

1. The IBM PS/2 Technical Reference Guide states that the Model 50's system board DRAM uses timing similar to 150ns Hitachi DRAMs. This results in the DRAM performing with 1-wait state.
2. The system board DRAM is an 8-bit device.

The Model 50 has two memory module connectors located on the system board. A 512KB memory module can be inserted in each of these connectors, yielding a maximum of 1MB of DRAM memory on the system board. Table 22-1 defines the signals found on each of these connectors.

The 80286 microprocessor running at 10MHz performs a 1-wait state bus cycle in 300ns. This results in 3.33 million transfers per second when accessing the 8-bit system board DRAM memory. Since the system board DRAM is only an 8-bit device, the microprocessor can read or write only 1 byte per transfer, resulting in a maximum transfer rate of 3.33MB/second.

Model 50Z

The Model 50Z is an improved version of Model 50. All of the improvements relate to the system board DRAM memory subsystem.

1. The 50Z system board DRAM memory has been upgraded from an 8-bit to a 16-bit device, allowing the 80286 microprocessor to transfer 2 bytes during each bus cycle.

TABLE 22-1   The Model 50 Memory Module Signals

Signal(s)	Description
D0:D7	Only the microprocessor's lower data path is connected to the memory module, thereby making system DRAM memory an 8-bit device. This severely limits its performance because the 16-bit 80286 microprocessor can read or write only 1 byte per bus cycle.
Parity Bit	This is the parity DRAM's data line.
A0:A8	This is the memory address bus. The fact that it is 9 bits wide means that the DRAM addressing logic can supply the DRAMs with any row or column address in the range from 0 through 511. Consequently, the DRAM on the memory modules is 256KB DRAM (512 rows x 512 columns). Since each memory module contains 512KB of DRAM, there are two 256KB banks of DRAM on each memory module.
WS#	Write strobe. This would more aptly be called the read/write control line. When high, it tells the DRAM that a memory read bus cycle is in progress; when low, a write is in progress.
CAS#	Column address strobe. When CAS# goes active, it causes the DRAM to latch the column address being presented to it on the memory address bus. This CAS# line goes to both banks of DRAM on a memory module.
RAS0, RAS1	Row address strobe for DRAM banks 0 and 1. RAS0 goes to DRAM bank 0 on the memory module, and RAS1 goes to bank 1. When one of these RAS lines goes active, it causes the DRAM to latch the row address being presented to it on the memory address bus.
Presence Detect 0 Presence Detect 1	Presence detect lines. During POST, these bits are checked to ensure that 1MB of DRAM is present in the two memory module connectors.

2. The 50Z can support either 1MB or 2MB of system board DRAM memory, as opposed to a 1MB limit for the Model 50.

3. The 50Z can support either 120ns or 85ns DRAM memory modules.

4. The 50Z can automatically detect the size and speed of memory module installed.

5. The 50Z can automatically enable or disable 1MB areas of system board DRAM memory.

The 50Z has one memory module connector located on the system board. Either a 1MB or a 2MB memory module can be inserted in this connector, yielding a maximum of 2MB of DRAM memory on the system board. Table 22-2 defines the signals found on this connector.

The 80286 microprocessor running at 10MHz performs a 0-wait state bus cycle in 200ns. This results in 5 million transfers per second when accessing the 16-bit system board DRAM memory. Since the system board DRAM is a 16-bit device, the microprocessor can read or write 2 bytes per transfer, resulting in a maximum transfer rate of 10MB/second.

Model 55SX

The Model 55SX system board DRAM memory consists of up to two memory modules of either 1MB or 2MB each, providing a maximum of 4MB of DRAM on the system board.

The IBM specifications state that the system board DRAM memory performs in the 0 to 2 wait state range. This means that either page mode or SCRAM memory is utilized, providing:

- 0-wait state accesses for sequential read accesses within the same row, or page, of memory

- 1-wait state accesses for sequential write accesses within the same row, or page, of memory

- 2-wait state access for accesses in different rows of memory

As of this printing, IBM has not published the memory module connector signal list.

The 80386SX microprocessor running at 16MHz performs a 0-wait state bus cycle in 125ns. This results in 8 million transfers per second when accessing the 16-bit system board DRAM memory. Since the system board DRAM is a 16-bit device, the microprocessor can read or write 2 bytes per transfer, resulting in a maximum transfer rate of 16MB/second.

TABLE 22-2 The Model 50Z Memory Module Signals

Signal(s)	Description
D0:D31	Although this memory module connector provides pins for D0:D31, the memory modules used in the 80286-based 50Z are 16-bit devices using only D0:D15.
Parity Data 0	This is the parity data bit associated with the lower data path, D0:D7, and even-addressed DRAM locations.
Parity Data 1	This is the parity data bit associated with the upper data path, D8:D15, and odd-addressed DRAM locations.
Parity Data 2	Not used.
Parity Data 3	Not used.
A0:A8	This is the memory address bus. The fact that it is 9 bits wide means that the DRAM addressing logic can supply the DRAMs with any row or column address in the range from 0 through 511. This means that the DRAM on the memory modules is 256KB DRAM (512 rows x 512 columns).
WE	Write enable. This would more aptly be called the read/write control line. When low, it tells DRAM that a memory read bus cycle is in progress; when high, a write is in progress.
CASP	This is the column address strobe line for the parity DRAM on the memory module. When CASP goes active, it causes the parity DRAM to latch the column address being presented to it on the memory address bus.
CAS0	Column address strobe. When CAS0 goes active, it causes DRAM bank 0 to latch the column address being presented to it on the memory address bus.
CAS1	Column address strobe. When CAS1 goes active, it causes DRAM bank 1 to latch the column address being presented to it on the memory address bus.
CAS2	Column address strobe. When CAS2 goes active, it causes DRAM bank 2 to latch the column address being presented to it on the memory address bus.
CAS3	Column address strobe. When CAS3 goes active, it causes DRAM bank 3 to latch the column address being presented to it on the memory address bus.

TABLE 22-2 Continued

Signal(s)	Description
RAS0	Row address strobe 0. When RAS0 goes active, it causes DRAM banks 0 and 2 to latch the row address being presented to them on the memory address bus.
RAS1	Row address strobe 1. When RAS1 goes active, it causes DRAM banks 1 and 3 to latch the row address being presented to them on the memory address bus.
RAS2	Not used.
RAS3	Not used.
Presence Detect	Presence detect lines 0 through 3. During the POST, these bits are checked to determine the size and speed of DRAM on the installed memory module. Table 22-3 describes their meaning.
Block Select	Block select lines 0 through 3. During the POST, these control lines are used to selectively enable or disable 1MB blocks of DRAM on the memory module.

TABLE 22-3 The Model 50Z Memory Module Presence Detect Lines

Interpretation	PD0	PD1	PD2	PD3
1MB, 120ns memory module	0	1	1	1
1MB, 85ns memory module	0	1	1	0
2MB, 85ns memory module	1	0	1	0

Model 60

The Model 60 system board DRAM memory subsystem is quite inefficient for two reasons.

1. The IBM PS/2 Technical Reference Guide states that the Model 60's system board DRAM uses timing similar to 150ns Hitachi DRAMs. This results in one wait state operation.

2. The system board DRAM is an 8-bit device.

The Model 60 has four memory module connectors located on the system board. A 256KB memory module can be inserted in each of these connectors, yielding a maximum of 1MB of DRAM memory on the system board. Table 22-4 defines the signals found on each of these connectors.

TABLE 22-4   The Model 60 Memory Module Signals

Signal(s)	Description
D0:D7	Only the microprocessor's lower data path is connected to the memory module, making system DRAM memory an 8-bit device. This severely limits its performance because the 16-bit 80286 microprocessor can read or write only 1 byte per bus cycle.
Parity Bit	This is the parity DRAM's data line.
A0:A8	This is the memory address bus. The fact that it is 9 bits wide means that the DRAM addressing logic can supply the DRAMs with any row or column address in the range from 0 through 511. This means that the DRAM on the memory modules is 256KB DRAM (512 rows x 512 columns). Since each memory module contains 256KB of DRAM, there is one 256KB bank of DRAM on each memory module.
WS#	Write strobe. This would more aptly be called the read/write control line. When high, it tells the DRAM that a memory read bus cycle is in progress; when low, a write is in progress.
CAS#	Column address strobe. When CAS# goes active, it causes the DRAM to latch the column address being presented to it on the memory address bus. This CAS# line goes to both banks of DRAM on a memory module.
RAS	Row address strobe for the DRAM Banks. When RAS goes active, it causes the DRAM to latch the row address being presented to it on the memory address bus. **See Note 1.**
Presence Detect 0 Presence Detect 1	Presence detect lines. During POST, these bits are checked to ensure that 1MB of DRAM is present in the four memory module connectors.

Note 1: RAS is not shown as attached to the memory module connector in the IBM PS/2 Technical Reference Guide, but it should be. DRAM memory will not work without both a RAS and a CAS.

The 80286 microprocessor running at 10MHz performs a 1-wait state bus cycle in 300ns. This results in 3.33 million transfers per second when accessing the 8-bit system board DRAM memory. Since the system board DRAM is only an 8-bit device, the microprocessor can read or write only 1-byte per transfer, resulting in a maximum transfer rate of 3.33MB/second.

Model 65SX

The Model 65SX has two memory module connectors on the system board, each of which can accept a 2MB DRAM memory module. This yields a maximum of 4MB of DRAM on the system board.

The DRAM used is 100ns access time page mode or SCRAM memory, as is evidenced by the quoted 0- to 2-wait state performance. The DRAM yields the following access times:

1. 0-wait state accesses for sequential read accesses within the same row, or page, of memory.

2. 1-wait state accesses for sequential write accesses within the same row, or page, of memory.

3. 2-wait state access for accesses in different rows of memory.

As of this printing, IBM has not published the Technical Reference Guide for the 65SX.

The 80386SX microprocessor running at 16MHz performs a 0-wait state bus cycle in 125ns. This results in 8 million transfers per second when accessing the 16-bit system board DRAM memory. Since the system board DRAM is a 16-bit device, the microprocessor can read or write 2 bytes per transfer, resulting in a maximum transfer rate of 16MB/second.

Model 70 Series

The Model 70 series includes the 16MHz Model 70E, the 20MHz Model 70, and the 25MHz Model 70A. The following sections describe the system board DRAM memory configurations of each.

Model 70E (16MHz)

The Model 70E is based on the 80386 microprocessor running at 16MHz. It has three memory module connectors, each of which can contain either a 1MB or 2MB memory module. This yields a maximum of 6MB of DRAM on the system board. The memory modules are populated with 100ns page mode or SCRAM memory. The DRAM yields the following access times:

1. 0-wait state accesses for sequential read accesses within the same row, or page, of memory.
2. 1-wait state accesses for sequential write accesses within the same row, or page, of memory.
3. 2-wait state access for accesses in different rows of memory.

Table 22-5 defines the signals found on each of these connectors.

The 80386 microprocessor running at 16MHz performs a 0-wait state bus cycle in 125ns. This results in 8 million transfers per second when accessing the 32-bit system board DRAM memory. Since the system board DRAM is a 32-bit device, the microprocessor can read or write 4 bytes per transfer, resulting in a maximum transfer rate of 32MB/second.

Model 70 (20MHz)

The Model 70 is based on the 80386 microprocessor running at 20MHz. It has three memory module connectors, each of which can contain either a 1MB or 2MB memory module. This yields a maximum of 6MB of DRAM on the system board. The memory modules are populated with 100ns or 85ns page mode or SCRAM memory. The DRAM yields the following access times:

1. 0-wait state accesses for sequential read accesses within the same row, or page, of memory.
2. 1-wait state accesses for sequential write accesses within the same row, or page, of memory.
3. 2-wait state access for accesses in different rows of memory.

Table 22-5 defines the signals found on each of these connectors.

TABLE 22-5   The Model 70 Memory Module Signals

Signal(s)	Description
D0:D31	The system board DRAM memory is a 32-bit device connected to all four 8-bit data paths. This means the microprocessor can transfer 4 bytes per bus cycle when communicating with system board DRAM memory.
Parity Data 0	This is the parity data bit associated with the lower data path, D0:D7, and the first location (byte 0) in a doubleword.
Parity Data 1	This is the parity data bit associated with the second data path, D8:D15, and the second location (byte 1) in a doubleword.
Parity Data 2	This is the parity data bit associated with the third data path, D16:D23, and the third location (byte 2) in a doubleword.
Parity Data 3	This is the parity data bit associated with the fourth data path, D24:D31, and the fourth location (byte 3) in a doubleword.
A0:A8	This is the memory address bus. The fact that it is 9 bits wide means that the DRAM addressing logic can supply the DRAMs with any row or column address in the range from 0 through 511. This means that the DRAM on the memory modules is 256KB DRAM (512 rows x 512 columns).
WE	Write enable. This would more aptly be called the read/write control line. When low, it tells DRAM that a memory read bus cycle is in progress; when high, a write is in progress.
CASP#	This is the column address strobe line for the parity DRAM on the memory module. When CASP# goes active, it causes the parity DRAM to latch the column address being presented to it on the memory address bus.
CAS0	Column address strobe. When CAS0 goes active, it causes DRAM bank 0 to latch the column address being presented to it on the memory address bus.
CAS1	Column address strobe. When CAS1 goes active, it causes DRAM bank 1 to latch the column address being presented to it on the memory address bus.

TABLE 22-5   Continued

Signal(s)	Description
CAS2	Column address strobe. When CAS2 goes active, it causes DRAM bank 2 to latch the column address being presented to it on the memory address bus.
CAS3	Column address strobe. When CAS3 goes active, it causes DRAM bank 3 to latch the column address being presented to it on the memory address bus.
RAS0	Row address strobe 0. When RAS0 goes active, it causes DRAM bank 0 to latch the row address being presented to it on the memory address bus.
RAS1	Row address strobe 1. When RAS1 goes active, it causes DRAM bank 1 to latch the row address being presented to it on the memory address bus.
RAS2	Row address strobe 2. When RAS2 goes active, it causes DRAM bank 2 to latch the row address being presented to it on the memory address bus.
RAS3	Row address strobe 3. When RAS3 goes active, it causes DRAM bank 3 to latch the row address being presented to it on the memory address bus.
Presence Detect	Presence detect lines 0 through 3. During the POST, these bits are checked to determine the size and speed of DRAM on the installed memory module. Table 22-6 describes their meaning.
Block Select	Block select lines 0 through 3. During the POST, these control lines are used to selectively enable or disable 1MB blocks of DRAM on the memory module.

The 80386 microprocessor running at 20MHz performs a 0-wait state bus cycle in 100ns. This results in 10 million transfers per second when accessing the 32-bit system board DRAM memory. Since the system board DRAM is a 32-bit device, the microprocessor can read or write 4 bytes per transfer, resulting in a maximum transfer rate of 40MB/second.

Model 70A (25MHz)

The Model 70A is based on the 80386 microprocessor running at 25MHz. It has two memory module connectors, each of which can contain a

TABLE 22-6   The Model 70 Memory Module Presence Detect
Lines

Interpretation	PD0	PD1	PD2	PD3
1MB, 100ns memory module	0	1	0	0
1MB, 85ns memory module	0	1	1	0
2MB, 85ns memory module	1	0	1	0

2MB or 4MB memory module. This yields a maximum of 8MB of DRAM on the system board. The memory modules are populated with 80ns DRAM memory.

As of this printing, IBM has not published the memory module connector signal list.

The Model 70A also incorporates a 64KB static RAM, or SRAM, cache and an Intel 82385 cache memory controller. When a read hit occurs, the requested information is supplied to the microprocessor at 0-wait states.

The 80386 microprocessor running at 25MHz performs a 0-wait state bus cycle in 80ns. This results in 12.5 million transfers per second when accessing the 32-bit cache memory. Since the cache memory is a 32-bit device, the microprocessor can read or write 4 bytes per transfer, resulting in a maximum transfer rate of 50MB/second.

Model P70 (Portable)

The Model P70 portable is based on the 80386 microprocessor running at 20MHz. It has four memory module connectors, each of which can contain a 2MB or 4MB memory module. This yields a maximum of 8MB of DRAM on the system board. The memory modules are populated with 85ns page mode or SCRAM memory. The DRAM yields the following access times:

1. 0-wait state accesses for sequential read accesses within the same row, or page, of memory.

2. 1-wait state accesses for sequential write accesses within the same row, or page, of memory.

3. 2-wait state access for accesses in different rows of memory.

As of this printing, IBM has not published the memory module connector signal list.

The 80386 microprocessor running at 20MHz performs a 0-wait state bus cycle in 100ns. This results in 10 million transfers per second when accessing the 32-bit system board DRAM memory. Since the system board DRAM is a 32-bit device, the microprocessor can read or write 4 bytes per transfer, resulting in a maximum transfer rate of 40MB/second.

Model 80 Series

The Model 80 series includes the 16MHz Model 80, the 20MHz Model 80, and the 25MHz Model 80A. The following sections describe the system board DRAM memory configurations of each.

Model 80 (16MHz)

The 16MHz Model 80 is based on the 80386 microprocessor running at 16MHz. It has two memory module connectors, each of which can contain either a 1MB or 2MB memory module. This yields a maximum of 4MB of DRAM on the system board. The memory modules are populated with 80ns DRAM memory that operates at 1-wait state.

Table 22-7 defines the signals found on each of these connectors.

The 16MHz Model 80 requires a minimum of 1MB of functional DRAM memory installed in either memory module slot.

The 80386 microprocessor running at 16MHz performs a 1-wait state bus cycle in 187.5ns. This results in 5.33 million transfers per second when accessing the 32-bit system board DRAM memory. Since the system board DRAM is a 32-bit device, the microprocessor can read or write 4 bytes per transfer, resulting in a maximum transfer rate of 21.32MB/second.

Model 80 (20MHz)

The 20MHz Model 80 is based on the 80386 microprocessor running at 20MHz. It has two memory module connectors, each of which can contain either a 1MB or 2MB memory module. This yields a maximum of 4MB of DRAM on the system board. The memory modules are populated with 80ns page mode or SCRAM memory. The DRAM yields the following access times:

TABLE 22-7   The Model 80 Memory Module Signals

Signal(s)	Description
MD0:MD31	The system board DRAM memory is a 32-bit device connected to all four 8-bit data paths. This means the microprocessor can transfer 4 bytes per bus cycle when communicating with system board DRAM memory.
MDP0	This is the parity data bit associated with the lower data path, D0:D7, and the first location (byte 0) in a doubleword.
MDP1	This is the parity data bit associated with the second data path, D8:D15, and the second location (byte 1) in a doubleword.
MDP2	This is the parity data bit associated with the third data path, D16:D23, and the third location (byte 2) in a doubleword.
MDP3	This is the parity data bit associated with the fourth data path, D24:D31, and the fourth location (byte 3) in a doubleword.
MA0:MA8	This is the memory address bus. The fact that it is 9 bits wide means that the DRAM addressing logic can supply the DRAMs with any row or column address in the range from 0 through 511. This means that the DRAM on the memory modules is 256KB DRAM (512 rows x 512 columns).
MW#	Memory write. This would more aptly be called the read/write control line. When high, it tells DRAM that a memory read bus cycle is in progress; when low, a write is in progress.
RAS0#	Row address strobe 0. When RAS0# goes active, it causes DRAM bank 0 to latch the row address being presented to it on the memory address bus.
RAS1#	Row address strobe 1. When RAS1# goes active, it causes DRAM bank 1 to latch the row address being presented to it on the memory address bus.
RAS2#	Row address strobe 2. When RAS2# goes active, it causes DRAM bank 2 to latch the row address being presented to it on the memory address bus.
RAS3#	Row address strobe 3. When RAS3# goes active, it causes DRAM bank 3 to latch the row address being presented to it on the memory address bus.
CAS0#	Column address strobe. When CAS0# goes active, it causes DRAM bank 0 to latch the column address being presented to it on the memory address bus.

TABLE 22-7 Continued

Signal(s)	Description
CAS1#	Column address strobe. When CAS1# goes active, it causes DRAM bank 1 to latch the column address being presented to it on the memory address bus.
CAS2#	Column address strobe. When CAS2# goes active, it causes DRAM bank 2 to latch the column address being presented to it on the memory address bus.
CAS3#	Column address strobe. When CAS3# goes active, it causes DRAM bank 3 to latch the column address being presented to it on the memory address bus.
BE0#	This is the byte enable 0 line from the microprocessor. The 80386 microprocessor sets it active when it is performing a data transfer with the first location in the currently addressed doubleword over the lowest data path, D0:D7.
BE1#	This is the byte enable 1 line from the microprocessor. The 80386 microprocessor sets it active when it is performing a data transfer with the second location in the currently addressed doubleword over the second data path, D8:D15.
BE2#	This is the byte enable 2 line from the microprocessor. The 80386 microprocessor sets it active when it is performing a data transfer with the third location in the currently addressed doubleword over the third data path, D16:D23.
BE3#	This is the byte enable 3 line from the microprocessor. The 80386 microprocessor sets it active when it is performing a data transfer with the fourth location in the currently addressed doubleword over the fourth data path, D24:D31.
CASP#	This is the column address strobe line for the parity DRAM on the memory module. When CASP# goes active, it causes the parity DRAM to latch the column address being presented to it on the memory address bus.
R	This is the memory module present line. It is read through POS register 3 during the POST.
T	This is DRAM type bit. Its state reflects the speed of the DRAM installed in the memory module slot. It is read through POS register 3 during the POST.

1. 0-wait state accesses for sequential read accesses within the same row, or page, of memory.

2. 1-wait state accesses for sequential write accesses within the same row, or page, of memory.

3. 2-wait state access for accesses in different rows of memory.

Table 22-7 defines the signals found on each of these connectors.

The 20MHz Model 80 requires a minimum of 1MB of functional DRAM memory installed in memory module slot 1.

The 80386 microprocessor running at 20MHz performs a 0-wait state bus cycle in 100ns. This results in 10 million transfers per second when accessing the 32-bit system board DRAM memory. Since the system board DRAM is a 32-bit device, the microprocessor can read or write 4 bytes per transfer, resulting in a maximum transfer rate of 40MB/second.

Model 80A (25MHz)

The 25MHz Model 80A is based on the 80386 microprocessor running at 25MHz. It has two memory module connectors, each of which can contain either a 1MB or 2MB memory module. This yields a maximum of 4MB of DRAM on the system board. The memory modules are populated with 80ns DRAM memory. This yields a maximum of 8MB of DRAM on the system board.

As of this printing, IBM has not published the memory module connector signal list.

The Model 80A also incorporates a 64KB static RAM, or SRAM, cache and an Intel 82385 cache memory controller. When a read hit occurs, the requested information is supplied to the microprocessor at 0-wait states.

The 80386 microprocessor running at 25MHz performs a 0-wait state bus cycle in 80ns. This results in 12.5 million transfers per second when accessing the 32-bit cache memory. Since the cache memory is a 32-bit device, the microprocessor can read or 4 four bytes per transfer, resulting in a maximum transfer rate of 50MB/second.

Summary

Each of the PS/2 products allows at least 1MB of DRAM memory to be installed on the system board using special memory modules. The remainder of the system SRAM, up to 16MB total, must be installed in micro channel slots.

Although PS/2 products based on the 32-bit 80386 and 80486 microprocessors can address up to 4GB (4 billion bytes) of memory address space, the DMA controller used throughout the current PS/2 product line is attached only to the lower 24 address lines, A0:A23. This means that it can perform DMA transfers only in the lower 16MB memory address range.

The 25MHz PS/2 products are the only products that incorporate cache memory. The Intel 82385 cache memory controller is used in these systems.

Additional information on system memory can be found in Chapters 21 and 23 through 26. Information regarding shadow RAM, split memory and DRAM setup are covered in Chapter 14.

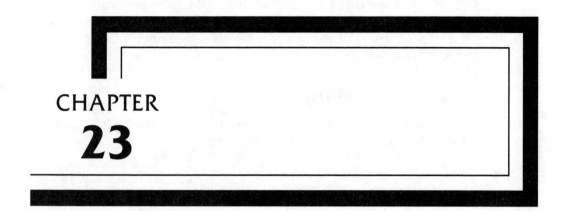

Cache Memory

Objectives: The PS/2 products based on 25MHz 80386 and 80486 microprocessors use cache memory to improve system performance. This chapter provides an introduction to cache systems in general and a detailed description of the Intel 82385 cache memory controller utilized in the PS/2 products.

Definitions for This Chapter

• The **cache directory** is used to keep track of the DRAM memory information currently stored in cache memory.

• The **cache memory** consists of a relatively small amount of fast access SRAM memory used to keep copies of data from DRAM memory.

• The **cache memory controller** copies information from DRAM memory into cache memory and maintains a directory of the information currently in cache memory.

• One of the most important goals of any cache memory controller is to maintain **coherency** between the DRAM memory and the copies in cache memory. They must always be mirror images.

• The cache memory controller's **FLUSH** input is activated to clear all cache directory entries.

• A **four-way set associative** directory structure keeps track of the information in four cache memory banks, or ways, using four directories.

• The cache memory controller's **hit rate** is the average percentage of 0-wait state memory reads that occur over a large number of memory accesses.

• The **least-recently used (LRU) algorithm** is used by the cache memory controller to decide which cache directory entry to use when storing information from a new memory page.

• The **least-recently used (LRU) switch** points to the oldest cache directory entry in the selected group of directory entries.

• A **line** of information is the fixed amount of data that a cache memory controller always fetches when accessing DRAM memory.

• A **line hit** occurs when a cache directory entry is checked and its tag valid bit is set, its tag field matches the currently addressed memory page address, and the line valid bit indicated by the currently addressed line is set.

• A **line miss** occurs when a cache directory entry is checked and its tag valid bit is set, its tag field matches the currently addressed memory page address, but the line valid bit indicated by the currently addressed line is not set.

• The **line valid bits** in a cache directory entry are used to indicate which lines from the respective set in this memory page are currently in cache memory.

• A **non-cacheable access** is a memory read from an area of memory that the cache memory controller cannot reliably keep track of.

• The cache memory controller views memory address space as consisting of a series of **pages** of a fixed length.

• A **posted write** is a write bus cycle that has been posted to (latched by) the posted write latch so that it can be run later.

• The **posted write latch** is used by the cache memory controller to memorize all of the information pertaining to a write bus cycle.

• A **read hit** occurs when the cache memory controller finds the requested information in the cache memory.

• A **read miss** occurs when the cache memory controller does not find the requested information in the cache memory.

• The cache memory controller views each page of memory address space as being subdivided into a fixed number of **sets**.

• The cache memory controller always **snoops** after surrendering its local buses to a bus master. This means that it observes the address bus and the bus cycle definition lines to see if the bus master is performing a memory write and altering the contents of a cached DRAM location.

- A **snoop hit** occurs when the cache memory controller sees that the current bus master is altering a DRAM location that has been cached.

- A **snoop miss** occurs when the cache memory controller observes a memory write bus cycle being performed by a bus master that does not alter a DRAM location that is cached.

- **Stale data** is data in cache memory that no longer matches the contents of its respective DRAM memory location.

- The **tag** is the same as the memory page address. It identifies the memory page currently being addressed.

- A **tag hit** occurs when a cache directory entry is checked and its tag valid bit is set and its tag field matches the currently addressed memory page address.

- A **tag miss** occurs when a cache directory entry is checked and either its tag valid bit is not set or its tag field does not match the currently addressed memory page address.

- A cache directory entry's **tag valid bit** is set to 1 to indicate that the entry is in use.

- A **two-way set associative** directory structure keeps track of the information in two cache memory banks, or ways, using two directories.

- A **way** is another word for a bank of cache memory.

- A **write hit** occurs when the cache memory controller has a copy of the target DRAM location during a memory write bus cycle.

- A **write miss** occurs when the cache memory controller does not have a copy of the target DRAM location during a memory write bus cycle.

- A cache memory controller with a **write through policy** always updates the copy in cache memory and the DRAM memory contents at the same time.

The Problem

When the IBM PC was introduced, it was based on the Intel 8088 microprocessor running at 4.77MHz. The 8088 took four ticks of its 4.77MHz PCLK to run a 0-wait state bus cycle; a 0-wait state bus cycle took 838ns (4 x 209ns = 838ns). Since virtually any DRAM or ROM on the market at the time could respond well within this period of time, wait states really were not an issue.

The access time of DRAM memory kept pace with the speed of the Intel processors up to and including the 16MHz version of the 80386 microprocessor. With the advent of the 20MHz 80386 microprocessor, however, the access times of available DRAM memory were being pushed to the limit. The PS/2 Models 70 and 80 running a 20MHz 80386 are rated at somewhere between 0- and 2-wait states for a DRAM memory access. This is because IBM used very fast access page mode or SCRAM memory that can respond quickly when sequential accesses are within the same page, or row, of the memory chips.

The Models 70 and 80 running a 25MHz 80386 or 80486, however, can run a 0-wait state bus cycle in 80ns, too fast for most DRAM memory available today. As a result, virtually every access to DRAM memory would involve one or more wait states, negating the speed advantage supplied by the 25MHz microprocessor.

One solution for this problem would be to populate the PS/2 with nothing but fast access SRAM memory. For several reasons, this solution is unacceptable.

- SRAM is typically ten times more expensive than DRAM memory.
- SRAM chips are typically larger than DRAMs, requiring more real estate for the same amount of memory.
- SRAMs consume more power than DRAMs and might require a more powerful and thus more expensive power supply.
- SRAMs generate more heat than DRAMs and might therefore require the inclusion of a larger cooling fan.

Introduction to Cache Memory Subsystems

The solution chosen by IBM and many other manufacturers of fast 80386 and 80486-based PCs is **cache memory**. Implementation of a cache memory subsystem is an attempt to achieve acceptable system cost and a high percentage of 0-wait state bus cycles when accessing DRAM memory.

A cache memory subsystem is implemented by populating main memory with relatively slow access, cheap DRAM, and also incorporating a relatively small amount of high cost, fast access SRAM into the system. The SRAM memory is referred to as cache memory and a **cache memory controller** attempts to maintain copies of information read from DRAM memory in the cache.

The cache memory controller uses a directory to keep track of the information it has copied into the cache memory. When the cache memory controller sees the microprocessor initiate a memory read bus cycle, it immediately checks its directory to see if it has a copy of the requested information in cache memory. If a copy is present, it reads the information from the cache, sends it back to the system board microprocessor over the microprocessor's data bus, and turns on the microprocessor's READY# signal. This is known as a **read hit**. The access can be completed in 0-wait states because the information is fetched from the fast access cache SRAM.

If, on the other hand, the cache memory controller checks its directory and sees it does not have a copy of the requested information in cache, it must then initiate a memory read bus cycle on its own buses to read the information from DRAM memory. This is known as a **read miss** and, due to the slow access time of the DRAM memory, entails wait states. The requested information is then sent back to the microprocessor to fulfill its request. In addition, the information is also copied into the cache memory by the cache memory controller and a **cache directory** entry is updated to reflect the presence of the new information.

On the surface, it may not be evident how this can speed up the microprocessor's memory accesses. Many programs, such as Lotus 1-2-3, contain program loops that are executed many times. (A program loop is a series of instructions that must be executed a number of times in succession to produce the desired results.) For example, Lotus 1-2-3 uses a program loop to recalculate spreadsheet cells. Depending on the number of calculations to be made during a Recalc, this program loop may need to be executed hundreds or even thousands of times.

Assume that the cache memory is empty. The first time the program loop is executed, the following series of events takes place:

1. The microprocessor initiates a memory read bus cycle to fetch the first instruction from memory.

2. The cache memory controller uses the memory address to check its directory to see if a copy of the requested information is already in the cache memory. Since the cache is initially empty, a copy does not exist and a read miss occurs.

3. The cache memory controller initiates a memory read bus cycle on its own buses to fetch the requested information (the instruction) from DRAM memory. This takes one or more wait states, depending on the access time of the DRAM.

4. The information from DRAM memory (the instruction) is sent back to the microprocessor and the cache memory controller also copies it into the cache memory and updates a cache directory entry to reflect the presence of the new information. No advantage was realized during this memory read because the information had to be read from slow DRAM memory.

6. Upon completing execution of the first instruction in the program loop, the microprocessor initiates a series of memory read bus cycles to fetch the remaining instructions in the program loop. If the cache is sufficiently large, all of the instructions in the program loop will be resident in cache memory after the last instruction in the loop has been read from DRAM memory and copied into the cache. Absolutely no advantage was realized during the first execution of this program loop.

7. The last instruction in a program loop is always an instruction to jump to the beginning of the loop and start over again.

8. When the microprocessor initiates the memory read bus cycle to fetch the first instruction again, the cache memory controller checks its cache directory and detects the presence of the requested information in cache memory. The cache memory controller immediately reads the information from the fast access SRAM that makes up the cache and sends it back to the microprocessor with no wait states incurred.

   The microprocessor is thus able to fetch and begin executing the instruction faster than it was able to the first time through the loop. This will prove true for the remaining instructions in the program loop as well. The second and subsequent times through the program loop, the microprocessor incurs no wait states in fetching the instructions, and the program runs substantially faster.

The following sections provide a detailed description of the cache memory architecture utilized in IBM PS/2 systems. It focuses on the Intel 82385, the cache memory controller used by IBM.

The Intel 82385 Cache Memory Controller Overview

Figure 23-1 illustrates the relationship of the cache memory controller to the remainder of the system. The cache memory controller resides between the system board microprocessor and the remainder of the system. The only device that the microprocessor can talk directly to without going through the cache memory controller is the Intel 80387 numeric coprocessor. The 80386 microprocessor is unaware of the 82385 cache memory controller.

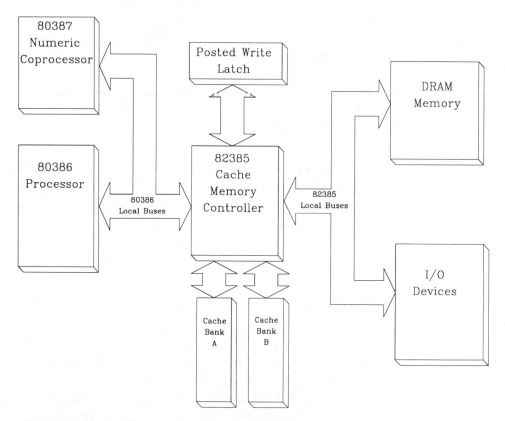

FIGURE 23-1   The Cache Memory Architecture

On one side, the 82385 is attached to the 80386 microprocessor's local buses (address, data, and control), and it can detect the type of bus cycle being initiated by the microprocessor. On the other side, the 82385 has a complete duplication of the 80386's buses. These are the 82385's local buses and are not connected to the 80386's buses in any way. The 80386 microprocessor can be fetching information from the cache memory or communicating with the 80387 numeric coprocessor while another bus master that has taken control of the 82385's local buses can be using them to transfer data simultaneously.

With the sole exception of the numeric coprocessor, the 80386 microprocessor is totally dependent on the 82385 cache memory controller to accomplish all communications with memory and I/O devices residing on the 82385's local buses. The 82385 also has another set of address, data, and control buses that it uses to communicate with cache memory, consisting of fast access SRAM memory.

Finally, the 82385 has a special set of buses it uses when the microprocessor is performing a write bus cycle. These buses are used to control logic referred to as the **posted write latch**.

Introduction to 82385 Operations

This section provides a description of each type of operation performed by the 82385 cache memory controller. Refer to Figure 23-1 throughout these discussions. The section following this one provides a more detailed description of each type of operation.

The Read Miss The following example instruction is used to demonstrate the series of actions that take place when a read miss occurs:

```
MOV AX,[0100]
```

Assume that the 80386 microprocessor's Data Segment register currently contains 0000_h and the processor is in real mode. This instruction tells the 80386 microprocessor to move the contents of memory locations 00000100_h and 00000101_h into the microprocessor's AX register (2 bytes because the target register is a 16-bit register).

When executed, the instruction causes the microprocessor to run a memory read bus cycle. Memory address 00000100_h is placed on A2:A31 of the microprocessor's local address bus, identifying the group of four locations (the doubleword) starting at memory location 00000100_h. The microprocessor also turns on BE0# and BE1# to request the contents of the first two locations in the doubleword, 00000100_h and 00000101_h. BE2# and BE3# are not turned on because the microprocessor does not require the contents of the last two locations in the doubleword, 00000102_h and 00000103_h.

1. When the 82385 detects the initiation of the memory read bus cycle on the 80386 microprocessor's local buses, it compares the memory address with those stored in its cache directory to determine if a copy of the requested information resides in cache memory. This check takes place during the 80386's address time, T_1.

2. If the requested information is not in cache memory, this is a read miss operation. The 82385 must fetch the requested information from DRAM memory by running a standard 80386-style bus cycle on the 82385's local buses. Since DRAM memory has such a slow access time, the resulting bus cycle will definitely entail one or more wait states.

3. Although the 80386 microprocessor turned on only two of its byte enable lines, BE0# and BE1#, when it placed the address on its local address bus, the 82385 always turns on all four of its byte enable lines when reading from DRAM memory. In other words, the 82385 always fetches a doubleword at a time when reading from DRAM memory; this is referred to as a **line** of information. In an effort to be more efficient, cache controllers always fetch a line of information whenever they are forced to read from slow DRAM memory. As noted above, the 82385's line size is 32-bits (a doubleword), but other cache memory controllers may use a different line size. For example, the cache memory controller built into the 80486 microprocessor has a line size of 16 bytes.

4. When the requested data comes back from DRAM memory over the 82385's local data bus, it is directed to the 80386 microprocessor's data bus to fulfill the microprocessor's request. The microprocessor's READY# input is then set active to tell the microprocessor that the requested data is present on its data bus.

5. At the same time, the line (doubleword) of information is stored in cache memory and a cache directory entry is updated to reflect the presence of the information in cache memory.

This completes the read miss operation. Since the requested data had to be read from slow DRAM memory, one or more wait states were incurred. A more detailed description of the cache directory lookup process can be found in this chapter in the section entitled "Cache Directory and Memory Usage."

The Read Hit

1. When the 82385 detects the initiation of the memory read bus cycle on the 80386 microprocessor's local buses, it compares the memory address with those stored in its cache directory to determine if a copy of the requested information resides in cache memory. This check takes place during the 80386's address time, T_1.

2. This is a read hit operation if the requested information is in cache memory.

3. The 82385 fetches the requested information from fast access cache memory and sends it back to the microprocessor over the system board microprocessor's local data bus.

4. The 82385 cache memory controller turns on the microprocessor's READY# input to indicate the presence of the requested data on the data bus.

5. The microprocessor reads the data when it samples READY# active at the end of data time (T_2).

This was a 0-wait state bus cycle because the data was retrieved from cache memory in two ticks of the microprocessor's PCLK, address time + data time.

The Write Miss and the Posted Write   When the microprocessor initiates a memory write bus cycle, the cache memory may or may not contain a copy of the target location's contents. This example of a memory write bus cycle assumes that it does not.

1. The microprocessor initiates a memory write bus cycle.

2. During the bus cycle's address time, T_1, the 82385 cache memory controller compares the memory address with those stored in its cache directory to determine if a copy of the target location is resident in cache memory.

3. This is a **write miss** operation if a copy does not exist.

4. The 82385 cache memory controller latches the data to be written, the memory address, and the bus cycle definition into the posted write latch. This is know as a **posted write**.

5. The 82385 sets the microprocessor's READY# input active, thereby tricking the microprocessor into believing that the memory write has been completed. This allows the microprocessor to perform 0-wait state memory write bus cycles when accessing DRAM memory.

6. Using the information latched into the posted write latch, the 82385 initiates the memory write bus cycle on its own local buses to accomplish the requested DRAM memory update.

If the microprocessor initiates another write bus cycle before the bus cycle in the posted write latch has been completed, the 82385 keeps the microprocessor's READY# input inactive until the first posted write has completed. This causes one or more wait states to be inserted into the second write bus cycle.

Having completed the posted write bus cycle on its local buses, the 82385 latches the information pertinent to the next write into the posted write latch and turns on the microprocessor's READY# input.

The Write Hit and Write Through Policy   When the microprocessor initiates a memory write bus cycle, the cache memory may or may not contain a copy of the target location's contents. This example of a memory write bus cycle assumes that it does.

1. The microprocessor initiates a memory write bus cycle.

2. During the bus cycle's address time, T_1, the 82385 cache memory controller compares the memory address with those stored in its cache directory to determine if a copy of the target location is resident in cache memory.

3. This is a **write hit** operation if a copy exists.

4. The 82385 cache memory controller latches the data to be written, the memory address, and the bus cycle definition into the posted write latch.

5. The 82385 sets the microprocessor's READY# input active, thereby tricking the microprocessor into believing that the memory write has been completed. This allows the micro-

processor to perform 0-wait state memory write bus cycles when accessing DRAM memory.

6. Using the information latched into the posted write latch, the 82385 initiates the memory write bus cycle on its own local buses to accomplish the requested DRAM memory update.

7. Simultaneously, the 82385 writes the data into the cache memory so that it will still match the contents of DRAM memory.

When a write hit occurs, the 82385 cache memory controller uses a **write through policy** to maintain **coherency** between DRAM and cache memory. Thus, the copy in cache is updated and the data is also written through to DRAM memory to ensure that they always match each other.

The I/O Write Because I/O operations are not cacheable, the cache memory controller will never attempt to maintain a copy of information read from I/O devices.

When the microprocessor initiates an I/O write bus cycle, the 82385 latches all of the bus cycle information into the posted write latch, and allows the microprocessor to think it is a 0-wait state bus cycle by turning on the microprocessor's READY# input. Using the information latched into the posted write latch, the 82385 initiates the I/O write bus cycle on its local buses to accomplish the requested I/O write.

The I/O Read As stated earlier, I/O operations are not cacheable. When the microprocessor initiates an I/O read bus cycle, the 82385 allows the bus cycle to immediately begin on its local buses. This bus cycle will entail one or more wait states due to the slowness of typical I/O devices. The data read from the I/O location(s) is routed to the 80386.

Bus Mastering and Snooping A device other than the system board microprocessor must become bus master when it requires the use of the buses to communicate with another device. Rather than assert HOLD to the microprocessor, however, it turns on the 82385's buffered hold request (BHOLD) input, thus forcing the cache memory controller to surrender its local buses. After disconnecting from its local buses, the 82385 turns on buffered hold acknowledge (BHLDA) to inform the requesting device that it is now bus master. This action introduces a potential problem. If the new bus master writes data to DRAM memory, it could cause mismatches, or a lack of coherency, between DRAM and copies of DRAM data in cache memory. The cache memory controller must have some way of handling this situation.

Upon becoming bus master, the new bus master begins a bus cycle. During the period of time that the bus master has control of the 82385's local buses, the 82385 **snoops.** It watches its local address bus and bus cycle definition lines to see if the bus master begins a memory write bus cycle. If it detects the start of a memory write bus cycle, the 82385 compares the memory address with the addresses stored in its cache directory to see if a copy of the target DRAM memory location exists in cache memory. If a copy exists, a **snoop hit** occurs. If a copy does not exist, a **snoop miss** occurs and the 82385 takes no further action.

In the case of a snoop hit, the current bus master is altering the contents of a DRAM memory location of which the cache is maintaining a copy. This could result in a lack of coherency between the cache copy and the DRAM's contents. Upon detecting a snoop hit, the 82385 marks the corresponding cache directory entry as invalid because the cache copy no longer matches the DRAM location's contents.

When the bus master has completed using the 82385's local buses, it surrenders the buses by turning off BHOLD. The 82385 then reassumes control of its buses and turns off BHLDA. If the microprocessor should attempt to read any of the DRAM memory locations that had caused snoop hits, read misses result because the corresponding cache directory entries were invalidated.

Concurrent Operations   A system designed around the 80386 microprocessor and the 82385 cache memory controller is capable of concurrent operation. In a best-case scenario, the 80386 microprocessor can be fetching and executing instructions from cache memory while the 82385's local buses are being used by another bus master (such as the DMA controller) to transfer data. The resulting concurrent operation can continue until the 82385 requires the use of its local buses to run a bus cycle.

Cache Directory and Memory Usage

The 82385's View of Memory   Figure 23-2 illustrates the concept of memory pages. The 82385 cache memory controller views the 80386's memory address space as a series of memory **pages**, each

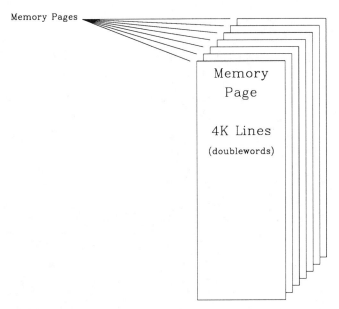

FIGURE 23-2 The 82385's View of Memory Address Space

consisting of 16KB. Since the 82385 always reads a doubleword, or line, of information from DRAM memory at a time, the 16KB page is actually viewed as a 4K doubleword memory page. The first page occupies the memory address space from 00000000_h–$00003FFF_h$, the second from 00004000_h–$00007FFF_h$, and so on.

Figure 23-3 illustrates the concept of sets and lines. The 82385 considers each 4K doubleword memory page to be divided into 512 **sets**, each consisting of eight lines, or doublewords. The sets are numbered 0 through 511 and the lines are numbered 0 through 7.

The Relationship Between the Cache Directory and DRAM Memory Refer to Figure 23-4. The 82385 cache memory controller contains two cache directories, referred to as Directories A and B. Their purpose is to keep track of the DRAM memory copies placed in cache memory. Each of these directories has 512 entries, numbered 0 through 511 and each directory entry corresponds to the same set number in a DRAM memory page. For example, entry 0 in each cache directory corresponds to Set 0 in a DRAM memory page.

The Relationship Between Cache Directory and Cache Memory Refer to Figure 23-5. The 82385 cache memory controller

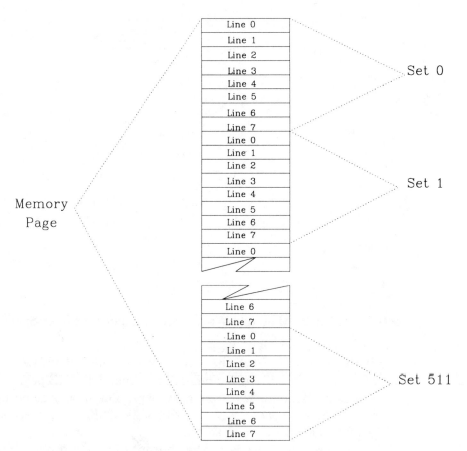

FIGURE 23-3 Sets and Lines

is designed to work with a 32KB cache memory, divided into two 16KB banks referred to as cache banks A and B. Just as the 82385 views DRAM memory as consisting of sets and lines, or doublewords, of storage, it also views the two cache memory banks as consisting of sets and lines. Instead of thinking of them as 16KB banks, it is more correct to regard them as two banks organized as 4K lines each. Each of the two cache banks is viewed as consisting of 512 sets, numbered 0 through 511, and each set as consisting of eight lines, numbered 0 through 7.

Each of the 512 directory entries in cache directory A is used to keep track of the information cached in the corresponding set of cache bank A. The same holds for cache directory B. Eight bits within each directory entry are used to keep track of the eight lines within the corresponding cache bank set.

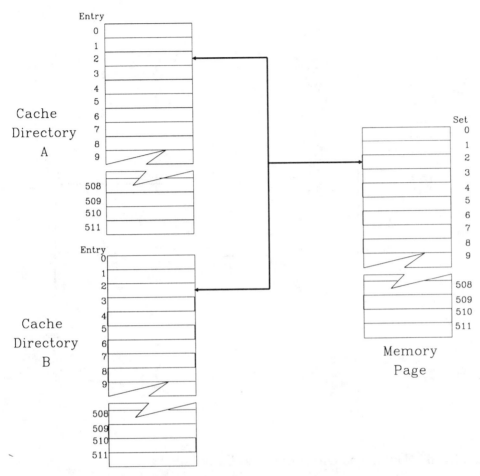

FIGURE 23-4 Relationship of Cache Directories to DRAM Memory

The 82385's Interpretation of the Memory Address The 82385 cache memory controller must look at the memory address under two circumstances.

1. When the 80386 microprocessor initiates a memory read or write bus cycle, the 82385 must interpret the memory address on the 80386's address bus.

2. When a bus master has taken over the 82385's local buses, the 82385 must snoop its local address bus.

Figure 23-6 illustrates the 82385's interpretation of the memory address. The 82385 views the memory address as three packets of information:

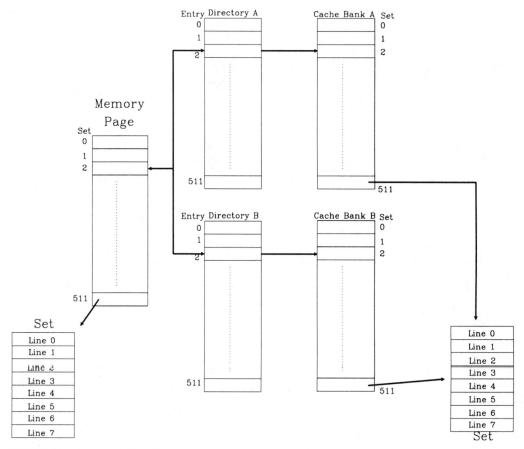

FIGURE 23-5   The Cache Directories and Banks

1. The set number. Address bits A5:A13 identify the set within the currently addressed DRAM memory page. This can be any set number between 0 and 511.

2. The page or **tag** number. Address bits A14:A31 identify the currently addressed DRAM memory page. This can be any number between 0 and 262,143.

3. The line number. Address bits A2:A4 identify the line within the set. This can be any line number between 0 and 7.

   The Format of the Cache Directory Entry   Figure 23-7 illustrates an 82385 cache directory entry. Each cache directory entry consists of three parts:

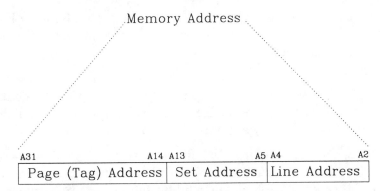

FIGURE 23-6   82385 Interpretation of the Memory Address

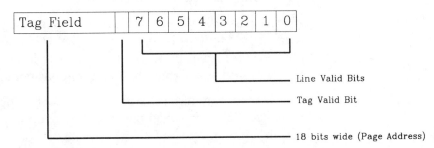

FIGURE 23-7   Format of the Cache Directory Entry

1. The tag, or page, address. This is an 18-bit field used to store the address of the DRAM memory page whose data is contained in the corresponding cache bank set.

2. The **tag valid bit**. This bit is set to a 1 whenever the corresponding cache bank set contains copies of any valid information from DRAM memory.

3. The **line valid bits**. This is an 8-bit field, designated as line valid bits 0 through 7. A line valid bit is set to a 1 if the corresponding line in the cache bank contains a line of valid data.

Checking the Directories for a Match   Refer to Figure 23-7 again. During any memory access, the cache memory controller uses the address as follows.

1. The set portion of the memory address, A5:A13, identifies the entry to be checked in both cache directories and the set in the currently addressed DRAM memory page.

2. Having identified the directory entry, the 82385 checks to see if the specified entry in either directory has its tag valid bit set to a 1. If the tag valid bit in neither directory entry is set to 1, it is a **tag miss** and the following conditions apply.

   If this is a memory read bus cycle, the operation turns into a read miss operation. The 82385 must fetch the requested data from DRAM memory by running a bus cycle on its own local buses. This process is described in more detail in this chapter in the section entitled "The Read Miss and the LRU Algorithm."

   If this is an 80386-initiated memory write bus cycle, it turns into a write miss operation. The 82385 latches the bus cycle information in the posted write latch and tells the microprocessor that the bus cycle has completed.

   If a bus master has control of the 82385's local buses while the 82385 is snooping, this is a snoop miss and no action is taken by the 82385.

3. If either, or both, tag valid bits are set to 1, the respective set in the respective cache bank contains something valid that may or may not be from the desired DRAM memory locations.

4. The 82385 then compares the tag, or page, portion of the memory address, A14:A31, to the tag address stored in the respective directory entry. If a miscompare results, it is a **tag miss**.

   If this is a memory read bus cycle, the operation turns into a read miss operation. The 82385 must fetch the requested data from DRAM memory by running a bus cycle on its own local buses. This process is described in more detail in this chapter in the section entitled "The Read Miss and the LRU Algorithm."

If this is an 80386-initiated memory write bus cycle, it turns into a write miss operation. The 82385 latches the bus cycle information in the posted write latch and tells the microprocessor the bus cycle has completed.

If a bus master has control of the 82385's local buses while the 82385 is snooping, this is a snoop miss and no action is taken by the 82385.

5. If the tag address compares on either directory entry, this is a **tag hit**, which means that the respective set in the respective cache memory bank contains information from the currently addressed memory set within the currently addressed memory page. However, it might not contain the requested line of information.

6. The 82385 then uses the line portion of the memory address, A2:A4, to identify the proper line valid bit in the directory entry that had a tag hit. If the respective line valid bit is set to a 1, this is a **line hit**. The requested line of information is located in the cache bank corresponding to either Directory A or B, whichever experienced both the tag and line hits. Within this cache memory bank, the requested line can be found within the set and line indicated by the set and line portions of the memory address.

7. Depending on the type of operation in progress when the line hit occurred, one of the following actions results.

If an 80386-initiated memory read bus cycle is in progress, the 82385 reads the requested information from the cache bank, sends it to the 80386 over the microprocessor's local data bus, and sets the microprocessor's READY# input active to indicate the presence of the requested data on the data bus.

If a bus master is running a memory write bus cycle, this is a snoop hit. The 82385 turns off the line valid bit to indicate that the line in cache no longer matches the line in DRAM memory that is being altered by the bus master. This old data is referred to as **stale data**.

If an 80386-initiated memory write bus cycle is in progress, this is a write hit. The microprocessor updates the line in cache with the data from the microprocessor and latches the bus cycle information into the posted write latch. The microprocessor's READY# input is set active to let the microprocessor end the bus cycle and the 82385 then initiates the memory write bus cycle on its local buses to update the line in DRAM memory.

The Read Miss and the LRU Algorithm   This section describes the actions taken by the 82385 cache memory controller when the 80386 microprocessor initiates a memory read bus cycle and the desired information is not found in the cache, thereby resulting in a read miss. Each read miss is actually either a tag miss or a **line miss**. Regardless of the type, the following actions take place:

1. The 82385 initiates a memory read bus cycle on its local buses to fetch the requested information from DRAM memory. Regardless of the byte enable lines set active by the 80386 microprocessor, the 82385 sets all four byte enable lines active to fetch a complete line, or doubleword, from DRAM memory.

2. The line, or doubleword, of information read from DRAM memory is sent to the microprocessor to fulfill its request for the information and to cache memory to store a copy of the data.

The cache memory controller must employ some type of decision-making process to select the cache memory location to store the copy in. This is known as the **least-recently used (LRU) algorithm**. The following steps outline this process. Figure 23-8 illustrates the LRU switches.

1. Just as before, the set portion of the memory address selects a pair of directory entries.

2. One of the following cases will be true:

   Neither directory entry has a tag match. The 82385 will set the tag valid bit in the directory entry pointed to by the pair's LRU switch. The 18-bit page, or tag, portion of the memory address is written into the directory entry's tag field. If this entry was already in use, the new tag address overwrites the old and all 8 LRU bits are turned off. The line portion of the memory address selects the proper line valid bit in the directory entry to set to a 1. The line of information is written into the cache

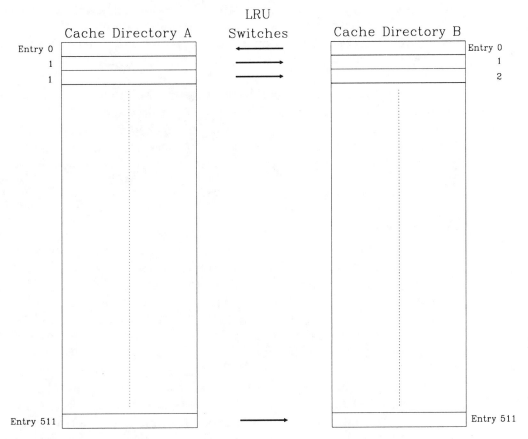

FIGURE 23-8 The LRU Switches

bank associated with this directory using the set and line number supplied by the memory address. Finally, the **least-recently used LRU switch** associated with the directory entry pair is then flipped to point to the other entry, identifying it as the least-recently used (the oldest) of the two entries.

One of the entries has a tag match. The directory entry whose tag matches the tag, or page, portion of the memory address is updated. The line portion of the memory address is used to select the proper line valid bit in the directory entry to set to a 1. The line of information is written into the cache bank associated with this directory using the set and line number supplied by the memory address. Finally, the LRU switch associated with the directory entry pair is flipped to point to the other entry, identifying it as the least-recently used of the two entries.

One directory entry can keep track of up to eight lines of data from the same set within the same page of DRAM memory.

This cache memory scheme is called **two-way set associative** because it uses two **ways**, or banks, of cache RAM and uses the set portion of the memory address to choose the set of cache memory to be used.

Non-Cacheable Address Space

There are certain areas of memory address space that the cache memory controller should not attempt to keep copies of. For example, there are network controller cards on the market that have memory located on the card. This memory is dual-ported in that it may be accessed by the microprocessor on the system board or another bus master, as well as by the network controller logic itself. The network controller can receive data over the network and write it into its local memory without any activity occurring on the MCA buses. As a result, the network controller can alter data in this memory without the knowledge of the cache memory controller on the system board or, for that matter, any other bus master's cache memory controller. If a cache memory controller attempts to maintain copies of the data stored in this area of memory, it is likely to end up with stale data that does not match the DRAM memory contents.

The solution is to somehow designate this memory address range as non-cacheable. The 82385 cache memory controller provides an input for this purpose: the non-cacheable access (NCA#) input. In order to implement this feature, the system board must have a memory address decoder capable of detecting all address ranges that are non-cacheable. When an address in this range is detected, the 82385's NCA# input is set active. When this occurs, the 82385 initiates the memory read bus cycle on its local buses to fetch the desired information directly from DRAM memory. The **non-cacheable access** memory address decoder is usually programmed during the Power-On Self-Test (or POST) from the information stored in configuration RAM memory.

Because the 82385 cache memory controller must be able to fetch a line, or doubleword, at a time from 32-bit DRAM memory in order to cache it, the 82385 is incapable of caching information from 16-bit memory. When a 16-bit memory card is addressed, its address decoder should assert CD DS 16# back to the system board, where it is used to inform the 80386 (via its BS16# input) that it can only converse over the lower 16 data lines. In addition, it should also cause the 82385's X16# input to go active, telling the 82385 to initiate the memory read bus cycle on its local buses to fetch the desired information directly from DRAM memory.

DRAM Memory Testing

Cache memory controllers present a potential problem when diagnostics are being run to test DRAM memory. The program may think it is accessing and testing DRAM when, in fact, the information is coming from cache memory.

Virtually every cache memory controller, the 82385 included, has a **FLUSH** input. When activated, it causes every tag valid bit in the directories to be turned off. If kept active, every memory read bus cycle causes a read miss and an actual access to the DRAM memory. In a system incorporating cache, the programmer is usually provided a special address that can be written to cause FLUSH to stay active so that testing can take place.

The Hit Rate

The actual percentage of cache read hits on a particular system is heavily dependent on the software currently running. An applications program that is comprised of fairly compact routines that are run multiple times will experience a relatively high hit rate, while a program that jumps around and randomly accesses memory a high percentage of the time will experience a very low hit rate.

The cache memory controller's **hit rate** is the average percentage of 0-wait state memory reads that occur over a large number of memory accesses.

The Actual PS/2 Implementation

The PS/2 products based on the 25MHz 80386 microprocessor incorporate the 82385 cache memory controller and 64KB of cache memory.

This may seem contradictory because it was stated earlier that the 82385 supports 32KB of cache memory. Since the PS/2 wiring diagrams are not released, one can only speculate regarding the actual implementation of a 64KB cache.

The cache memory is organized as two banks of 32KB each, rather than 16KB each. Each can still hold 4096 lines of information (512 sets x 8 lines per set), but each line is now a quadword (8 bytes) in length rather than a doubleword (4 bytes).

Figure 23-9 illustrates the cache memory bank organization. DRAM memory is organized as one 64-bit bank. Whenever the 82385 cache memory controller experiences a read miss and must fetch a line of information from DRAM memory, it actually fetches a quadword from

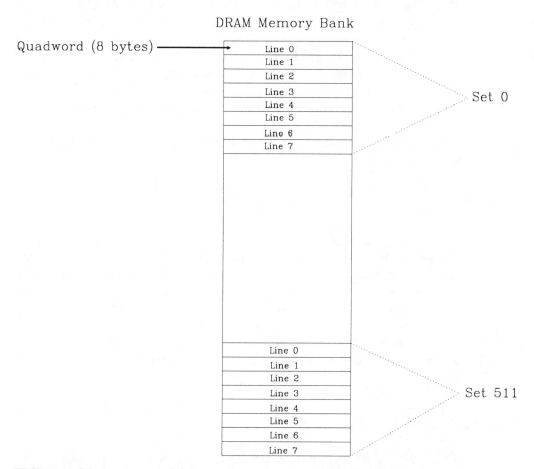

FIGURE 23-9 DRAM Memory Organized As One 64-Bit Bank

DRAM starting at the requested memory address, sends it back to the microprocessor and writes it into the cache line. This is twice as efficient as fetching a doubleword at a time because each directory entry can keep track of 64 bytes of DRAM data, rather than 32.

Any 80486-based product incorporates cache because the 80486 microprocessor incorporates a **four-way set associative** 8KB cache into the microprocessor chip itself. Currently, only the IBM power platform option for the Model 70 uses the 80486.

Summary

Microprocessor-based systems running at 25MHz or greater require cache memory controllers to provide acceptable performance when accessing DRAM memory. Implementation of a cache memory subsystem is an attempt to achieve acceptable system cost and a high percentage of 0-wait state bus cycles when accessing DRAM memory.

The cache memory controller uses a directory to keep track of the information it has copied into the cache memory. When the cache memory controller sees the microprocessor initiate a memory read bus cycle, it immediately checks its directory to determine if it has a copy of the requested information in cache memory. If a copy is present, it immediately reads the information from the cache, sends it back to the system board microprocessor over the microprocessor's data bus, and turns on the microprocessor's READY# signal; this is a read hit. The access can be completed in 0-wait states because the information is fetched from the fast access cache SRAM.

The actual percentage of cache read hits on a particular system is heavily dependent on the software currently running. An applications program that is comprised of fairly compact routines that are run multiple times will experience a relatively high hit rate, while a program that jumps around and randomly accesses memory a high percentage of the time experiences a very low hit rate.

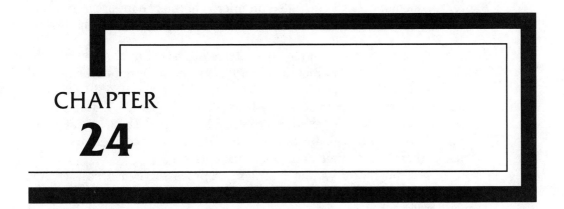

CHAPTER
24

Channel Memory

Objectives: This chapter provides information regarding channel memory, the memory that is installed on micro channel adapter cards rather than in the proprietary memory module slots on the system board.

Memory installed on MCA cards is referred to as channel memory. The total amount of memory installed in a PS/2 system cannot exceed 16MB because the DMA controller on the system board can only generate memory addresses up to 16MB. Although more than 16MB of DRAM memory can be installed in an 80386- or 80486-based PS/2, any attempt to perform a DMA transfer between an I/O device and memory above the 16MB address range does not work correctly.

Although the system board microprocessor can access DRAM memory located on the system board at the full rated speed of the microprocessor, access to channel memory is substantially slower in many PS/2 products. This slowdown in access time has two causes.

1. When a bus cycle initiated by the system board microprocessor is accessing an MCA device, the bus cycle must pass through the system board bus control logic to be seen on the micro channel.

2. As previously described in Chapter 16, the fastest type of bus cycle permissible on the micro channel is typically the 10MHz default bus cycle. The one exception to this is the matched memory cycle.

Table 24-1 illustrates the fastest DRAM memory accesses that can occur when the system board microprocessor attempts to access channel memory.

In the PS/2's with processors that run at more than 10MHZ, a substantial penalty is incurred when accessing channel memory versus system board memory. When a parity error is incurred while reading a channel memory location, the card generates a channel check condition by turning on the MCA's CHCK# signal. This causes an NMI to the system board microprocessor. The programmer may read bit 6 of system control port B at I/O address 0061 to determine if channel check was the cause of the NMI (1 = channel check).

Summary

A pre-defined amount of DRAM memory can be installed on the system board using special memory modules. Additional memory can be added

TABLE 24-1   Channel Memory Access Times

Model	CPU Speed	Access Time	Maximum Transfer Rate	Notes
50	10MHz	200ns	10MB/s	
50Z	10MHz	200ns	10MB/s	
60	10MHz	200ns	10MB/s	
70	16MHz	250ns	16MB/s	
70	20MHz	200ns	20MB/s	
80	16MHz	250ns	16MB/s	Accessing card that does not support matched memory cycles
80	16MHz	187.5ns	21.3MB/s	Accessing card that supports matched memory cycles
80	20MHz	200ns	20MB/s	

to the system by installing MCA memory cards in MCA slots. This allows the user to expand DRAM memory up to 16MB. It should be noted that a substantial penalty is incurred when accessing channel memory versus system board memory in the PS/2's with processors that run at more than 10MHZ.

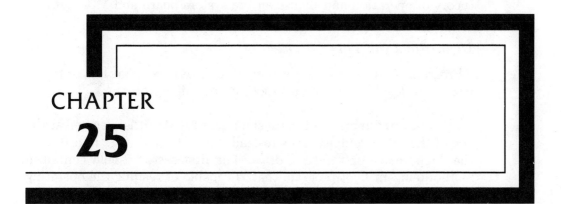

ROM Memory: On the System Board and MCA Cards

Objectives: This chapter provides information regarding ROM memory theory of operation and its use on the system board and MCA cards.

Definitions for This Chapter

• Programs written in assembly language must be **assembled**, or translated, into the hex code understood by the microprocessor.

• The **boot program** is in the system board ROM. It is executed at the end of the POST and attempts to read the first sector (512 bytes) from the floppy drive or the hard drive. The first sector should contain a more intelligent boot program that is capable of reading the operating system software from the disk to memory. Once loaded, the boot program jumps to the beginning of the operating system software and executes it.

• **Checksumming** is the method used to ensure that the information stored in ROM memory has not changed. Checksumming is accomplished by adding the contents of every ROM location together and checking for a result of 0.

• Programs written in high-level languages such as C must be **compiled**, or translated, into the hex code understood by the microprocessor.

• A **device ROM** is located on an MCA card. It contains the self-test, BIOS, and interrupt service routines for the card, as well as initialization code.

• **Erasable programmable read-only memory (EPROM)** is a ROM that can be erased and reprogrammed many times. A floating gate is used to produce a 1 or a 0 at the bit cell level.

• A **floating gate** is a small piece of conductor surrounded by a thin layer of insulating material. It is charge is used to control the conduction of the transistor in an EPROM's bit cell.

• A **fusible-link PROM** uses a fuse at the bit cell level to represent a 0 or a 1.

• **Machine language** is the hex series of numbers that the microprocessor treats as instructions and data.

• A **masked ROM** is a mass-produced, pre-programmed ROM. A photographic image is used to reproduce large quantities of ROMs with the desired series of opens and shorts to represent 0's and 1's.

• A **read-only memory (ROM)** chip can only be read when installed in the system. It is non-volatile; that is, it retains its stored information indefinitely when power is removed.

• A **ROM programmer** is a device used to write hex information into ROMs before their installation in a system.

• The **ROM scan** is the POST process that automatically detects the device ROMs, tests them, and executes the initialization programs for every installed MCA card that has a device ROM on it.

ROM Memory: Theory of Operation

One of the primary operational characteristics of **read-only memory (ROM)** is that, once installed in a system, it can only be read from. Its other primary operational characteristic is that it is non-volatile memory; that is, it retains its stored information indefinitely after power is removed from the system.

The ROM memory chips used in the PS/2 products contain 1 byte of information per internal storage location. Figure 25-1 illustrates the ROM's internal layout. Each storage location consists of 8 bit cells, each of which can store a 1 or a 0.

The information stored in a ROM typically consists of both programs and data to be used by the programs. The programs and data are developed by a programmer and are then **assembled** or **compiled** into **machine language**. Machine language is the actual series of hex numbers that the microprocessor treats as instructions and data.

The machine language representation of the programs and data must then be loaded into a device called a **ROM programmer**. This is typically accomplished by transmitting the information to the ROM programmer using a serial or parallel communications link. The ROM is then placed into a socket on the ROM programmer and the proper information is written into each storage location. Once placed in the target unit such as a PS/2, the ROM can only be read from.

The following sections discuss the three types of ROMs that may be found in a PS/2:

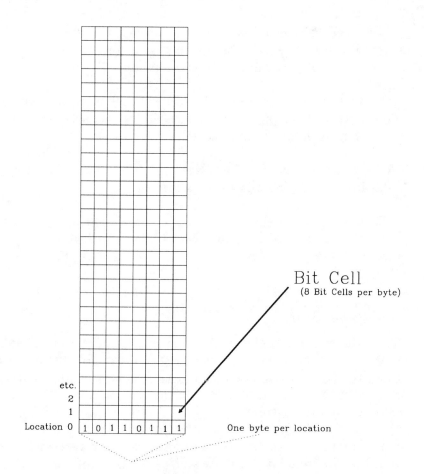

FIGURE 25-1   The ROM Bit Cell

- Fusible-Link PROM
- Masked ROM
- EPROM

Fusible-Link PROM

Figure 25-2 illustrates a **fusible-link PROM** storage location. When a PROM is received from the chip manufacturer, every bit cell contains a fuse, or fusible-link. In order to write the programs and data into the PROM's storage locations, it must be placed into the socket on the ROM programmer. When the programming process begins, a byte is written into each location by blowing, or vaporizing, the fuses in some bit cells

FIGURE 25-2

0 1 1 0 0 1 0 1   The PROM Bit Cells

and leaving others intact. When the PROM is placed into the PS/2, the microprocessor can only read from it. When a PROM storage location is read from, the pattern of 1's and 0's represented by the eight fuses is simultaneously output onto the data bus and sent back to the microprocessor.

Because some of the fusible-links are physically vaporized during the programming process, a PROM cannot be reprogrammed with new information after its initial programming. For this reason, PROMs should not be used if a systems manufacturer intends to update the information stored in the ROMs periodically.

The Masked ROM

The **masked ROM** is a variation of the fusible-link PROM. If the systems manufacturer is absolutely certain that the information in the ROMs will never change, it may choose to have the ROM chip manufacturer pre-program the information into the ROMs for them. The systems manufacturer sends the memory chip manufacturer a copy of the information to be stored in the ROM. The memory chip manufacturer then produces a photographic mask that represents the opens and shorts that would be produced by blowing some fuses and leaving other intact. This mask is then used to etch thousands of pre-programmed ROMs.

EPROM

If the systems manufacturer wants to reserve the option of re-programming the ROMs at some time in the future, it uses **erasable programmable read-only memory (EPROMs)** instead of PROMs or masked ROMs. When an EPROM is received from the memory chip manufacturer, it is blank (contains no information). As with the PROM, the information must be written into it using a ROM programmer.

Figure 25-3 illustrates an EPROM bit cell. At the bit cell level, the EPROM basically consists of a transistor, which is nothing more than a switch. With a certain voltage, or charge, on its base, the transistor provides a path for current flow through its collector and emitter.

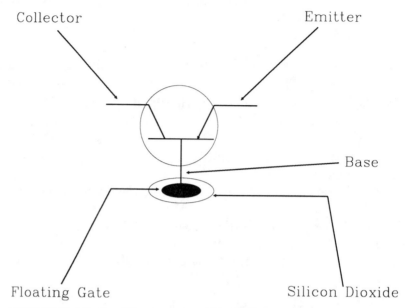

FIGURE 25-3   The EPROM Bit Cell

In other words, the switch is closed, allowing current flow. With a different charge on its base, however, the transistor ceases to conduct.

The base of the transistor in the EPROM's bit cell is connected to a small piece of conductor, known as a **floating gate**, surrounded by a thin layer of silicon dioxide. Since silicon dioxide is an insulator and it does not conduct electricity, a charge placed on the floating gate has nowhere to go and tends to stay there.

When the EPROM is placed in the ROM programmer and the programming process is initiated, a bit is written into a bit cell by either placing a charge on the floating gate or not placing a charge on it. At the completion of the programming process, some of the bit cells have had charges placed on their floating gates and some have not.

The EPROM is removed from the ROM programmer and placed in the PS/2. When the microprocessor attempts to read from one of the EPROM's storage locations, some of the eight transistors that make up the storage location will conduct and others will not as a result of the charge (or lack of a charge) placed on their floating gates. It acts just like a series of eight switches, producing a group of eight bits of information. The eight bits of information are then driven out onto the data bus and sent back to the microprocessor.

If the information in the EPROM must be changed, the EPROM is removed from the PS/2 and placed under a special ultra-violet light. An EPROM can be easily identified by the small, rectangular crystal window on its upper surface. The EPROM is left under the light for approximately 21 minutes. During this period of time, every floating gate is bombarded with high energy ultra-violet light and a charge begins to build on every gate. Eventually, by the end of the 21 minute period, every floating gate has built up a charge sufficiently high to jump the thin layer of silicon dioxide and discharge. In this way, all of the data in the EPROM is cleared. The EPROM is then removed from the light source and may be reprogrammed with new information.

The ROM's Interface to the System

Figure 25-4 illustrates ROM's interface to the system, consisting of the signals described in Table 25-1.

For example, assume that the ROM in Figure 25-4 is a 64KB ROM and the ROM's address decoder is designed to detect the memory address range from $F0000_h$ to $FFFFF_h$. The ROM address decoder observes the upper address lines, A16:A19, to detect an F_h as the uppermost digit in the memory address. When an F_h is detected, the ROM address decoder chip-selects the ROM by turning on its CE# input. The ROM responds by using its address inputs, A0:A15, to select the exact location

TABLE 25-1 The ROM's Interface Signals

Signal(s)	*Description*
CE#	Chip-enable or chip-select. This signal is set active by the ROM address decoder when it detects a memory address within the range of addresses assigned to the ROM. When CE# is set active, the ROM then uses its address inputs to select the target location to be read.
Address lines	Once CE# is detected, the ROM uses the address present on its address inputs to select the target location to be read.
OE#	Output enable. When OE# is set active, the ROM outputs the byte of information from the target location onto the data bus lines to be sent back to the microprocessor.
Data lines	Used by the ROM to send the byte read from the target location back to the microprocessor.

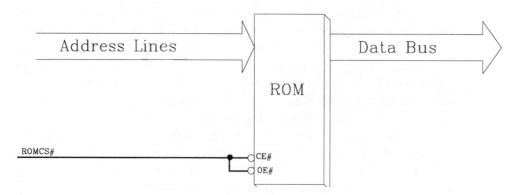

FIGURE 25-4   The ROM's Interface to the System

within the 64K locations of storage within the ROM. If the ROM's output enable (OE#) input is also active, the ROM reads the byte from the target location and drives it onto the data bus lines to be sent back to the microprocessor.

System Board ROM Memory

The PS/2 system board contains 128KB of ROM memory. This ROM contains the following.

1. The power-on self-test, or POST. This includes the automatic POS register configuration routines.
2. The BIOS routines for the standard I/O devices integrated onto the system board.
3. The interrupt service routines for the standard I/O devices integrated onto the system board.
4. The BASIC language interpreter that is executed if the **boot program** fails to find a valid operating system on either the floppy or hard drive.
5. The boot program used to read the operating system software, such as PC-DOS or OS/2, from the floppy or hard drive.

Address Range

The system board ROM occupies the memory address space defined in Table 25-2.

TABLE 25-2 The System Board ROM Address Range

PS/2 Model	Memory Address Ranges Occupied (in hex)
50	0E0000 to 0FFFFF and FE0000 to FFFFFF
50Z	0E0000 to 0FFFFF and FE0000 to FFFFFF
60	0E0000 to 0FFFFF and FE0000 to FFFFFF
70	000E0000 to 000FFFFF and FFFE0000 to FFFFFFFF
80	000E0000 to 000FFFFF and FFFE0000 to FFFFFFFF

For example, the first location in the Model 50's system board ROM may be read from either memory address $0E0000_h$ or $FE0000_h$, the second from either $0E0001_h$ or $FE0001_h$, and so on.

Testing

Parity checking is not done on ROM memory. To perform parity checking, a parity generator must create the parity bit and store it in memory when data is written to a memory location. Since ROM memory is read-only, parity makes no sense.

Checksumming is used to check ROMs for proper operation. When the programmer originally develops the programs and data to be written to the ROM, a simple utility program adds the contents of every ROM location together using a process called exclusive-or'ing. When 2 bytes are exclusive-or'ed, each bit position in the 2 bytes is exclusive-or'ed and the resulting bit is only a 1 if the 2 bits are different. The following example illustrates the process:

```
Byte 1: 1011 1001
Byte 2: 1001 1110
Result: 0010 0111
```

The programmer always stores a value in one location in the ROM that will force the result to 0. For example, assume that exclusive-or'ing every ROM location but the last resulted in DA_h ($1101\ 1010_b$). The programmer would store the same value in the last ROM location to cause the overall result to be 0:

```
Running Total : 1101 1010
```

```
Last Byte : 1101 1010
Resulting Checksum: 0000 0000
```

During the POST, the program reads the contents of every system board ROM location and exclusive-or's them together. If the result is not 0, this indicates that either the data in the ROM has changed (which it never should) or the system cannot properly read from the ROM. In either case, the ROM cannot be reliably read from and an error is generated.

Shadow RAM

The PS/2 products based on the 80386 and 80386SX microprocessors (the Models 55SX, 65SX, 70 and 80), all copy the system board ROM contents into shadow RAM during the POST. This is done to compensate for the notoriously slow access time of ROMs. This subject is covered in Chapter 14.

System Board ROM Configuration

The system board ROMs in selected PS/2 products are configured as shown in Table 25-3.

Figures 25-5 and 25-6 illustrate the ROM configuration found in the PS/2 products utilizing 32KB and 64KB ROMs, respectively.

The 32KB System Board ROM Configuration

In Figure 25-5, the ROMs are divided into two pairs, one of which responds to the address range from $E0000_h$ to $EFFFF_h$ and the other to

TABLE 25-3   System Board ROM Configuration

PS/2 Model	Number of ROMs	Individual ROMs Capacity
50	4	32KB
50z	2	64KB
60	4	32KB
70	2	64KB
80-16MHz	4	32KB
80-20MHz	2	64KB

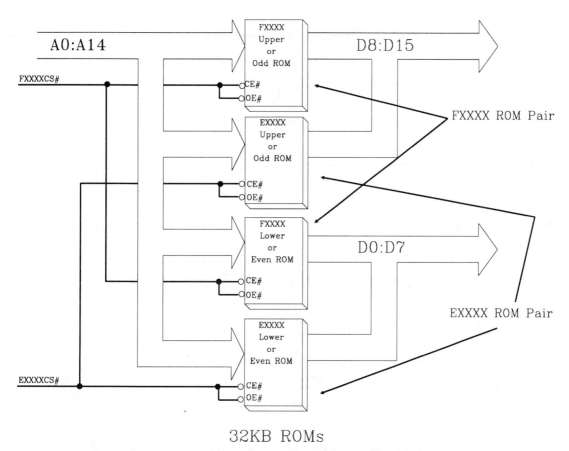

32KB ROMs

FIGURE 25-5   System Board ROM Configuration with 32KB ROMs

the address range from F0000$_h$ to FFFFF$_h$. Each of these pairs consists of two 32KB ROMs designated as the "upper or odd ROM" and the "lower or even ROM".

The "upper or odd ROM" is so named because it is connected to the upper data path, D8:D15, and because all of the odd-addressed ROM locations are within this ROM. This is evident because it is connected to the upper data path and the microprocessor always communicates with odd addresses over the upper data path.

The "lower or even ROM" is so named because it is connected to the lower data path, D0:D7; and because all of the even-addressed ROM locations are within this ROM. This is evident because it is connected to the lower data path and the microprocessor always communicates with even addresses over the lower data path.

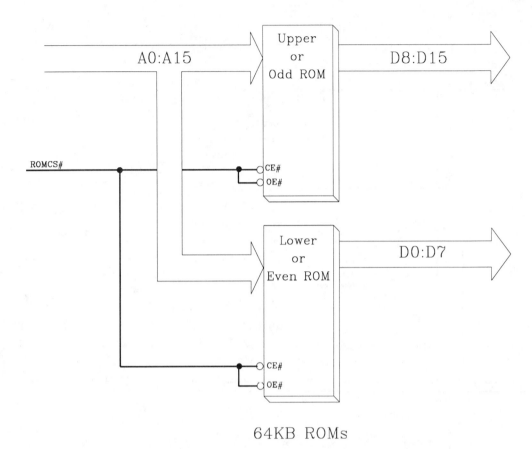

64KB ROMs

FIGURE 25-6   System Board ROM Configuration with 64KB ROMs

When the programmer loads the data into the ROMs using the ROM programmer, a utility program is first executed that divides the information in half. All of the information to be stored in even addresses is programmed into the "lower or even ROM," and all information to be stored in odd-addressed locations is programmed into the "upper or odd ROM."

Whenever an address in the range from $E0000_h$ to $EFFFF_h$ is detected by the system board ROM address decoder, the EXXXXCS# line (chip-select for E0000-EFFFF range) is set active by the decoder. This enables the EXXXX ROM pair. The two ROMs then use the lower part of the address from the microprocessor, A0:A14, to select one of 32K locations in each of the two ROMs. Since the EXXXXCS# signal is also connected to the output enable pin on both ROMs, OE#, each of the ROMs outputs the byte from the addressed location onto the data bus. The "lower or even ROM" outputs the byte from the even address onto the lower data path, D0:D7, and the other ROM outputs the byte from the odd address onto the upper data path, D8:D15.

The FXXXX ROM pair responds to the address range from F0000$_h$ to FFFFF$_h$.

The 64KB System Board ROM Configuration

In Figure 25-6, there are two 64KB ROMs that respond to the address range from E0000$_h$ to FFFFF$_h$. They are designated as the "upper or odd ROM" and the "lower or even ROM." This designation is explained in the previous section.

Whenever an address in the range from E0000$_h$ to FFFFF$_h$ is detected by the system board ROM address decoder, the ROMCS# line (ROM chip-select) is set active by the decoder. This enables the ROM pair. The two ROMs then use the lower part of the address from the microprocessor, A0:A15, to select one of 64K locations in each of the two ROMs. Since the ROMCS# signal is also connected to the output enable pin on both ROMs, OE#, each of the ROMs outputs the byte from the addressed location onto the data bus. The "lower or even ROM" outputs the byte from the even address onto the lower data path, D0:D7, and the other ROM outputs the byte from the odd address onto the upper data path, D8:D15.

Limited Data Transfer Capability in 80386 Units

It should be noted that all of the ROM configurations for the PS/2 products listed in Table 25-3 show the ROM as a 16-bit device, connected only to the lower two data paths, D0:D7 and D8:D15. This means that the ROM transfer rate in the 80386-based products, the Models 70 and 80, is limited to 2 bytes per transfer rather than the possible 4 allowed by the overall width of the 80386's data bus.

ROMs on MCA Cards (Device ROMs)

As already pointed out, the system board ROM contains:

- the POST for the standard devices.

- the BIOS routines for the standard devices.
- the interrupt service routines for the standard I/O devices.

A card designed to be installed in an MCA slot also needs to be tested during POST and may require a BIOS routine and an interrupt service routine. The card designer can include a ROM on the MCA card and place its self-test program, BIOS routine, and interrupt service routine in it. This is called a **device ROM**.

IBM provided a way to automatically execute the MCA card's self-test during POST and to automatically update the interrupt table in RAM to point to the card's BIOS routine and interrupt service routine.

During the POST, a process called **ROM Scan** is performed. Starting at memory address $C0000_h$ and going to $DFFFF_h$, the POST program looks for Device ROMs. The process is simple:

1. The POST reads the 2 bytes from memory locations $C0000_h$ and $C0001_h$. If it is an AA_h and a 55_h, this identifies it as the first two locations of a device ROM on an MCA card.

2. POST reads the next byte from location $C0002_h$. This location contains the length of the device ROM in increments of 512 bytes. For example, a 2KB device ROM would have a 04_h in its third location ($4 \times 512 = 2048$, or 2KB).

3. Knowing the start address and the length of the device ROM, POST then checksums it to ensure it can be read from properly. The result should be 0. If it is not, a checksum error is displayed on the screen along with the segment start address. For example:

   CHECKSUM ERROR C000:000

   is interpreted as a device ROM checksum error for an MCA card whose device ROM starts at memory address C000:0000 (Segment:Offset format).

4. If the ROM checksum is OK, the POST program jumps to the fourth location in the device ROM, in this case, location $C0003_h$. This is the start address of the initialization code, or program, in the ROM.

5. The initialization code:

   - Runs a self-test on the card.

- Writes the start address of its BIOS routine into the proper slot in the interrupt table.
- Writes the start address of its interrupt service routine into the proper slot in the interrupt table.
- Initializes any programmable I/O registers on the card to set it up for normal operation.
- Returns to the POST program.

In this way, the device ROM is automatically detected and tested, and its BIOS and interrupt service routine pointers are installed in the interrupt table.

The POST then adds 2K (0800_h) to the start address, $C0000_h$, and checks for another ROM starting at $C0800_h$. If another device ROM is detected, the process is repeated. This process is repeated at 2K address intervals up to location $DFFFF_h$, the end of the ROM scan address range.

When the ROM scan is completed, the POST has automatically detected and tested every MCA card with a device ROM and executed their initialization programs.

Summary

The PS/2 system board contains 128KB of ROM memory. This ROM contains the power-on self-test (POST). This includes the automatic POS register configuration routines. The BIOS routines and interrupt service routines for the standard I/O devices integrated onto the system board are also contained in the system board ROM. The BASIC language interpreter that is executed if the boot program fails to find a valid operating system on the first sector of either the floppy or the hard drive is in ROM, as well as the boot program used to read the operating system software, such as PC-DOS or OS/2, from the floppy or hard drive.

A card designed to be installed in an MCA slot also needs to be tested during POST and may require a BIOS routine and an interrupt service routine. The card designer can include a ROM on the MCA card and place its self-test program, BIOS routine and interrupt service routine in it. This is called a device ROM.

Using a procedure known as ROM Scan, the POST can automatically detect the device ROMs, test them, and execute the initialization programs for every installed MCA card that has a device ROM on it.

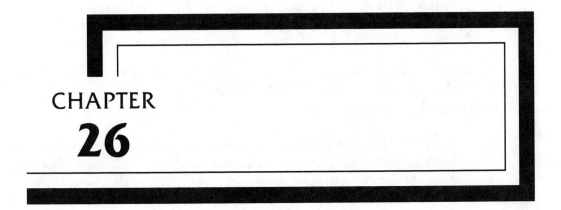

The Real-Time Clock and Configuration RAM

Objectives: Every time a PS/2 is powered up, information stored in battery backed-up CMOS RAM is used to automatically configure the unit. This chapter describes the CMOS RAM. It also describes the real-time clock function performed by the configuration RAM chip.

The Motorola MC146818 Real-Time Clock and Configuration RAM Chip

Every PS/2 contains either a Motorola MC146818 real-time clock and configuration RAM chip or a Dallas semiconductor equivalent. This chip consists of two functional areas:

1. 64 locations of CMOS low power RAM memory that retains stored information after power-down via a battery backup. In the case of the Motorola version, the battery is external, mounted on the same frame as the speaker. The Dallas semiconductor chip has the battery built in. This means that the Dallas semiconductor chip must be replaced approximately every ten years.

2. The real-time clock function automatically keeps track of the date and time.

The first ten RAM locations are used by the real-time clock function to keep track of the date (day and month) and time. The next four locations are used to control the real-time clock function. The remaining 50 locations are used to store system configuration information and the century portion of the date.

Accessing the RAM Locations

The RAM locations inside the chip are accessed via I/O operations. It is a two-step process:

1. The programmer first identifies which of the 64 RAM locations is to be accessed by writing the RAM address to I/O port 70_h, the chip's address port. The address must be in the range from 00_h to $3F_h$. Caution should be exercised when writing the address to port 70_h because port 70_h has a second function by which bit 7 controls the enabling or disabling of NMI interrupts to the microprocessor (0 = enable NMI).

2. Next, the programmer either reads the contents of the previously identified CMOS RAM location from the chip's data port, I/O port 71_h, or writes the desired data byte to the data port.

For example, the proper sequence to read the contents of CMOS RAM location 5 is

1. Write the RAM address, 05, to the address port at I/O port 70_h.

2. Read RAM location 5's contents by performing an I/O read from the data port, I/O port 71_h.

Caution must be exercised to always follow a write to the address port with either a read from or a write to the data port. Failure to do so may result in unreliable operation of the real-time clock.

The Real-Time Clock Function

The first ten RAM locations are used by the real-time clock function and are defined in Table 26-1.

TABLE 26-1   The Real-Time Clock Bytes

Address	Function
0	Seconds
1	Seconds alarm
2	Minutes
3	Minutes alarm
4	Hours
5	Hours alarm
6	Day of week
7	Date of month
8	Month
9	Year

Locations 1, 3, and 5 can be used to specify an alarm event to occur once per day. Locations A_h through D_h are referred to as Status registers A through D and are used to control the operational characteristics of the real-time function. Table 26-2 defines the function of the bits in the four Real-Time Clock Status registers.

Using the BIOS to Control the Real-Time Clock

The recommended method for controlling the real-time clock chip is through BIOS function calls. INT $1A_h$ can be used to call the time-of-day BIOS routine. A complete description of this BIOS routine's use can be found in either of the following publications:

- *The IBM PS/2 and Personal Computer BIOS Interface Technical Reference* published by IBM.

- *CBIOS For IBM PS/2 Computers and Compatibles* by Phoenix Technologies Ltd., published by Addison-Wesley.

The Configuration RAM Usage

Table 26-3 defines the usage of the 50 configuration RAM locations in the MC146818 chip.

Table 26-4 further defines the use of some of the configuration RAM locations mentioned in Table 26-3.

The 2KB Configuration RAM Extension

In PS/2s having more than four MCA slots, an additional 2KB of battery backed-up CMOS configuration RAM is supplied.

Accessing the Extended Configuration RAM Locations

The extended configuration RAM locations are accessed via I/O operations. It is a two-step process:

1. The programmer first identifies which of the 2048 RAM locations is to be accessed by writing the RAM address to I/O ports 74_h and 75_h, the lower and upper address ports, respec-

TABLE 26-2 The Real-Time Clock Status Registers

Status Register	Bit(s)	Description
A	7	Update in progress. When set to 1, indicates that the chip is updating the time and date.
	6-4	22-stage divider. Indicate timebase in use. In PS/2s, always set to 010_b to indicate a 32.768KHz timebase.
	3-0	Rate selection bits. Allow selection of an output frequency. In all PS/2s, set to 0110, selecting a 1.024KHz square-wave output frequency and a 976.562 microsecond periodic interrupt rate on IRQ8#.
B	7	Set bit. When 0, this bit allows the date/time to be updated normally at the rate of once-per-second. When set to a 1, updates are disallowed and the programmer can set the date and time without interference from updates.
	6	Periodic interrupt enable. When set to 1, allows IRQ8# to occur at the 1.024KHz rate specified in Status register A. This bit is normally 0.
	5	Alarm interrupt enable. When set to 1, this bit allows an IRQ8# to be generated at the selected alarm date/time. This bit is normally 0.
	4	Update-ended interrupt enable. When set to 1, the chip generates an IRQ8# each time a date/time update is completed in the device's RAM. This bit is normally 0.
	3	Square-wave enabled. When set to 1, this bit enables the generation of the output frequency selected in Status register A. This bit is normally 0.
	2	Date mode. This bit defines whether the date and time will be represented in binary or BCD formats. A 1 selects binary mode. This bit is normally 0.
	1	24-hour mode. This bit defines whether the hours byte is presented in 24- or 12-hour format. A 1 selects 24-hour mode. This bit is normally 1.
	0	Daylight-savings enabled. A 1 enables daylight-savings time mode. This bit is normally 0.

TABLE 26-2 Continued

Status Register	Bit(s)	Description
C	7	Interrupt request flag. This bit is set to a 1 when the chip has generated an interrupt on IRQ8#. Bits 4, 5, and 6 of this register can then be checked to ascertain the cause of the interrupt.
	6	Periodic interrupt flag. Set to 1 when an periodic interrupt is generated.
	5	Alarm interrupt flag. Set to 1 when an alarm interrupt is generated.
	4	Update-ended interrupt flag. Set to 1 when an update-ended interrupt is generated.
	3-0	Not used.
D	7	RAM valid. When set to 0, indicates that the battery is dead or disconnected and RAM data has therefor been lost.
	6-0	Not used.

tively. The address must be in the range from 000_h to $7FF_h$. This is a two-step process:

    a. Write the least-significant byte of the RAM address to port 74_h.

    b. Write the most-significant byte of the RAM address to port 75_h.

2. Next, the programmer either reads the contents of the previously identified CMOS RAM location from the data port, I/O port 76_h, or writes the desired data byte to the data port.

Table 26-5 defines the use of some of these RAM locations.

Summary

Either a Motorola MC146818 or a Dallas semiconductor battery backed-up configuration RAM is used to hold system configuration information

TABLE 26-3 Configuration RAM Usage

Location (Hex)	Description of use
0E	Diagnostic status byte
0F	Shutdown status byte
10	Diskette drive type byte
11	First fixed disk drive type byte
12	Second fixed disk drive type byte
13	Password configuration
14	Equipment byte
15-16	Low and high base memory bytes
17-18	Low and high expansion memory bytes
19	Low byte of adapter ID for card in MCA slot 0
1A	High byte of adapter ID for card in MCA slot 0
1B	Low byte of adapter ID for card in MCA slot 1
1C	High byte of adapter ID for card in MCA slot 1
1D	Low byte of adapter ID for card in MCA slot 2
1E	High byte of adapter ID for card in MCA slot 2
1F	Low byte of adapter ID for card in MCA slot 3
20	High byte of adapter ID for card in MCA slot 3
21	POS 2 configuration byte for card in MCA slot 0
22	POS 3 configuration byte for card in MCA slot 0
23	POS 4 configuration byte for card in MCA slot 0
24	POS 5 configuration byte for card in MCA slot 0
25	POS 2 configuration byte for card in MCA slot 1
26	POS 3 configuration byte for card in MCA slot 1
27	POS 4 configuration byte for card in MCA slot 1
28	POS 5 configuration byte for card in MCA slot 1
29	POS 2 configuration byte for card in MCA slot 2
2A	POS 3 configuration byte for card in MCA slot 2
2B	POS 4 configuration byte for card in MCA slot 2
2C	POS 5 configuration byte for card in MCA slot 2

TABLE 26-3   Configuration RAM Usage

Location (Hex)	Description of use
2D	POS 2 configuration byte for card in MCA slot 3
2E	POS 3 configuration byte for card in MCA slot 3
2F	POS 4 configuration byte for card in MCA slot 3
30	POS 5 configuration byte for card in MCA slot 3
31	Copy of system board POS 2
* 32-33	Configuration CRC bytes. CRC of locations 10-31
34	Miscellaneous information
35	Low byte of actual expansion memory size
36	High byte of actual expansion memory size
37	Date century byte in BCD
38-3E	Power-on password
3F	Power-on password checksum

* Note: CRC means "cyclic redundancy check." This is a checksum of the indicated RAM locations contents.

and maintain the date and time. Both of these chips have 64 RAM locations, sufficient to hold the configuration information for a PS/2 that has four or fewer MCA slots. PS/2 models with more than four MCA slots have an additional 2KB of configuration RAM.

TABLE 26-4   Configuration RAM Byte Definitions

Location (hex)	Name	Bit	Description
0E	Diagnostic byte	7	Real-time chip power. A 1 indicates the chip lost power.
		6	Checksum valid. A 1 indicates the checksum is invalid.
		5	Configuration incorrect. A 1 indicates configuration is incorrect.
		4	Memory size miscompare. A 1 indicates that the POST found the actual memory size differed from that specified in configuration RAM.
		3	When set to 1, indicates that fixed disk drive C or its controller failed to power up correctly.
		2	Time status indicator. A 1 indicates the date/time is invalid.
		1	Adapter configuration miscompare. A 1 indicates that the installed MCA adapters do not match the configuration information.
		0	Adapter ID timeout. When 1, indicates that the ID being read from an MCA adapter card did not change from 0000_h to a valid ID within one second after power up.
10	Diskette type	7-4	First diskette drive type
			Bit 7654
			0000 No drive
			0001 DS, 360KB, 48TPI
			0011 720KB
			0100 1.44MB
		3-0	Second diskette drive type. See bits 7-4 for breakdown.

TABLE 26-4 Continued

Location (hex)	Name	Bit	Description
11-12	Fixed drive type	00	= no drive installed
14	Equipment byte	7-6	Number of diskette drives
			00 One
			01 Two
		5-4	Display operating mode
			01 40 column mode
			10 80 column mode
			11 monochrome mode
		3-2	Not used
		1	1 = Math coprocessor present
		0	1 = Diskette drive installed
15-16	Base memory bytes		Define the amount of memory in the lower 640K of memory address space. Binary value = number of 1KB blocks. Example: 280_h = 640KB.
17-18	High memory bytes		Define the amount of memory above 1MB. Binary value = number of 1KB blocks. Example: 800_h = 2048KB.

TABLE 26-5 Usage of the Extended Configuration RAM

Location(s) (hex)	Description
000	Low byte of adapter ID for card in MCA slot 0
001	High byte of adapter ID for card in MCA slot 0
002	Number of POS registers used
003	POS 2 configuration byte for card in MCA slot 0
004	POS 3 configuration byte for card in MCA slot 0
005	POS 4 configuration byte for card in MCA slot 0
006	POS 5 configuration byte for card in MCA slot 0
007-022	Reserved
023	Low byte of adapter ID for card in MCA slot 1
024	High byte of adapter ID for card in MCA slot 1
025	Number of POS registers used
026	POS 2 configuration byte for card in MCA slot 1
027	POS 3 configuration byte for card in MCA slot 1
028	POS 4 configuration byte for card in MCA slot 1
029	POS 5 configuration byte for card in MCA slot 1
02A-045	Reserved
046	Low byte of adapter ID for card in MCA slot 2
047	High byte of adapter ID for card in MCA slot 2
048	Number of POS registers used
049	POS 2 configuration byte for card in MCA slot 2
04A	POS 3 configuration byte for card in MCA slot 2
04B	POS 4 configuration byte for card in MCA slot 2
04C	POS 5 configuration byte for card in MCA slot 2
04D-068	Reserved
069	Low byte of adapter ID for card in MCA slot 3
06A	High byte of adapter ID for card in MCA slot 3
06B	Number of POS registers used
06C	POS 2 configuration byte for card in MCA slot 3
06D	POS 3 configuration byte for card in MCA slot 3
06E	POS 4 configuration byte for card in MCA slot 3
06F	POS 5 configuration byte for card in MCA slot 3

TABLE 26-5 Continued

Location(s) (hex)	Description
070-08B	Reserved
08C	Low byte of adapter ID for card in MCA slot 4
08D	High byte of adapter ID for card in MCA slot 4
08E	Number of POS registers used
08F	POS 2 configuration byte for card in MCA slot 4
090	POS 3 configuration byte for card in MCA slot 4
091	POS 4 configuration byte for card in MCA slot 4
092	POS 5 configuration byte for card in MCA slot 4
093-0AE	Reserved
0AF	Low byte of adapter ID for card in MCA slot 5
0B0	High byte of adapter ID for card in MCA slot 5
0B1	Number of POS registers used
0B2	POS 2 configuration byte for card in MCA slot 5
0B3	POS 3 configuration byte for card in MCA slot 5
0B4	POS 4 configuration byte for card in MCA slot 5
0B5	POS 5 configuration byte for card in MCA slot 5
0B6-0D1	Reserved
0D2	Low byte of adapter ID for card in MCA slot 6
0D3	High byte of adapter ID for card in MCA slot 6
0D4	Number of POS registers used
0D5	POS 2 configuration byte for card in MCA slot 6
0D6	POS 3 configuration byte for card in MCA slot 6
0D7	POS 4 configuration byte for card in MCA slot 6
0D8	POS 5 configuration byte for card in MCA slot 6
0D9-0F4	Reserved
0F5	Low byte of adapter ID for card in MCA slot 7
0F6	High byte of adapter ID for card in MCA slot 7
0F7	Number of POS registers used
0F8	POS 2 configuration byte for card in MCA slot 7
0F9	POS 3 configuration byte for card in MCA slot 7
0FA	POS 4 configuration byte for card in MCA slot 7
0FB	POS 5 configuration byte for card in MCA slot 7
0FC-7FF	Reserved

The System Board
Peripheral Devices

Introduction to Part VIII

Part VIII consists of Chapters 27 through 32. It provides a description of the peripheral devices that are an integral part of the PS/2 system board.

An in-depth programmer's guide for each of the devices is not provided because a wealth of information has already been published on this subject.

The following is a synopsis of each chapter.

Chapter 27: The Floppy Disk Interface. This chapter provides a block-level description of the floppy disk subsystem and the I/O registers used to control it.

Chapter 28: The Serial Port. This chapter provides an overview of the serial port's capabilities, the number of serial ports supported, the IRQ lines used, and a description of the I/O registers used to control the serial port.

Chapter 29: The Parallel Port. This chapter provides an overview of the parallel port's capabilities, the IRQ lines used, and a description of the I/O registers used to control the parallel port.

Chapter 30: The Keyboard/Mouse Interface. This chapter provides an overview of the keyboard/mouse interface's capabilities and a description of the I/O registers used to control the keyboard/mouse interface.

Chapter 31: The VGA Display Interface. This chapter focuses on the relationship of the VGA chip to the video memory, digital-to-analog converter (DAC), and the video extension used by the IBM 8514A advanced display adapter.

Chapter 32: The Numeric Coprocessor. This chapter describes the relationship between the microprocessor and the numeric coprocessor. Performance of floating-point operations both with and without the numeric coprocessor are discussed.

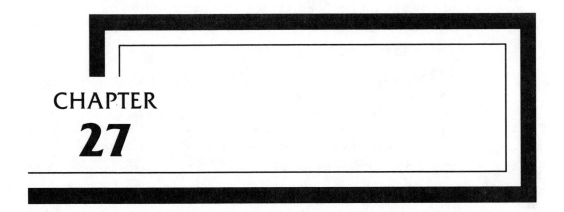

CHAPTER
27

The Floppy Disk Interface

Objectives: This chapter provides a block-level description of the floppy disk subsystem and the I/O registers used to control it.

Definitions for This Chapter

• **Clock bits** frame the start and end of bit cells when writing data on the diskette surface.

• A **data separator** is a device that determines the point at which the floppy disk controller should sample the combined clock/data stream on the read data line to capture a data bit.

• A **data window** signal is generated by the data separator logic to tell the floppy disk controller when to sample the combined clock/data stream on the read data line to capture a data bit.

• The **floppy disk controller** is the programmable device that receives commands from the microprocessor and controls one or two drive units.

• **Frequency modulation (FM)** recording is used in low-density mode and places a clock bit at the leading edge of each bit cell.

• **High-density** recording uses a clock pulse frequency of 500KHz when writing bit cells on the diskette surface.

• The **index** pulse is generated by the drive unit once per revolution. It marks the start of a track.

• **Low-density** recording uses a clock pulse frequency of 250KHz when writing bit cells on the diskette surface.

• **Modified frequency modulation (MFM)** recording is used in high-density mode. It does not place a clock bit at the leading edge of a bit cell if either the previous bit cell or the bit cell about to be written contains a 1.

• A **phase-locked loop (PLL)** acts as an electronic flywheel that maintains its momentum, or frequency, for some time before it begins to drift off frequency. It is used to generate the data window signal to the floppy disk controller when MFM recording is in use (high-density mode).

- A **read/write coil** writes data on and reads data from the disk surface.

- The **recalibrate** command causes the floppy disk controller to reposition the heads over track 0.

- A **sector** is a data area on the diskette that can hold 512 bytes of data.

- **Sector address marks** are written on the diskette surface during low-level formatting to identify individual sectors.

- The **seek** command causes the floppy disk controller to position the head mechanism over the desired track.

- **Settling time** is the amount of time that must be allowed for the head assembly to stop vibrating after the heads are positioned over a particular track.

- **Step** pulses are issued by the floppy disk controller and cause the drive unit to move the heads one track for each step pulse received.

- The **stepper band** is manipulated by the stepper motor to move the read/write head mechanism.

- A **track** is the concentric ring traversed by the head while positioned over a particular point on the diskette surface.

- **Track 0** is the outermost track on the diskette and is considered the home track.

- The **write protect window** is the small opening near the corner of a 3.5″ diskette that can either be opened to write-protect a diskette or closed to allow writing.

The Diskette

Figure 27-1 illustrates a typical diskette. The diskettes used in the PS/2 have a diameter of 3.5″, are protected by a plastic carrier, and are coated with ferric oxide on both sides. Ferric oxide consists of iron particles that can be magnetized. When the diskette is inserted in the drive unit,

FIGURE 27-1 The Diskette

a sliding door on the carrier automatically opens and exposes the diskette surface to the drive mechanism. The drive unit's spindle motor engages the center hub of the diskette. When activated, the spindle motor rotates the diskette at approximately 300RPM. The drive unit produces a signal known as **index** once for each revolution of the diskette. The use of the index signal is discussed later in this chapter.

The small, sliding tab near one of the corners of the plastic diskette carrier is the write protect tab. When the tab is positioned so that the **write protect window** opening appears, the drive unit generates the write protect signal to send back to the **floppy disk controller** on the system board. This prevents programs from writing on a write-protected diskette. Information may be recorded on both sides, or surfaces, of the diskette.

Head Mechanism

The **read/write coil** records information on the diskette surface and reads information from its surface. When information is written on the diskette, an electrical current passes through the coil to create a magnetic field around it. Because the coil is close to the spinning diskette surface, the resulting magnetic field magnetizes the ferric oxide on the diskette surface directly under the coil.

When reading information from the diskette surface, the drive unit does not pass any current through the coil. The coil is once again positioned close to the diskette surface. As previously magnetized points on the diskette surface pass under the coil, each of their magnetic fields induces a momentary current flow in the coil. These rather weak pulses are amplified and shaped (cleaned up) by the drive electronics and are passed back to the floppy disk controller on the system board.

Figure 27-2 illustrates the read/write head actuator. There are actually two read/write coils, one associated with each surface of the diskette. The drive unit uses an electromechanical device known as the

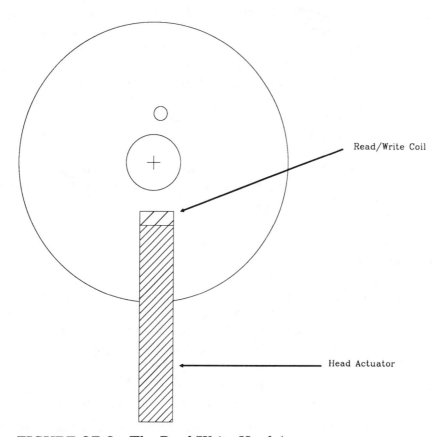

FIGURE 27-2 The Read/Write Head Actuator

read/write head actuator to position the coils over the desired point on the diskette surfaces.

The head actuator moves the read/write coils in towards the spindle or out towards the edge of the disk under the control of the floppy disk controller on the system board. A stepper motor actuator is used in PS/2 drive units.

Unlike a normal motor that spins freely when power is applied, the stepper motor has four or more field coils. Special control logic built into the drive electronics is used to select the next coil to energize each time a **step** pulse is received from the floppy disk controller. This causes the motor's rotor to move a small, precise amount to line up its magnetic poles with the new field orientation. The net result is that the rotor moves in small, magnetically-detented steps as the electromagnetic field rotates around the central axis. The motor's shaft is then used to drive a **stepper band** that is attached to the arm holding the read/write coils.

Each step pulse positions the read/write coil over the next **track**. When the head mechanism is fully retracted towards the outer edge of the diskette, the heads, or coils, are positioned over **track 0**. This is considered to be the home position for the heads. The innermost track is track 79, making a total of 80 tracks per surface.

The advantage of the of stepper actuator is its inherent accuracy; its major disadvantage is its slowness. The average track-to-track access time for this type of actuator mechanism is 60 to 100ms. The access time for fixed disk drives can be 15ms or less.

When the head actuator mechanism moves the heads to a new track, the system must allow a certain length of **settling time** for the heads to stop vibrating.

Diskette Usage

Both diskette surfaces must be formatted before recording data. Many diskettes are sold pre-formatted. The low-level formatting process is initiated by issuing the format command to the floppy disk controller on the system board. The formatting process proceeds as follows:

1. The heads are retracted to track 0 by issuing the Recal (**Recalibrate** to track 0) command to the floppy disk controller.

2. The floppy disk controller waits until the index mark is sensed. This marks the beginning of a track.

3. Figure 27-3 illustrates the concept of tracks divided into sectors. The floppy disk controller writes a series of special address patterns along track 0 on the selected surface. These are known as **sector address marks** and each marks the beginning of a data storage area on the track. Each of these data storage areas is a **sector** and can contain 512 bytes of data. A **low-density** diskette is formatted with 9 sectors per track; a **high-density** diskette is formatted with 18 sectors per track.

4. When the track formatting has been completed on both surfaces, a **Seek** command is issued to the floppy disk controller to position the heads over track 1.

5. The process is repeated for each track on both surfaces until the format of track 79 has been completed. This completes the low-level format of the diskette.

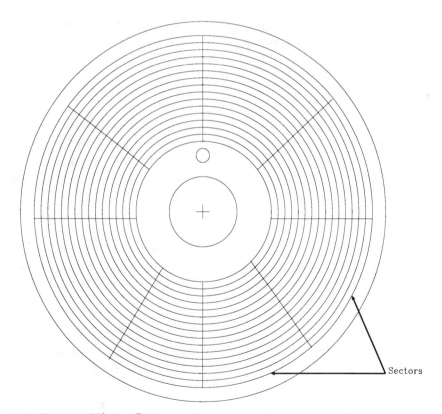

FIGURE 27-3 Sectors

The overall storage capacity of low- and high-density diskettes can be computed from the information supplied above. The low-density diskette capacity is computed as follows:

512 bytes/sector
× 9 sectors/track
× 80 tracks/surface
× 2 surfaces = 737,280 bytes formatted capacity (720KB)

The high-density diskette capacity is computed as follows:

512 bytes/sector
× 18 sectors/track
× 80 tracks/surface
× 2 surfaces = 1,474,560 bytes formatted capacity (1.44MB)

Recording Format

Frequency modulation (FM) and **modified frequency modulation (MFM)** are the two recording formats used on the floppy drives used in the PS/2 products. Descriptions of each follow.

Frequency Modulation (FM) Recording

The FM data recording technique is used in low-density mode. The floppy disk controller frames each bit (a 1 or a 0) in a bit cell when sending the data to the disk drive. If the disk controller wants to write only 0's on the disk, it sends nothing over the write data line except **clock bits** consisting of a fixed-frequency signal. The clock pulses are then written on the disk. Figure 27-4 illustrates this pattern.

One cycle of the clock signal defines the limits of a bit cell. A cycle is the interval from one rising edge to the next rising edge. When the disk controller wants the disk drive to write a 1 on the disk, it inserts the 1 (a pulse) in the middle of the bit cell. When it wants to write a 0, nothing is inserted in that bit cell. Figure 27-5 illustrates two sample series of bits. This means that the frequency of the data going to the disk drive varies, or modulates, from bit cell to bit cell. Bit cells containing 1's are double the frequency of bit cells containing 0's—hence the term frequency modulation (FM). FM is also called low-density recording.

When the information is read back from the disk and sent to the disk controller over the read data line, it consists of a composite

Bit Cells

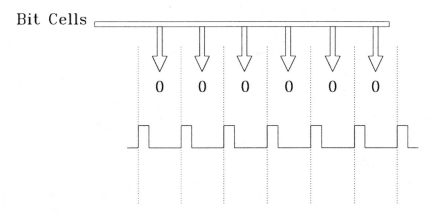

FIGURE 27-4   All 0's Pattern

Clock Bit

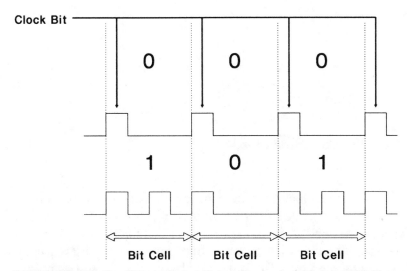

Bit Cell   Bit Cell   Bit Cell

FIGURE 27-5   Example of Data Recorded Using FM Recording

read data signal with intermingled clocks and data. The disk controller is associated with logic that can separate out the data from the clocks. This logic is called a **data separator**. Refer to Figure 27-6.

The job of the data separator is to create a **data window** signal to tell the floppy disk controller when a data bit (either a 1 or a 0) is present in the composite clock/data stream on the read data line. Having identified the time slot during which the 1 or 0 can be read from the read data line, the floppy disk controller can capture the data bits and assemble them into bytes to be sent to system memory.

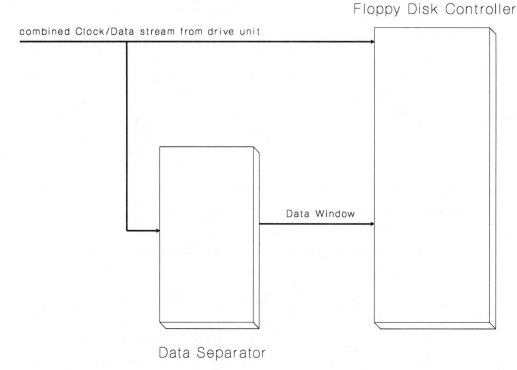

Floppy Disk Controller

combined Clock/Data stream from drive unit

Data Window

Data Separator

FIGURE 27-6 FM Data Separator

The FM clock rate used in low-density mode is 250KHz. This means that one cycle of the clock is 4 microseconds in length. Since a bit cell is one cycle of clock in duration, the bit cell is also 4 microseconds in length. The clock bit remains high for the first microsecond of the bit cell. The data bit (if it is a 1) is always written in the middle of the bit cell, centered between the trailing edge of the clock bit at the bit cell start and the leading edge of the clock bit that delineates the end of the bit cell. This means the one microsecond-wide pulse (representing a 1) or the lack of a pulse (representing a 0) can be found during the third microsecond of the 4 microsecond-wide bit cell.

The FM data separator therefore generates a data window signal that goes active one microsecond after each clock bit and lasts for two microseconds. The data window signal is left active for two microseconds to allow for a one bit that has drifted slightly (due to rotational speed variations).

Modified Frequency Modulation (MFM) Recording

The modified frequency modulation (MFM) recording technique is used when high-density mode is chosen. MFM is a variation on FM that effectively doubles the frequency of the clock, thereby doubling the density of the data written on the disk. Instead of using a 250KHz clock (as in FM), MFM uses a 500KHz clock rate. At 500KHz, a bit cell is two microseconds instead of four microseconds wide.

In addition, a clock bit is written at the leading edge of a bit cell only if a 1 was not written in the previous bit cell and a 1 will not be written in the present bit cell. If bit cells contain a 1, the clock bits and the 1 bit are very close together at this higher frequency and may confuse the drive's read logic. Refer to Figure 27-7 for an example.

MFM presents two problems:

1. Only some bit cells contain a clock bit, thereby losing the fixed reference for the start of a bit cell that the FM technique offers.

2. The bit cell in MFM is one-half the duration of the bit cell in FM. This shorter bit cell means that MFM cannot tolerate

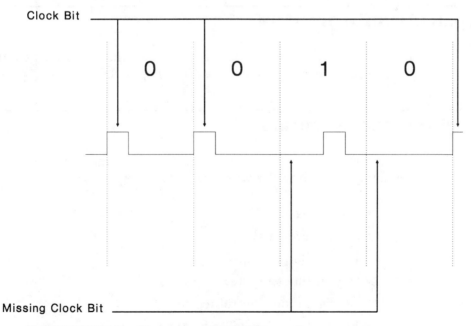

FIGURE 27-7 Example of MFM Recording

as large a playback data-shift (due to variations in spindle motor speed) as FM can.

Because of the missing clock bits, a more sophisticated data separator must be used to create the data window signal when MFM is used. The circuit used is a **phase-locked loop** (PLL) that is constantly re-synchronized to the incoming composite clock/data stream on the read data line.

When a low-level format is performed, a series of 0 bit cells is written at the beginning of every track and every sector on the track. This is done because bit cells containing 0's always have a clock bit at the leading edge. These clock bits are used to synchronize the PLL to the clock. When missing clock bits start to appear, the PLL continues to supply the data window signal to the floppy disk controller so it can accurately identify the data bits in the composite read data. The PLL acts as an electronic flywheel that maintains its momentum, or frequency, for some time before it begins to drift off frequency. Before that occurs, it encounters bit cells that have clock bits and uses them to resync itself to the proper frequency.

Controller/Drive Interface

The signals in Table 27-1 are used to connect the floppy disk controller on the system board to one or two 3.5″ floppy drive units.

Registers and Commands

The programmer uses seven registers to control and sense the status of the floppy disk controller with one or two drive units.

- Status register A
- Status register B
- Digital Output register
- Digital Input register
- Configuration Control register
- Floppy Disk Controller Status register
- Floppy Disk Controller Data register

TABLE 27-1 The Floppy Disk Controller to Drive Unit Interface

Signal	Description
HIGH DENSITY SELECT#	When 0, the drive unit uses the MFM recording technique at a frequency of 500KHZ.
2ND DRIVE INSTALLED#	Goes low when a second drive unit is installed.
INDEX#	Goes active briefly once per revolution.
DRIVE SELECT#	Selects this drive unit when low. This signal and MOTOR ENABLE# must both be active in order to control the drive unit or check its status.
MOTOR ENABLE#	When low, drive unit's spindle motor is turned on. This signal and DRIVE SELECT# must both be active in order to control the drive unit or check its status.
DIRECTION IN#	When low, the head mechanism moves towards the spindle when STEP pulses are received from the floppy disk controller.
STEP#	The drive unit moves the head mechanism one track in the direction selected by the state of the DIRECTION IN# signal when a step pulse is received.
WRITE DATA#	During a disk write operation, the combined clock/data stream is sent to the drive unit (from the floppy disk controller) over this line.
WRITE ENABLE#	During a disk write operation, the floppy disk controller sets this line active to enable the drive unit's write logic.
TRACK 0#	This line is set low by the drive unit when the read/write heads are positioned over track 0.
WRITE PROTECT#	This line is set low by the drive unit when the Write Protect window on the diskette is open. The diskette may not be written to when this signal is active, but it may be read from.
READ DATA#	During a disk read operation, the combined clock/data stream is sent to the floppy disk controller (by the drive unit) over this line.
HEAD 1 SELECT#	0 = head/surface 1 selected. 1 = head/surface 0 selected.

TABLE 27-1 Continued

Signal	Description
DISKETTE CHANGE#	When low, the user has removed and inserted a new diskette. The operating system software should read the new diskette's directory into memory.
+5vdc	Power for the logic on the drive unit.
−12vdc	Spindle motor power.

A drive unit must be selected and its spindle motor turning in order to check its status or issue commands to it.

The Floppy Disk Controller Status register and the Floppy Disk Controller Data register are within the Intel 8272A floppy disk controller chip. The other five are external to the controller. The following sections describe the function of the seven registers.

The I/O Registers External to the Floppy Disk Controller

The following five registers are external to the Intel 8272A floppy disk controller chip:

- Status register A
- Status register B
- Digital Output register
- Digital Input register
- Configuration Control register

Table 27-2 defines the bits in Status register A, a read-only register at I/O address $03F0_h$.

Table 27-3 defines the bits in Status register B. It is a read-only register at I/O address $03F1_h$.

The Digital Output register (DOR) is a write-only register at I/O address $03F2_h$. Table 27-4 defines the function of the bits in this register.

The Digital Input register is a read-only register at I/O address $03F7_h$. Table 27-5 defines the function of the bits in this register.

The Configuration Control register is a write-only register at I/O address $03F7_h$. Table 27-6 defines the function of the bits in this register.

TABLE 27-2 Status Register A

Bit	Function
7	Interrupt pending. This bit is set to 1 when the floppy disk controller is generating IRQ6#. If the IRQ6# line is shared by multiple devices, the IRQ6# interrupt service routine should check this bit to see if a floppy disk controller interrupt is pending.
6	Second drive installed. Set to 0 if the second drive unit is installed.
5	Step. Set to 1 if the STEP command line to the drive unit is active. This capability is provided for diagnostic programs so the operability of the STEP# line can be ascertained.
4	Track 0. Set to 0 if the read/write heads are positioned over track 0.
3	Head 1 select. Set to 1 if head/surface 1 is currently selected. This capability is provided for diagnostic programs so the operability of the HEAD 1 SELECT# line can be ascertained.
2	Index. Set to 0 if the INDEX status line from the selected drive unit is active. Diagnostics can check this bit to ascertain that the diskette spindle motor is turning and up to speed.
1	Write protect. Set to 0 if the Write Protect window in the diskette is open and the diskette is write-protected.
0	Direction select. Indicates the current state of the DIRECTION IN# command line to the drive unit. This capability is provided for diagnostic programs so that the operability of the DIRECTION IN# line can be ascertained.

The I/O Registers Internal to the Floppy Disk Controller

The Intel 8272A floppy disk controller contains two I/O registers, the Floppy Disk Controller Status register and the Floppy Disk Controller Data register.

The Floppy Disk Controller Status register is a read-only register at I/O address $03F4_h$. Table 27-7 defines the function of the bits in this register.

The Floppy Disk Controller Data register at I/O address $03F5_h$ accepts data, commands, and parameters (such as the sector number) from the microprocessor, and sends status information to the microprocessor.

TABLE 27-3 Status Register B

Bit(s)	Function
7-6	Not used.
5	Drive select. Indicates the drive unit that is currently selected. This capability is provided for diagnostic programs so the operability of the DRIVE SELECT# line can be ascertained. 0 = drive 0 1 = drive 1
4	Write data. Set to 1 by a rising edge on the WRITE DATA# signal. This capability is provided for diagnostic programs so that the operability of the WRITE DATA# line can be ascertained.
3	Read data. Set to 1 by a rising edge on the READ DATA# signal. This capability is provided for diagnostic programs so that the operability of the READ DATA# line can be ascertained.
2	Write enable. Reflects the current state of the WRITE ENABLE# command line to the drive unit. This capability is provided for diagnostic programs so that the operability of the WRITE ENABLE# line can be ascertained. 0 = Disabled 1 = Enabled
1	Motor enable 1. Reflects the current state of the MOTOR ENABLE 1# command line to the drive unit. This capability is provided for diagnostic programs so that the operability of the MOTOR ENABLE 1# line can be ascertained. 0 = Motor off 1 = Motor on
0	Motor enable 0. Reflects the current state of the MOTOR ENABLE 0# command line to the drive unit. This capability is provided for diagnostic programs so that the operability of the MOTOR ENABLE 0# line can be ascertained. 0 = Motor off 1 = Motor on

TABLE 27-4   The Digital Output Register

Bit(s)	Function
7-6	Not used.
5	Motor enable 1. 1 = Drive unit 1's spindle motor on 0 = Drive unit 1's spindle motor off
4	Motor enable 0. 1 = Drive unit 0's spindle motor on 0 = Drive unit 0's spindle motor off
3	Not used.
2	Floppy disk controller reset. When set to 1, applies a reset to the floppy disk controller chip. Used to clear error conditions. Must be 0 in order to communicate with the floppy disk controller.
1	Not used.
0	Drive select. 0 = Select drive 0 1 = Select drive 1

TABLE 27-5   The Digital Input Register

Bit(s)	Function
7	Diskette change.
6-1	Not used.
0	Reflects the current density selection. 0 = High density 1 = Low density

Commands and Status

The execution of any command by the floppy disk controller involves three separate and distinct phases:

1. **The Command Phase**. The microprocessor issues the command and any required command parameters to the floppy

TABLE 27-6 The Configuration Control Register

Bit(s)	Function
7-2	Not used.
1-0	Data rate select.
	00 = 500KHz
	01 = Not used
	10 = 250KHz
	11 = Not used

TABLE 27-7 The Floppy Disk Controller Status Register

Bit(s)	Function
7	Request for master. When set to 1, the Floppy Disk Controller Data register is ready to accept data from or has data for the microprocessor.
6	Data input/output mode.
	0 = Floppy Disk Controller Data register is ready to accept data from the microprocessor.
	1 = Floppy Disk Controller Data register has data to be transferred to the microprocessor.
5	Non-DMA mode. When set to 1, the floppy disk controller is in the non-DMA mode.
4	Floppy disk controller busy. When set to a 1, the floppy disk controller is performing a disk read or write.
3-2	Not used.
1	Drive 1 busy. 1 = Drive 1 is busy seeking to the target track.
0	Drive 0 busy. 1 = Drive 0 is busy seeking to the target track.

disk controller. For example, a command to perform a disk read also requires the following parameters:

a. The head/surface number (0 or 1).

b. The track number (0 through 79).

c. The sector number (1 through 9, or 1 through 18).

d. The number of sectors of information to transfer.

2. **The Execution Phase**. The floppy disk controller executes the command.

3. **The Result Phase**. After completion of the command, the floppy disk controller supplies status information back to the microprocessor.

The command and any required parameters are written to the Floppy Disk Controller Data register by the microprocessor. A command consists of 1 byte; the number of parameter bytes required is specific to the command issued. The number of bytes of status supplied by the floppy disk controller after command execution is also specific to the command executed. Table 27-8 lists the valid commands.

A detailed explanation of the commands and resulting status can be found in Intel's publication *Microprocessor and Peripheral Handbook, Volume II Peripheral* in the section on the 8272A floppy disk controller.

BIOS Routine

The recommended method for controlling the floppy disk subsystem is through BIOS function calls. INT 13_h can be used to call the floppy disk BIOS routine. A complete description of this BIOS routine's use can be found in *The IBM PS/2 and Personal Computer BIOS Interface Technical Reference* published by IBM and *CBIOS For IBM PS/2 Computers and Compatibles* by Phoenix Technologies Ltd., published by Addison-Wesley.

DMA Transfers

The floppy disk controller uses DMA channel 2 to transfer data between itself and memory. For more information on DMA transfers, refer to Chapter 20.

Summary

The floppy disk controller used in the PS/2 product line can handle one or two drive units. It is based on the Intel 8272A floppy disk controller and is built into the system board.

TABLE 27-8 Floppy Disk Controller Commands

Command	Description
Read Data	Reads a sector of information, 512 bytes, from the specified Head/track/sector.
Read Deleted Data	Allows the programmer to read 512 bytes of information from a sector previously marked as deleted.
Read a Track	Reads a complete track's worth of information from the specified head/track.
Read ID	Allows the programmer to determine the current position of the selected read head by reading the next sector ID encountered.
Write Data	Writes a sector of information, 512 bytes, to the specified head/track/sector.
Write Deleted Data	Marks the specified sector as deleted, but the data within the sector is not actually deleted. The sector ID is altered to indicate the data has been marked as deleted.
Format a Track	Performs a low-level format on the specified head/track.
Scan Equal	Compares the data within the specified sector to data in memory to see if they are equal.
Scan Low or Equal	Compares the data within the specified sector to data in memory and reports whether the data from the disk is numerically less than or equal to the data in memory.
Scan High or Equal	Compares the data within the specified sector to data in memory and reports whether the data from the disk is numerically greater than or equal to the data in memory.
Recalibrate	The floppy disk controller sets the direction line and issues the required number of step pulses to get the heads back to track 0.
Sense Interrupt Status	Allows the programmer to determine the cause of an IRQ6# from the floppy disk controller.
Specify Command	Allows the programmer to specify the following operational characteristics of the floppy disk controller: • Head load time in milliseconds • Head unload time in milliseconds • The rate at which step pulses are issued • Whether the controller should use DMA

TABLE 27-8 Continued

Command	Description
Sense Drive Status	Allows the programmer to obtain the status of the specified drive unit.
Seek Command	Commands the floppy disk controller to step the specified drive unit's head mechanism to the specified track.

A diskette has two surfaces, each divided into 80 tracks and either 9 or 18 sectors. Each sector holds 512 bytes of data. The drive unit uses a movable read/write head assembly to position the heads over the desired track. The beginning of a track is sensed by the index mark. Each sector is identified by a special address mark written on the diskette by performing a low-level format command.

In low-density mode, there are 9 sectors per track and the diskette capacity is 737,280 bytes. In high-density mode, there are 18 sectors per track and the diskette capacity is 1,474,560 bytes.

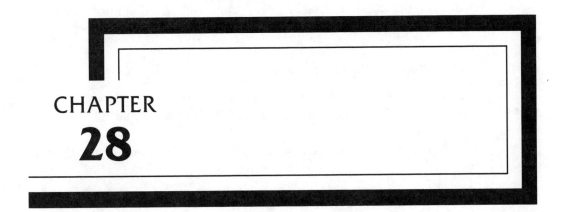

CHAPTER
28

The Serial Port

Objectives: This chapter provides an overview of the serial port's capabilities, the number of serial ports supported, the IRQ lines used, and a description of the I/O registers used to control the serial port.

Definitions for This Chapter

• The **baud rate** is the rate at which serial data is transmitted or received by a serial port. Baud stands for bits per second.

• **Demodulation** is the act of converting FM information to 1's and 0's.

• **FIFO** stands for first in, first out buffer. The first byte to be placed in the buffer is the first one to be output from it.

• A **mark** is a logic 1 on the transmit data line to the modem.

• A **modem** is a device that converts FM data to 1's and 0's or visa versa. It is used to interface a serial port to the telephone lines.

• **Modulation** is the act of varying a base, or carrier, frequency to represent information.

• The **RS-232 standard** defines the signals and voltage levels that link the serial port to the modem and the modem to the telephone lines.

• The **start bit** precedes a byte of serial data. Together with the stop bit, it frames the serial data byte.

• The **stop bit** always follows a byte of serial data. It may actually consists of 1, 1.5, or 2 bits. Together with the start bit, it frames the serial data byte.

Purpose of the Serial Port: Telephone Communications

In this context, the word port signifies a communications port, or device, rather than an I/O address. The serial port exists to allow the system to communicate with other devices via the telephone lines. Refer to

Figure 28-1. The serial port is connected to the **modem** which is connected to the telephone lines. The function of the modem is defined later in this chapter. The two primary functions performed by a serial port are as follows.

1. The microprocessor deals with information a byte (8 bits) at a time, and the phone lines provide only one wire for transmission and one for reception. The serial port must therefore provide parallel-to-serial and serial-to-parallel conversion capability.

   During data transmission, the serial port must send a byte to the telephone lines 1 bit at a time (parallel-to-serial); during reception, it must receive data 1 bit at a time until a byte has been assembled (serial-to-parallel). The byte is then given to the microprocessor.

2. The voltage levels used to represent 0's and 1's inside the system are 0Vdc and +5Vdc, respectively; those understood by the modem are

   a. 0 = a voltage greater than +3Vdc

   b. 1 = a voltage less than −3Vdc.

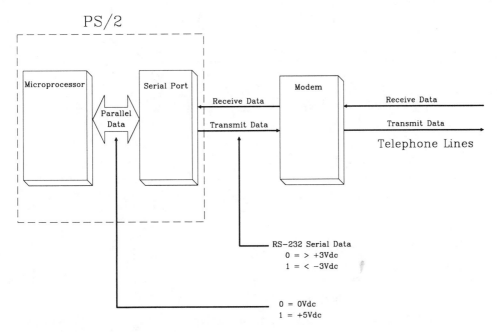

FIGURE 28-1   Block Diagram

The Modem

Modem stands for modulator/demodulator. It uses frequency **modulation** (FM) to send and receive data over the telephone lines. If a 1 is represented on the phone lines as a pulse and a 0 as the lack of a pulse, the data stream resembles Figure 28-2.

Using this method, it is very easy to identify the 1's, but the 0's are a problem. How many 0's are there between the 1 bits and where are they? Because there is no point of reference, it is impossible to tell.

Figure 28-3 illustrates the actual transmission method. Using FM, clock bits at a specific frequency are used to establish points of reference. Every bit sent (a 1 or a 0) is prefaced by a clock bit. The period of time from the leading-edge of one clock bit to the leading-edge of the next is known as a bit cell. Within a bit cell, a 0 is represented

FIGURE 28-2   Stream of 1's and 0's

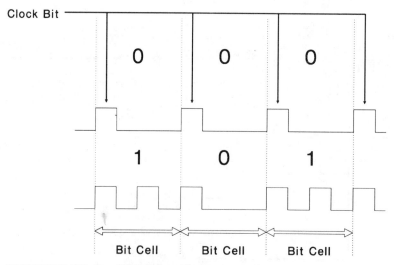

FIGURE 28-3   FM Data Representation

by the lack of a pulse between two clock bits; a 1 is represented by a pulse. If sending nothing but 0's, just the clock bits are sent. In other words, 0's are represented by the clock, or carrier, frequency. Bit cells containing 1 bits, however, are represented by a frequency double that of the clock. It is called frequency modulation because the frequency is varied (modulated) to represented 0's and 1's.

Introduction to Data Transmission and Reception

When the system is transmitting data to another system:

1. The microprocessor writes a data byte to the serial port.

2. The serial port serializes the data and feeds it to the modem one bit at a time. The serial port also converts the 1's and 0's to the voltage levels understood by the modem.

3. The modem converts the 1's and 0's to FM and sends it over the telephone line to the other computer system.

4. The serial port interrupts the microprocessor to request another byte.

When the system is receiving data from another system:

1. The modem receives the FM data over the telephone line, converts it through **demodulation** back to 1's and 0's, and sends the serial bit stream to the serial port.

2. The serial port converts the 1's and 0's to the voltage levels understood by the system: $0 = 0\text{Vdc}$ and $1 = +5\text{Vdc}$.

3. The serial port interrupts the microprocessor when it has assembled 8 bits into a byte.

4. The microprocessor jumps to the serial port's interrupt service routine.

5. The interrupt service routine inputs the data byte and stores it in memory.

The RS-232 Interface

The **RS-232 standard** defines the signals and voltage levels that link the serial port and the modem and the modem and the telephone lines. The PS/2's serial port uses a subset of the RS-232 signals. Table 28-1 defines theses signals.

The RS-232 standard defines the signals and voltage levels that link the serial port and the modem and the modem and the telephone lines.

TABLE 28-1   PS/2 RS-232 Signal Usage

Signal Name	Pin	Description
TD	2	Transmit data. Serial data to modem from serial port.
RD	3	Receive data. Serial data from modem to serial port.
RTS	4	Request to send. Control signal from serial port to modem. Commands modem to turn on its carrier frequency in preparation to send data.
CTS	5	Clear to send. Status signal from modem to the serial port. Modem is ready to send data.
DSR	6	Data set ready. Status signal from modem to the serial port. Indicates the modem is powered on and functional.
DCD	8	Data carrier detect. Status signal from modem to serial port. Indicates the modem has turned on its carrier frequency on the telephone transmit line in response to the RTS command line from the serial port. The modem has checked the telephone transmit line and the carrier appears to be within tolerance.
DTR	20	Data terminal ready. Status line from the serial port to the modem. Tells the modem that the system is powered on and ready to communicate.
RI	22	Ring indicator. Status signal from modem to the serial port. Goes active when ring voltage is detected on the phone line.

The Handshake

Prior to data transmission from the PS/2, the following actions must take place.

1. The microprocessor issues a command to the serial port to turn on DTR and RTS. DTR indicates to the modem that the PS/2 is powered up and ready to communicate. RTS commands the modem to prepare to send data.
2. The modem should already have DSR turned on to indicate that it is powered on and ready to communicate.
3. The modem responds to RTS by turning on its transmit carrier on the telephone transmit line and testing it. If it appears to be within tolerance, the modem sends back CTS and DCD to the serial port.
4. The microprocessor reads the modem status to ascertain that DSR, CTS, and DCD are all turned on.

The serial port and modem are now ready to send data supplied by the microprocessor.

Prior to data transmission from the PS/2, the following actions must take place.

1. The microprocessor issues a command to the serial port to turn on DTR. DTR indicates to the modem that the PS/2 is powered up and ready to communicate.
2. The modem should already have DSR turned on to indicate that it is powered on and ready to communicate.

The serial port and modem are now ready to receive data from another system and supply it to the microprocessor.

Data Format

When not transmitting data, the serial port's transmit data output is kept in the **mark** state. This means that it is kept in the logic 1 state.

Figure 28-4 illustrates the data transmission format. When a byte of information is serialized by the serial port, it is transmitted to the modem in the following sequence:

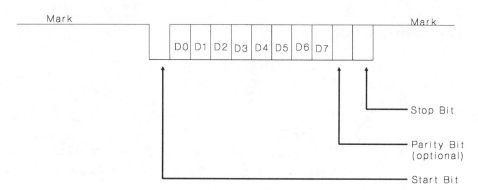

FIGURE 28-4   Data Format

1. A **start bit** to indicate the start of a byte. The start bit is a logic 0.

2. The data bits. This field may be 5, 6, 7, or 8 bits wide.

3. An optional even or odd parity bit.

4. The **stop bit**. This field may be 1, 1.5, or 2 stop bits wide.

The rate at which data is transmitted is software-selectable from 50 to 19.2K Baud, where baud stands for bits-per-second.

Both the transmitting and the receiving serial ports must be set up for the same **baud rate**, number of data bits, parity on or off, even or odd parity, and the number of stop bits.

Setup

During the POST, the serial port on the system board is configured as either serial port 1 or 2.

Serial port 1 responds to the I/O addresses in the range from $03F8_h$ to $03FF_h$. It uses the IRQ4# interrupt request line.

Serial port 2 responds to the I/O addresses in the range from $02F8_h$ to $02FF_h$. It uses the IRQ3# interrupt request line.

For more information regarding setup of the system board serial port, refer to Chapter 14.

FIFO Operation

FIFO stands for first in, first out buffer. This capability did not exist in the PC product line and is not present in the entire PS/2 product line. Table 28-2 identifies some PS/2 products that incorporate the FIFO feature.

In the earlier PC products, the serial port had a 1-byte buffer. During transmission the serial port could hold and serialize only 1 byte at a time. When receiving, it could hold only one byte received from the modem.

The problem with the earlier serial port implementation involved data overrun and underrun conditions. A data overrun condition occurs when data is received by the serial port faster than the microprocessor can read it. With the earlier serial ports, a byte received by the serial port could be overwritten by the next byte from the modem if the microprocessor was slow in reading the first byte from the serial port. A data underrun condition occurs when the microprocessor cannot write data bytes to the serial port as quickly as the serial port serializes and transmits them. The earlier serial ports (and the system on the other end of the telephone line) were idled while waiting for the microprocessor to catch up.

The FIFO capability provides a 16-byte receive buffer and a 16-byte transmit buffer. This allows the serial port to transmit bytes from one end of the transmit buffer while the microprocessor loads (writes) bytes into the other end. The first byte placed in the buffer is the first one transmitted, hence the name FIFO. The serial port can continue to transmit data if the microprocessor falls somewhat behind, thus eliminating underrun conditions. The FIFO also allows data bytes to be

TABLE 28-2 FIFO Feature

Model	FIFO Supported?
50	no
50Z	no
60	yes
70	yes
80	yes

received and placed in one end of the FIFO receive buffer while the microprocessor reads bytes from the other end of it. This eliminates overrun conditions when the microprocessor is slightly tardy in accepting the data.

I/O Registers

The serial port contains 11 I/O registers that are used to control, sense the status of, and transfer data with the serial port. Table 28-3 provides a brief description of each of these registers.

A complete breakdown of the individual bits in these registers is beyond the scope of this book. It may be found in the *IBM PS/2 Hardware Interface Technical Reference* published by IBM.

BIOS Routine

The recommended method for controlling the serial ports is through BIOS function calls. INT 14_h can be used to call the serial port BIOS routine. A complete description of this BIOS routine's use can be found in *The IBM PS/2 and Personal Computer BIOS Interface Technical Reference* published by IBM and *CBIOS For IBM PS/2 Computers and Compatibles* by Phoenix Technologies Ltd., published by Addison-Wesley.

Summary

The serial port exists to allow the system to communicate with other computer systems via the telephone lines. The serial port provides serial-to-parallel conversion when receiving data and parallel-to-serial conversion when transmitting data.

The serial port on the system board is compatible with the serial port found in the earlier PC product line. The serial port in some PS/2 models, however, has been enhanced with FIFO buffers to minimize or eliminate overrun and underrun conditions.

The IBM PS/2 product line supports up to four serial ports, numbered 1 through 4, one of which is integrated onto the system board. The system board serial port can be configured as either serial port 1 or 2 using the system board POS register. Serial port 1 uses IRQ4# and serial port 2 uses IRQ3#.

TABLE 28-3 The Serial Port Registers

Register Name	Hex I/O Address	Description
Transmitter Holding	* 0nF8	This write-only register contains the next character to be transmitted. **
Receiver Buffer	* 0nF8	This read-only register contains the received character. **
Divisor Latch, Low Byte	* 0nF8	This read/write register contains the lower byte of the 16-bit baud rate divisor. **
Divisor Latch, High Byte	* 0nF9	This read/write register contains the upper byte of the 16-bit baud rate divisor. **
Interrupt Enable	* 0nF9	This read/write register allows the programmer to selectively enable or disable the four possible sources of serial port interrupts.
Interrupt ID	* 0nFA	This read-only register identifies the pending interrupt condition that has the highest priority.
FIFO Control	* 0nFA	This write-only register allows the programmer to initialize the FIFO logic. This register is not available in all PS/2 models.
Line Control	* 0nFB	This read/write register allows the programmer to customize the data transmission/reception format.
Modem Control	* 0nFC	This read/write register allows the programmer to initiate a diagnostic loop-back, select the IRQ line to be used, and issue RTS and DTR to the modem.
Line Status	* 0nFD	This read-only register provides the programmer with status about the data transfer (such as parity error).
Modem Status	* 0nFE	This read-only register provides the current state of the status lines from the modem.
Scratch	* 0nFF	This read/write register is not used by the serial port and is available for use as a temporary holding register.

* Note: n = 3 for serial port 1 and 2 for serial port 2.
** Note: Bit 7 in the Line Control register controls access to these registers. If bit 7 is a 0, the programmer can access the Receiver Buffer, Transmitter Holding, and Interrupt Enable registers at the indicated I/O addresses. If bit 7 is a 1, the Divisor Latch registers can be accessed at the indicated I/O addresses.

Serial ports other than the one on the system board are installed in the MCA slots. Serial port 3 responds to the I/O address range from 3220_h through 3227_h and uses IRQ4#. Serial port 4 responds to the I/O address range from 3228_h through $322F_h$ and uses IRQ3#.

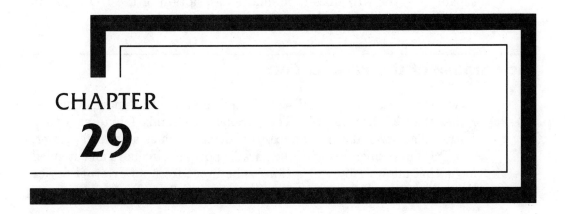

CHAPTER
29

The Parallel Port

Objectives: This chapter provides an overview of the parallel port's capabilities, the IRQ lines used, and a description of the I/O registers used to control the parallel port.

The Purpose of the Parallel Port

As with the serial port, "port" signifies a communications port, or device, rather than an I/O address. The parallel port sends 1 byte at a time (rather than serial data) to an external device such as a parallel printer. The PS/2 implementation of the parallel port also includes an extended mode that allows 1 byte at a time to be input from an external device through the parallel port.

Setup

By programming the system board POS register, the parallel port integrated onto the system board can be set up to respond as parallel port 1, 2, or 3 and, extended mode can be enabled or disabled. The default selection made by the POST sets it up to respond as parallel port 1 in compatibility mode. Selecting compatibility mode means that the port is compatible with the parallel port as implemented in the earlier PC product line: extended mode is disabled and the port is output only.

When set up as parallel port 1, the parallel port uses interrupt request line IRQ7#. When set up as parallel port 2, the parallel port uses interrupt request line IRQ5#.

For more information regarding set up of the system board parallel port, refer to Chapter 14.

The Parallel Port Signals

Table 29-1 defines the signals present on the parallel port connector.

I/O Registers

Three I/O registers are used to control, sense the status of, and transfer data with the parallel port. Table 29-2 defines the I/O addresses assigned to parallel ports 1, 2, and 3.

TABLE 29-1   The Parallel Port Signal Description

Pin	Signal Name	Description
1	STROBE#	Data strobe. Set active under software control, STROBE# causes the external device (such as a parallel printer) to latch the byte present on pins 2 through 9.
2-9	DATA O:DATA 7	The parallel port presents the data byte to the external device (such as a parallel printer) on these eight lines.
10	ACK#	Status line set active by the external device (such as a parallel printer) when it has received a data byte and is ready for another.
11	BUSY	Status line set active by the external device (such as a parallel printer) when the device is busy and cannot accept data.
12	PE	Status line set active by the external device (such as a parallel printer) when an out-of-paper (or similar condition) occurs. PE stands for "paper end."
13	SLCT	Status line set active by the external device (such as a parallel printer) when the external device has been selected.
14	AUTO FD XT#	Auto feed XT command line. When set active by software, causes the printer to advance the paper one line for each carriage return character ($0D_h$) received.
15	ERROR#	Status line set active by the external device (such as a parallel printer) when the external device has encountered an error condition.
16	INIT#	Initialize command line. When set active by software, causes the printer to be placed on-line.
17	SLCT IN#	Select In command line. When set active by software, causes the printer to be selected.

The status port can be read to determine the current status of the parallel port. Table 29-3 defines the bit assignment for the status port.

TABLE 29-2 Parallel Port Address Assignment

Port Number	Data Port	Status Port	Command Port
1	03BC	03BD	03BE
2	0378	0379	037A
3	0278	0279	027A

TABLE 29-3 The Parallel Port's Status Port Bit Assignment

Bit	Description
7	BUSY#. Status line set active (low) by the external device (such as a parallel printer) when the device is busy and cannot accept data.
6	ACK#. Status line set active (low) by the external device (such as a parallel printer) when it has received a data byte and is ready for another.
5	PE. Status line set active (high) by the external device (such as a parallel printer) when an out-of-paper (or similar condition) occurs. PE stands for "paper end."
4	SLCT. Status line set active (high) by the external device (such as a parallel printer) when the external device has been selected.
3	ERROR#. Status line set active (low) by the external device (such as a parallel printer) when the external device has encountered an error condition.
2	IRQ Status. Set active (low) by the parallel port to indicate that the printer has accepted the previous character and is ready for another.
1-0	Not used.

The command port sends commands to the parallel port. Table 29-4 defines the bit assignment for the command port.

In compatibility mode, writing a character to the data port causes the character to be presented to the printer. In extended mode, bit 5 in the command port can be used to select the direction of the data port.

BIOS Routine

The recommended method for controlling the parallel ports is through BIOS function calls. INT 17_h can be used to call the parallel port BIOS

TABLE 29-4   The Parallel Port's Command Port Bit Assignment

Bit	Description
7-6	Not used. Should be 0.
5	Direction select line. In compatibility mode, this line is set to 0 and the data port is write-only. If it is set to 1 and the parallel port is in extended mode, the data port is readable.
4	IRQ enable. When set to 1, the parallel port generates an interrupt request each time the printer accepts a character. When 0, the parallel port does not generate any interrupt requests.
3	Select in. When set to 1, the SLCT IN# signal is set active and the printer is selected. SLCT IN# is set inactive when this bit is 0.
2	Initialize. When set to 0, the INIT# line is set active and printing starts.
1	Auto feed XT. When set to 1, the AUTO FD XT# signal is set active and the printer advances the paper one line each time a carriage return character ($0D_h$) is received.
0	Data strobe. When set to 1, the STROBE# signal is set active and the printer accepts the character being presented to it on the data lines.

routine. A complete description of this BIOS routine's use can be found in *The IBM PS/2 and Personal Computer BIOS Interface Technical Reference*, published by IBM and *CBIOS For IBM PS/2 Computers and Compatibles* by Phoenix Technologies Ltd., published by Addison-Wesley.

Summary

The parallel port sends one byte at a time (rather than serial data) to an external device such as a parallel printer. The PS/2 implementation of the parallel port also includes an extended mode that allows 1 byte at a time to be input from an external device through the parallel port.

By programming the system board POS register, the parallel port integrated onto the system board can be set up to respond as parallel port 1, 2, or 3 and extended mode can be enabled or disabled.

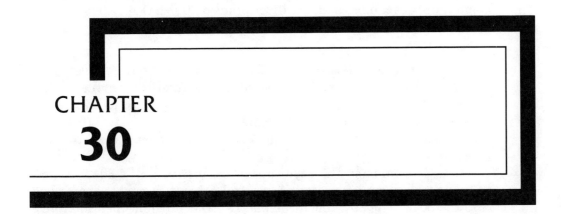

CHAPTER
30

The Keyboard/Mouse Interface

Objectives: This chapter provides an overview of the keyboard/mouse interface's capabilities and a description of the I/O registers used to control the keyboard/mouse Interface.

Figure 30-1 illustrates the keyboard/mouse interface. Every IBM PS/2 includes a combined keyboard/mouse interface on the system board. It consists of an Intel 8042 microcomputer with its own RAM, ROM, and I/O. The 8042 is a self-contained computer system that communicates with the system board microprocessor by way of two I/O registers.

To command the keyboard/mouse interface (the 8042) to perform a task, the microprocessor uses an I/O write to send the command to the 8042. The 8042 microcomputer's ROM program then interprets the command and jumps to the appropriate subroutine (series of instructions) to accomplish the requested task.

The 8042 communicates with the keyboard and the mouse using two independent serial interfaces. The keyboard and the mouse both receive their power from the system board.

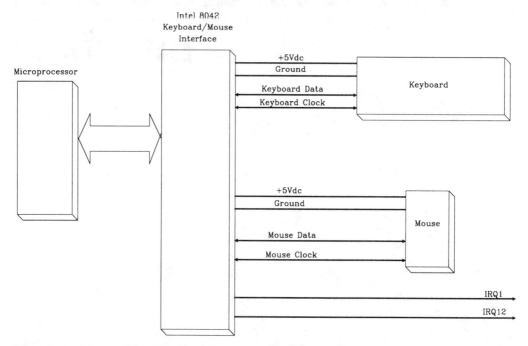

FIGURE 30-1   The Keyboard/Mouse Interface

The IBM keyboard incorporates its own 8042 microcomputer. The key switches are laid out in rows and columns within the keyboard. The 8042 is constantly scanning the key matrix to see if a key has been pressed. When a key is pressed, the 8042 within the keyboard assembly creates an 8-bit scan code that represents the key pressed. The scan code is then converted to a serial bit stream and sent to the keyboard/mouse interface on the system board.

Once the entire 8-bit scan code has been received, the keyboard/mouse interface generates an interrupt request (IRQ1#) to alert the microprocessor. The microprocessor jumps to the keyboard interrupt service routine and an I/O read is performed to read the scan code from the system board 8042. IRQ1# remains active until the scan code is read from the 8042 and is then turned off or reset.

The Keyboard and Mouse Interface Signals

Table 30-1 defines the signal lines present on both the keyboard and mouse connectors.

The I/O Registers

The microprocessor communicates with the keyboard and/or mouse by issuing commands to the keyboard/mouse command port at I/O address 0064_h. The keyboard/mouse data port at I/O address 0060_h is used to send data to the keyboard and read the scan code sent from the keyboard

TABLE 30-1 The Keyboard and Mouse Interface Connectors

Pin	Signal	Description
1	Data	This is the keyboard or mouse data line. Serial data (1's and 0's) are sent and/or received over this line.
3	Ground	Pins 3 and 4 supply power and ground to the keyboard or mouse.
4	+5Vdc	See pin 3.
5	Clock	Each data bit sent or received over the data line (pin 1) is framed by clock bits on this signal line.

or mouse. The keyboard/mouse status port at I/O address 0064$_h$ is used to read the status of the 8042 keyboard/mouse interface.

Table 30-2 lists all the possible commands that can be sent to the 8042 keyboard/mouse interface's command port.

More comprehensive information on programming the keyboard/mouse interface can be found in *IBM PS/2 Hardware Interface Technical Reference*, published by IBM.

The 8042 Keyboard/Mouse Interface's Local I/O Ports

Table 30-3 defines the bit assignment for the 8042's local input I/O port. Table 30-4 defines the bit assignment for the 8042's local output I/O port.

BIOS Routine

The recommended method for controlling the keyboard/mouse interface is through BIOS function calls. INT 09$_h$ and INT 16$_h$ can be used to call the keyboard/mouse BIOS routine. A complete description of this BIOS routine's use can be found in *The IBM PS/2 and Personal Computer BIOS Interface Technical Reference* published by IBM and *CBIOS For IBM PS/2 Computers and Compatibles* by Phoenix Technologies Ltd., published by Addison-Wesley.

Summary

The keyboard/mouse interface is integrated onto the system board and consists of a specially programmed Intel 8042 microcomputer with its own RAM, ROM, and I/O. It handles all communication with the keyboard and mouse, as well as some miscellaneous functions. These miscellaneous functions include gate address bit 20, generating hot reset to reset the CPU (used to switch the 80286 microprocessor from protected to real mode), and the password feature.

TABLE 30-2   8042 Keyboard/Mouse Interface Command List

Command (hex)	Description
20-3F	Bits 0 through 5 of this command designate 1 of 32 possible 8042 internal RAM locations to be read. For example, 23_h causes internal RAM location 03_h to be read. Its contents are placed in the data port at I/O address 0060_h so the microprocessor can read it.
60-7F	Bits 0 through 5 of this command designate 1 of 32 possible 8082 internal RAM locations to be written. The next byte written to the data port at I/O address 0060_h is written to the designated internal RAM location. For example, 63_h causes internal RAM location 03_h to be written. The next byte written to the data port at I/O address 0060_h is written to the designated location.
A4	Test password installed. This command checks for a password installed in the 8042's internal RAM. FA_h is placed in the data port at I/O address 0060_h if the password is installed. A $F1_h$ indicates it is not installed.
A5	Load password. Initiates the password load procedure. The 8042 then accepts input from the data port at I/O address 0060_h until a null (00_h) is received.
A6	Enable password feature.
A7	Disable mouse interface.
A8	Enable mouse interface.
A9	Mouse interface test. Tests the mouse clock and data lines. Result is placed in the 8042's data port at I/O address 0060_h.
AA	Self-test. Runs an 8042 self-test. 55_h placed in the data port at I/O address 0060_h if no errors are detected.
AB	Keyboard interface test. Tests the keyboard clock and data lines. Result is placed in the 8042's data port at I/O address 0060_h.
AD	Disable keyboard interface.
AE	Enable keyboard interface.
C0	Read input port. Allows the programmer to read the contents of the 8042's local input I/O port. The result is placed in the data port at I/O address 0060_h.
C1	Poll input port low. Bits 0-3 of the 8042's local input I/O port are read and placed in bits 4-7 of the Status register at I/O address 0064_h.

TABLE 30-2 Continued

Command (hex)	Description
C2	Poll input port high. Bits 4-7 of the 8042's local input I/O port are read and placed in bits 4-7 of the status register at I/O address 0064_h.
D0	Read output port. Causes the 8042 to read the current state of its local output I/O port and place the result in the data port at I/O address 0060_h.
D1	Write output port. The next byte written to the data port at I/O address 0060_h is written to the 8042's local output I/O port.
D2	Write keyboard output buffer. The next byte written to the data port at I/O address 0060_h causes a keyboard interrupt on IRQ1# (if the keyboard interface is enabled). The byte is supplied as the keyboard scan code when the data port is read.
D3	Write mouse output buffer. The next byte written to the data port at I/O address 0060_h causes a mouse interrupt on IRQ12# (if the mouse interface is enabled). The byte is supplied as the mouse scan code when the data port is read.
D4	Write to mouse. The next byte written to the data port at I/O address 0060_h is transmitted to the mouse.
E0	Read test inputs. Causes the 8042 to read the current state of the keyboard and mouse clock lines. The results are stored in bits 0 and 1, respectively, of the data port at I/O address 0060_h.
F0-FF	Pulse output port. Bits 0-3 of the 8042's local output I/O port are pulsed low for approximately 6 microseconds. Bits 0-3 of this command indicate which bits are to be pulsed. 0 indicates the respective bit should be pulsed; 1 indicates the respective bit should not be altered.

TABLE 30-3   The Keyboard/Mouse Interface's Local Input I/O Port

Bit	Description
7-2	Not used.
1	Mouse data input line.
0	Keyboard data input line.

TABLE 30-4   The Keyboard/Mouse Interface's Local Output I/O Port

Bit	Description
7	Keyboard data output line.
6	Keyboard clock output line.
5	IRQ12#.
4	IRQ1#.
3	Mouse clock output line.
2	Mouse data output line.
1	Gate address bit 20.
0	Reset microprocessor. Generates hot reset.

CHAPTER

31

The VGA Display Interface

Objectives: This chapter focuses on the relationship of the VGA chip to the video memory, digital-to-analog converter (DAC), and the video extension used by the IBM 8514A advanced display adapter.

Definitions for This Chapter

• An **attribute byte** is associated with each text character to be displayed on the screen. This byte defines the foreground and background color of the character, as well as underlining, blinking, and high intensity.

• The **attribute controller** is part of the VGA chip. It combines the attribute information read from video memory with the dot definition of the text character (in text modes) or the PEL (in graphics modes) to create the final dot definition.

• The **character box** is the rectangle of phosphor dots on the screen that is used to display a text character.

• The **character generator** combines the ASCII representation of a text character read from video memory with the scan line counter output to address font memory (also see **scan line counter**).

• The **digital-to-analog converter (DAC)** uses the palette address output by the VGA controller to index into its 256 palette registers. The contents of the addressed palette register is then used to select the voltage level to be placed on the red, green, and blue gun outputs to the display when the dot clock signal goes active.

• The **electron gun** in the display unit is controlled by the output voltage from the VGA's DAC. The magnitude of the input voltage defines the power, or intensity, of the electron beam emitted by the gun towards the phosphor dots on the face of the display screen.

• A **font** is the typeface used to display each text character on the screen.

• **Horizontal retrace** is performed at the end of each horizontal scan line. When the horizontal sync pulse is received from the VGA controller, the display electronics turns off the electron beams and repositions the electron beams back to the start of the next horizontal scan line on the left side of the screen.

• A **horizontal scan line** consists of all the PELs, or phosphor dot triads, along one horizontal line on the display screen. The display's beam deflection electronics scans the electron beams along the scan line from left-to-right to irradiate the phosphor dots along the line.

• The **horizontal sync** pulse is generated by the VGA controller and sent to the display. It tells the display unit's electronics when the end of a horizontal scan line has been reached. In response, the display electronics turns off the electron beams and performs a horizontal re-trace back to the start of the next horizontal scan line on the left side of the screen.

• The **palette** is the selection of video colors available in a particular color video mode. The palette is set up by pre-loading the palette registers in the DAC with the color information. Each palette register is pre-loaded with three 6-bit values representing the voltage levels to be placed on the three electron gun outputs to the display when the dot clock signal goes active.

• The **palette bus** loads color information into the DAC's 256 palette registers and addresses the DAC palette register that defines the three color combination for the current screen dot.

• The **palette registers** are contained within the DAC. Each of the 256 Palette registers are pre-loaded with three 6-bit values representing the voltage levels to be placed on the three electron gun outputs to the display when the dot clock signal goes active.

• A **phosphor** is a substance that emits visible light of a specific fre-quency, or color, when bombarded with electrons. The exact chemical consistency of the phosphor defines the color of the light emitted.

• A **picture element (PEL)** is also commonly referred to as a pixel. It consists of a phosphor dot triad (red, green, and blue phosphor dots) on the screen face.

• The **scan line counter** is contained within the VGA chip. Each text character to be displayed must be painted using rows of dots on multiple scan lines. Starting with a count of 0, the scan line count, in conjunction with the ASCII text character from video memory, is presented to the font memory as an address. The font memory outputs the pattern of

1's and 0's representing the dots for the first line of the character. As the counter is then incremented, the dot definition for each successive scan line is output from the font memory.

• **Vertical retrace** is performed at the end of each screen output. When the vertical sync pulse is received from the VGA controller, the display electronics turns off the electron beams and repositions the electron beams back to the top left corner of the screen to start painting the screen again.

• The **vertical sync** pulse is generated by the VGA controller and sent to the display. It tells the display unit's electronics when the bottom of the screen has been reached. In response, the display unit turns off the electron beams and performs a vertical retrace back to the top left corner of the screen.

The VGA Video Subsystem's Job

The VGA video subsystem's job is to read information from video memory and convert it to the format understood by the display unit.

Block Diagram of Video Subsystem

Figure 31-1 illustrates the video subsystem. The video subsystem consists of the following major parts:

- **The VGA chip.** Reads information from video memory and converts it to **palette** information for the **digital-to-analog converter** (DAC).
- **The video memory.** Contains the information to be displayed on the screen.
- **The video digital-to-analog converter (DAC).** Converts the color palette information supplied by the VGA chip to the correct voltages to be placed on the red, green, and blue gun outputs to the display unit.
- **The video extension, or auxiliary video, connector.** Allows another display adapter, such as the IBM 8514/A, to take the place of the VGA chip on the system board.
- **The display.**

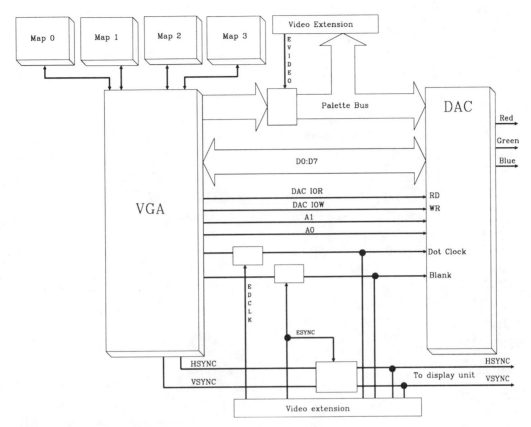

FIGURE 31-1 The VGA Logic Block Diagram

The Display

Figure 31-2 illustrates a typical display tube. The inside surface of the display tube is coated with dots of electroluminescent **phosphor**. When an electron beam hits one of these dots, it emits visible light of a specific frequency, or color. The electron beam is generated by an **electron gun** at the rear of the display tube.

Figure 31-3 illustrates a typical phosphor dot arrangement. The dots are distributed in triads. Within a triad, each of the three dots is composed of a different type of phosphor. When stimulated by an electron beam, one emits red light, another green, and the third blue. These

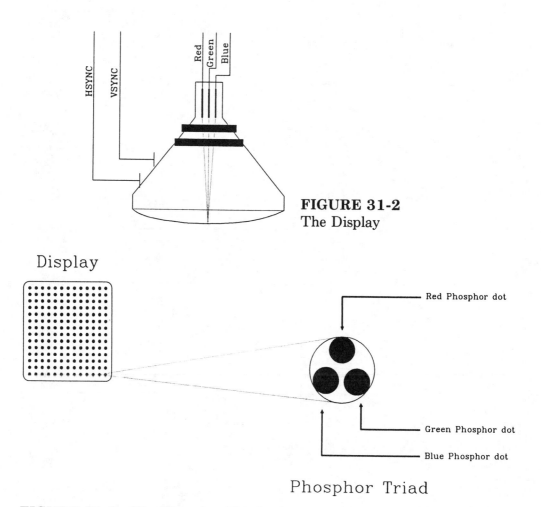

FIGURE 31-2
The Display

Display

Phosphor Triad

FIGURE 31-3   The Phosphor Triads

are the three primary colors that can be used to form any other color. In a color display, there are actually three separate electron guns: a red, a green, and a blue gun. Each gun is focused so that it hits only the dots corresponding to its respective color.

The power of the electron beam determines the amount of visible light emitted by a phosphor dot. By varying the power of the beam, the intensity of the dot's visible output can be chosen.

The triads are laid out in **horizontal scan lines**. When a picture is to be painted on the screen, the three electron beams are positioned at the top left corner of the display by the VGA logic on the system board. The beams are then moved, or scanned, from left to right across the first horizontal scan line by electronics inside the display tube. As they pass each triad, each of the three electron guns is either turned completely off or produces an electron beam at a selected power level. The control of the three guns is handled by the VGA logic on the system board.

The movement of the electron beams across the screen is controlled by magnetic fields generated by passing current through coils located around the outside neck of the display tube. When the beams get to the right end of the horizontal scan line, a **horizontal sync**, or synchronization, pulse produced by the VGA logic causes electronics within the display unit to retrace, or re-position, the beams to the start of the next horizontal scan line on the left side of the screen. The VGA logic also activates a signal called BLANK that turns off the three electron guns during the retrace period.

Under control of the electronics within the display unit, the beams then traverse the second scan line, and the guns are turned off and on under the control of the VGA logic to paint this display line on the screen.

This process of horizontal scanning and **horizontal retrace** continues until the beams get to the end of the last scan line on the screen. The VGA logic then produces a **vertical sync**, or synchronization, signal pulse that causes the display unit to perform a **vertical retrace** and position the beams back up to the top left corner of the screen. During the vertical retrace period, the VGA logic activates the BLANK signal to turn off the three electron guns during the retrace period.

To summarize, the VGA logic on the system board uses five signals to control the display unit:

- Red gun
- Green gun
- Blue gun
- HSYNC
- VSYNC

Introduction to Text Generation

Information can be displayed as either text or graphics. When displaying text, the programmer specifies the character to be displayed, (for ex-

ample, the letter "A") by writing its 8-bit ASCII equivalent into video
memory. In order to be displayed, however, the character must be converted into a series of dots.

Figure 31-4 illustrates a character box. When displaying text,
the VGA views the screen as consisting of a series of character boxes.
A text character is represented by turning on the proper combination
of dots within the character box. Each character box consists of a number of horizontal scan lines and picture elements (**PELs**) along the scan
line. A PEL is simply a dot triad on the screen. The exact size of the
character box depends on the display mode selected by software. Table
31-1 defines the box size when displaying 25 lines of text each consisting
of 80 text characters in the various 80 x 25 text display modes.

The VGA display adapter is backward-compatible with previous
IBM display adapters:

- Monochrome display adapter (MDA). This is the original IBM
  PC's monochrome display adapter.

PEL

Character Box
(with the character "A" drawn it in)

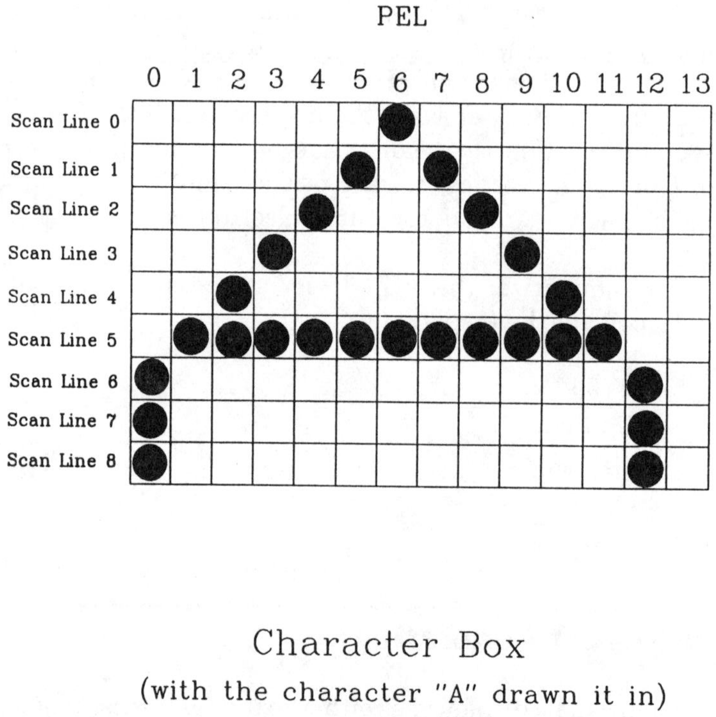

FIGURE 31-4   The Character Box

TABLE 31-1   The Character Box Size in 80 x 25 Mode

VGA Mode	Horizontal Scan Lines	PELs per Scan Line	Box Width (PELs/80)	Box Height Mode (Scan Lines/25)
MDA	350	720	9	14
CGA	200	640	8	8
EGA	350	640	8	14
MCGA	400	640	8	16
VGA	400	720	9	16

- Color graphics adapter (CGA).
- Enhanced graphics adapter (EGA).
- Video graphics array (VGA). This is the large chip on the system board that contains most of the VGA logic.

Older IBM display adapters used fewer dots spaced further apart to draw a character than do the later adapters. For example, the CGA used an 8 x 8 box, while VGA uses a 9 x 16 box. The later adapters create a significantly crisper character display.

Each character box consists of a number of scan lines. To display a row of text characters on the screen, the VGA logic must paint the dots representing the top scan line of each character box across the entire scan line, followed by the second scan line of each box. This process continues until the last scan line of the row's boxes have been painted.

Any particular text character can be drawn many ways. In the printing industry, there are literally hundreds of different typefaces, or **fonts**, to choose from. Bit patterns representing the pattern of screen dots for each displayable text character are stored in a special area of video RAM memory known as font memory.

Figure 31-5 illustrates the character generator logic. When the VGA logic must draw a row of text characters on the screen, the following procedure must occur:

1. The **scan line counter** is reset to 0 at the start of a text line, or row. In text modes, the scan line counter is used to

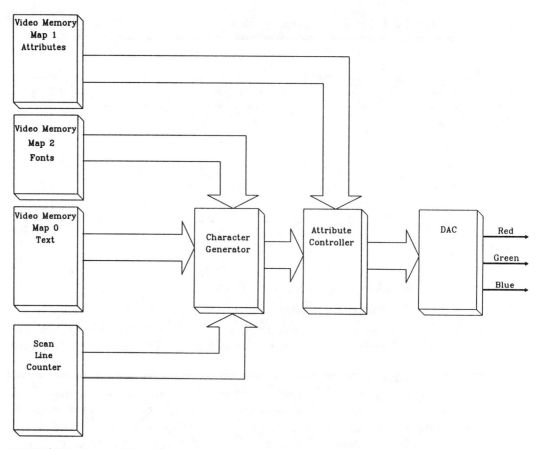

FIGURE 31-5   The Character Generation Logic

identify the scan line (relative to the top of the character box) currently being scanned.

2. The first text character in the row is read from memory and latched by the VGA controller. In addition, every text character stored in video memory also has a second byte of information associated with it known as its **attribute byte**. This 8-bit value describes color, underline, and blinking information for the text character. The character's attribute byte is also read from video memory at this time. Figure 31-6 illustrates the text attribute byte.

3. The 8-bit text character read from memory and the current output of the scan line counter are used as address inputs to the character generator.

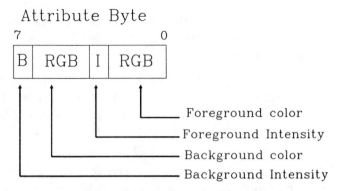

FIGURE 31-6　The Text Attribute Byte

4. The **character generator** uses the character plus the scan line counter output to address its font memory. The contents of the addressed font memory location contains the series of 1's and 0's representing the dots to be turned on and off to paint scan line 0 of the character box.

5. The dot pattern for scan line 0 of the character box is presented to the VGA logic's **attribute controller**. Its job is to add the character's color, underline, and cursor information to the dot data being presented to it by the character generator.

6. The attribute controller then outputs one 8-bit value for each dot in the current scan line of the character box to be displayed onto the **palette bus**.

7. The digital-to-analog converter (DAC) samples the palette bus and the BLANK signal from the VGA on the rising edge of dot clock (see Figure 31-1).

8. The DAC uses the 8-bit value to address one of the 256 palette registers inside the DAC. The addressed palette register contains 18 bits of information, broken up into three 6-bit fields. Each of these 6-bit values describes the output voltage to be placed on one of the DAC's gun outputs.

    Note: The DAC's 256 palette registers must be loaded with the desired color palette information prior to displaying data.

9. The resultant voltages present on the red, green, and blue gun DAC outputs causes the display unit's three electron guns

to irradiate the dot triad currently at the focal point of the three beams. As a result, the dot triad luminesces with the desired color mix.

10. When all of the dots for the first scan line of the first character box have been scanned out to the display, the VGA controller reads the next text character and its attribute byte from video memory and repeats steps 2 through 9.

11. When the top scan line of every character box has been displayed, the beams are retraced to the beginning of the next horizontal scan line on the left side of the display.

12. The scan line counter increments to 1.

13. Every one of the row's characters and their attributes must then be re-read in sequence to paint the second scan line of every character box in the row.

14. This process is repeated until the last scan line of every character box in the row has been painted on the screen.

15. The scan line counter is then reset to 0 and the VGA controller proceeds to paint the next row of 80 character boxes on the screen.

The attribute byte associated with each text character is defined as illustrated in Figure 31-6.

Video Memory Organization

The PS/2 system contains a total of 256KB of video RAM memory located on the system board. The 128KB memory address range from $A0000_h$ to $BFFFF_h$ is reserved for video memory. The 256KB of video RAM memory is divided into four maps, or banks, of 64KB each, referred to as maps 0 through 3. The exact start memory address and length of the maps is automatically selected depending on the current display mode. Only two of the four video memory maps are addressable in the 128KB address space assigned to video memory. The other two maps are addressed through special VGA registers.

In text modes, the video memory is used as follows:

• **Map 0**. Stores the character data to be displayed.

- **Map 1**. Stores the attribute bytes associated with the data stored in map 0.

- **Map 2**. This is the font memory. Bit patterns representing the pattern of screen dots for each displayable text character is stored in map 2.

- **Map 3**. Not used in text modes.

Text Modes

Table 31-2 defines the text modes available when using the VGA.

Video Memory Use in Text Modes

In text modes 0 and 1, map 0, the map containing the text, consists of the even addresses starting at location B8000$_h$ and covers a 16KB address range; 8KB of this range are even addresses. A complete 40 x 25 character screen image can be stored in 1000 locations. This means that map 0 can contain a total of eight 40 x 25 screen images. These are referred to as text pages and they are numbered 1 through 8. The programmer can choose which page, or video memory area, to display.

TABLE 31-2 VGA Text Modes

Mode (hex)	Colors	Text Format	Video Memory Start	Box Size	Screen Format
0,1	16	40 x 25	B8000	8 x 8	320 x 200
0,1	16	40 x 25	B8000	8 x 14	320 x 350
0,1	16	40 x 25	B8000	9 x 16	360 x 400
2,3	16	80 x 25	B8000	8 x 8	640 x 200
2,3	16	80 x 25	B8000	8 x 14	640 x 350
2,3	16	80 x 25	B8000	9 x 16	720 x 400
7	0	80 x 25	B0000	9 x 14	720 x 350
7	0	80 x 25	B0000	9 x 16	720 x 400

The attribute map, map 1, for these text pages consists of the odd addresses starting at location B8001$_h$ and covers a 16KB address range. Map 1 can contain the attributes for a total of eight 40 x 25 screen images. Table 31-3 defines the start and end addresses for each of the eight data pages and its corresponding attribute page.

In text mode 2 and 3, map 0, the data map, consists of the even addresses starting at location B8000$_h$ and covers a 32KB address range; 16KB of this range are even addresses. A complete 80 x 25 character screen image can be stored in 2000 locations. This means that map 0 can contain a total of eight 80 x 25 screen images. These are referred to as text pages and they are numbered 1 through 8. The programmer can choose which page to display.

The attribute map, map 1, for these text pages consists of the odd addresses starting at location B8001$_h$ and covers a 32KB address range. Map 1 can contain the attributes for a total of eight 80 x 25 screen images. Table 31-4 defines the start and end addresses for each of the eight data pages and its corresponding attribute page.

In text mode 7, map 0, the data map, consists of the even addresses starting at location B0000$_h$ and covers a 32KB address range; 16KB of this range are even addresses. A complete 80 x 25 character screen image can be stored in 2000 locations. This means that map 0 can contain a total of eight 80 x 25 screen images. These are referred to as text pages and they are numbered 1 through 8. The programmer can choose which page to display.

TABLE 31-3   Video Memory Use in Text Modes 0 and 1

Page Number	Map 0 Start	Map 0 End	Map 1 Start	Map 1 End
1	B8000	B87CE	B8001	B87CF
2	B8800	B8FCE	B8801	B8FCF
3	B9000	B97CE	B9001	B97CF
4	B9800	B9FCE	B9801	B9FCF
5	BA000	BA7CE	BA001	BA7CF
6	BA800	BAFCE	BA801	BAFCF
7	BB000	BB7CE	BB001	BB7CF
8	BB800	BBFCE	BB801	BBFCF

TABLE 31-4   Video Memory Use in Text Modes 2 and 3

Page Number	Map 0 Start	Map 0 End	Map 1 Start	Map 1 End
1	B8000	B8F9E	B8001	B8F9F
2	B9000	B9F9E	B9001	B9F9F
3	BA000	BAF9E	BA001	BAF9F
4	BB000	BBF9E	BB001	BBF9F
5	BC000	BCF9E	BC001	BCF9F
6	BD000	BDF9E	BD001	BDF9F
7	BE000	BEF9E	BE001	BEF9F
8	BF000	BFF9E	BF001	BFF9F

TABLE 31-5   Video Memory Use in Text Mode 7

Page Number	Map 0 Start	Map 0 End	Map 1 Start	Map 1 End
1	B0000	B0F9E	B0001	B0F9F
2	B1000	B1F9E	B1001	B1F9F
3	B2000	B2F9E	B2001	B2F9F
4	B3000	B3F9E	B3001	B3F9F
5	B4000	B4F9E	B4001	B4F9F
6	B5000	B5F9E	B5001	B5F9F
7	B6000	B6F9E	B6001	B6F9F
8	B7000	B7F9E	B7001	B7F9F

The attribute map, map 1, for these text pages consists of the odd addresses starting at location $B0001_h$ and covers a 32KB address range. Map 1 can contain the attributes for a total of eight 80 x 25 screen images. Table 31-5 defines the start and end addresses for each of the eight data pages and its corresponding attribute page.

Soft-Fonts

In VGA text modes, video memory map 2 is used to store the font to be used by the character generator. When a text display mode is chosen via the BIOS, the default font is automatically copied from the system board ROMs to map 2 of video memory. Up to eight fonts can be loaded into the 64KB map 2.

Introduction to Graphics

In text mode, the VGA must translate the data stored in video memory into the dot pattern to be displayed. The VGA's role is altered when in a graphics mode and a translation stage becomes necessary. The information stored in video memory describes individual PELs rather than entire characters. IBM's generic name for graphics modes is all points addressable (APA) modes. The programmer can build a display picture out of thousands of individual dots, describing each dot individually. This allows the programmer to build any image desired.

Graphics Modes

Table 31-6 defines the primary characteristics of each of the VGA graphics modes.

The resolution column defines the number of PELs per scan line (first number) and the number of scan lines used (second number).

The total PELs column is the total number of PELs used (PELs per scan line x number of scan lines) for a screen image.

The PELs/byte column indicates the number of PELs defined in each location of video memory. An N/A entry indicates that more than one memory map is used to define a PEL.

The map(s) used column indicates the video memory maps used in the indicated video graphics mode.

The total video memory column indicates the total amount of video RAM memory available to define PELs. Where the pages column indicates that more than one screen image, or page, can be stored, divide the number of pages into the total video memory required to yield the memory required for one screen image.

The following sections provide a description of each of the graphics modes.

TABLE 31-6   VGA Graphics Modes

Mode (hex)	Resolution	Total PELs	Colors	PELs/Byte	Map(s) Used	Total Video Memory	Pages
4,5	320X200	64.0K	4	4	0,1	16.0K	1
6	640X200	128.0K	2	8	0	16.0K	1
D	320X200	64.0K	16	N/A	0-3	64.0K	8
E	640X200	128.0K	16	N/A	0-3	256.0K	4
F	640X350	224.0K	2	N/A	0,2	112.0K	2
10	640X350	224.0K	16	N/A	0-3	224.0K	2
11	640X480	307.2K	2	8	0	38.4K	1
12	640X480	307.2K	16	N/A	0-3	153.6K	1
13	320X200	64.0K	256	N/A	0-3	64.0K	1

Graphics Modes 4 and 5 (320 X 200, 4 Colors)

Modes 4 and 5 are CGA-compatible. They operate identically to the 320 x 200, 4 color mode available with the IBM CGA display adapter.

Figure 31-7 illustrates video memory usage in modes 4 and 5. Video memory maps 0 and 1 are used to store the image. The data defining all of the PELs to be displayed on even-numbered scan lines is stored in one memory address range, and the PELs to be displayed on odd-numbered scan lines are stored in another range. Map 0 consists of all the even addresses within the 16KB range, and map 1 consist of all the odd addresses.

Each memory location defines the color of four PELs, using 2 bits per PEL. The most-significant 2 bits in a location define the color of the first PEL.

Example 1: The PEL in the top left corner of the screen is on scan line 0, an even-numbered scan line. Its color is defined in bits 6 and 7 of memory location B8000$_h$ in map 0.

Example 2: The second PEL in the top left corner of the screen is also on scan line 0. Its color is defined in bits 4 and 5 of memory location B8000$_h$ in map 0.

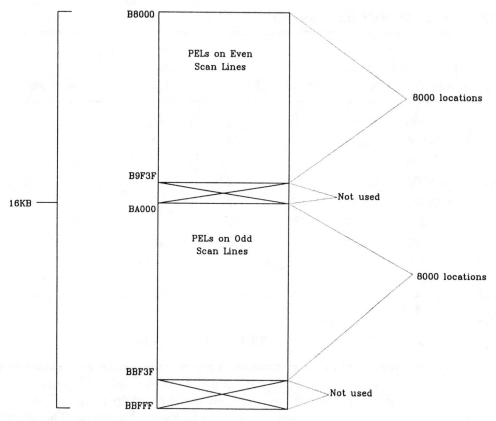

FIGURE 31-7   Mode 4 and 5 Video Memory Use

Example 3: The fifth PEL in the top left corner of the screen is also on scan line 0. Its color is defined in bits 6 and 7 of memory location B8001$_h$ in map 1.

Example 4: The first PEL on scan line 1, an odd-numbered scan line, is defined in bits 6 and 7 of memory location BA000$_h$.

The PEL color selected with the 2 bits depends on the color set used. Color Set 1 is the default, but the programmer can select from other color sets.

Graphics Mode 6 (640 x 200, 2 Color)

Graphics mode 6 is compatible with the 640 x 200 black and white mode on the IBM CGA display adapter.

Figure 31-8 illustrates video memory usage in mode 6. Video memory map 0 is used to store the image. The data defining all of the PELs to be displayed on even-numbered scan lines is stored in one memory address range, and the PELs to be displayed on odd-numbered scan lines are stored in another range.

Each memory location defines the status of eight PELs, using one bit per PEL (1 = white, 0 = black). The most-significant bit in a location defines the color of the first PEL.

Example 1: The PEL in the top left corner of the screen is on scan line 0, an even-numbered scan line. Its color is defined in bit 7 of memory location B8000$_h$ in map 0.

Example 2: The second PEL in the top left corner of the screen is also on scan line 0. Its color is defined in bit 6 of memory location B8000$_h$ in map 0.

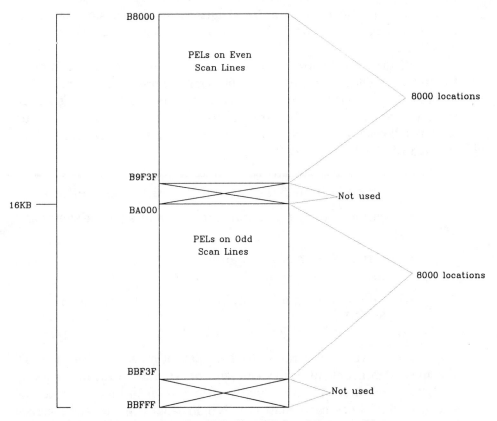

FIGURE 31-8 VGA Graphic Mode 6 Video Memory Use

Example 3: The ninth PEL in the top left corner of the screen is also on scan line 0. Its color is defined in bit 7 of memory location B8001$_h$ in map 0.

Example 4: The first PEL on scan line 1, an odd-numbered scan line, is defined in bit 7 of memory location BA000$_h$.

Graphics Mode D$_h$ (320 x 200, 16 Color)

The VGA chip can perform a data transfer with all four video memory maps simultaneously (see Figure 31-1). In mode D$_h$, each video memory map is 64KB in length.

Mode D$_h$ takes 4 bits of information to define the mix of the 3 primary colors and the intensity for each PEL to be displayed. This allows the specification of 1 of 16 possible colors for each PEL (8 colors without intensity and the same 8 with intensity). Each video memory location defines the color of 8 PELs. This means it takes a total of 32-bits of information (4 bits/PEL $\times$ 8 PELs/location) to define the color of 8 PELs.

Figure 31-9 illustrates video memory usage in mode D$_h$. In mode D$_h$, all four memory maps reside in the same address range, from A0000$_h$ to AFFFF$_h$. When the VGA reads a video memory location, it is simultaneously reading from the same location in all four maps. They are used as follows (N = a video memory address in the range from A0000 through AFFFF$_h$):

- Location N in map 0 contains blue bits for eight PELs.

- Location N in map 1 contains the green bits for the same eight PELs.

- Location N in map 2 contains the red bits for the same eight PELs.

- Location N in map 3 contains the intensity bits for the same eight PELs.

Figure 31-10 illustrates the PEL definition format in mode D. The most-significant bit corresponds to the left-most PEL in the group of eight represented. It takes 8000 locations in each map to store one screen image. Since each map is 64KB in length, up to eight screen images, or pages, can be stored. Within a page, PEL definitions are stored

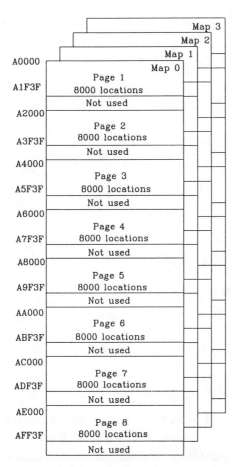

FIGURE 31-9

Mode D_h Video Memory Map Use

sequentially (that is, the eight PELs in the top left corner of the screen are stored in location $A0000_h$, the next eight in $A0001_h$, and so on).

Graphics Mode E_h (640 x 200, 16 Color)

Mode E_h is almost identical to Mode D_h. The only difference is that sufficient memory must be used to define the color for 640 PELs per line versus 320 in Mode D_h. This doubles the amount of memory necessary.

Because double the number of PELs are used per screen, only four pages, or screen images, can be stored. The page size is increased from 8000 locations to 16000 locations. The PEL color definition is identical to mode D_h. Figure 31-11 illustrates video memory usage in mode E_h.

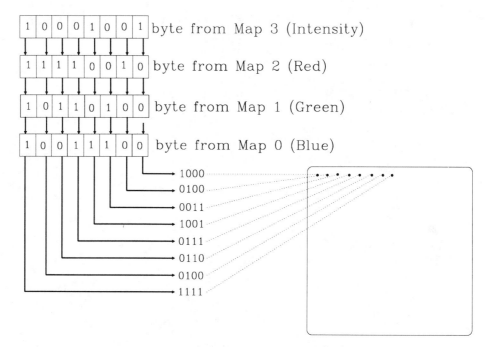

FIGURE 31-10 Mode D_h PEL Definition Format

Graphics Mode F_h (640 x 350, 2 Color)

Mode F_h is similar to modes D_h and E_h in that it also uses overlapping video memory maps. However, it uses two maps, each 32KB in length, rather than four, of which only 28000 locations are used in each. It takes 28000 locations to define the 224000 PELs (640 x 350) in a screen image. Two pages, or screen images, can be stored in video memory.

Each PEL uses 2 bits and can be defined as black, white, blinking, or intensified. When the VGA reads from a video memory location while in mode F_h, it simultaneously reads a byte from the specified location in map 0 and a byte from the same location in map 2. The 2 bits from bit 7 in both locations define the left-most PEL in the group of 8, and the 2 bits from bit 0 in both locations defines the right-most PEL in the group of 8. Figure 31-12 illustrates video memory usage in mode F_h.

Graphics Mode 10_h (640 x 350, 16 Color)

Mode 10_h is very similar to modes D_h, E_h, and F_h in its use of video memory. The only difference is that sufficient memory must be used to define the color for 640 PELs per line versus 320 in mode D_h, and 350

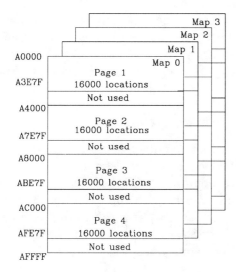

FIGURE 31-11
Mode E$_h$ Video Memory Map Use

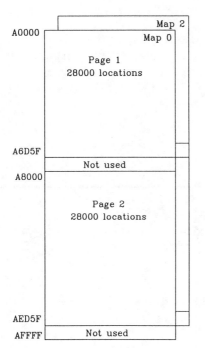

FIGURE 31-12
Mode F$_h$ Video Memory Map Use

vs. 200 scan lines. This increases the amount of memory necessary. Because more PELs are used per screen, only two pages, or screen images, can be stored. The page size is increased from 8000 locations to 28000 locations. The PEL color definition is identical to mode D_h. Figure 31-13 illustrates video memory usage in mode 10_h.

Graphics Mode 11$_h$ (640 x 480, 2 Color)

In Mode 11_h, only one video memory map is used, map 0. It is 64KB in length, of which only 38400 locations are used. In each location each bit defines whether its corresponding PEL is off (black) or on (white). Eight PELs are defined per location, with bit 7 defining the left-most PEL in the group of eight and bit 0 the right-most. Using 38400 locations to define eight PELs each allows 307200 PELs to be defined (640 x 480). Figure 31-14 illustrates video memory usage in mode 11_h.

Graphics Mode 12$_h$ (640 x 480, 16 Color)

Mode 12_h is very similar to modes D_h, E_h, and 10_h in its use of video memory. The only difference is that sufficient memory must be used to

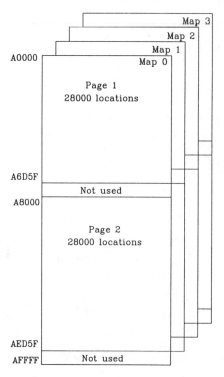

FIGURE 31-13
Mode 10_h Video Memory Map Use

Video Map 0

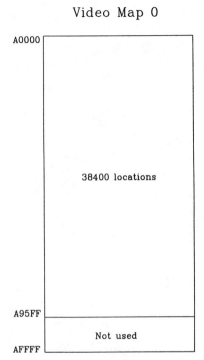

A0000

38400 locations

A95FF

Not used

AFFFF

FIGURE 31-14
Mode 11_h Video Memory Map Use

define the color for 640 PELs per line versus 320 in mode D_h, and 480
vs. 200 scan lines. This increases the amount of memory necessary.
Because more PELs are used per screen, only one page, or screen image,
can be stored. The page size is increased from 8000 locations to 38400
locations. The PEL color definition is identical to mode D_h. Figure 31-
15 illustrates video memory usage in mode 12_h.

Graphics Mode 13_h (320 x 200, 256 Color)

Mode 13_h allows the programmer to define the colors for 64000 PELs
(320 x 200). One of 256 possible colors can be defined for each PEL.
     The video memory is divided into four maps of 16KB each.
Figure 31-16 illustrates video memory usage in mode 13_h. Each location
contains one byte of information that defines its respective PEL's color.
This allows the selection of 1 of 256 possible colors (00_h to FF_h).
     The overall address range of the video memory used is 64KB
from $A0000_h$ to $AFFFF_h$. The maps are organized as follows:

• Map 0: A0000, A0004, A0008, and so on.

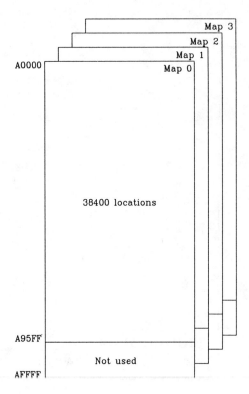

FIGURE 31-15
Mode 12ₕ Video Memory Map
Use

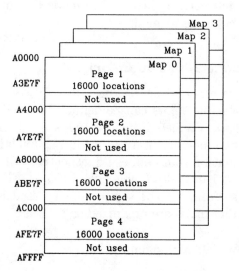

FIGURE 31-16
Mode 13ₕ Video Memory Map
Use

- Map 1: A0001, A0005, A0009, and so on.
- Map 2: A0002, A0006, A000A, and so on.
- Map 3: A0003, A0007, A000B, and so on.

The contents of address A0000$_h$ defines the PEL in the top left corner of the screen, A0001$_h$ defines the next sequential PEL, and so on.

Setup

The video subsystem may be placed into setup mode through bit 5 of the System Board Enable/Setup register at I/O address 0094$_h$. Once in setup mode, bit 0 of POS register 2 at I/O address 0102$_h$ is the video enable bit. Setting bit 0 to 1 enables the VGA logic. The VGA logic must then be taken out of setup mode with bit 5 of the System Board Enable/ Setup register.

Registers

The VGA adapter contains 73 I/O registers that are used to control, sense the status of, and transfer data with the VGA adapter. As a result, programming the VGA adapter is quite an involved task. A complete definition of the VGA I/O registers can be found in the IBM *PS/2 Hardware Interface Technical Reference*. There are also a number of excellent books on the market that provide a full programmer's reference guide to the VGA adapter. To reproduce this information here would constitute an unnecessary reproduction of available information. In addition, this information is not necessary for understanding how the VGA adapter functions and its relation to the overall architecture of the system.

The Display Connector

Table 31-7 defines the display unit connector signals.

The Video Extension

See the video extension connector illustrated in Figure 31-1; also see Chapter 17.

TABLE 31-7 Display Unit Connector

Pin	Description
1	Red. This is the DAC's red gun output to the display unit.
2	Green. This is the DAC's green gun output to the display unit.
3	Blue. This is the DAC's blue gun output to the display unit.
6	Red ground. Completes the red gun circuit.
7	Green ground. Completes the green gun circuit.
8	Blue ground. Completes the blue gun circuit.
11	Monitor sense 0. Pins 11 and 12 are used by the VGA to automatically sense the type of monitor installed.
12	Monitor sense 1. See pin 11.
13	HSYNC. The VGA generates horizontal sync pulses on this line.
14	VSYNC. The VGA generates vertical sync pulses on this line.

Interrupts

The VGA chip can be programmed to generate an interrupt request (IRQ9) each time that vertical retrace begins. The programmer can use this period of time to update the information in video memory. Since the beams are turned off during vertical retrace, the programmer can update video memory without causing any "snow," or visual interference, to appear on the screen.

BIOS Routine

The recommended method for controlling the VGA is through BIOS function calls. INT 10_h can be used to call the VGA BIOS routine. A complete description of this BIOS routine's use can be found in *The IBM PS/2 and Personal Computer BIOS Interface Technical Reference* published by IBM and *CBIOS For IBM PS/2 Computers and Compatibles* by Phoenix Technologies Ltd., published by Addison-Wesley.

Limitations

The VGA chip on the system board is an 8-bit device. Since video memory operations can be performed only by the VGA chip, the programmer can only write a byte at a time to video memory when updating screen information. This results in slow screen updates.

Summary

The VGA display adapter is integrated onto the system board of all PS/2 products. It is backward-compatible with the MDA, CGA, MCGA, and EGA display adapters and provides several new and enhanced display modes.

Information to be displayed is stored in video RAM memory by the programmer. This information is then read from video memory by the VGA chip, converted to palette addresses for the DAC, and sent to the display unit over the red, green, and blue gun lines along with the required timing information on the HSYNC and VSYNC lines.

The user can substitute a different display adapter, such as the IBM 8514/A, by installing it into a 16-bit MCA connector that has the video extension. Insertion of the new card automatically disconnects the VGA chip from the DAC and allows the new display adapter card to supply the palette addresses and synchronization signals to the DAC.

The Numeric Coprocessor

Objectives: This chapter describes the relationship between the microprocessor and the numeric coprocessor. Performance of floating-point operations both with and without the numeric coprocessor installed are discussed.

History

When Intel was designing the 8088/8086 microprocessor, they had to decide whether or not to provide it with the ability to perform floating-point mathematics (floating-point numbers are numbers with decimal places). This capability would substantially increase the price of the microprocessor, and marketing information indicated that most users did not need it. Consequently, floating-point capability was not included in the final processor design; the microprocessor can perform whole number calculations, but not floating-point.

Rather than completely eliminate the floating-point capability, Intel included hooks on the microprocessor that would enable users to include a companion floating-point processor in designs that required this capability. The companion processor, or coprocessor, was the 8087 numeric coprocessor. It is also referred to as a processor extension because it extends the microprocessor's instruction set. When the 80286 and 80386 microprocessors were introduced, the same approach was used: the 80286 can be coupled with the 80287 and the 80386 with the 80387 numeric coprocessor.

The microprocessor treats the numeric coprocessor as an I/O device. When the microprocessor fetches an instruction from memory and senses that it is an instruction for the coprocessor, it automatically performs a series of one or more I/O writes to forward the instruction to the coprocessor, which then executes the instruction. The I/O address range from $00F8_h$ through $00FF_h$ are assigned to the coprocessor.

Setup

At the beginning of the POST, the programmer checks the configuration RAM to see if a numeric coprocessor is installed. Bits 1 and 2 of the microprocessor's Machine Status Word (MSW) register are then set according to Table 32-1.

TABLE 32-1 The Numeric Coprocessor Bits in the MSW Register

Bit 2 (EM)	Bit 1 (MP)	Description
0	0	Ignore instructions for the coprocessor.
0	1	Coprocessor is installed. Forward all coprocessor instructions to the coprocessor.
1	0	Coprocessor not installed. Emulate coprocessor.
1	1	Invalid.

Note: In the 80386 microprocessor, the MSW register is found in the lower half of control register 0 (CR0).

Operation with Numeric Coprocessor Installed

Figure 32-1 illustrates the coprocessor's relationship to the system. When the coprocessor is installed and the MP bit is set to 1, the following actions take place when the microprocessor fetches a coprocessor instruction from memory.

1. If execution of the coprocessor instruction requires a memory read or a memory write operation, the microprocessor saves the memory address and notes whether a read or write is required.

2. The microprocessor then performs one or more I/O writes to forward the instruction to the coprocessor. Simple instructions that are only 1 or 2 bytes in length can be transferred in a single I/O write bus cycle; more complex instructions consisting of 3 or more bytes require additional I/O write bus cycles.

3. When the coprocessor starts execution of the instruction, it turns on its BUSY# output. The microprocessor will not attempt to forward another instruction to the coprocessor until BUSY# is turned off.

4. If execution of the instruction requires that a memory read or memory write bus cycle take place, the coprocessor turns on processor extension request (PEREQ) to ask the microprocessor to run the bus cycle.

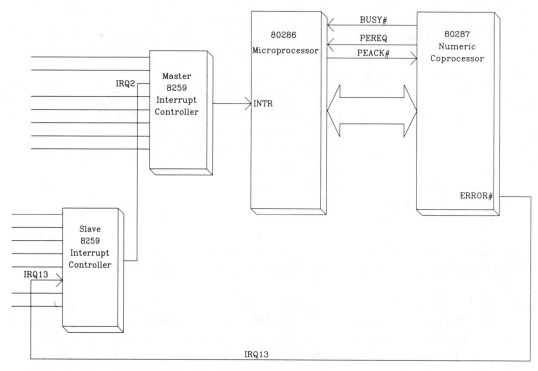

FIGURE 32-1   The Numeric Coprocessor

5. The 80286 microprocessor responds with processor extension acknowledge (PEACK#) to inform the coprocessor that the requested bus cycle has been initiated. The 80386 microprocessor has eliminated the PEACK# line because it was unnecessary. The microprocessor has no choice when PEREQ goes active but to run the requested bus cycle.

6. If the requested bus cycle is a memory write, the microprocessor initiates the bus cycle, but the data is supplied by the coprocessor. If the requested bus cycle is a memory read, the bus cycle is run by the microprocessor, but the data is read by the coprocessor. The microprocessor ignores the data.

7. If the coprocessor incurs an error while executing the instruction, its ERROR# and BUSY# outputs are turned on. This generates an IRQ13# to the microprocessor and prevents the microprocessor from forwarding another coprocessor instruction. In the IRQ13# interrupt service routine, the programmer reads the coprocessor status register to ascertain the cause of

the error. Any coprocessor error can be reset by writing 00_h to I/O address 00F0, which causes just the coprocessor to be reset, thereby clearing any error conditions.

8. When the coprocessor completes execution of the instruction, it turns off its BUSY# output to inform the microprocessor that it is ready to accept another coprocessor instruction.

Detailed information about coprocessor programming may be found in the following Intel manuals: *iAPX 286 Hardware Reference Manual, iAPX 286 Programmer's Reference Manual including the iAPX 286 Numeric Supplement,* and *80386 Hardware Reference Manual.*

Operation Without Numeric Coprocessor Installed (Emulation)

When a PS/2 running Lotus 1-2-3 recalculates a spreadsheet, the decimal portion of the numbers are calculated correctly, even if the coprocessor is not installed. This does not seem possible since the microprocessor can only perform integer mathematics. However, in this case, the floating-point calculations are performed by special routines known as floating-point emulation routines. These routines are supplied as part of the applications program (such as Lotus 1-2-3).

Using the standard instruction set, floating-point calculations can be performed through laborious manipulation of floating-point numbers stored in memory. This process is much less efficient than the floating-point instruction capability embedded within the coprocessor. Where the coprocessor can directly execute a single floating-point instruction with its hardware, an emulation routine must execute hundreds of instructions to accomplish the same goal. When running applications programs that are floating-point intensive, the performance improvement provided by the coprocessor can be quite dramatic. Improvements in the 100% to 500% range are not uncommon.

Floating-point emulation requires inclusion of a set of emulation routines in the applications program (like Lotus 1-2-3). It also requires that the EM bit must be set to 1 and the MP bit set to 0 in the MSW register.

This section describes the actions taken when a coprocessor is not installed and the EM bit is set to 1 in the MSW register.

1. The microprocessor fetches a coprocessor instruction from memory. When the microprocessor decodes the instruction and senses that it belongs to the coprocessor, it checks the MP bit in the MSW register to see if a coprocessor is installed. If it is not (MP = 0), it checks the EM bit to see if the coprocessor instruction is to be emulated. In this case, it is (EM = 1).

2. The microprocessor internally generates an Exception 7 interrupt request. As with any interrupt, the microprocessor responds by pushing the contents of the CS, IP, and Flag registers into stack memory. The stored CS and IP values point to the coprocessor instruction that caused the exception.

3. The microprocessor jumps to the Exception 7 interrupt service routine. In the routine, the programmer reads the address of the coprocessor instruction from the stack and determines the type of instruction (such as a floating-point divide). The programmer then jumps to the routine (in the package of emulation routines) that emulates that particular type of instruction.

4. Upon conclusion of the instruction emulation, the programmer alters the Stack Pointer (SP) register's contents to point to the instruction immediately following the coprocessor instruction that caused the exception.

5. The programmer executes an IRET (interrupt return) instruction. The microprocessor responds by reloading the CS, IP, and Flag registers from the stack and resuming normal operation (in other words, the microprocessor fetches the next instruction from the memory location pointed to by CS and IP). This is the instruction after the coprocessor instruction that caused the exception.

Summary

The numeric coprocessor extends the microprocessor's instruction set to include floating-point math functions. It acts as an I/O device and the microprocessor uses I/O writes to send instructions to it for execution. Since the coprocessor is not connected to the address bus, it can execute bus cycles. If it must read data from or write data to memory when executing an instruction, it must rely on the microprocessor to perform the memory access for it.

If the coprocessor isn't installed and a coprocessor instruction is encountered, software can be written to emulate, or simulate, the coprocessor's execution of the instruction. The coprocessor can perform a floating-point math function in one instruction; it takes the microprocessor hundreds of instructions to perform that same function. Consequently, applications programs that rely heavily on coprocessor instructions are much more efficient when a coprocessor is installed. (On the other hand, if applications programs only perform an occasional floating-point math function, a coprocessor is a waste of money.)

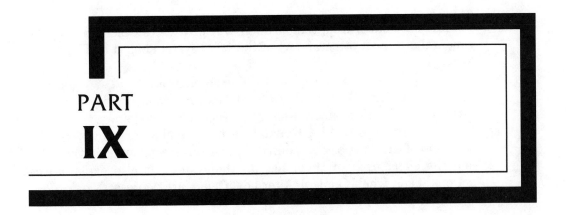

Miscellaneous Subjects

Introduction to Part IX

Part IX consists of Chapters 33 and 34. It provides a description of the timers that are an integral part of the PS/2 system board and the reset logic.

The following is a synopsis of each chapter:

Chapter 33: The PS/2 Timers. This chapter provides a description of the four timers present in each PS/2 system.

Chapter 34: The Reset Logic. This chapter provides a description of the five possible sources for various reset signals in the PS/2 and the effect each of them has on the system. It also explains the actions taken when Control/Alternate/Delete are depressed.

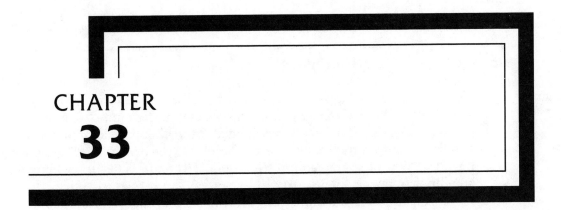

CHAPTER
33

The PS/2 Timers

Objective: This chapter provides a description of the four timers present in each PS/2 system.

The System Timer, Timer 0

The system timer, or timer 0, is actually a programmable frequency source. A 1.19318MHz signal provides its input clock rate. The programmer specifies a divisor to be divided into the input clock to yield the desired output frequency. During the POST, the divisor $FFFF_h$ (decimal 65535) is programmed into timer 0 at I/O address 0040_h, yielding an output frequency of 18.20Hz.

Figure 33-1 illustrates the system timer. Timer 0's output is connected to the IRQ0 latch. When timer 0's output goes active, the latch is set, sending IRQ0# to the Master 8259 Interrupt Controller. In the IRQ0# interrupt service routine, the programmer can turn off IRQ0# by setting bit 7 of system control port B at I/O address 0061_h to a 1.

At a frequency of 18.20Hz, IRQ0# is generated every 54.9ms, which causes the IRQ0# interrupt service routine to be executed once every 54.9ms.

In the original IBM PC and XT, this interrupt service routine was used to maintain the date and time in RAM memory. In the IBM PC/AT, a real-time clock chip was added to perform this function, but timer 0 is still available to be used as a general purpose timer by programmers. It serves the same purpose in the PS/2 product line.

There's an interesting story attached to this timer. In 1989, a number of industry publications reported the astounding news that a

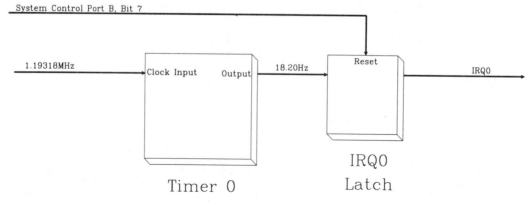

FIGURE 33-1   The System Timer, Timer 0

532

designer in Taiwan had altered a PC/AT so that it could perform at the positively awesome rate of 100 mips (million instructions per second). A number of benchmark (performance verification) programs had been run on the system to verify his claims. Quite a few people in the industry were reeled in, hook, line, and sinker. All this designer had done was reprogram timer 0 to tick at a different rate. Since the benchmark programs used this interrupt as their timebase, it altered the results. Red faces all around.

The Refresh Timer, Timer 1

The refresh timer (timer 1) is (or rather, was) a programmable frequency source. The following discussion describes the function of the refresh timer in the earlier PC product line.

The same 1.19318MHz signal (used by timer 0) provides the refresh timer's input clock. The programmer specifies a divisor to be divided into the input clock to yield the desired output frequency. During the POST, a divisor of 0012_h (decimal 18) is written to the refresh timer. The input clock frequency of 1.19318MHz is then divided by 18 to yield an output frequency of 66287.77KHz, or a pulse every 15.0857 microseconds.

This is the refresh request signal that triggers the DRAM refresh logic to become bus master once every 15.0857 microseconds so that it can refresh another row in DRAM memory throughout the system. For more information on DRAM refresh, refer to Chapter 21.

In 1988, a number of industry publications included brief but dangerous articles that addressed the issue of the refresh timer. It was revealed that this demon timer "steals" the buses from your computer every 15 microseconds to refresh DRAM memory. A small program was provided to reprogram this timer so that it could not ask for the buses quite so frequently and would thereby give more bus time to your computer.

This approach was extremely dangerous. It is entirely possible that users who implemented this change occasionally experienced mysterious RAM parity errors and lost all data in RAM because the unit locked up after outputting the message. To avoid this problem in the PS/2 product line, IBM made the refresh timer non-programmable. It still lives at the same I/O address, 0041_h, but nothing actually happens if you perform an I/O write to it. It is fixed at the frequency of 66287.77KHz in hardware and begins running when the unit is powered up.

The Speaker Data Timer, Timer 2

The speaker data timer, timer 2, resides at I/O address 0042_h and, like timer 0, is a programmable frequency source derived from the 1.19318MHz timebase. The programmer specifies a divisor to be divided into the input clock to yield the desired output frequency. The divisor is written to timer 2 at I/O address 0042_h. Figure 33-2 illustrates timer 2.

In order for timer 2 to actually use the input clock, bit 0 of system control port B at I/O address 0061_h must be a 1. The timer then divides the timebase by the programmer-specified divisor, yielding an output frequency that is applied to one input of a two-input AND gate. If the other AND gate input is a 1 (from bit 1 of system Control B at I/O address 0061_h), the timer 2 output frequency is gated through the AND gate and applied to the speaker driver chip. It is amplified and applied to the speaker.

To sum it up, the output frequency of timer 2 is applications-specific: it can be programmed to make happy or sad sounds, depending

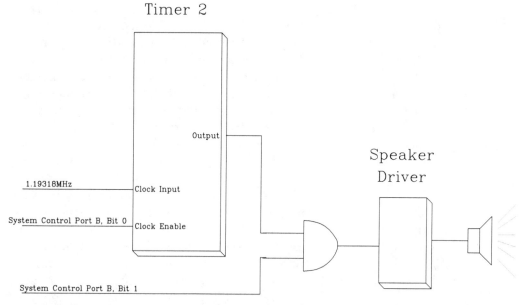

FIGURE 33-2   The Speaker Data Logic

on the occasion. For additional information regarding the speaker data logic, refer to Chapter 17.

The Watchdog Timer, Timer 3

The watchdog timer, timer 3, detects ill-behaved programs. It lives at I/O address 0044_h. Problems could result if a multitasking operating system, like OS/2, were to give control to a program that disables interrupt recognition for an extended period of time. The various devices generating interrupt requests to obtain microprocessor servicing could experience problems if they were not serviced on a timely basis.

One of the interrupt requests that would not be serviced is the system timer interrupt, IRQ0#. The system timer, or timer 0, requires servicing every 54.9ms. The watchdog timer is designed to detect a cessation of IRQ0# servicing.

Figure 33-3 illustrates the watchdog timer. The watchdog timer at I/O address 0044_h is programmed with a count (number). The output of timer 0 is connected to the IRQ0 latch and to the clock input of the

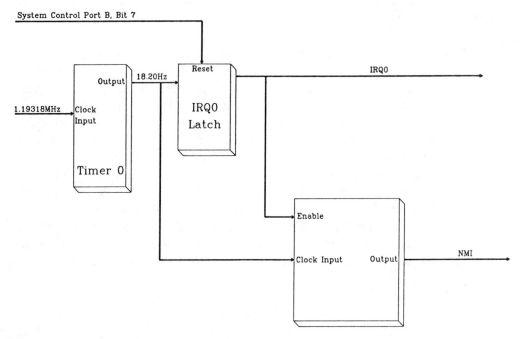

FIGURE 33-3 The Watchdog Timer

watchdog timer. When timer 0 generates a pulse, it sets the IRQ0 latch and generates IRQ0# to the interrupt controller. When IRQ0# goes active, it enables the watchdog timer. Starting with the next timer 0 output pulse, the watchdog timer begins to count down once for each pulse received on its clock input.

In the IRQ0 interrupt service routine, the programmer should set bit 7 of system control port B to a 1 to reset the IRQ0 latch, thereby turning off IRQ0#. When turned off, it disables the watchdog timer so it cannot count down any more. The programmer should also reload the start count into the watchdog timer.

If interrupt recognition has been disabled for an extended period of time by an ill-behaved program, IRQ0# will not be reset. The watchdog timer will therefore continue to be count down towards 0 by the repeated timer 0 output pulses. If the count goes to 0, the watchdog timer's output goes active, setting NMI active to the microprocessor.

In the NMI interrupt service routine, the programmer can check bit 4 of system control port A at I/O address 0092_h to see if the watchdog timer was the source of the NMI. It will be set to 1 if it was. Writing a new count to the watchdog timer will turn off NMI.

Summary

The IBM PS/2 product line incorporates four timers, three of which are programmable. The system timer, timer 0, is a general purpose timer. It is programmed during the POST to generate an IRQ0# once every 54.9ms. It is programmable at I/O address 0040_h. The refresh timer, timer 1, is not programmable. It generates a refresh request once every 15.0857 microseconds to request the use of the buses to refresh the next row in DRAM memory throughout the system. The speaker data timer, timer 2, is programmable at I/O address 0042_h. Its frequency output is applied to the speaker if bits 0 and 1 of system control port B are both 1's. The watchdog timer, timer 3, is programmable at I/O address 0044_h. If the microprocessor ceases to service IRQ0# (the system timer) the watchdog timer begins to count down towards 0. If it gets to 0 before IRQ0# is serviced, it generates an NMI to the microprocessor.

CHAPTER

34

The Reset Logic

Objectives: This chapter provides a description of the five possible sources for various reset signals in the PS/2 and the effect each of them has on the system. It also explains the actions taken when Control/Alternate/Delete are depressed.

The purpose of a reset signal is twofold: 1) To keep a device or devices from doing anything until power has stabilized and 2) to force a device or devices to a known state.

The PS/2 products have six separate resets, one of which is generated only by the hardware; the other five are initiated by software commands.

The Power Supply Reset

The power supply provides the operating voltages necessary for system operation. When the power switch is first placed in the ON position, it takes some time for the power supply's output voltages to reach their proper operating levels. Erratic operation would result if the system components were allowed to begin operating before the voltages have stabilized.

Every PC and PS/2 power supply produces an output signal commonly called POWERGOOD. On the system board, the POWERGOOD signal is used to produce the RESET signal. During the period required for stabilization of the output voltages, the POWERGOOD signal is kept inactive by the power supply. While POWERGOOD is inactive, the RESET signal is kept active.

While RESET is active, it has two effects on the microprocessor and other system components: 1) It keeps any activity from occurring until power has stabilized and 2) It presets the microprocessor and other system devices to a known state prior to letting them begin their jobs. This ensures that the machine will always start up the same way.

When POWERGOOD goes active, the RESET signal goes inactive and the microprocessor can begin to fetch and execute instructions. The first instruction is always fetched from the power-on restart address, which is always located 16 locations from the very top of the memory address space. This is $FFFF0_h$ for the 8088 microprocessor, $FFFFF0_h$ for the 80286 microprocessor, and $FFFFFFF0_h$ for the 80386 and 80486 microprocessors. This location contains the first instruction of the POST.

Hot Reset

PC-DOS was written specifically for the Intel 8088 microprocessor using 8088-specific instructions. Since the 8088 has only 20 address lines, it cannot generate a memory address greater than $FFFFF_h$ (1MB). Also, since protected mode was not introduced until the advent of the 80286 microprocessor, PC-DOS can address only the lower 1MB and does not understand protected mode.

When an 80286 is powered up, it operates in real mode (that is, it operates like an 8088 and therefore understands only 8088 instructions). As a result, it is limited to the lower 1MB when in real mode even though it has 24 address lines and can physically address up to 16MB of memory address space.

Most current applications programs are written to run under PC-DOS. Many of these programs require access to more memory space than allowed under PC-DOS. For example, many Lotus 1-2-3 spreadsheets require very large amounts of memory space, far in excess of that allowed under PC-DOS and the 8088 microprocessor.

If a system is based on the 80286 microprocessor, the problem can be solved by switching the microprocessor into protected mode. This allows the microprocessor to access up to 16MB of memory space. PC-DOS presents a problem because it does not understand protected mode and cannot generate addresses above 1MB.

Special software that understands protected mode operation must prepare the segment descriptor tables in memory prior to switching into protected mode. It also must save the address of the next instruction to be executed when the microprocessor returns to real mode so that PC-DOS can continue to run at the point where it went to protected mode. The 80286 is then switched into protected mode and the extended memory above 1MB accessed (for example, to store spreadsheet data).

Once the extended memory access is complete, the microprocessor must be switched back into real mode so that the applications program can continue to run under PC-DOS. Here is where the problem comes in: In order to switch the 80286 microprocessor from protected mode to real mode, the microprocessor must be reset. To do this, the following actions must be accomplished:

1. A special value is stored in a configuration CMOS RAM location to indicate the reason for the reset.

2. The hot reset command must be issued to the keyboard/mouse interface. This is accomplished by writing a FE_h to the keyboard/mouse interface's command port at I/O address 0064_h.

3. In response, the keyboard/mouse interface pulses its hot reset output one time. This causes the hardware to generate a reset just to the 80286 microprocessor.

4. When the reset goes inactive, the microprocessor begins to fetch and execute instructions at the power-on restart address exactly as if a power up had just occurred.

5. At the beginning of the POST, the programmer reads the value stored in the configuration RAM location to ascertain the reset's cause. In this case, the value indicates that it was caused by hot reset to get back to real mode and continue program execution.

6. POST then retrieves the previously stored real mode address pointer and jumps to the indicated address and picks up where it left off in real mode.

Alternate Hot Reset

The alternate hot reset command performs the same function as the hot reset command. The microprocessor is reset more quickly using alternate hot reset. The hot reset command must be interpreted by the ROM program inside of the keyboard/mouse interface, but the alternate hot reset command is executed by the hardware immediately (within 13.4 microseconds).

Alternate hot reset is generated by setting bit 0 in system control port A (I/O port 92_h) to a 1. This generates a pulse on alternate hot reset which, in turn, causes a pulse on hot reset. This resets the microprocessor. For a more extensive explanation of hot reset, see the previous section.

Channel Reset

The CHRESET signal on the MCA connectors resets all installed MCA cards. It is asserted during the period when the POWERGOOD signal is not yet active, but can also be turned on under software control. This provides the programmer with a method for clearing error conditions on MCA cards without resetting the system board and the system board microprocessor.

CHRESET is turned on by writing a 1 to bit 7 of the Adapter Enable/Setup register at I/O address 0096_h. Bit 3 should be kept off (0) to keep from placing any of the MCA cards into setup mode.

Numeric Coprocessor Reset

Coprocessor error conditions can be cleared by performing an I/O write of all 0's to I/O address $00F0_h$. This causes just the coprocessor to be reset.

Control/Alternate/Delete: Soft Reset

When the Control/Alternate/Delete key combination is depressed, an IRQ1# keyboard interrupt request is generated. In the keyboard interrupt service routine, the scan code is read from the keyboard interface's data port at I/O address 0060_h. The scan code that represents Control/Alternate/Delete causes the keyboard interrupt service routine to take the following actions:

1. Store a special value in RAM to indicate that Control/Alternate/Delete was sensed.

2. Jump to the power-on restart address and start execution of the POST.

3. At the beginning of the POST, the programmer reads the value stored in the RAM location to ascertain the reset's cause. In this case, the value indicates that it was caused by Control/Alternate/Delete.

4. As a result, only a subset of the POST is executed.

Summary

The purpose of a reset signal is to keep a device or devices from doing anything until power has stabilized and to force a device or devices to a known state.

The PS/2 products have six separate resets, one of which is generated only by the hardware and the other five of which can be initiated by software commands. The POWERGOOD signal, generated by the power supply, resets the entire system, including MCA cards. The Hot Reset command is generated by the keyboard/mouse interface under software control. It resets just the microprocessor. It is provided because some AT-specific software uses this method to switch the 80286 microprocessor from protected mode to real mode. The alternate hot reset command performs the same function as the hot reset command but performs it more quickly. The channel reset command is generated under software control and can be used to clear error conditions on MCA cards. The numeric coprocessor reset command is generated under software control and resets just the numeric coprocessor. It is used to clear coprocessor error conditions. Control/Alternate/Delete does not generate any reset signals. It simulates a partial hardware reset by performing part of the POST.

APPENDIX
A

Logic Primer

Objectives: Very few portions of this book require a background in digital logic. This appendix prepares the reader for those sections that do require some prior knowledge. Readers who are unfamiliar with basic digital logic symbols or who would benefit from a brief review should read this chapter.

The Bit

Figure A-1 illustrates the concept of a bit. Information can be represented on many different levels within a digital system. When studying those levels, however, one sees that all levels are based on the bit, which is the lowest level at which information can be represented.

In the digital world, the bit can possess one of two values, a **0** or a **1**. Each of these two values is represented by pre-defined voltage levels. Most systems (including IBM computers and compatibles) use what are known as transistor - transistor logic (TTL) voltage levels, in which a 0 bit is represented by a voltage of $0V_{dc}$, and a 1 bit is represented by a voltage of $+5V_{dc}$.

Using this standard, any device can send a 1 bit or a 0 bit over a piece of wire to another device by applying a voltage of $+5V_{dc}$ or $0V_{dc}$ to the wire (or trace on a printed circuit board).

A digit in the binary numbering system may be either a 1 or a 0. The location of a digit in a binary number is known as its bit position within the number. Any bit may be a 1 or a 0, then. In a digital system, a bit may be trans—ferred over a wire from one device to another. A 0 is usually represented by 0Vdc and a 1 by +5Vdc.

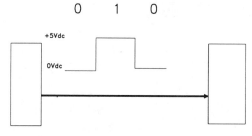

FIGURE A-1 The Bit

The AND Gate

Figure A-2 illustrates an AND gate. The AND gate pictured has two input pins and one output pin. In the figure, pins 1 and 2 are the inputs and pin 3 is the output. AND gates may have any number of inputs, but only one output.

Truth tables describe the function of a digital logic component. A truth table illustrates the resulting output(s) for every possible combination of inputs. Table A-1 is the truth table for a two-input AND gate.

To summarize the two-input AND gate's function: it takes a 1 **AND** a 1 to get a 1 out. Any low (0) input causes the output to be low (0). An AND gate with more than two inputs functions the same way. All inputs must be high (1's) in order to have a high on the output.

The Inverter

Figure A-3 illustrates an inverter. The inverter has one input and one output. Its function is to place the inversion, or opposite, of the input state onto the output pin.

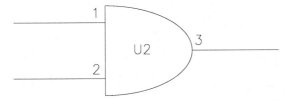

FIGURE A-2   The Two-Input AND Gate

TABLE A-1   Truth Table for a Two-Input AND Gate

	Inputs		Output
	Pin 1	*Pin 2*	*Pin 3*
	0	0	0
	0	1	0
	1	0	0
	1	1	1

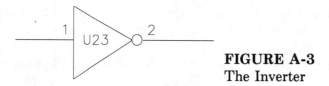

FIGURE A-3
The Inverter

TABLE A-2   Truth Table for an Inverter

Input	Output
Pin 1	Pin 2
0	1
1	0

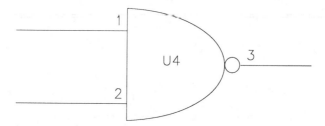

FIGURE A-4   The Two-Input NAND Gate

Table A-2 is the truth table for the inverter.

The state indicator (bubble) on the output represents the inversion performed by the inverter.

The NAND (Negative AND) Gate

Figure A-4 illustrates a NAND gate. The NAND gate pictured has two inputs and one output. Pins 1 and 2 are the inputs and pin 3 is the output. As with AND gates, NAND gates can have any number of inputs but only one output. Table A-3 is the truth table for a two-input NAND gate.

The state indicator on output pin 3 indicates that the output will go low (0) when input 1 **AND** input 2 are high (1's). In other words, the NAND gate acts as an AND gate that inverts the output of the AND gate, hence the name negative AND gate. A NAND gate with more than two inputs functions the same way. All inputs must be high (1's) in order to have a low (0) on the output.

The OR Gate

Figure A-5 illustrates an OR gate. The OR gate pictured has two inputs and one output. Pins 1 and 2 are the inputs and pin 3 is the output. As with AND gates, OR gates may have any number of inputs but only one output. Table A-4 is the truth table for a 2-input OR gate.

If either input 1 **OR** input 2 is high, output 3 will be high. In other words, if any input to an OR gate is high, the output will be high.

TABLE A-3   Truth Table for a Two-Input NAND Gate

	Inputs		Output
	Pin 1	*Pin 2*	*Pin 3*
	0	0	1
	0	1	1
	1	0	1
	1	1	0

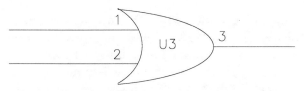

FIGURE A-5   The Two-Input OR Gate

TABLE A-4   Truth Table for a Two-Input OR Gate

	Inputs		Output
	Pin 1	*Pin 2*	*Pin 3*
	0	0	0
	0	1	1
	1	0	1
	1	1	1

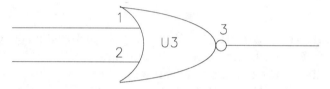

FIGURE A-6   The Two-Input NOR Gate

TABLE A-5   Truth Table for a Two-Input NOR Gate

	Inputs		Output
	Pin 1	*Pin 2*	*Pin 3*
	0	0	1
	0	1	0
	1	0	0
	1	1	0

The NOR (Negative OR) Gate

Figure A-6 illustrates a NOR gate. The NOR gate pictured has two inputs and one output. Pins 1 and 2 are the inputs and pin 3 is the output. As with OR gates, NOR gates can have any number of inputs but only one output. Table A-5 is the truth table for a two-Input NOR gate.

If either input 1 **OR** input 2 is high, output 3 will be low. In other words, if any input to an NOR gate is high, the output will be low.

Device Designators

Board designers place a device designator within or near a digital symbol on a schematic to indicate the actual chip on the board that contains this digital device. For example, the OR gate in Figure A-5 has a U3 device designator written inside the symbol. The designer then also labels the chip on the board as U3. Many manufacturers use U-numbers, but other designators are sometimes used as well. To refer to pin 3 on the OR gate in Figure A-5, U3-3 would be used.

APPENDIX

B

The Communications Language: Binary and Hex

Objectives: This appendix provides the reader with a brief tutorial on the binary and hexadecimal numbering systems. An understanding of this subject is necessary in order to understand how information is represented on the address and data buses. To ensure that the reader has the proper background understanding, a number of aspects of data format are covered, from the lowest level of digital data transmission, the bit, up to the doubleword (32 bits).

The Bit

Figure B-1 illustrates the bit. Information can be represented on many different levels within a digital system. All levels are based on the bit, which is the lowest level at which information can be represented.

In the digital world, the bit can possess one of two values, a 0 or a 1. Each of these two values is represented by pre-defined voltage levels. Most systems, including IBM systems and compatibles, use transistor-transistor logic (TTL) voltage levels, in which a 0 bit is represented by a voltage of $0V_{dc}$, and a 1 bit is represented by a voltage of $+5V_{dc}$.

Using this standard, any device can send a 1 bit or a 0 bit over a piece of wire to another device by applying a voltage of $+5V_{dc}$ or $0V_{dc}$ to the wire (or trace on a printed circuit board).

The Nibble

Figure B-2 illustrates the concept of the nibble. The next higher level at which information can be represented is the nibble. A nibble consists

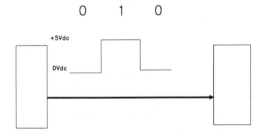

A digit in the binary numbering system may be either a 1 or a 0. The location of a digit in a binary number is known as its bit position within the number. Any bit may be a 1 or a 0, then. In a digital system, a bit may be transferred over a wire from one device to another. A 0 is usually represented by 0Vdc and a 1 by +5Vdc.

FIGURE B-1 The Bit

A nibble is made up of four, grouped bits (binary digits). In any group of bits, the right—most is referred to as the Least—Significant Bit (LSB), while the left—most is the Most—Significant Bit (MSB).

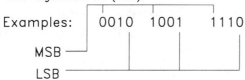

FIGURE B-2 The Nibble

TABLE B-1 The Nibble

Nibble Value
0000
0001
0010
0011
0100
0101
0110
0111
1000
1001
1010
1011
1100
1101
1110
1111

of a logical grouping of 4 bits. An example would be 4 adjacent bits on the address or data bus. Each of these bits can assume the 1 or 0 state. The lowest-valued pattern of information that can be represented on 4 wires is a 0000_b, and the highest is a 1111_b. This yields 16 possible values as illustrated in Table B-1.

Binary-Weighted Values

The numbering system in common use is known as the decimal (base 10) numbering system because it is based on ten numbers, 0 through 9. The numbering system used in the digital world is called the binary (base two) numbering system. The entire binary numbering system is based on the numbers 1 and 0, the two numbers that can be represented by a single bit.

In turn, the binary-weighted numbering system is built upon the numbers 1 and 0. This numbering system is based on the idea that each 1-bit within a group of bits assumes a predefined value based on its position in the group of bits. A 0 in any bit position always has a value of 0.

The bit position with the lowest value within the group is referred to as the least significant bit (LSB) position, and the bit position with the highest value is referred to as the most significant bit (MSB) position. The LSB position is commonly referred to as Bit 0, the next higher bit position as Bit 1, the next as Bit 2, and so on.

When represented in written form, Bit 0 (the LSB) is usually the right-most bit in a group. The value assigned to the LSB position is a decimal 1. Each bit position above that one increases in value by a power of two. In other words, the LSB position is assigned the decimal value 1, the next higher bit the decimal value 2, the next decimal value 4, and so on. This assigning of values (also referred to as weighting) continues up to the MSB position in the group of bits.

By adding up the decimal values of any bit position containing a binary 1 bit, the total equivalent decimal value of that group of bits can be ascertained. For example, Figure B-3 illustrates a nibble with the binary value 1001_b. In this example, both the LSB (bit 0) and the MSB (bit 3) are 1's, and bits 1 and 2 are 0's. To find the total decimal value of this bit grouping, add up the values assigned to the bit positions that have 1's in them. The bit positions are assigned the decimal values illustrated in Table B-2.

In the bit group 1001_b, bits 0 and 3 contain 1 bits; thus, the total decimal value of this nibble (group of 4 bits) is $8 + 1 = $ **9**. A bit pattern of 0110_b has a decimal value of **6** $(4 + 2)$, and a pattern of 0100_b has a decimal value of **4**. The situation is handled in the same manner when working with a wider group of bits (for example, 8, 16, 20, 24, or 32 bits wide).

In Binary, each bit position is assigned a value. The LSB is assigned a value of 1 and each bit afterwards has a value double that of the bit to its right.

To ascertain the total value of a group of bits, add the assigned values of each bit position with a 1 in it. The sum is the decimal value of the bit grouping.

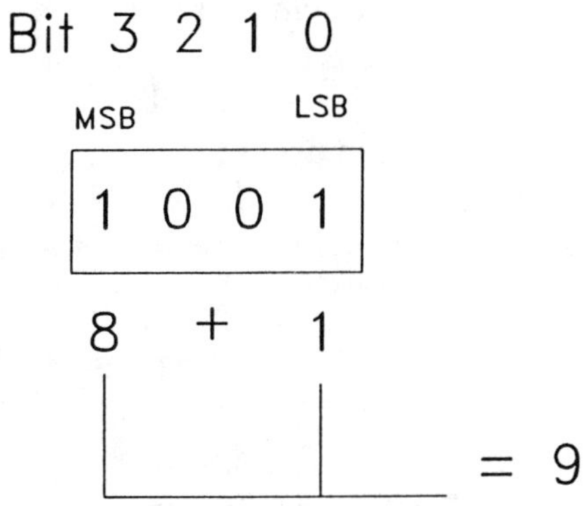

Bit 3 2 1 0

MSB   LSB

| 1 | 0 | 0 | 1 |

8 + 1

= 9

FIGURE B-3   Binary Weighting

TABLE B-2   Bit Weighting

	Bit	3 2 1 0
	Value	8 4 2 1
		MSB LSB

Hexadecimal Notation

In the digital world, information transmitted over the microprocessor address and data buses is usually considered in hexadecimal (base 16) rather than decimal. Just as binary (base 2) is represented by two digits,

0 and 1, and decimal (base 10) by ten digits, 0 through 9, hexadecimal (base 16) is represented by 16 digits, 0 through F.

Table B-3 shows the relationship between binary, hex (as it is commonly referred to), and decimal. The hex digits 0 through 9 are identical to the decimal digits 0 through 9. Adding one to hex 9, though, results in **A**, not **10**.

Counting proceeds as follows in hex:

```
0 1 2 3 4 5 6 7 8 9 A B C D E F 10 11 12 etc.
```

Conveniently, a nibble (group of 4 bits) can represent any of the 16 possible hex digits from 0 through F. Since the number of bits on all microprocessor address and data buses is divisible by 4, it is handy to think of an address or data as being made up of a number of nibbles. It is just an additional small step to think of address and data in the form of hex numbers. For example, the following 16-bit pattern

TABLE B-3   Relationship Between Binary, Hex, and Decimal

Binary	Hex	Decimal
0000	0	0
0001	1	1
0010	2	2
0011	3	3
0100	4	4
0101	5	5
0110	6	6
0111	7	7
1000	8	8
1001	9	9
1010	A	10
1011	B	11
1100	C	12
1101	D	13
1110	E	14
1111	F	15

```
1100101000110111
```

can be rewritten as

```
1100 1010 0011 0111
```

to re-group it as nibbles, and then finally as

$CA37_h$

pronounced as: Charlie Alpha Three Seven.

If asked what information is currently on the microprocessor's address bus, it is a lot easier to respond:

$CA37_h$

then

```
1100 1010 0011 0111.
```

The most common way of pronouncing the hex digits A_h through F_h is Alpha, Baker, Charlie, Dog, Easy, and Fox.

As stated earlier, the number of bits on virtually all address and data buses is a multiple of 4 and therefore easily represented as hex numbers. A 16-bit bus is made up of 4 nibbles (16 divided by 4), each of which can represent 1 hex digit. A 32-bit bus is made up of 8 nibbles (32 divided by 4), each of which can represent 1 hex digit.

The Byte

Just as a group of 4 bits is known as a nibble, a group of 8 bits is known as a byte. A byte consists of 8 bits and is made up of 2 nibbles of 4 bits each. In other words, a byte may be represented by two hex digits. For example,

```
1011 1101
```

is a byte that can also be represented as a BD_h.

The Word

A word is 16-bits in length and consists of 2 bytes, or 4 nibbles. A word can be represented as 4 hex digits (for example, $98EA_h$).

The Doubleword

The doubleword is 32 bits in length and consists of 2 words (4 bytes; 8 nibbles). A doubleword can be represented as 8 hex digits (for example, $98EA3215_h$).

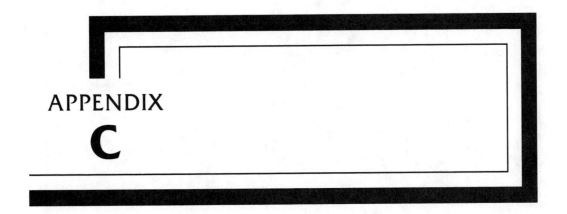

APPENDIX
C

The I/O Address Map

I/O Port	R/W	Note	Bit 7	Bit 6	Bit 5	Bit 4	Bit 3	Bit 2	Bit 1	Bit 0
0000_h	R/W	Master DMA Channel 0 Memory Address Register	lower 16-bits of memory address written as 2 successive bytes							
0001_h	R/W	Master DMA Channel 0 Transfer Count Register	lower 16-bits of memory address written as 2 successive bytes							
0002_h	R/W	Master DMA Channel 1 Memory Address Register	lower 16-bits of memory address written as 2 successive bytes							
0003_h	R/W	Master DMA Channel 1 Transfer Count Register	lower 16-bits of memory address written as 2 successive bytes							
0004_h	R/W	Master DMA Channel 2 Memory Address Register	lower 16-bits of memory address written as 2 successive bytes							
0005_h	R/W	Master DMA Channel 2 Transfer Count Register	lower 16-bits of memory address written as 2 successive bytes							
0006_h	R/W	Master DMA Channel 3 Memory Address Register	lower 16-bits of memory address written as 2 successive bytes							
0007_h	R/W	Master DMA Channel 3 Transfer Count Register	lower 16-bits of memory address written as 2 successive bytes							
0008_h	R	Master DMA Status Register (Channels 0-3)	1 = Channel 3 request	1 = Channel 2 request	1 = Channel 1 request	1 = Channel 0 request	1 = Channel 3 Terminal Count	1 = Channel 2 Terminal Count	1 = Channel 1 Terminal Count	1 = Channel 0 Terminal Count
$000A_h$	R/W	Master DMA Mask Register (Channels 0-3)	reserved					0 = clear mask bit 1 = set mask bit	00 = select Channel 0 01 = select Channel 1 10 = select Channel 2 11 = select Channel 3	
$000B_h$	W	Master DMA Mode Register (Channels 0-3)	00 = demand transfer mode 01 = single transfer mode 10 = block transfer mode 11 = cascade mode		reserved		00 = verify operation 01 = write operation 10 = read operation 11 = reserved		00 = select Channel 0 01 = select Channel 1 10 = select Channel 2 11 = select Channel 3	
$000C_h$	W	Master DMA Clear Byte Pointer	not used							
$000D_h$	W	Master DMA Master Clear	not used							
$000E_h$	W	Master DMA Clear Mask Register for Channels 0-3	not used							
$000F_h$	W	Master DMA Write Mask Register	reserved				0 = unmask Channel 3 1 = mask Channel 3	0 = unmask Channel 2 1 = mask Channel 2	0 = unmask Channel 1 1 = mask Channel 1	0 = unmask Channel 0 1 = mask Channel 0
0018_h	W	Master DMA Extended Function Register	0_h = I/O Address Register access 1_h = reserved 2_h = Memory Address Register Write 3_h = Memory Address Register Read 4_h = Transfer Count Register Write 5_h = Transfer Count Register Read 6_h = Status Register Read 7_h = Mode Register 8_h = Arbus Register 9_h = Mask Register set single bit A_h = Mask Register reset single bit B_h-C_h = reserved D_h = Master Clear E_h-F_h = reserved				reserved			

I/O Port	R/W	Note	Bit 7	Bit 6	Bit 5	Bit 4	Bit 3	Bit 2	Bit 1	Bit 0
001Ah	R/W	Master DMA Extended Function execute	not used							
0020h	R	Master Interrupt Request Register	0 = IR7 not active 1 = IR7 active	0 = IR6 not active 1 = IR6 active	0 = IR5 not active 1 = IR5 active	0 = IR4 not active 1 = IR4 active	0 = IR3 not active 1 = IR3 active	0 = IR2 not active 1 = IR2 active	0 = IR1 not active 1 = IR1 active	0 = IR0 not active 1 = IR0 active
0020h	R	Master 8259 In-Service Register	0 = IR7 not currently being serviced 1 = IR7 being serviced	0 = IR6 not currently being serviced 1 = IR6 being serviced	0 = IR5 not currently being serviced 1 = IR5 being serviced	0 = IR4 not currently being serviced 1 = IR4 being serviced	0 = IR3 not currently being serviced 1 = IR3 being serviced	0 = IR2 not currently being serviced 1 = IR2 being serviced	0 = IR1 not currently being serviced 1 = IR1 being serviced	0 = IR0 not currently being serviced 1 = IR0 being serviced
0020h	W	Master 8259 ICW1	must = 000 (only used in 8080/8085 mode)			must = 1	1 = Level-sensitive mode	0 = interrupt vectors are separated by 8 locations	0 = cascade mode	1 = ICW4 not needed
0021h	W	Master 8259 ICW2	upper 5 bits of Interrupt Vector (master = 00001)	slave = 01110					always = 000	
0021h	W	Master 8259 ICW3	0 (I/O device attached to IRQ7)	0 (I/O device attached to IRQ6)	0 (I/O device attached to IRQ5)	0 (I/O device attached to IRQ4)	0 (I/O device attached to IRQ3)	1 (Slave 8259 attached to IRQ2)	0 (I/O device attached to IRQ1)	0 (I/O device attached to IRQ0)
0021h	W	Master 8259 ICW4	reserved (should be 000)			0 = fully-nested mode off 1 = fully-nested mode on	00 = non-buffered mode 01 = non-buffered mode 10 = buffered mode/slave 11 = buffered mode/master		0 = normal EOI 1 = Auto EOI	0 = 8080/8085 mode 1 = 8086 mode
0021h	R/W	Master Interrupt Mask Register (OCW1)	0 = enable IR7 1 = mask out IR7	0 = enable IR6 1 = mask out IR6	0 = enable IR5 1 = mask out IR5	0 = enable IR4 1 = mask out IR4	0 = enable IR3 1 = mask out IR3	0 = enable IR2 1 = mask out IR2	0 = enable IR1 1 = mask out IR1	0 = enable IR0 1 = mask out IR0
0021h	W	Master 8259 OCW2	000 = rotate in Auto EOI Mode (clear) 001 = non-specific EOI 010 = no operation 011 = specific EOI 100 = rotate in Auto EOI Mode (set) 101 = rotate on non-specific EOI command 110 = set priority command 111 = rotate on specific EOI command			reserved		Interrupt Request to which the command applies: 000 = IR0 001 = IR1 010 = IR2 011 = IR3 100 = IR4 101 = IR5 110 = IR6 111 = IR7		
0020h	W	Master 8259 OCW3	reserved	00 = nop 01 = nop 10 = reset special mask 11 = set special mask		reserved		0 = not poll command 1 = poll command	00 = nop 01 = nop 10 = read Interrupt Request Register on next read from port 20h 11 = read In-Service Register on next read from port 20h	
0040h	R/W	Interval Timer #1/System Timer 0	Read or write Counter 0							
0042h	R/W	Interval Timer #1/Speaker Timer	Read or write Counter 2							
0043h	W	Interval Timer #1 Mode Control Register	00 = select Counter 0 01 = reserved 10 = select Counter 2		00 = Counter latch command 01 = read/write counter bits 0-7 only 10 = read/write counter bits 8-15 only 11 = read/write counter bits 0-7 first followed by bits 8-15		000 = mode 0 (interrupt on terminal count) 001 = mode 1 (hardware retriggerable one-shot) 010 or 110 = mode 2 (rate generator) 011 or 111 = mode 3 (square wave generator) (system timer and speaker timer mode) 100 = mode 4 (software retriggerable strobe) 101 = mode 5 (hardware retriggerable strobe)			0 = 16-bit binary counter 1 = BCD counter
0044h	W	Interval Timer #2/Watchdog Timer	read or write counter 3							

I/O Port	R/W	Note	Bit 7	Bit 6	Bit 5	Bit 4	Bit 3	Bit 2	Bit 1	Bit 0
0047h	W	Interval Timer #2 Mode Control Register	00 = select counter 3 01 = reserved 10 = reserved 11 = reserved		00 = counter latch command 01 = read/write counter bits 0-7 only 10 = reserved 11 = reserved		000 = mode 0 (interrupt on terminal count) (watchdog timer mode) 001 = mode 1 (hardware retriggerable one-shot) 010 or 110 = mode 2 (rate generator) 011 or 111 = mode 3 (square wave generator) (system timer and speaker mode) 100 = mode 4 (software retriggerable strobe) 101 = mode 5 (hardware retriggerable strobe)			0 = 16-bit binary counter 1 = BCD counter
0060h	R/W	Keyboard/Mouse Interface Data Port	see IBM Technical Reference Guide							
0061h	R	System Control Port B	1 = System Board RAM parity check	1 = Channel Check	1 = timer 2 (speaker) output is high	Refresh Request toggle	0 = Channel Check enabled	0 = System Board Parity Check enabled	1 = speaker data enabled	1 = Timer 2 speaker gate enabled
0061h	W	System Control Port B	1 = reset Timer 0 Interrupt Request (IRQ0)	reserved			0 = enable Channel Check	0 = enable System Board RAM Parity Check	1 = enable speaker data	1 = enable Timer 2 speaker gate
0064h	W	Keyboard/Mouse Interface Command Port								
0064h	R	Keyboard/Mouse Interface Status Port	1 = Parity Error	1 = general timeout	1 = Mouse output buffer full	0 = Keyboard password protected	0 = Keyboard data port accessed 1 = Keyboard command port accessed	system flag bit	1 = Keyboard Interface input buffer full	1 = Keyboard Interface output buffer full
0070h	W	RTC/CMOS RAM Address Port	0 = NMI enable 1 = NMI disable	CMOS RAM address						
0071h	R/W	RTC/CMOS RAM Data Port	data to be read or written							
0074h	W	Extended CMOS RAM Address Port	LSB of address							
0075h	W	Extended CMOS RAM Address Port	MSB of address							
0076h	R/W	Extended CMOS RAM Data Port	data to be read or written							
0081h	R/W	Channel 2 DMA Page Register	upper 8-bits of memory address							
0082h	R/W	Channel 3 DMA Page Register	upper 8-bits of memory address							
0083h	R/W	Channel 1 DMA Page Register	upper 8-bits of memory address							
0087h	R/W	Channel 0 DMA Page Register	upper 8-bits of memory address							
0089h	R/W	Channel 6 DMA Page Register	upper 8-bits of memory address							
008Ah	R/W	Channel 7 DMA Page Register	upper 8-bits of memory address							
008Bh	R/W	Channel 5 DMA Page Register	upper 8-bits of memory address							
008Fh	R/W	Channel 4 DMA Page Register	upper 8-bits of memory address							
0090h	R	Central Arbitration Control Point (CACP) Status Register	1 = system microprocessor Bus Cycles enabled	1 = NMI caused ARB/GNT# to be set high	1 = Bus Timeout	reserved	arbitration level of current Bus Master			

I/O Port	R/W	Note	Bit 7	Bit 6	Bit 5	Bit 4	Bit 3	Bit 2	Bit 1	Bit 0
0090$_h$	W	Central Arbitration Control Point (CACP) Command Register	1 = enable system microprocessor Bus Cycles during arbitration	1 = force ARB/GNT# high	1 = enable extended arbitration (600ns Arbitration Cycle)	reserved				0 = Card Selected signal active on previous Bus Cycle or a system board I/O device accessed by an I/O Bus Cycle
0091$_h$	R	Feedback Register	reserved							
0092$_h$	R/W	System Control Port A	1 = Fixed disk LED on (write only bit)	1 = Fixed disk LED on (write only bit)	reserved	1 = Watchdog Timer timeout (read-only bit)	1 = Security lock (password) engaged	reserved	1 = set Alternate Gate Address bit 20 active	1 = set Alternate (Fast) Hot Reset active
0094$_h$	R/W	System Board Enable/Setup Register	0 = place system board in Setup mode 1 = place system board in Enabled mode	reserved	0 = place VGA in Setup mode 1 = place VGA in Enabled mode	reserved				
0096$_h$	R/W	Adapter Enable/Setup Register	1 = activate Channel Reset signal	reserved			1 = allow card setup selection using bits 0-2	card slot (slot number minus 1) to be placed in Setup mode		
00A0$_h$	R/W	Slave Interrupt Controller	see bit definitions for Port 0020$_h$							
00A1$_h$	R/W	Slave Interrupt Controller	see bit definitions for Port 0021$_h$							
00A1$_h$	W	Slave ICW3 Register contains the Slave ID (02$_h$)	0	0	0	0	0	0	1	0
00C0$_h$	R/W	Slave DMA Channel 4 Memory Address Register	lower 16-bits of memory address written as 2 successive bytes							
00C2$_h$	R/W	Slave DMA Channel 4 Transfer Count Register	lower 16-bits of memory address written as 2 successive bytes							
00C4$_h$	R/W	Slave DMA Channel 5 Memory Address Register	lower 16-bits of memory address written as 2 successive bytes							
00C6$_h$	R/W	Slave DMA Channel 5 Transfer Count Register	lower 16-bits of memory address written as 2 successive bytes							
00C8$_h$	R/W	Slave DMA Channel 6 Memory Address Register	lower 16-bits of memory address written as 2 successive bytes							
00CA$_h$	R/W	Slave DMA Channel 6 Transfer Count Register	lower 16-bits of memory address written as 2 successive bytes							
00CC$_h$	R/W	Slave DMA Channel 7 Memory Address Register	lower 16-bits of memory address written as 2 successive bytes							
00CE$_h$	R/W	Slave DMA Channel 7 Transfer Count Register	lower 16-bits of memory address written as 2 successive bytes							
00D0$_h$	R	Slave DMA Status Register (Channels 4-7)	1 = Channel 7 request	1 = Channel 6 request	1 = Channel 5 request	1 = Channel 4 request	1 = Channel 7 Terminal Count	1 = Channel 6 Terminal Count	1 = Channel 5 Terminal Count	1 = Channel 4 Terminal Count

I/O Port	R/W	Note	Bit 7	Bit 6	Bit 5	Bit 4	Bit 3	Bit 2	Bit 1	Bit 0
00D4h	R/W	Slave DMA Mask Register (Channels 4-7)	reserved					0 = clear mask bit 1 = set mask bit	00 = select Channel 4 01 = select Channel 5 10 = select Channel 6 11 = select Channel 7	00 = select Channel 4 01 = select Channel 5 10 = select Channel 6 11 = select Channel 7
00D6h	W	Slave DMA Mode Register (Channels 4-7)	00 = Demand Transfer Mode 01 = single transfer mode 10 = block transfer mode 11 = cascade mode		reserved		00 = verify operation 01 = write operation 10 = read operation 11 = reserved			
00D8h	W	Slave DMA Clear Byte Pointer	not used							
00DAh	W	Slave DMA Master Clear	not used							
00DCh	W	Slave DMA Clear Mask Register for Channels 4-7	not used							
00DEh	W	Slave DMA Write Mask Register	reserved				0 = unmask Channel 7 1 = mask Channel 7	0 = unmask Channel 6 1 = mask Channel 6	0 = unmask Channel 5 1 = mask Channel 5	0 = unmask Channel 4 1 = mask Channel 4
00E0h	R/W	Model 70 Memory Encoding Register 2	reserved	reserved	0 = enable 2nd 1MB block in slot 3	0 = enable 1st 1MB block in slot 3	starting with bit 3 these four bits supply the high-order digit of the Split Memory Block's start address.			
00E0h	R/W	16MHz Model 80 Split Address Register	reserved				starting with bit 3 these four bits supply the high-order digit of the Split Memory Block's start address.			
00E0h	R/W	20MHz Model 80 Memory Encoding Register 2	reserved			00 = 2MB card enabled in slot 2 01 = 1st 1MB disabled on 2MB card in slot 2 10 = 2nd 1MB disabled on 2MB card in slot 2 11 = all memory disabled or no card present	starting with bit 3 these four bits supply the high-order digit of the Split Memory Block's start address.			
00E1h	R/W	Model 70 Memory Encoding Register 1	0 = enable 2nd 1MB memory block in slot 2	0 = enable 1st 1MB memory block in slot 2	0 = enable 2nd 1MB memory block in slot 1	0 = enable 1st 1MB memory block in slot 1	0 = Enable Split Memory Block	0 = split at 640KB	1 = ROM enabled 0 = Shadow RAM enabled	0 = enable System Board RAM parity checking
00E1h	R/W	16MHz Model 80 Memory Encoding Register	10 = 1MB memory card enabled in slot 2 11 = Memory card disabled or no card present in slot 2	10 = 1MB memory card enabled in slot 1 11 = Memory card disabled or no card present in slot 1	0 = enable Split Memory Block	0 = split at 640KB	1 = ROM enabled 0 = Shadow RAM enabled	0 = enable System Board RAM parity checking		

564

I/O Port	R/W	Note	Bit 7	Bit 6	Bit 5	Bit 4	Bit 3	Bit 2	Bit 1	Bit 0
00E1h	R/W	20MHz Model 80 Memory Encoding Register 1	reserved			00 = 2MB memory card enabled in connector 1 01 = 1st 1MB disabled on 2MB card in slot 1 10 = 2nd 1MB disabled on 2MB card in slot 1 11 = invalid	0 = enable Split Memory Block	0 = split at 640KB	1 = ROM enabled 0 = Shadow RAM enabled	0 = enable System Board RAM parity checking
00F1h	W	Numeric Coprocessor Reset	all bits = 0							
00F8-00FCh	R/W	Numeric Coprocessor Ports		see IBM Technical Reference Guide						
0100h	R	Adapter card POS Register 0		LSB of Option ID						
0101h	R	Adapter card POS Register 1		MSB of Option ID						
0102h	R/W	System Board POS Register 2	0 = Parallel Port Extended Mode 1 = disable Parallel Port Extended Mode	00 = Parallel Port responds as Parallel Port 1 01 = parallel port responds as Parallel Port 2 10 = parallel port responds as Parallel Port 3 11 = reserved		if bit 0 = 1 1 = enable Parallel Port	0 = Serial Port responds as Serial Port 2 and uses IRQ3 1 = serial port responds as Serial Port 1 and uses IRQ4	if bit 0 = 1 1 = enable serial port	if bit 0 = 1, 1 = enable diskette interface	0 = disable system board devices 1 = allow bits 4/2/1 to control system board devices.
0102h	R/W	Adapter card POS Register 2	1 = card enable							
0103h	R/W	System board POS Register 3	PS/2 model-dependent	device-dependent						
0103h	R/W	Models 50 and 60 POS Register 3	reserved							1 = enable System Board RAM.
0103h	R/W	Model 70 POS Register 3	reserved	1 = 2MB memory card installed in slot 3 0 = 1MB memory card installed in slot 3	0 = memory card present in slot 3	reserved	1 = 2MB memory card installed in slot 2 0 = 1MB memory card installed in slot 2	0 = memory card present in slot 2	1 = 2MB memory card installed in slot 1 0 = 1MB memory card installed in slot 1	0 = memory card present in slot 1
0103h	R/W	16MHz Model 80 POS Register 3	reserved				0 = 1MB memory card installed in slot 2	0 = memory card present in slot 2	0 = 1MB memory card installed in slot 1	0 = memory card present in slot 1
0103h	R/W	20MHz Model 80 POS Register 3	reserved				1 = 2MB memory card installed in slot 2	0 = memory card present in slot 2	1 = 2MB memory card installed in slot 1	0 = memory card present in slot 1
0103h	R/W	Adapter Card POS Register 3	device-dependent							
0104h	R/W	Adapter card POS Register 4	device-dependent							
0105h	R/W	Adapter card POS Register 5	0 = Channel Check active on a read, Note: on a write 1 = reset Channel Check condition (also see bit 6)	0 = Channel Check available from POS Registers 6 and 7 1 = no channel check status available	device-dependent					

I/O Port	R/W	Note	Bit 7	Bit 6	Bit 5	Bit 4	Bit 3	Bit 2	Bit 1	Bit 0
0106h	R/W	Adapter Card POS Register 6	device-dependent							
0107h	R/W	Adapter Card POS Register 6	device-dependent							
0278h	R/W	Parallel Port 3 Data Port	data read from or written to the data port							
0279h	R	Parallel Port 3 Status Port	0 = Printer Busy	0 = Printer Acknowledge	1 = Out-of-Paper	1 = Printer Selected	0 = Printer Error	0 = Printer Interrupt Request pending	reserved	
027Ah	R/W	Parallel Port 3 Command Port	reserved		0 = Output Port (default) 1 = Input Port (Extended Mode)	1 = enable Interrupt Request	1 = select printer	0 = initialize printer	1 = auto line feed	1 = Printer Strobe active
02F8h	W	(when DLAB bit = 0) Serial Port 2 Transmit Holding Register	byte to transmit							
02F8h	R	(when DLAB bit = 0) Serial Port 2 Receive Buffer Register	receive character							
02F8h	R/W	(when DLAB bit = 1) LSB of Serial Port 2 Divisor Latch	LSB of baud rate divisor							
02F9h	R/W	(when DLAB bit = 1) MSB of Serial Port 2 Divisor Latch	MSB of baud rate divisor							
02F9h	R/W	(when DLAB bit = 0) Serial Port 2 Interrupt Enable Register	reserved				1 = enable Modem Status interrupt	1 = enable Receiver Line Status interrupt	1 = enable Transmit Holding Register Empty interrupt	1 = enable Receive Data Available interrupt. In FIFO mode also enables time-out interrupt.
02FAh	R	Serial Port 2 Interrupt ID Register	11 = FIFO feature present 10 = FIFO feature not present		reserved		000 = Modem Status interrupt 001 = transmit Holding Register Empty interrupt 010 = receive Data Available interrupt 011 = receive Line Status interrupt 110 = FIFO timeout interrupt			0 = Interrupt Pending
02FAh	W	Serial Port 2 FIFO Control Register	Receiver FIFO Register Trigger 00 = 1 byte 01 = 4 bytes 10 = 8 bytes 11 = 14 bytes		reserved			1 = Transmit FIFO Register cleared; counter cleared; bit is self-clearing	1 = Receive FIFO Register cleared; counter cleared; bit is self-clearing	0 = clears Receive and Transmit FIFO Registers and enters Character Mode 1 = Receive and Transmit FIFOs enabled
02FBh	R/W	Serial Port 2 Line Control Register	DLAB (Divisor Latch Access Bit) 0 = Receive Buffer/Transmit Holding/Interrupt Enable Register access enabled 1 = Divisor Latch access enabled	1 = Set Break enable	Stick Parity	1 = Even Parity enable	1 = Parity enable	Number of Stop Bits 0 = 1 Stop Bit 1 = 1.5 Stop Bits with character length of 5 bits 1 = 2 Stop Bits with character length of 6/7/8 bits	00 = character length is 5 bits 01 = Character length is 6 bits 10 = Character length is 7 bits 11 = Character length is 8 bits	

I/O Port	R/W	Note	Bit 7	Bit 6	Bit 5	Bit 4	Bit 3	Bit 2	Bit 1	Bit 0
$02FC_h$	R/W	Serial Port 2 Modem Control Register	reserved			1 = Loopback mode	1 = enable OUT2 interrupt	1 = force OUT1 output active	1 = set Request-to-Send (RTS) active	1 = set Data Terminal Ready (DTR) active
$02FD_h$	R	Serial Port 2 Line Status Register	reserved	1 = Transmit Shift and Holding Registers empty	1 = Transmit Holding Register empty	1 = Break interrupt	1 = Framing error	1 = Parity error	1 = Overrun error	1 = Data Ready
$02FE_h$	R	Serial Port 2 Modem Status Register	1 = Data Carrier Detect (DCD) active	1 = Ring Indicator (RI) active	1 = Data Set Ready (DSR) active	1 = Clear-to-Send (CTS) active	1 = change detected on Data Carrier Detect (DCD) line	1 = trailing edge of Ring Indicator signal detected	1 = change detected on Data Set Ready (DSR) line	1 = change detected on Clear-to-Send (CTS) line
$02FF_h$	R/W	Serial Port 2 Scratch Register	can be used by the microprocessor to hold a byte. It's not used by the Serial Port at all.							
0378_h	R/W	Parallel Port 2 Data Port	see address 0278_h							
0379_h	R	Parallel Port 2 Status Port	see address 0279_h							
$037A_h$	R/W	Parallel Port 2 Command Port	see address $027A_h$							
$03B4_h$	R/W	VGA CRT Controller Address Register (mono)	see Tech Ref Guide							
$03B5_h$	R/W	VGA CRT Controller Data Register (mono)	see Tech Ref Guide							
$03BA_h$	R	VGA Input Status Register 1 (mono)	see Tech Ref Guide							
$03BA_h$	W	VGA Feature Control Register (mono)	see Tech Ref Guide							
$03BC_h$	R/W	Parallel Port 1 Data Port	see address 0278_h							
$03BD_h$	R	Parallel Port 1 Status Port	see address 0279_h							
$03BE_h$	R/W	Parallel Port 1 Command Port	see address $027A_h$							
$03C0_h$	R/W	VGA Attribute Controller Address Register	see Tech Ref Guide							
$03C0_h$	W	VGA Attribute Controller data register (write address)	see Tech Ref Guide							
$03C1_h$	R	VGA Attribute Controller data register (read address)	see Tech Ref Guide							
$03C2_h$	W	VGA Miscellaneous Output Register	see Tech Ref Guide							
$03C2_h$	R	VGA Input Status Register 0	see Tech Ref Guide							
$03C3_h$	R/W	VGA Video Subsystem Enable Register	see Tech Ref Guide							
$03C4_h$	R/W	VGA Sequencer Address Register	see Tech Ref Guide							
$03C5_h$	R/W	other VGA Sequencer data register	see Tech Ref Guide							
$03C6_h$	R/W	Video DAC PEL Mask	see Tech Ref Guide							
$03C7_h$	W	Video DAC Palette Address/Read Mode	see Tech Ref Guide							
$03C7_h$	R	Video DAC State Register	see Tech Ref Guide							
$03C8_h$	R/W	Video DAC Palette Address/Write Mode	see Tech Ref Guide							
$03C9_h$	R/W	Video DAC Palette Data Register	see Tech Ref Guide							

I/O Port	R/W	Note	Bit 7	Bit 6	Bit 5	Bit 4	Bit 3	Bit 2	Bit 1	Bit 0
03CA$_h$	R	VGA Feature Control Register	see Tech Ref Guide							
03CC$_h$	R	VGA Miscellaneous Output Register	see Tech Ref Guide							
03CE$_h$	R/W	VGA Graphics Controller Address Register	see Tech Ref Guide							
03CF$_h$	R/W	VGA Graphics Controller Address Register	see Tech Ref Guide							
03D4$_h$	R/W	VGA CRT Controller Address Register (color)	see Tech Ref Guide							
03D5$_h$	R/W	VGA CRT Controller Data Register	see Tech Ref Guide							
03DA$_h$	R	VGA Color Input Status Register 1	see Tech Ref Guide							
03DA$_h$	W	VGA Color Feature Control Register	see Tech Ref Guide							
03F0$_h$	R	Floppy Status Register A	1 = Interrupt Pending	0 = Second drive installed	1 = Step signal active	0 = Track 0 sensor active	0 = Head 0 selected / 1 = Head 1 selected	0 = Index sensor active	0 = Write Protect sensor active	state of Direction Select signal
03F1$_h$	R	Floppy Status Register B	reserved		0 = Drive 0 Select signal active / 1 = Drive 1 Select signal active	1 = Write Data signal active	1 = Read Data signal active	1 = Write Enable signal active	1 = Motor 1 On signal active	1 = Motor 0 On signal active
03F2$_h$	W	Floppy Digital Output Register (DOR)	reserved		1 = set Motor 1 On signal active	1 = set Motor 0 On signal active	0 = enable interrupts	0 = reset Floppy Disk Controller	reserved	0 = set Drive 0 Select signal active / 1 = set Drive 1 Select signal active
03F4$_h$	R	Floppy Disk Controller (FDC) Status Register	1 = FDC Data Register is ready	0 = transfer is from microprocessor to FDC / 1 = transfer is from FDC to microprocessor	1 = non-DMA mode	1 = FDC busy	reserved		1 = drive 1 is in Seek mode	1 = drive 0 is in Seek mode
03F5$_h$	R/W	Floppy Disk Controller (FDC) Data Register	see Tech Ref Guide							
03F7$_h$	R	Floppy Digital Input Register	1 = Diskette has been changed since last access							
03F7$_h$	W	Floppy Configuration Control Register	reserved						00 = 500kbs mode (High Density Mode) / 01 = reserved / 10 = 250kbs (Low Density Mode) / 11 = reserved	0 = High Density selected / 1 = Low Density selected
03F8$_h$	W	Serial Port 1 Transmit Holding Register	see address 02F8$_h$							

I/O Port	R/W	Note	Bit 7	Bit 6	Bit 5	Bit 4	Bit 3	Bit 2	Bit 1	Bit 0
$03F8_h$	R	Serial Port 1 Receive Buffer Register	see address $02F8_h$							
$03F8_h$	R/W	Serial Port 1 LSB of Divisor Latch	see address $02F8_h$							
$03F9_h$	R/W	Serial Port 1 MSB of Divisor Latch	see address $02F9_h$							
$03F9_h$	R/W	Serial Port 1 Interrupt Enable Register	see address $02F9_h$							
$03FA_h$	R	Serial Port 1 Interrupt ID Register	see address $02FA_h$							
$03FA_h$	W	Serial Port 1 FIFO Control Register	see address $02FA_h$							
$03FB_h$	R/W	Serial Port 1 Line Control Register	see address $02FB_h$							
$03FC_h$	R/W	Serial Port 1 Modem Control Register	see address $02FC_h$							
$03FD_h$	R	Serial Port 1 Line Status Register	see address $02FD_h$							
$03FE_h$	R	Serial Port 1 Modem Status Register	see address $02FE_h$							
$03FF_h$	R/W	Serial Port 1 Scratch Register	see address $02FF_h$							
0680_h	W	Manufacturing Checkpoint Port	Checkpoint character							
$3220\text{-}3227_h$		Serial Port 3	see $02F8\text{-}02FF_h$							
$3228\text{-}322F_h$		Serial Port 4	see $02F8\text{-}02FF_h$							
$4220\text{-}4227_h$		Serial Port 5	see $02F8\text{-}02FF_h$							
$4228\text{-}422F_h$		Serial Port 6	see $02F8\text{-}02FF_h$							
$5220\text{-}5227_h$		Serial Port 7	see $02F8\text{-}02FF_h$							
$5228\text{-}522F_h$		Serial Port 8	see $02F8\text{-}02FF_h$							

APPENDIX

D

Memory Address Map

Objectives: Provides a list of memory locations used by the IBM PS/2 hardware. A listing of software use of memory is not provided because it is defined by the type and version of operating system and the applications programs running on the system.

Table D-1 describes memory use. Memory is used as follows.

- The first 1KB of memory address space contains the interrupt table.
- 639KB is assigned to the system board RAM memory.
- 128KB area assigned to the video RAM memory on the system board.
- 128KB area reserved for device ROMs located on MCA cards.
- 128KB assigned to the system board ROMs and the shadow RAM.
- 15MB of extended memory.

In Table D-1, the first two memory locations of each interrupt table slot contain the 16-bit value to be placed in the microprocessor's IP register. The second two locations contain the 16-bit value to be placed in the microprocessor's CS register. In addition, the IP and CS register values are stored in reverse order, least-significant byte first.

TABLE D-1   Interrupt Table Usage

Memory Address Range	Use
000000–000003	Interrupt table slot 00. Points to the Divide-by-Zero Exception Interrupt Service routine.
000004–000007	Interrupt table slot 01. Points to the trap or Single-Step Exception Interrupt Service routine in the debug program.
000008–00000B	Interrupt table slot 02. Points to the NMI Interrupt Service routine.
00000C–00000F	Interrupt table slot 03. Points to the Breakpoint Exception Interrupt Service routine.
000010–000013	Interrupt table slot 04. Points to the Overflow Detected Exception Interrupt Service routine.

000014–000017	Interrupt table slot 05. Points to the Print Screen Interrupt Service routine.
000018–00001B	Interrupt table slot 06. Points to the Invalid Opcode Exception Interrupt Service routine.
00001C–00001F	Interrupt table slot 07. Points to the Numeric Coprocessor Not Available Exception Interrupt Service routine.
000020–000023	Interrupt table slot 08. Points to the IRQ0 System Timer Interrupt Service routine. This interrupt request is generated once every 55ms by timer 0. Also used to report double exception conditions.
000024–000027	Interrupt table slot 09. Points to the Keyboard Interrupt Service routine. This interrupt request is generated each time a key is pressed. Also used by the numeric coprocessor segment overrun interrupt.
000028–00002B	Interrupt table slot 0A. Points to the IRQ2 Interrupt Service routine. Since the slave interrupt controller uses the master's IRQ2 input as a cascade input, IRQ2 is never really generated. Also used by the invalid task state segment (TSS) interrupt.
00002C–00002F	Interrupt table slot 0B. Points to the IRQ3 Interrupt Service routine. IRQ3 is normally used by serial port 2. Also used by the segment not present interrupt.
000030–000033	Interrupt table slot 0C. Points to the IRQ4 Interrupt Service routine. IRQ4 is normally used by serial port 1. Also used by the stack segment overrun or not present interrupt.
000034–000037	Interrupt table slot 0D. Points to the IRQ5 Interrupt Service routine. IRQ5 is normally used by parallel port 2. Also used by the general protection interrupt.
000038–00003B	Interrupt table slot 0E. Points to the IRQ6 Interrupt Service routine. IRQ6 is normally used by the floppy disk interface.
00003C–00003F	Interrupt table slot 0F. Points to the IRQ7 Interrupt Service routine. IRQ7 is normally used by parallel port 1.
000040–000043	Interrupt table slot 10. Points to the Video BIOS routine.
000044–000047	Interrupt table slot 11. Points to the Equipment List Interrupt Service routine. When executed, this routine returns the contents of RAM location 0000410_h, which indicates the equipment installed in the unit.
000048–00004B	Interrupt table slot 12. Points to the Memory Size Interrupt Service routine. When executed, this routine returns the amount of base memory (up to 640KB) installed in the unit.

00004C–00004F	Interrupt table slot 13. Points to the BIOS routine for the fixed and floppy disk subsystems.
000050–000053	Interrupt table slot 14. Points to the serial port BIOS routine.
000054–000057	Interrupt table slot 15. Points to the Systems Services BIOS routine.
000058–00005B	Interrupt table slot 16. Points to the keyboard BIOS routine.
00005C–00005F	Interrupt table slot 17. Points to the Parallel Printer BIOS routine.
000060–000063	Interrupt table slot 18. Points to ROM BASIC.
000064–000067	Interrupt table slot 19. Points to the bootstrap loader program.
000068–00006B	Interrupt table slot 1A. Points to the System Timer and RTC Interrupt Service routine.
00006C–00006F	Interrupt table slot 1B. Points to the Keyboard Break Handler routine.
000070–000073	Interrupt table slot 1C. Available for use.
000074–000077	Interrupt table slot 1D. Available for use.
000078–00007B	Interrupt table slot 1E. Contains the start address of the diskette parameters table in memory.
00007C–00007F	Interrupt table slot 1F. Contains the start address of the video graphics character table in memory.
000080–0000FF	Interrupt table slots 20 through 3F. Reserved for PC-DOS function calls.
000100–000103	Interrupt table slot 40. When a fixed disk is installed, points to the Floppy Disk Interrupt Service routine.
000104–000107	Interrupt table slot 41. Points to the fixed disk parameter table for drive 0.
000108–00010B	Interrupt table slot 42. Points to the EGA BIOS routine.
00010C–00010F	Interrupt table slot 43. Contains the start address of the video graphics character table in memory.
000110–000117	Interrupt table slots 44 and 45. Reserved.
000118–00011B	Interrupt table slot 46. Points to the fixed disk parameter table for drive 1.
00011C–000127	Interrupt table slots 47 through 49. Reserved.
000128–00012B	Interrupt table slot 4A. Points to the start address of the user-supplied RTC Alarm Interrupt Service routine.
00012C–00017F	Interrupt table slots 4B through 5F. Reserved.

000180–00019B	Interrupt table slots 60 through 66. Available for use by user programs.
00019C–00019F	Interrupt table slot 67. Points to the Expanded Memory Management (EMM) Interrupt Service routine.
0001A0–0001BF	Interrupt table slots 68 through 6F. Reserved.
0001C0–0001C3	Interrupt table slot 70. Points to the IRQ8 Interrupt Service routine. IRQ8 is used by the alarm output of the RTC chip.
0001C4–0001C7	Interrupt table slot 71. Points to the IRQ9 Interrupt Service routine. IRQ9 substitutes for IRQ2, which is used to cascade, or connect, the slave interrupt controller to the master interrupt controller. The pointer stored in slot 71 points to the IRQ2 Interrupt Service routine.
0001C8–0001CB	Interrupt table slot 72. Points to the IRQ10 Interrupt Service routine. IRQ10 is available for use by MCA add-in I/O cards.
0001CC–0001CF	Interrupt table slot 73. Points to the IRQ11 Interrupt Service routine. IRQ11 is available for use by MCA add-in I/O cards.
0001D0–0001D3	Interrupt table slot 74. Points to the IRQ12 Interrupt Service routine. IRQ12 is used by the mouse interface.
0001D4–0001D7	Interrupt table slot 75. Points to the IRQ13 Interrupt Service routine. IRQ13 is used by the error output of the numeric coprocessor.
0001D8–0001DB	Interrupt table slot 76. Points to the IRQ14 Interrupt Service routine. IRQ14 is normally used by the fixed disk adapter.
0001DC–0001DF	Interrupt table slot 77. Points to the IRQ15 Interrupt Service routine. IRQ15 is available for use by MCA add-in I/O cards.
0001E0–0001FF	Interrupt table slots 78 through 7F. Available for use by user programs.
000200–0003C3	Interrupt table slots 80 through F0. Used by BASIC.
0003C4–0003FF	Interrupt table slots F1 through FF. Available for use by user programs.
000400–09FFFF	639KB of system board RAM.
0A0000–0BFFFF	128KB assigned to video RAM memory.
0C0000–0DFFFF	ROM scan area. Device ROMs located on MCA cards must reside within this range.

0E0000–0FFFFF	System board ROM memory and shadow RAM.
100000–FFFFFF	15MB of extended memory. Only accessible when the microprocessor is in protected mode.

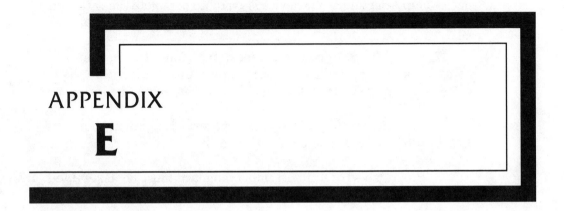

APPENDIX
E

Glossary of Terms

Access time is defined as the amount of time that elapses from device chip-select until the device is ready to complete the data transfer (either a read or a write).

An **address decoder** decodes (examines) the current address being output by the microprocessor to determine if it is within the range of memory or I/O addresses assigned to its respective device.

An **address map** represents the overall range of memory and/or I/O locations addressable by a particular microprocessor.

Programs written in assembly language must be **assembled**, or translated, into the hex code understood by the microprocessor.

An **attribute byte** is associated with each text character to be displayed on the screen. This byte defines the foreground and background color of the character, as well as underlining, blinking, and high intensity.

The **attribute controller** is part of the VGA chip. It combines the attribute information read from video memory with the dot definition of the text character (in text modes) or the PEL (in graphics modes) to create the final dot definition.

The **baud rate** is the rate at which serial data is transmitted or received by a serial port. Baud stands for bits per second.

A **BIOS routine** is a routine supplied by the system manufacturer, usually in system ROM. The BIOS routine is designed to interact with a specific I/O device, causing it to perform specified functions upon request. The applications programmer can control, sense the status of, or channel data to or from a specific I/O device by placing a request number in the AH register and calling the device-specific BIOS routine. The BIOS routine interprets the request number, instructs the I/O device to perform the requested function, and returns the results to the caller.

Bit cell is the name given to the logic in a memory device that stores a 1 or a 0.

The **boot program** is in the system board ROM. It is executed at the end of the POST and attempts to read the first sector (512 bytes) from the floppy drive or the hard drive. The first sector should contain a more intelligent boot program that is capable of reading the operating system software from the disk to memory. Once loaded, the ROM boot program jumps to the beginning of the operating system boot and executes it.

Bus cycle refers to the overall sequence of events on the Address, Control, and Data buses during a read or write.

The **cache directory** is used to keep track of the DRAM memory information currently stored in cache memory.

The **cache memory** consists of a relatively small amount of fast access SRAM memory used to keep copies of data from DRAM memory.

The **cache memory controller** copies information from DRAM memory into cache memory and maintains a directory of the information currently in cache memory.

CAS access time is the time elapsed from the activation of CAS# until the DRAM chip is ready to complete a data transfer.

The **cascade bus** is used by the master interrupt controller to command the slave interrupt controller to send the interrupt slot number to the microprocessor.

Channel memory is DRAM memory installed on micro channel adapter cards rather than in the proprietary memory module slots on the system board.

The VGA's **character generator** combines the ASCII representation of a text character read from video memory with the scan line counter output to address font memory (also see **scan line counter**).

Checksumming is the method used to ensure that the information stored in ROM memory has not changed. Checksumming is accomplished by adding the contents of every ROM location together and checking for a result of 0.

A device's **chip-select** signal line is turned on by the address decoder when an address assigned to its device is detected. An active level on the chip-select line informs the device that the microprocessor is reading from or writing to a location within the device.

Clock bits frame the start and end of bit cells when writing data on the diskette surface.

One of the most important goals of any cache memory controller is to maintain **coherency** between the DRAM memory and the copies in cache memory. They must always be mirror images.

The **column address decoder** is the device in a DRAM chip that interprets the column address latched into the DRAM's column latch and activates the proper column line within the DRAM.

The **column address latch** is the device in a DRAM chip that latches the column address presented on the memory address bus when CAS# goes active.

The **column address strobe (CAS#)** is the signal the DRAM addressing logic generates to latch the column address into the DRAM chips.

Programs written in high-level languages such as C must be **compiled,** or translated, into the hex code understood by the microprocessor.

A **cycle** of PCLK is the period of time between its positive-going edges (low-to-high transitions).

Cycle time is the combination of a DRAM's RAS access time and its pre-charge delay. It defines how frequently a DRAM may be accessed.

Data bus contention occurs when two devices occupy the same address space. A read performed from one device also selects the other, thus causing them to attempt simultaneous use of the data bus. This results in garbled data and, possibly, hardware damage.

A **data separator** is a device that determines the point at which the floppy disk controller should sample the combined clock/data stream on the read data line to capture a data bit.

A **data window** signal is generated by the data separator logic to tell the floppy disk controller when to sample the combined clock/data stream on the read data line to capture a data bit.

Demodulation is the act of converting FM information to 1's and 0's.

A **device ROM** is located on an MCA card. It contains the self-test, BIOS, and interrupt service routines for the card, as well as initialization code.

The **digital-to-analog converter (DAC)** uses the palette address output by the VGA controller to index into its 256 Palette registers. The contents of the addressed Palette register is then used to select the voltage level to be placed on the red, green, and blue gun outputs to the display when the dot clock signal goes active.

Don't care bits are the address lines that need not be examined by an address decoder in order to determine if the address currently on the address bus is assigned to its respective device.

A **DMA channel** is the hardware interface between I/O devices and memory.

The **DMA controller (DMAC)** gives an I/O device the ability to directly access memory without the intervention of the microprocessor.

A **doubleword** is a group of four contiguous locations starting at an address that is divisible by four.

DRAM access time is the period of time from the activation of the RAS# line until the DRAM chip is ready to complete the data transfer. The DRAM access time is also referred to as the RAS access time.

The **DRAM addressing logic** translates the address output by the current bus master to the row and column addresses expected by DRAM memory chips. It presents the row and column address to the DRAM chips in the proper sequence.

Under control of the DRAM addressing logic, the **DRAM address multiplexer (MUX)** selects either the row portion or the column portion of the current bus master's address to route to the DRAM chips.

A **DRAM bank** is created by addressing the same location within a series of DRAM chips simultaneously. This enables the current bus master to transfer one or more bytes during a single bus cycle.

Dynamic RAM (DRAM) memory is so named because it must be refreshed on a dynamic, ongoing basis or it loses the information stored in it.

The **electron gun** or guns in the display unit are controlled by the output voltage from the VGA's DAC. The magnitude of the input voltage defines the power, or intensity, of the electron beams emitted by the guns towards the phosphor dots on the face of the display screen.

Erasable programmable read-only memory (EPROM) is a ROM that can be erased by ultraviolet light and reprogrammed many times.

An **exception interrupt** is generated when the execution of an instruction results in an error. The interrupt causes the microprocessor to jump to the interrupt service routine written to handle the particular type of error condition.

FIFO stands for first in, first out buffer. This means the first byte to be placed in the buffer is the first one to be output from it.

Floating the buses is the term used to describe the process whereby the current bus master electrically disconnects itself from the address, control, and data buses.

A **floating gate** is a small piece of conductor surrounded by a thin layer of insulating material. Its charge is used to control the conduction of the transistor in an EPROM's bit cell.

The **floppy disk controller** is the programmable device that receives commands from the microprocessor and controls one or two drive units.

The cache memory controller's **FLUSH** input is activated to clear all cache directory entries.

A **font** is the typeface used to display each text character on the screen.

A **four-way set associative** directory structure keeps track of the information in four cache memory banks, or ways, using four directories.

Frequency modulation (FM) recording is used in low-density mode and places a clock bit at the leading-edge of each bit cell when writing to the disk.

A **fusible-link ROM** uses a fuse at the bit cell level to represent a 0 or a 1.

High-density recording uses a clock pulse frequency of 500KHz when writing bit cells on the diskette surface.

The **hi/lo byte copier** copies data between the upper and lower system data (SD) bus paths when odd-addressed information is being transferred between the microprocessor and an 8-bit device.

The cache memory controller's **hit rate** is the average percentage of 0-wait state memory reads that occur over a large number of memory accesses.

Horizontal retrace is performed at the end of each horizontal scan line. When the horizontal sync pulse is received from the VGA controller, the display electronics turns off the electron beams and repositions them back to the start of the next horizontal scan line on the left side of the screen.

A **horizontal scan line** consists of all the PELs, or phosphor dot triads, along one horizontal line on the display screen. The display's beam deflection electronics scans the electron beams along the scan line from left-to-right to irradiate the phosphor dots along the line.

The **horizontal sync** pulse is generated by the VGA controller and sent to the display. It tells the display unit's electronics when the end of a horizontal scan line has been reached. In response, the display electronics turns off the electron beams and performs a horizontal retrace back to the start of the next horizontal scan line on the left side of the screen.

An **I/O device** is any device (except a memory device) that the microprocessor can read data from or write data to.

An **I/O port** is an I/O address or location.

The **index** pulse is generated by the drive unit once per revolution. It marks the start of a track.

In-line code fetching is the term used to describe the sequential nature of instruction fetching performed by computers.

Interleaved memory architecture is used to speed up access to sequential DRAM memory locations. What would ordinarily be one bank of DRAM memory is split up into two banks. Support logic within the interleaved memory logic keeps track of which bank was accessed last. Using address pipelining, the subsystem can detect that the upcoming access is to the same bank or the other bank. If it is the other bank, the memory logic need not allow for the pre-charge delay and can let the microprocessor access it immediately.

An **interrupt** is a condition internal or external to the microprocessor that causes execution of the current program to be temporarily interrupted. The microprocessor is then forced to execute another program to service the interrupting device or internal condition. At the completion of the interrupt servicing, the microprocessor then returns to its original program flow.

Intel microprocessors automatically generate two back-to-back **interrupt acknowledge** bus cycles to request the interrupt slot number from the Intel 8259 Programmable Interrupt Controller. At the trailing edge of the second interrupt acknowledge bus cycle, the microprocessor reads the slot number from the lower data path, D0:D7.

The **interrupt controller** prioritizes concurrent interrupt requests and forwards them to the microprocessor one at a time, in order of priority.

The **interrupt instruction (INT)** allows the programmer to call a routine without knowing its start memory address. The number specified after the INT instruction is the slot number in the interrupt table. When executed, the INT instruction causes the microprocessor to react as if an interrupt request had been sensed on the INTR line. The only difference is that the interrupt slot number is supplied by the INT instruction rather than by the 8259 interrupt controller.

The **interrupt request** signal line is used by an I/O device to inform the microprocessor that it requires service.

The **interrupt return (IRET)** instruction must be the last instruction in every interrupt service routine (ISR). When executed, it causes the microprocessor to reload the CS, IP, and Flag registers from stack memory, causing the microprocessor to resume execution of the interrupted program at the point where it was interrupted.

The **interrupt service routine (ISR)** is a special program written to handle the servicing of interrupt requests from a specific device type.

The **interrupt slot number** is the 8-bit number sent to the microprocessor to identify the ISR that must be run to service the current interrupt request. It identifies a slot, or entry, in the interrupt table in RAM memory. It is also referred to as the interrupt vector, interrupt ID, or interrupt type code.

The **interrupt table** is located in RAM memory and contains pointers to as many as 256 ISRs. In real mode, each table entry consists of 4 bytes of information—a 2 byte CS value and a 2 byte IP value.

A **JUMP instruction** is an instruction that causes the microprocessor to alter its program flow.

The **least-recently used (LRU) algorithm** is used by the cache memory controller to decide which cache directory entry to use when storing information from a new memory page.

The **least-recently used (LRU) switch** points to the oldest cache directory entry in the selected group of directory entries.

A **line** of information is the fixed amount of data that a cache memory controller always fetches when accessing DRAM memory.

A **line hit** occurs when a cache directory entry is checked and its tag valid bit is set, its tag field matches the currently addressed memory page address, and the line valid bit indicated by the currently addressed line is set.

A **line miss** occurs when a cache directory entry is checked and its tag valid bit is set, its tag field matches the currently addressed memory page address, but the line valid bit indicated by the currently addressed line is not set.

The **line valid bits** in a cache directory entry are used to indicate which lines from the respective set in this memory page are currently in cache memory.

The **local address bus** consists of the address bus lines connected directly to the microprocessor.

The **local data bus** consists of the data bus lines connected directly to the microprocessor.

Low-density recording uses a clock pulse frequency of 250KHz when writing bit cells on the diskette surface.

Machine language is the hex series of numbers that the microprocessor treats as instructions and data.

A **mark** is a logic 1 on the transmit data line to the modem.

The **maskable interrupt request (INTR)** is an input that informs the microprocessor when an external hardware device requires servicing.

A **masked ROM** is a mass-produced, pre-programmed ROM where a photographic image is used to reproduce large quantities of ROMs with the desired series of opens and shorts to represent 0's and 1's.

The **memory address bus** supplies the row and column address to the DRAM chips. These addresses are derived from the address being output by the current bus master and are routed onto the memory address bus by the MUX under the control of the DRAM addressing logic.

A **modem** is a device that converts FM data to 1's and 0's or visa versa. It is used to interface a serial port to the telephone lines.

Modified frequency modulation (MFM) recording is used when in high-density mode. It does not place a clock bit at the leading edge of a bit cell if either the previous bit cell or the bit cell about to be written contains a 1.

Modulation is the act of varying a base, or carrier, frequency to represent information.

A **non-cacheable access** is a memory read from an area of memory that the cache memory controller cannot reliably keep track of.

Non-maskable interrupt (NMI) is an input that causes the microprocessor to jump to the NMI interrupt service routine. Slot 2 in the interrupt table is dedicated to NMI. In a PS/2, NMI is used to report hardware failures (such as a RAM parity error) to the microprocessor.

Non-volatile memory is memory that does not lose its data when power is lost.

The cache memory controller views memory address space as consisting of a series of **pages** of a fixed length.

Sequential **page mode DRAM** locations are laid out or distributed sequentially along a row. When the current bus master performs a series of bus cycles to access locations within the same row, the page mode DRAM requires only the column portion of the address. Since the RAS/CAS delay can therefore be skipped, the access time is substantially reduced. The CAS# line must be activated for each new column address presented to the page mode DRAM chips.

The **Palette** is the selection of video colors available in a particular color video mode. The palette is set up by pre-loading the Palette registers in the DAC with the color information. Each Palette register is pre-loaded with three 6-bit values representing the voltage levels to be placed on the three electron gun outputs to the display when the dot clock signal goes active.

The **palette bus** loads color information into the DAC's 256 Palette registers and addresses the DAC Palette register that defines the three color combination for the current screen dot.

The **Palette registers** are contained within the DAC. Each of the 256 Palette registers are pre-loaded with three 6-bit values representing the voltage levels to be placed on the three electron gun outputs to the display when the dot clock signal goes active.

When a byte of information is written into RAM memory, an additional **parity** bit is appended to it by the parity generation logic. If necessary, the parity bit is set to a 1, forcing the number of 1 bits in the 9-bit pattern to an even number. When a RAM memory location is read from, the byte of data is sent back to the requesting bus master and is also applied to the parity checking logic with the parity bit from memory. If an odd number of 1 bits is detected, the parity logic generates a RAM parity check error, thereby causing an NMI to the system board microprocessor.

A **phantom, or ghost interrupt** can occur in the PC/XT/AT product line when a noise spike on an interrupt request line registers as a pending interrupt request. This problem has been eliminated in the PS/2 product line (with MCA) by making the interrupt request lines active low and placing pull-up resistors on them.

A **phase-locked loop (PLL)** acts as an electronic flywheel that maintains its momentum, or frequency, for some time before it begins to drift off frequency. It is used to generate the data window signal to the floppy disk controller when MFM recording is in use (high-density mode).

A **phosphor** is a substance that emits visible light of a specific frequency, or color, when bombarded with electrons. The exact chemical consistency of the phosphor defines the color of the light emitted.

A **picture element (PEL)** is also commonly referred to as a pixel. It consists of a phosphor dot triad (red, green, and blue phosphor dots) on the screen face.

A **POP operation** causes the microprocessor to read 2 bytes from memory starting at the location pointed to by the Stack Pointer (SP) register. These 2 bytes are then placed in the target register, and the SP register is incremented by 2 to point to the next data item stored in stack memory.

A **posted write** is a write bus cycle that has been posted to (latched by) the posted write latch by the cache memory controller so that it can be run later.

The **posted write latch** is used by the cache memory controller to memorize all of the information pertaining to a write bus cycle.

The **power-on restart address** is the memory location from which the microprocessor always fetches its first instruction after power-up.

The **pre-charge delay** is the length of time it takes a DRAM to charge up after it has been read from. If the DRAM is accessed during this period of time, faulty data may be returned.

A **PUSH operation** causes the microprocessor to decrement the Stack Pointer (SP) register by 2 to point to the next available location in stack memory. The microprocessor then performs a memory write bus cycle to write the contents of the specified register into stack memory.

A **queue** is a temporary holding area, or buffer.

The **RAS/CAS delay** is the delay between activation of RAS# and activation of CAS#. It is necessary to ensure proper operation of the DRAM chip.

A **read-only memory (ROM)** chip can only be read from once installed in the system. It is non-volatile; that is, it retains its stored information indefinitely when power is removed.

A **read/write coil** writes data on and reads data from the disk surface.

A **read hit** occurs when the cache memory controller finds the requested information in the cache memory.

A **read miss** occurs when the cache memory controller does not find the requested information in the cache memory.

The **Recalibrate** command causes the floppy disk controller to reposition the heads over track 0.

DRAM storage locations require **refresh** on a periodic basis in order to retain the information stored in them. A row of locations within a DRAM memory chip is refreshed by setting the DRAM's R/W# pin to the read state and latching the row address into the DRAM's row latch with RAS#.

The **refresh row counter** contains the address of the next row to be refreshed within the DRAM memory chips. It is located on the system board and outputs a new row address onto the address bus every 15 microseconds. When the last row address has been refreshed, the refresh row counter rolls over to row 0 and starts over again.

The **refresh timer** is located on the system board and outputs an active signal every 15 microseconds to request the buses to run a refresh bus cycle. This timer is not programmable in the PS/2 product line.

A **register** is an individual storage location found either inside the microprocessor or an I/O device.

A **ROM programmer** is a device used to write hex information into ROMs before their installation in a system.

The **ROM scan** is the POST process that automatically detects the device ROMs, tests them, and executes the initialization programs for every installed MCA card that has a device ROM on it.

The **row address decoder** is located inside the DRAM chips and selects the row line to be activated during a bus cycle.

The DRAM addressing logic uses the **row address strobe (RAS)** signal to latch the row address into the DRAM chips.

The **row comparator** is found in DRAM memory systems utilizing page mode or static column (SCRAM) memory chips. Using address pipelining, it compares the row to be addressed in the upcoming bus cycle to the row already latched into the DRAM chips. If they are equal, this is a row, or page, hit and it is only necessary to present the new column address to the DRAM chips.

Page mode and static column (SCRAM) DRAM memory subsystems also include a **row latch** used to hold the same row address currently latched into the DRAM chips. The row comparator compares this row address to the row to be addressed in the upcoming bus cycle. Also see row comparator definition.

Every DRAM chip contains an internal **row latch** used to hold the row address currently being accessed.

The **RS-232 standard** defines the signals and voltage levels that link the serial port and the modem and the modem and the telephone lines.

The **scan line counter** is contained within the VGA chip. Each text character to be displayed must be painted using rows of dots on multiple scan lines. Starting with a count of 0, the scan line count, in conjunction with the ASCII text character from video memory, is presented to the font memory as an address. The font memory outputs the pattern of 1's and 0's representing the dots for the first line of the character. As the counter is then incremented, the dot definition for each successive scan line is output from the font memory.

A **sector** is a data area on the diskette that holds 512 bytes of data.

Sector address marks are written on the diskette surface during low-level formatting to identify individual sectors.

The **seek** command causes the floppy disk controller to position the head mechanism over the desired track.

Serial DMA is the transfer methodology utilized by the current PS/2 DMA controller. The DMA controller must actually perform two bus cycles in sequence (or serially) in order to transfer a byte or a word between an I/O device and memory.

The cache memory controller views each page of memory address space as being subdivided into a fixed number of **sets**.

Settling time is the amount of time that must be allowed for the head assembly to stop vibrating after the heads are positioned over a particular track.

Shadow RAM is the RAM memory that the entire system ROM is copied to during the POST, thus relocating the BIOS and interrupt service routines to faster, RAM memory.

PS/2 products with the micro channel have **shareable interrupts**. This means that multiple I/O devices can be attached to the same interrupt request signal line without causing damage to each other.

The **slave** is the device being addressed by the current bus master.

A **snoop hit** occurs when the cache memory controller sees that a bus master is altering a DRAM location that has been cached.

A **snoop miss** occurs when the cache memory controller observes a memory write bus cycle being performed by a bus master which does not alter a DRAM location that is cached.

The cache memory controller always **snoops** after surrendering its local buses to a bus master. This means that it observes the address bus and the bus cycle definition lines to see if the bus master is performing a memory write and altering the contents of a cached DRAM location.

The **stack** is an area of RAM memory set aside as scratchpad memory. One way the microprocessor uses stack memory is to store the Flag, CS, and IP register contents when servicing an interrupt. CS and IP are saved so the microprocessor knows the memory address at which to resume execution of the interrupted program.

Stale data is data in cache memory that no longer matches the contents of its respective DRAM memory location.

The **start bit** precedes a byte of serial port data. Together with the stop bit, it frames the serial data byte.

Sequential **static column RAM (SCRAM)** locations are laid out or distributed sequentially along a row. When the current bus master performs a series of bus cycles to access locations within the same row, the SCRAM requires only the column portion of the address. Since the RAS/CAS delay can therefor be skipped, the access time is substantially reduced. The CAS# line is kept active (or static) for each new column address presented to the SCRAM chips.

Static RAM (SRAM) memory does not require refreshing at regular intervals in order to maintain the information stored in memory. This is because SRAM uses single-bit latches known as D-flip flops, unlike DRAM, which uses capacitors to store information. In addition, SRAM chips have very fast access times because they do not require that the address be split into a row and column and presented in sequence.

Step pulses are issued by the floppy disk controller and cause the selected drive unit to move the heads one track for each step pulse received.

The **stepper band** is manipulated by the stepper motor to move the read/write head mechanism.

The **stop bit** always follows a byte of serial port data. It may actually consists of 1, 1.5, or 2 bits. Together with the start bit, it frames the serial data byte.

The **tag** is the same as the same as the memory page address. It identifies the memory page currently being addressed.

A **tag hit** occurs when a cache directory entry is checked and its tag valid bit is set and its tag field matches the currently addressed memory page address.

A **tag miss** occurs when a cache directory entry is checked and either its tag valid bit is not set or its tag field does not match the currently addressed memory page address.

A cache directory entry's **tag valid bit** is set to 1 to indicate that the entry is in use.

A **track** is the concentric ring traversed by the head while positioned over a particular point on the diskette surface.

Track 0 is the outermost track on the diskette and is considered to be the home track.

A **transceiver** passes information from left-to-right, from right-to-left, or keep the two sides separate.

A **two-way set associative** directory structure keeps track of the information in two cache memory banks, or ways, using two directories.

Vertical retrace is performed at the end of each screen output. When the vertical sync pulse is received from the VGA controller, the display electronics turns off the electron beams and repositions them back to the top left corner of the screen to start painting the screen again.

The **vertical sync** pulse is generated by the VGA controller and sent to the display. It tells the display unit's electronics when the end of the screen has been reached. In response, the display unit turns off the electron beams and performs a vertical retrace back to the top left corner of the screen.

Volatile memory is memory that does not retain stored information when power is lost.

A **wait state** is an extra data time inserted into a bus cycle by the microprocessor to allow more time for the currently addressed device to respond to a data transfer request.

A **way** is another word for a bank of cache memory.

A **write hit** occurs when the cache memory controller has a copy of the target DRAM location's contents during a memory write bus cycle.

A **write miss** occurs when the cache memory controller does not have a copy of the target DRAM location's contents during a memory write bus cycle.

The **write protect window** is the small opening near the corner of a 3.5″ diskette that can either be opened to write-protect a diskette or closed to allow writing.

A cache memory controller with a **write through policy** always updates the copy in cache memory and the DRAM memory contents at the same time.

A **0-wait state bus cycle** occurs when the microprocessor samples READY# active at the end of the first data time in a bus cycle.

An **8-bit device (or board)** is a device that is connected only to the lower data path, D0:D7.

An **8-bit slave** is a slave installed in a 16-bit MCA slot and that can use only the lowest data path, D0:D7 during data transfers.

A **16-bit bus master** is installed in a 16-bit MCA slot and can therefore only use the lower two data paths, D0:D7 and D8:D15, during data transfers.

A **16-bit device (or board)** is connected to both the upper (D8:D15) and the lower (D0:D7) data paths.

A **16-bit slave** is a slave installed in a 16-bit MCA slot and that can use the lower 2 data paths, D0:D7 and D8:D15 during data transfers.

A **32-bit bus master** is a bus master that is installed in a 32-bit MCA slot and can use all 4 data paths during data transfers.

A **32-bit slave** is a slave installed in a 32-bit MCA slot and that can use all 4 data paths: D0:D7, D8:D15, D16:D23 and D24:D31 during data transfers.

APPENDIX

F

MCA Signal Glossary

The 16-Bit MCA Signals

Table F-1 defines the signals found on the 16-bit MCA connectors.

TABLE F-1 The 16-Bit MCA Signals

Signal(s)	Description
A0:A23	Address bits 0 through 23. A2:A23 are generated by the current bus master. A0 and A1 are generated by 16-bit bus masters, but are generated by the system board translation logic when the bus cycle is being run by a 32-bit bus master.
SBHE#	System bus high enable. Set active when the current bus master is going to use D8:D15 during a bus cycle. Generated by 16-bit bus masters, but generated by the system board translation logic when the bus cycle is being run by a 32-bit bus master.
MADE24	Memory address enable 24. Set active by the current bus master whenever a memory address within the first 16MB of address space is on the address bus. MADE24 should be used as an enable by the address decoders on memory cards installed in 16-bit MCA slots.
	If a memory bus cycle is in progress and MADE24 is inactive, it means that the current bus master is reading from or writing to a memory address greater than 16MB. All memory cards installed in 16-bit MCA slots should therefore ignore the address. This will prevent 16-bit memory cards from incorrectly responding to addresses greater than 16MB that are addressing memory cards installed in 32-bit MCA slots.
D0:D7	The lower 8-bit data path. Used by 16-bit bus masters to communicate with even addresses. Used by 32-bit bus masters to communicate with the first location in the currently addressed doubleword.
D8:D15	The second data path. Used by 16-bit bus masters to communicate with odd addresses. Used by 32-bit bus masters to communicate with the second location in the currently addressed doubleword.
M/IO#	Memory or I/O. M/IO#, S0#, and S1# are the bus cycle definition lines. They are generated by the current bus master and indicate the type of bus cycle in progress.

M/IO#	S0#	S1#	Bus Cycle Type
0	0	0	Interrupt Acknowledge
0	0	1	I/O Write
0	1	0	I/O Read
1	0	0	Halt or Shutdown
1	0	1	Memory Write
1	1	0	Memory Read

S0#	See M/IO#.
S1#	See M/IO#.
ADL#	Address decode latch. The current bus master sets ADL# active during address time (T_s) to indicate that a valid address and bus cycle definition are present on the micro channel. The currently addressed slave may latch the address on either the leading or trailing edge of ADL#. ADL# is not active during matched memory bus cycles.
CD CHRDY (n)	Card channel ready signal for MCA slot 'n'. The currently addressed slave sets this normally active signal inactive when it first detects that it is being addressed. It is kept inactive until the slave is ready to end the bus cycle. If a read bus cycle is in progress, CD CHRDY (n) is kept inactive until the addressed slave has placed the data on the data bus for the bus master to read. If a write bus cycle is in progress, CD CHRDY (n) is kept inactive until the addressed slave has accepted the data on the data bus.
CHRDYRTN	Channel ready return. In addition to being routed to the system board microprocessor, the CD CHRDY (n) signal is turned around on the system board and sent out over this line so that the current bus master, no matter where it is physically located, can see ready and know when to end the bus cycle.
CMD#	The command signal is set active by the current bus master to indicate that it is data time (T_c) (In other words, time to transfer the data). The trailing edge (end) of CMD# indicates the end of the bus cycle. CMD# is not active during matched memory bus cycles (see MMC CMD#).
CD DS 16 (n)#	Card data size 16 signal from MCA slot n. Set active when a 16-bit MCA card's address decoder detects an address within the range assigned to the card. Informs the system board data bus steering and translation logic that the addressed device is connected to the lower two data paths and requires address bits A0, A1, and SBHE#. Also see DS 16 RTN#.

DS 16 RTN#	Data size 16 return. On the system board, the CD DS 16 (n)# signal is turned around and sent back to all the MCA slots to inform the current bus master, wherever it is physically located, that the addressed device is connected to the lower two data paths and requires address bits A0, A1, and SBHE#.
ARB0:ARB3	This is the 4-bit arbitration bus that competing bus masters place their arbitration priority codes on during an arbitration cycle.
ARB/GNT#	The arbitrate/grant line identifies the start and end of an arbitration cycle for competing bus masters. The arbitration cycle begins when ARB/GNT# goes high and ends when it goes low.
PREEMPT#	The preempt line is used by the DMA controller and competing bus masters to request the use of the buses.
BURST#	Bursting bus masters use the burst line to inform the central arbitration control point (CACP) that they require the use of the buses to run multiple bus cycles, rather than just a single bus cycle.
CHRESET	Channel reset. When active, causes all MCA cards to be reset, thereby preventing the cards from doing anything and initializing all cards to a known state. Set active when the POWERGOOD signal from the power supply is inactive and, under software control, by setting bit 7 in the adapter enable/setup register at I/O port 0096_h.
TC#	Transfer complete. Generated by the DMA controller when the transfer count has been exhausted. Generated by an I/O device when an error condition has been encountered during a DMA transfer. When generated by an I/O device, causes the DMA controller to abort the DMA transfer in progress. The I/O device also generates an interrupt request to inform the microprocessor that the transfer has completed.
IRQ3#	Interrupt request 3. Used by serial port 2, but may be shared by other I/O devices.
IRQ4#	Interrupt request 4. Used by serial port 1, but may be shared by other I/O devices.
IRQ5#	Interrupt request 5. Used by parallel port 2, but may be shared by other I/O devices.
IRQ6#	Interrupt request 6. Used by floppy disk interface, but may be shared by other I/O devices.
IRQ7#	Interrupt request 7. Used by parallel port 1, but may be shared by other I/O devices.

IRQ9#	Interrupt request 9. Used by VGA to indicate start of vertical retrace, but may be shared by other I/O devices.
IRQ10#	Interrupt request 10. May be shared by a number of I/O devices.
IRQ11#	Interrupt request 11. May be shared by a number of I/O devices.
IRQ12#	Interrupt request 12. Used by mouse interface, but may be shared by other I/O devices.
IRQ14#	Interrupt request 14. Used by hard disk interface, but may be shared by other I/O devices.
IRQ15#	Interrupt request 15. May be shared by a number of I/O devices.
CD SETUP (n)#	Card setup line for the MCA card in MCA slot n. Normally inactive, thereby allowing the MCA card to function normally. Can be set low by writing the appropriate value to the Adapter Enable/Setup register at I/O port 0096_h. When low, places the selected MCA card in setup mode so its POS registers can be accessed. Refer to Chapter 14.
CHCK#	Channel check. Used by MCA cards to report error conditions. When active, causes an NMI interrupt to the system board microprocessor.
AUDIO	Can be used by an MCA card to send a signal of the desired frequency to the speaker.
AUDIO GND	Audio ground. Completes the circuit for the AUDIO signal. See AUDIO, above.
REFRESH#	Generated by the refresh logic on the system board when it has become bus master and is performing a memory read bus cycle to refresh the next row of DRAM memory throughout the system. When sensed active by channel memory cards, they route the row address from the address bus directly through their DRAM address MUXs onto their memory address buses and activate their RAS# lines. Every DRAM memory chip in the system then latches the row address and activates the specified row line within the DRAM, refreshing all storage locations along the row. For additional information, refer to Chapter 21.
OSC	The oscillator signal is a free-running 14.31818MHz signal, generated on the system board and made available to MCA cards for general use. It was used by the color graphics adapter (CGA) card in the PC/XT/AT as the source for the display's color burst signal.

CD SFDBK(n)#   Refer to Figure 17-13. Card selected feedback for MCA slot 'n' goes active whenever the address decoder on the MCA card installed in slot 'n' detects an address within its assigned range. Feedback is described in Chapter 14.

The 32-Bit MCA Signals

Table F-2 defines the signals found on the 32-bit MCA connectors.

TABLE F-2   The 32-Bit MCA Signals

Signal(s)	*Description*
A24:A31	Address line 24 through 31. Transmits the upper 8 bits of the address to the addressed 32-bit device. When a 16-bit bus master is running the bus cycle, A24:A31 are not used. When a 32-bit bus master is running the bus cycle, A24:A31 are generated by the bus master.
BE0#:BE3#	Byte enable lines. Tells the addressed 32-bit device the locations within the currently addressed doubleword with which the bus master wishes to communicate. When a 16-bit bus master is running the bus cycle, the translation logic on the system board generates BE0#:BE3# by interpreting the A0, A1, and SBHE# signals generated by the 16-bit bus master. When a 32-bit bus master is running the bus cycle, BE0#:BE3# are generated by the bus master.
D16:D23	The third data path. Used by 32-bit bus masters to communicate with the third location in the currently addressed doubleword.
D24:D31	The fourth data path. Used by 32-bit bus masters to communicate with the fourth location in the currently addressed doubleword.
TR32	TR32 is a normally active signal driven inactive (low) only when a 32-bit bus master is running a bus cycle. An inactive level informs the system board's translation logic that the bus master will be generating A2:A31 and the proper byte enable lines.
	When the translation logic senses TR32 inactive (high), it converts the signals A0, A1, and SBHE# to the proper levels on the byte enable lines, BE0#:BE3#, so that the 16-bit bus master can correctly address a 32-bit device.

CD DS 32 (n)#   Card data size 32 signal from MCA slot n. Set active when a 32-bit MCA card's address decoder detects an address within the range assigned to the card. Informs the system board data bus steering and translation logic that the addressed device is connected to all four data paths. Also see DS 32 RTN#.

DS 32 RTN#   Data size 32 return. On the system board, the CD DS 32 (n)# signal is turned around and sent back to all the 32-bit MCA slots to inform the current bus master, wherever it is physically located, that the addressed device is connected to all four data paths.

The Matched Memory Extension Signals

Table F-3 defines the signals found on the matched memory extension connector.

TABLE F-3   The Matched Memory Extension Signals

Signal(s)	Description
MMC#	Matched Memory Cycle. On the 16 MHz PS/2 Model 80, generated when the system board microprocessor is bus master and is placing an address on the address bus. Indicates that the system board microprocessor supports matched memory bus cycles. Also generated by the 20MHz Model 80 and the Model 70s, but the system boards in these systems do not support matched memory bus cycles.
MMCR#	Matched Memory Cycle Request. Generated by a matched memory card in response to MMC# when its address decoder detects an address within its assigned range. Indicates that the card supports matched memory cycles. On the 16MHz PS/2 Model 80, causes the system board microprocessor to use matched memory bus cycles when communicating with the matched memory card.
MMC CMD#	Matched Memory Command. During matched memory bus cycles, generated by the system board logic to indicate that it is data time. Due to the abbreviated data time used during matched memory bus cycles, MMC CMD# is substituted for CMD#.

The Video Extension Signals

Table F-4 defines the signals found on the video extension connector.

TABLE F-4   The Video Extension Signals

Signal(s)	Description
P0:P7	Palette Bus. Used by the VGA or the 8514/A advanced video interface to address the DACs Palette registers or to send data to the DAC's Palette registers.
HSYNC	Horizontal Sync. Generated by the VGA or the 8514/A advanced video interface at the end of a horizontal scan line to inform the display unit that the electron beams should be retraced, or re-positioned, back to the start of the next horizontal scan line on the left side of the screen.
VSYNC	Vertical Sync. Generated by the VGA or the 8514/A advanced video interface to inform the display unit that the electron beams should be retraced, or re-positioned, back to the start of the screen at the top left corner of the screen.
BLANK	Generated by the VGA or the 8514/A advanced video interface. Causes the DAC to turn off its three electron gun outputs during a retrace period.
EDCLK	When set low (grounded), this normally active signal causes the VGA to electrically disconnect itself from the dot clock line to the DAC so that the advanced video card can provide dot clock instead.
EVIDEO	When set low (grounded), this normally active signal causes the VGA to electrically disconnect itself from the palette bus going to the DAC. This allows the advanced video card, rather than the VGA, to provide Palette register addresses and data to the DAC.
ESYNC	When set low (grounded), this normally active signal causes the VGA to electrically disconnect itself from the three synchronization signals. This allows the advanced video card, rather than the VGA, to provide HSYNC and VSYNC to the display and BLANK to the DAC.

Bibliography

Phoenix Technologies, Inc., *CBIOS for IBM PS/2 Computers and Compatibles*, Reading, MA: Addison-Wesley, 1989.

Phoenix Technologies, Inc., *ABIOS for IBM PS/2 Computers and Compatibles*, Reading, MA: Addison-Wesley, 1989.

Phoenix Technologies, Inc., *System BIOS for IBM PC/XT/AT Computers and Compatibles*, Reading, MA: Addison-Wesley, 1989.

IBM Personal System/2 Hardware Interface Technical Reference: IBM.

IBM PS/2 and Personal Computer BIOS Interface Technical Reference: IBM.

Intel Corporation, Microprocessor and Peripheral Handbook, Volume II.

Intel Corporation, *iAPX 286 Hardware Reference Manual*.

Intel Corporation, *iAPX 286 Programmer's Reference Manual Including the iAPX 286 Numeric Supplement*.

Intel Corporation, *80386 Hardware Reference Manual*.

Index